Introduction to **International** & **Global Studies**

INTRODUCTION TO

International & Global Studies

THIRD EDITION

SHAWN SMALLMAN

KIMBERLEY BROWN

The University of North Carolina Press Chapel Hill

Manufactured in the United States of America
Designed and Set in Scala and Scala Sans with Champion
by Rebecca Evans.

The University of North Carolina Press has been a
member of the Green Press Initiative since 2003.

Cover illustration: © iStockphoto.com/Vit_Mar

Library of Congress Cataloging-in-Publication Data
Names: Smallman, Shawn C., author. | Brown, Kimberley, 1966– author.
Title: Introduction to international and global studies / Shawn C. Smallman, Kimberley Brown.
Description: Third edition, revised and expanded. | Chapel Hill : The University of North Carolina Press, 2020. | Includes bibliographical references and index.
Identifiers: LCCN 2019054498 | ISBN 9781469659992 (paperback) | ISBN 9781469660004 (ebook)
Subjects: LCSH: Globalization. | World citizenship. | International cooperation. | International relations.
Classification: LCC JZ1318 .S597 2020 | DDC 327—dc23
LC record available at https://lccn.loc.gov/2019054498

To Mina, Paige, and Audrey,

with faith in your ability to make a difference

Contents

Maps, Tables, Photographs, and Figure

MAPS

TABLES

PHOTOGRAPHS

FIGURE

ONE Introduction

Lauren grew up in a suburb of Minneapolis, Minnesota. While an undergraduate, she arranged with one of her professors to conduct an independent research project and traveled to Liberia in West Africa for a summer. Upon her return, she worked as an intern for an international nongovernmental agency and, as she completed a political science degree, made plans for a career in the areas of philanthropy and leadership. Following graduation, she joined the Peace Corps and traveled to Cape Verde, where she worked in family health. These experiences helped her choose to earn a graduate degree in public health, as well as a graduate certificate in nonprofit management. In graduate school, she met her future husband, an Indian national. She is now part of a bicultural family in which she and her husband both are working to expose their children to the plethora of cultures around the world through travel and education. She also remains deeply engaged in international philanthropy. Lauren had not initially known where her undergraduate program of study would lead her; she knew only that she thrived on making contact with individuals from other cultures, even as she came to know her own culture better.

Fekade is Ethiopian. His parents emigrated to the United States when he was eight years old. Raised bilingually and biculturally, he attended public elementary and high schools in the Pacific Northwest. His original intention was to find a way to return to Ethiopia to work in some type of international service. Following his undergraduate work in international studies, he has since decided to focus his graduate work on public health and immigrant communities in the United States. He has organized students at his university to participate in activities that focus on the United Nations' Millennium Development Goals and to try to make informed choices about everything they do. Contact with other cultures has transformed both his education choices and career choices.

The life trajectories of Lauren and Fekade (whose stories are real but whose names have been changed here) are not unusual. Many people are profoundly touched by their own concern for international questions. Perhaps you will also find your life transformed by your cultural contacts and program of study. But whether or

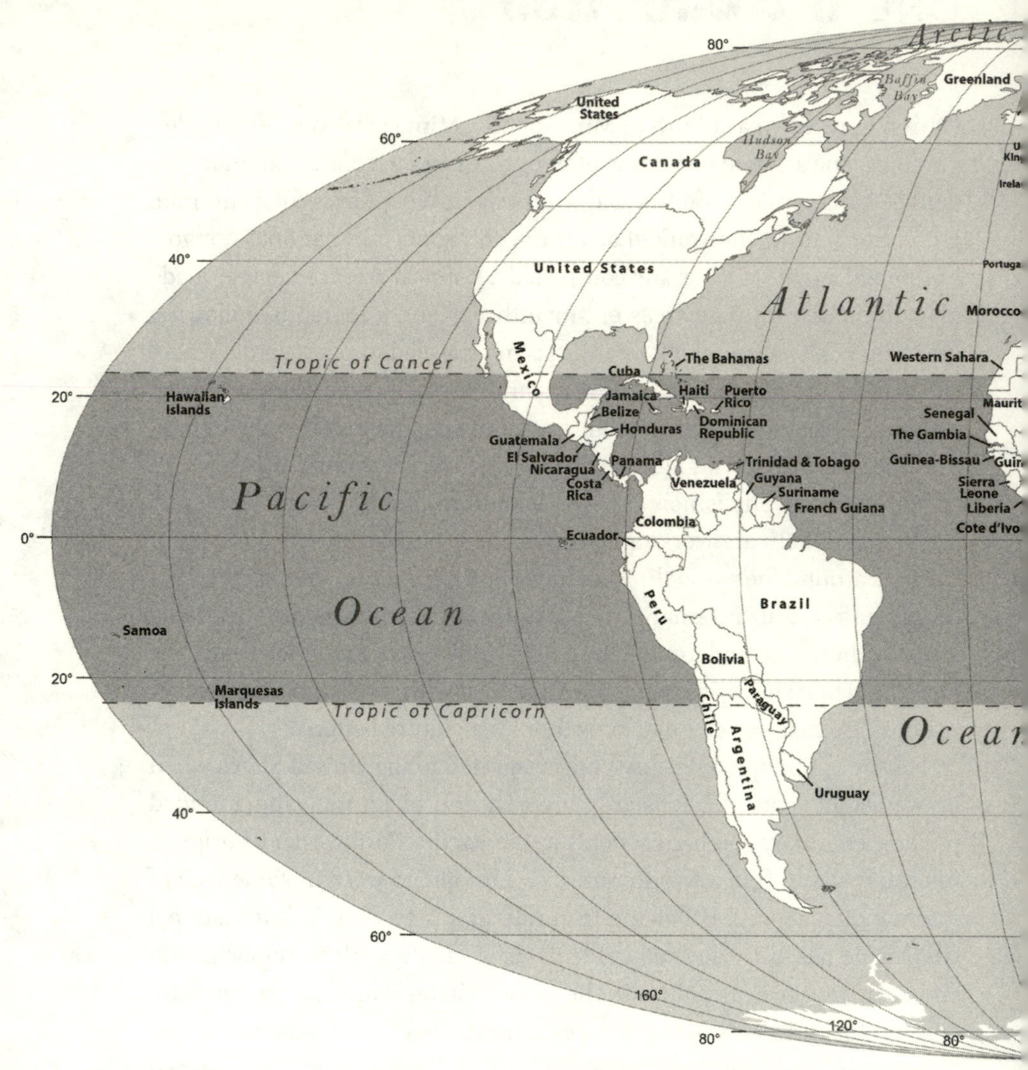

Map 1 The World (Steph Gaspers 2008)

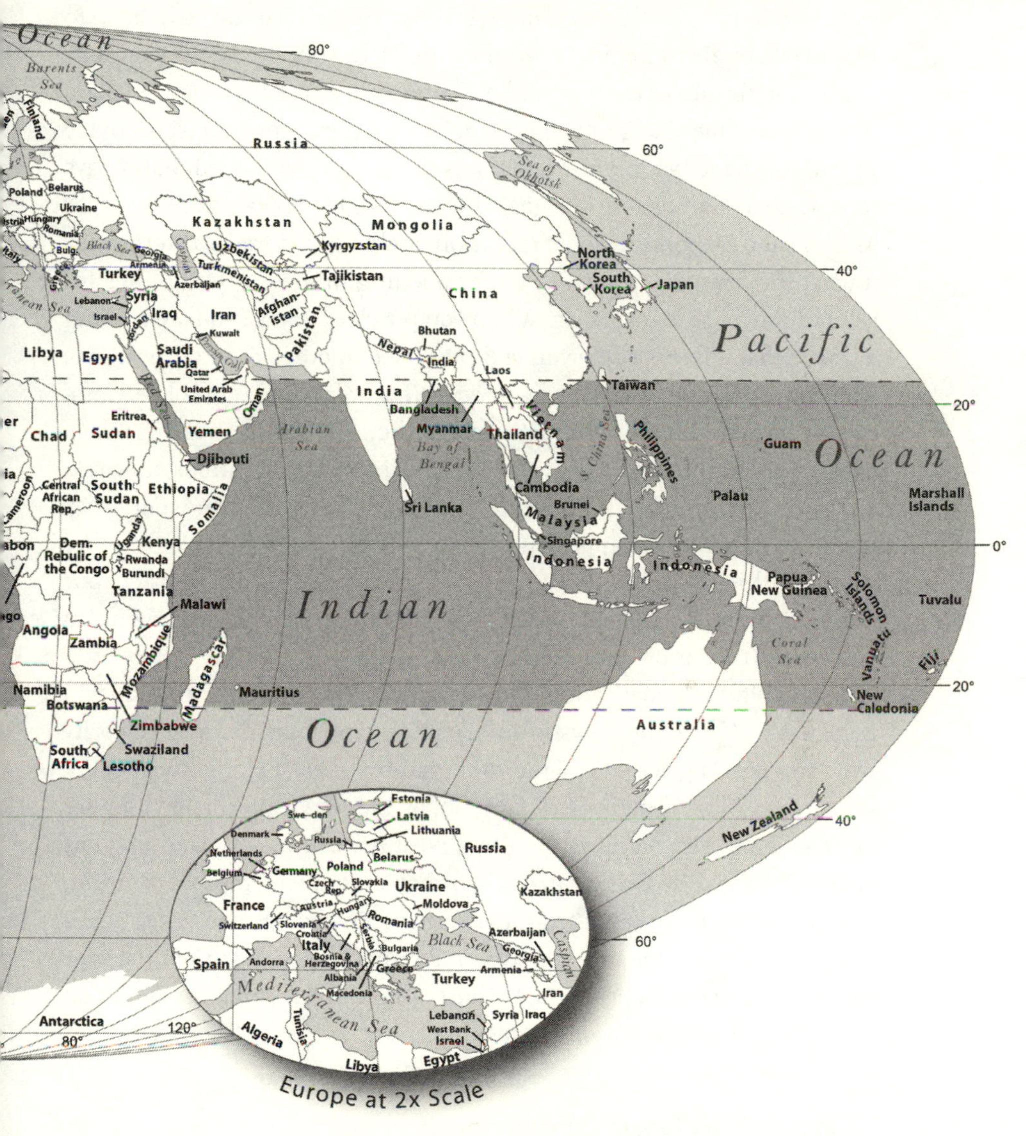

Ocean
Barents Sea
Finland
Russia
Sea of Okhotsk
Poland
Belarus
Ukraine
Hungary
Romania
Bulg.
Black Sea
Georgia
Armenia
Azerbaijan
Italy
Greece
Turkey
Kazakhstan
Caspian
Uzbekistan
Turkmenistan
Kyrgyzstan
Tajikistan
Mongolia
North Korea
South Korea
Japan
China
Syria
Lebanon
Israel
Jordan
Iraq
Iran
Kuwait
Afghanistan
Pakistan
Nepal
Bhutan
India
Libya
Egypt
Saudi Arabia
Qatar
United Arab Emirates
Oman
Red Sea
Pacific
Laos
Taiwan
Bangladesh
Myanmar
Thailand
Vietnam
Philippines
S. China Sea
Chad
Sudan
Eritrea
Yemen
Arabian Sea
Bay of Bengal
Djibouti
Guam
Ocean
Central African Rep.
South Sudan
Ethiopia
Somalia
Cameroon
Sri Lanka
Cambodia
Palau
Marshall Islands
Brunei
Malaysia
Singapore
Gabon
Dem. Rebulic of the Congo
Uganda
Kenya
Rwanda
Burundi
Indonesia
Papua New Guinea
Solomon Islands
Tanzania
Tuvalu
Malawi
Indian
Angola
Zambia
Mozambique
Madagascar
Coral Sea
Vanuatu
Fiji
Namibia
Botswana
Mauritius
New Caledonia
Zimbabwe
Australia
Ocean
South Africa
Swaziland
Lesotho
New Zealand
Antarctica
Estonia
Latvia
Lithuania
Swe-den
Denmark
Russia
Netherlands
Belarus
Belgium
Germany
Poland
Czech Rep.
Slovakia
Ukraine
Moldova
Kazakhstan
France
Austria
Hungary
Romania
Switzerland
Slovenia
Croatia
Serbia
Black Sea
Azerbaijan
Caspian
Italy
Bosnia & Herzegovina
Bulgaria
Georgia
Spain
Andorra
Albania
Greece
Armenia
Turkey
Macedonia
Iran
Mediterranean Sea
Tunisia
Lebanon
Syria
Iraq
Algeria
West Bank
Israel
Libya
Egypt
80°
60°
40°
20°
0°
20°
40°
60°
120°
80°
Europe at 2x Scale

not you choose to look for international career opportunities, your life will be affected by global trends. Some issues, such as those surrounding epidemic disease, may impact you on a deeply personal level. For example, as new strains of influenza emerge, you and your family may have to make choices about finding a vaccine. Similarly, your life is influenced by changes in the global economy. The Chinese government owns a substantial portion of the U.S. government's debt. That means that decisions made in Beijing shape the interest rate that someone in the United States pays for a student loan or a mortgage. Whether you live in Halifax, Canada, or Manchester, England, a global recession or changes in trade patterns may impact the company you work for by opening up new opportunities for sales or moving jobs overseas. When you purchase foods, you are making a choice that affects people you will never see in other parts of the globe, whether you decide to buy shade-grown coffee or fair-trade chocolate. Commodity chains for other products—such as energy—also shape our daily lives. If political unrest closes the Strait of Hormuz, oil importers could see gasoline rationing. At the same time, European wind companies may invest in turbines that appear near you in Kentucky or Calgary, whether you view this positively or not. Security concerns also will impact your life, perhaps when friends or family are deployed overseas or when you encounter frustration with security measures while traveling.

With cultural globalization, our literature, art, music, trade, and technology are affected by flows of information. You may follow a celebrity twitter in Los Angeles, FaceTime your grandmother in Hong Kong, check your friend's Facebook page in London, or follow an international figure on Instagram. Or you may listen to a West African fusion band that has been influenced by Celtic music. You may emigrate someday, or immigrants may shape your community. Perhaps no age has been as touched by global trends as the one you live in. For this reason, it is important for you to learn about international studies, the multidisciplinary field that examines major international issues.

What Is International/Global Studies?

International/global studies (IGS) is an increasingly common major, not only in liberal arts colleges but also in public institutions. What unites all of these programs is that they try to interpret major global trends in a manner that is multidisciplinary; that is, they draw on faculty and ways of looking at the world that come from many different areas (Ishiyama and

Breuning 2004; Hey 2004). A scholar in IGS might utilize the writing of political philosophers to describe the global economy or consider how films reflect new trends in cultural globalization. This cross-pollination among multiple disciplines is central to the field. IGS programs also share certain common characteristics, such as an emphasis on language competence and various dimensions of globalization.

The related term "global studies" is preferred by some scholars because it removes the focus on the nation-state and places it instead on the transnational processes and issues that are key in an era defined by globalization. Global studies programs also often stress the importance of race, class, and gender in international affairs, as well as the importance of social responsibility. Both international studies and global studies programs share a commitment to interdisciplinary work, a focus on globalization and change, and an emphasis on how global trends impact humanity. They both also differ from international relations, an older discipline within political science that emphasizes ties between nations and topics with clear importance to nation-states, such as war, economics, and diplomacy. Finally, both international and global studies share a concern with global citizenship.

Global Citizenship

During the 2008 election campaign in the United States, then presidential candidate Barack Obama declared himself to be a "citizen of the world." Former House Speaker Newt Gingrich criticized this position as "intellectual nonsense and stunningly dangerous" (Gerzon 2009). This exchange encapsulated a debate about the nature of citizenship that stretches back to ancient Greece. The philosopher Socrates (469–399 B.C.E.) allegedly said, "I am a citizen, not of Athens or Greece, but of the world." His student Aristotle thought seriously about the meaning of citizenship, as did the Stoic philosophers. At the core of this idea of world citizenship was the idea that individuals have a duty to other people outside of their state because of their shared humanity. This debate about the nature of citizenship—and the ideal of cosmopolitanism, the belief that we need to view affairs from our perspective as global citizens—has been a thread through the writing of many scholars. It was central to the thinking of Enlightenment philosophers such as the German Immanuel Kant, who spoke of an individual's membership in a universal community as a basis for global peace (Kant, "Essay on Theory and Practice," in Brown, Nardin, and Rengger 2002,

441–50). It even shaped the thought of European philosophers during the Age of Empire. For example, the Italian thinker Giuseppe Mazzini wrote at length about an individual's duties to humanity and the fact that an individual's loyalty cannot be determined by his or her nationality alone (Mazzini, *On the Duties of Man*, in Brown, Nardin, and Rengger 2002, 476–85). Martha Nussbaum (1998) and Kwame Anthony Appiah (2006, 2008) have written influential works in defense of cosmopolitanism, which describe it as a perspective that can best serve the ethical and political needs of people in an era of globalization.

While this ideal has been enduring, it has also been contested, because global citizenship is not a legal status. Critics argue that it is a vaguely defined term that appeals to people's sentiments and emotions but has little meaning in an anarchical world—that is, in an international order that lacks a central power to impose law. They portray it as a "hands across the cultures" ideal that sounds appealing but lacks any grounding in reality. Others suggest that the idea ignores the reality that there are power differentials between those nation-states, groups, and individuals that enjoy privilege and power and those that don't. For example, Kevin Lyons and his colleagues (2011) characterize well-intentioned but often naive international gap year tourism/service as part of a broader neoliberal agenda. Kate Simpson suggests, "The current gap year volunteer industry does not address issues of Western privilege and power and actively promotes the simplistic binaries of 'us' and 'them'" (2004, 690).

This book is not the place to encapsulate this broader debate. But global citizenship remains a powerful idea, and as authors we believe it has deep meaning. As a citizen, you will face complex global issues, from trade to war, commanding your attention and calling for you to make decisions. One goal of this text is to help you critically reflect on global issues and identify the contexts where your loyalty, responsibility, and connection to others will make a difference. Perhaps the notion of global citizenship seems too strong or exclusive to you. If this is so, what about the notion of being a globally minded individual?

You are living in what Mary Louise Pratt (1996) terms a "contact zone"; that is, your ideas come in contact with other people and other ideas all the time. In order to negotiate this space, you have to be able to "imaginatively step into the world view of the other" (Bennett 1998). In a sense, this mindset will mean that you will have a bigger "tool kit" to deal with problems. A global perspective changes not just what you think but what you do.

The Authors and IGS

We are faculty members who have taught IGS for over twenty years and served as directors of an IGS department at a large urban institution. Kim Brown became interested in international studies as an undergraduate while studying anthropology, French, and geography at Macalester College. During that time, she was able to co-teach an international studies senior seminar with a visiting German Fulbrighter, Dr. Gotz von Houwald, whose area of specialization was Central American Indigenous peoples. This experience led her to become passionate about the international learning experience. She is now a professor of applied linguistics who has expertise in world Englishes—the different forms of English spoken globally—as well as in intercultural communication and education and development. She lived and worked in Iran during the late 1970s, a time of turmoil that included the 1979 Revolution, the beginning of the decade-long Iran-Iraq war, and the now-infamous takeover of the U.S. embassy and ensuing hostage crisis. She has maintained a close cultural connection to Iran ever since.

Shawn Smallman became interested in international affairs while he was an undergraduate at Queen's University, where he became fascinated with Latin America during a history class taught by Catherine LeGrand. He is now a professor of IGS. He has published books examining the history of military terror in Brazil and the evolution of the AIDS pandemic in Latin America. For the latter project, he carried out fieldwork in Brazil, Cuba, and Mexico, during which he interviewed drug traffickers, crack addicts, sex workers, doctors, and gay leaders. More recently, he has done work on influenza and global health, such as viral sample sharing in Indonesia (Smallman 2013). He is particularly interested in how conspiracy theories and fake news impact people's willingness to be vaccinated.

We have both taught outside of our own countries (in Germany and Iran) and have traveled widely. From this background, we have the experience of crossing cultural boundaries, from Rio de Janeiro to Tehran. We speak or read Farsi, French, Portuguese, and Spanish. We have also served as administrators: Brown was vice provost for international affairs, while Smallman was the dean of undergraduate studies and vice provost of instruction and later department chair. Both of us have worked to internationalize undergraduate education and have presented the results of our work at professional meetings. Our teaching, travel, disciplines, work experience, and language competence have shaped how we have written this book. We have a shared belief in the value of a liberal arts education, the importance of clear learning outcomes, and the necessity of Universal Design for Learning (UDL), a learning framework incorporating specific techniques such as multimodal presentation of information to enable all learners to profit from the classroom space.

Learning Outcomes and Competing Worldviews

We want you to finish this text having achieved a number of learning outcomes: to see yourselves as members of global as well as local communities, to be aware of major world regions and the nation-states within them, to be open to intercultural contact, to place issues in historical and ideological context, and to be able to judge information about major global trends and issues. Additionally, we hope you will be able to situate your prior and current experiences in informing your approach to global engagement. We expect that as you work through this text, you will come to understand key global issues and the perspectives held by different cultures regarding these issues. We also want you to be able to think critically about competing worldviews. This goal is critical to many disciplines, but it is particularly essential in IGS. For this reason, you will see global issues presented from different perspectives throughout this text.

In the chapters that follow, we will introduce material from all major world regions. You will see ideas and information from scholars whose ideas conflict with each other as well as from scholars whose ideas reinforce common understandings of particular issues. You will not see chapters on every global issue, although there are many key topics that might have filled entire sections, such as water, religion, and women. No comprehensive selection of chapters was possible because of the breadth of international issues. Instead, chapters 2 through 7 focus on history, globalization (economic, political, and cultural), development, and security to give you a broad understanding of the context of global issues. The second block of chapters focuses on global topics in which you may more readily see yourself as an actor. The subjects covered in these chapters are, in order, food, health, energy, and environment. Chapter 12 considers the many career opportunities in international fields, and the conclusion will place what you have learned in context.

References

Andreotti, V. 2014. Soft versus critical global citizenship education. *Development education, policy, and practice 3* (1): 22–31. Retrieved April 3, 2019, from http://www.osdemethodology.org.uk/texts/softcriticalvan.pdf.

Appiah, K. A. 2006. *Cosmopolitanism: Ethics in a world of strangers*. New York: W. W. Norton.

———. 2008. Education for global citizenship. *Yearbook of the National Society for the Study of Education* 107 (1): 83–99.

Bennett, J. 1998. Transition shock: Putting culture shock in perspective. In *Basic concepts of intercultural communication*, edited by M. Bennett, 215–24. Yarmouth, Maine: Intercultural Press.

Brown, C., T. Nardin, and N. Rengger, eds. 2002. *International relations in political thought: Texts from the ancient Greeks to the First World War*. New York: Cambridge University Press.

Carter, D., and S. Gradin. 2001. *Writing as reflective action: A reader*. New York: Longman.

Gerzon, M. 2009. Going global: The Gingrich-Obama "global citizen" debate. June 23. http://www.ewi.info/going—global-gingrich-obama-%E2%80%9Cglobal-citizen%E2%80%9D-debate.

Hey, J. 2004. Can international studies research be the basis for an undergraduate international studies curriculum? A response to Ishiyama and Breuning. *International Studies Perspectives* 5:395–99.

Hoopes, D. 1979. Intercultural communication concepts and the psychology of intercultural experience. In *Multicultural education: A cross-cultural training approach*, edited by M. D. Pusch, 10–38. Yarmouth, Maine: Intercultural Press.

Ishiyama, J., and M. Breuning. 2004. A survey of international studies programs at liberal arts colleges and universities in the Midwest: Characteristics and correlates. *International Studies Perspectives* 5:134–46.

Lyons, K., J. Hanley, S. Wearing, and J. Neil. 2012. Gap year volunteer tourism: Myths of global citizenship? *Annals of Tourism Research 39* (1): 361–78.

Nussbaum, M. 1998. *Cultivating humanity: A classical defense of reform in liberal education*. Boston: Harvard University Press.

Pratt, M. L. 1996. Arts of the contact zone. In *Resources for teaching ways of reading: An anthology for writers*, edited by D. Bartholomae and A. Petrosky, 440–60. Boston: Bedford Books.

Simpson, K. 2004. "Doing development": The gap year, volunteer-tourists and a popular practice of development. *Journal of International Development 16*:681–92.

Smallman, S. 2013. Biopiracy and vaccines: Indonesia and the World Health Organization's new pandemic influenza plan. *Journal of International and Global Studies* 4 (2): 20–36.

Stevenson, R. W. 2002. Middle path emerges in debate on Africa aid. *New York Times*, June 9.

Suarez-Orozco, M., and D. Qin-Hilliard. 2004. *Globalization: Culture and education in the new millennium*, 1–37. Berkeley: University of California Press.

TWO **History**

➤ SYNOPSIS

Technological and military changes led to the unexpected rise of Europe and the birth of modern imperialism beginning in the late fifteenth century. Although the rise of nationalism ultimately destroyed European empires, nearly five centuries of European imperialism have deeply shaped our world's demography, economy, and culture. Now the international system is defined by the nation-state, which is increasingly challenged by the power of globalization. These two forces—the nation-state and globalization—have created tension in the current period between populism and nationalism on the one hand and migration and financial globalization on the other. Europe has also entered into a relative economic and political decline, which is being matched by the dramatic growth of some Asian nations, particularly China.

➤ SCAFFOLDING

As you read through this chapter, think about how you would answer each of the questions below.

When you started this chapter, how much did you know about the history of imperialism? How has the legacy of imperialism shaped our world?

In chapter 1, you were introduced to the idea of global citizenship, which is not a new idea. In what ways might it have been easier for people in an earlier era to think of themselves as global citizens?

Whose histories were missing from this chapter? What information could have been added?

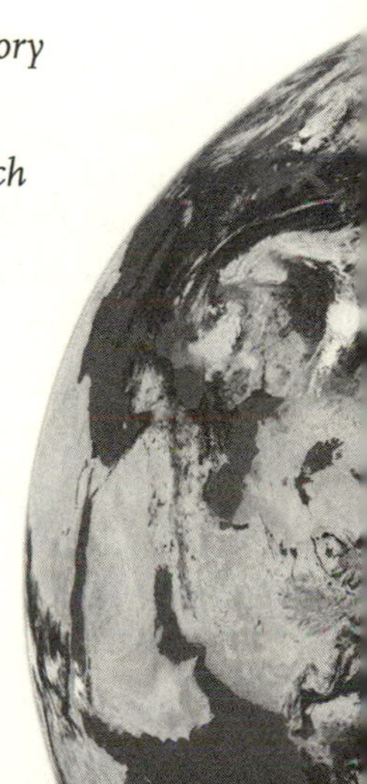

➤ CORE CONCEPTS

Why was Europe's rise unexpected? How would you describe European empires, and what factors led to their end?

What are the similarities and differences between different eras of globalization?

What do you think the future of the nation-state is likely to be, based on the information from this chapter? What might replace the nation-state?

In what ways does this history help us to understand the rise of populism and nationalism in the contemporary period?

Our knowledge of the world has been shaped by the stories we have been told and the contexts we have lived in. While many would say there is an absolute set of true facts regarding world events, others would argue that the lenses we put on shape both what we see and what we look for. We do not generally read an account of an event and ask, "Who wrote this?," "Is something missing?," or, "Are there equally compelling alternative explanations of the same phenomenon?" We learn what we are taught. In international studies, we strive to understand how local contexts and cultural issues may shape our understanding of information. Two cases, based on our own experiences with academic institutions in Brazil and Iran, illustrate how a historical context shapes the presentation of information during times of revolution and struggle.

How people understand their world is shaped by the stories they have been told and the way in which they understand their past as an individual, a family member, and a citizen. This reality became clear to me (Smallman) in the summer of 1990, when I did intensive language training in Portuguese in Brazil. At one point, I was seated on a lawn on a university campus, speaking with a group of friends who were all university students. I told them that the way that their university was laid out made no sense. They had to take a bus to travel from their residence hall to their classrooms, and then take another bus to travel to the cafeteria for lunch. Why hadn't the architects designed a space in which people could walk from one place to another throughout their day? My friends then told me that this was no accident. During military rule in Brazil (1964–85), the armed forces had feared that students could form a source of opposition to the regime. Accordingly, military officers had deliberately designed the university's layout to make it as difficult as possible for students to congregate. When I told this story to a faculty member later to learn if it was true, the professor told me that the changes the military had made during this period went much deeper than the buildings themselves. The university had also changed its curriculum, so that history classes now ended with Brazilian independence in the 1820s. The generals had not wanted university students to study more contemporary social issues. What was strange, the faculty member told me, was that since democratization in 1985, the curriculum had not changed because both faculty members and students had internalized this definition of history. When I spoke with my student friends later, they disagreed with this interpretation. They claimed that history courses ended in the early nineteenth century because anything more recent was not truly history. With time, as I researched a book on how the Brazilian military shaped historical memory to achieve its political goals, I came to understand the deep legacies that military rule had on Brazilian academia, popular memory, and society.

These issues also were relevant half a world away. In March 1979 the Ayatollah Khomeini returned to Iran. Universities were closed for a period of more than three years as the government developed a plan to Islamize the curriculum. Students who needed fewer than nine credits to finish their degree were allowed to graduate. Others had to wait three and a half years and submit proof that they were strong Muslims who had not engaged in any antigovernment activity during the time the universities were closed or immediately preceding the closure. At the high school level, social studies textbooks were the first to undergo a rewriting process. Pictures of the shah were stripped from the front page and replaced with pictures of the Ayatollah Khomeini; photos of burning tires and demonstrations were placed within the contemporary history chapter. The shah was denounced in the textbook, and the virtues of the new Islamic Republic were laid out. At the elementary school level, all illustrations beginning with the first grade text were changed: illustrations of a family eating a meal at a table were replaced with images of a family seated on a carpet with a large tablecloth spread on the floor; instead of a small girl lying in a bed with her blankets pulled up, hair askew around her face, the textbook had an image of a child lying on a pallet on the floor with a head scarf on. These changes were completed within a twelve-month period. The government was heavily invested in rewriting history and framing what was to come.

Governments care about how you understand the past because it shapes your decisions politically and your engagement in the world around you.

Because multiple forces will try to shape your understanding, it is very important to learn to critically interpret the past. This chapter will focus on the surprising rise of Europe in the fifteenth century, the Age of Imperialism and its legacy, the emergence of nationalism, the roots of current globalization, and the continued importance of the nation-state. Our intent is to provide you with one perspective of world history that will allow you to frame later information in the text.

The Unexpected Rise of Europe

If a dispassionate observer had studied the globe in the fourteenth century, it would have been unlikely that he or she would have chosen Europe as the region that would dominate international affairs for the next five centuries. Nothing predestined Europe's rise. Barbara Tuchman titled her 1978 history of this period *A Distant Mirror: The Calamitous 14th Century* with good reason. The Black Death so depopulated Paris that wolves roamed its empty suburbs. The division of the papacy plunged Christendom into a prolonged political crisis, while the Hundred Years' War (1337–1453) absorbed the energies of two major states (England and France) for generations. The start of the fourteenth century saw the onset of the Little Ice Age, which perhaps explains why the Norse colonies in Greenland disappeared. Famine was a frequent challenge for European states during this period, which was so politically and socially difficult that some Europeans thought that the world might be ending. The Crusades had failed, and Europe was on the defensive.

While Europe staggered from one crisis to the next, Islam had undergone centuries of expansion during an earlier epoch of cultural and religious globalization, which had created a shared world that stretched from the Atlantic to Central Asia and from Iraq to Indonesia. The impact of this experience was enduring: "[T]he Arab conquests inaugurated a thousand-year era, lasting from the seventh to the seventeenth century, when all the major civilizations of the Old World—Greco-Roman, Irano-Semitic, Sanskritic, Malay-Javanese, and Chinese—were for the first time brought into contact with one another by and within a single overarching civilization" (Eaton 1990, 17). New cities sprang up from Baghdad to Cordova, as an urban, sophisticated civilization spread throughout the Old World (19).

Travelers such as Ibn Battuta could travel with ease in the fourteenth century, during which he "crisscrossed North and West Africa, the Middle East, the steppes of Central Asia, India, Southeast Asia, and China, for an estimated total of 73,000 miles" (Eaton 1990, 44). For centuries, Islamic scholars had translated works from Greek, studied mathematics, and rethought agronomy. Islamic victories allowed them to experiment with new crops, including "fruits such as banana, sour orange, lemon, lime, mango, watermelon, and the coconut palm" (23). Equally important was the diffusion of new technologies, such as paper (22). Many Europeans feared that Christendom could not withstand Islam's waxing power. In 1453 Byzantium, which for eight centuries had shielded Europe from Islamic invasion, fell to the Turks because its famous walls could not withstand cannon fire. This defeat blocked the old spice trade to the East along the Silk Road and left Europe isolated.

At the same time that Islam was rising, China was expanding its power from Asia into the Indian Ocean. In 1421 Imperial China sent out a massive fleet—which contained many vessels that dwarfed the greatest European ships—on a nearly three-year expedition to India, East Africa, and Indonesia (Abu-Lughod 1993, 10). Chinese technology was advanced, as were the country's population and resources. But even for China, this fleet was so expensive that its construction created controversy. By the time the expedition's survivors returned, China was turning inward, and the great fleet was disbanded. This ended an important opportunity for Chinese expansion: "Although the reasons for this reversal of policy remain shrouded in mystery and enigma, and scholars are far from agreeing on an explanation, the results were clear and disastrous for the prospects of continued Asian independence" (16). One of the outcomes of this inward turn, both in China and Japan, was that it permitted Russia to extend its authority across Siberia to the Pacific. It also meant that expanding European empires did not face competition in India, East Africa, or Indonesia. For this reason, Janet Lippman Abu-Lughod has argued that China's turn inward was fundamental to the success of European expansionism (16).

This expansion began in the unlikeliest of places: Portugal, a small, lightly populated nation on the edge of the Western world. When the Silk Road was closed to the West, Europeans began to wonder if they could reach the East by sea. This idea proved especially attractive to Henry the Navigator, the monarch of Portugal who spent his fortune and his life encouraging scholarship in the era of navigation and ship design. During this period the Portuguese created the caravel, based on earlier Arab designs. This ship had lateen sails that enabled them to travel against the winds that prevailed along the West African coast. Throughout the 1400s, the Portuguese expanded out into the Atlantic to the Azores (1427), the Cape

Verde Islands (1455–56), and the west coast of Africa (McGhee 1991, 79). This exploration helped Europeans to develop and hone their naval skills while China was turning inward. At the same time that political divisions and other problems sapped the strength of Islamic Spain (Andalusia), the states of Christian Spain moved toward unity, especially after the marriage of Ferdinand and Isabella in 1467. With the fall of Granada—the last Islamic state in Spain—to the combined forces of Castile and Aragon in 1492, Spain was freed to direct its energies into the Atlantic.

While the new unity and naval knowledge of Iberia prompted European expansionism, an equally important force was a revolution in military affairs that made European armies vastly more powerful than their counterparts. In the fourteenth century, there had been little to distinguish European armies from those of Africa, the Islamic Empire, or China. This changed in the following three centuries. Gunpowder was a Chinese creation that the Islamic world and Europe adopted in the 1300s. At Nicopolis in September 1396, the Turks destroyed a French army, proving that European forces had no relative advantage over those of the Ottomans. A century later, however, gunpowder had brought profound changes to Europe. Mounted knights were no longer effective against foot soldiers with matchlocks. Different states began to experiment with combining pikemen with gunners. The rise of cannons made castles outmoded. With the introduction of cannons into naval warfare, even small Portuguese ships could challenge Islamic fleets in the Indian Ocean. The change took place over centuries, and the Islamic world, in particular, adopted many of the same practices and technologies. But the trend was clear: "By 1700 the disproportion between European and other styles of warfare had become pronounced and, in conjunction with parallel improvements in naval management and equipment, allowed Europeans to expand their power literally around the globe in the course of the eighteenth and nineteenth centuries" (McNeill 1989, 2). The timing of this military revolution was important, for it took place at the same moment that Europe expanded into the Atlantic and beyond.

The Americas

The New World likely had been visited by other cultures prior to Columbus. Certainly, the native populations of North America had trading relationships with their counterparts in eastern Siberia, as well as with the Norse in Greenland, which means that some archaeological finds of iron and bronze goods in northern Canada predate Columbus's arrival (Sutherland 2000, 244–47; Schledermann 2000; Pringle 2012). Archaeologists have found Norse ships in Greenland that were built of Canadian wood (Seaver 2000, 273). So the term "discovery" must be a qualified one, as flows of people and goods had taken place for thousands of years. Still, Columbus's arrival in 1492 in the Caribbean was an epoch-making event and marked the true birth of Europe's rise to global dominance. For thirty years, the Spanish expanded throughout the Caribbean, with disastrous results for local peoples. On the island of Hispaniola, the Tainos' numbers plummeted from perhaps more than 1 million to at most a few thousand in 1531. Between 1519 and 1521, Spanish troops led by Hernán Cortés overthrew the Aztec Empire; a decade later, Spanish troops under Francisco Pizarro overthrew the Incas, the greatest empire then known: "[B]igger by far than any European state, the Inca dominion extended over a staggering thirty-two degrees of latitude—as if a single power held sway from St. Petersburg to Cairo" (Mann 2006, 71). As a result, Spain gained access to the silver, gold, crops, and resources of the New World.

The reasons for the Europeans' victory were manifold, as Jared Diamond (1997), Alfred Crosby (1972, 35–63), and others have explained, despite the cultural richness of New World peoples. The Aztec and Incan Empires reflected masterful political organization. The Incas were an ethnic group that came to dominate the Andean region of South America in the 1400s and 1500s. They were engineers who could build roads and bridges to unite their empire from one end of the Andes Mountain chain to the other, while they constructed buildings out of stones so carefully worked that no mortar was needed. The astronomical knowledge in Meso-America may have been equal to that of Europe at the time. Anyone who has visited the Museum of Gold in Bogotá—which holds but a tiny fraction of the cultural wealth of pre-contact Andean peoples—must stand in awe of its riches. But none of these achievements changed the fact that New World peoples had not been exposed to smallpox and other diseases (Alchon 2003). Nor had they seen horses, steel, or gunpowder. In 542 the Byzantine Empire's efforts to reclaim the Western Roman Empire had collapsed in the face of one illness: bubonic plague (Rosen 2007, 3). The Aztecs and Incas had to deal simultaneously with smallpox, gunpowder, and cavalry. The populations of these empires underwent a stunning demographic collapse (Mann 2006, 143–44).

While the Spanish conquered the Aztec and Incan Empires, the Portuguese expanded into Africa and began the slave trade. After Vaco de Gama successfully passed the southern tip of Africa in 1498, the Portuguese gained access to the trade markets of Asia, which undercut the old spice road. In 1516 the Portuguese destroyed Islamic forces in the Arabian Sea (Abu-Lughod 1993, 9). The Islamic world was no longer the key connection of East and West. Timbuktu in West Africa was a center renowned both for its wealth and for its scholarship in the fourteenth century (Eaton 1990, 41). But that wealth depended on trade, and Portuguese galleons were more efficient than camel caravans. Portugal, which was a marginal state on the rim of Europe, controlled an empire that stretched from Goa, India, to Mozambique, Africa. Its colony of Brazil would one day come to encompass half of South America. No longer was the Mediterranean the center of a global trading system (Abu-Lughod 1993, 18). Instead, Europeans dominated global trade—at the core of which was slavery.

The Spanish could count initially on the labor of the large Indigenous populations that they had conquered in Mexico and Peru. As these populations declined, however, they turned to African slaves from Portuguese colonies in Africa. Because of the collapse of Caribbean populations, African slavery was always fundamental to the region's development during the colonial period. Likewise, the Portuguese—who dominated the slave trade—turned to African slaves as the main labor source in Brazil, where sugar plantations in the northeast created fabulous wealth. Similarly, the British colonies in the New World soon embraced slavery to obtain the labor that underlay an economy based on plantation agriculture. This trade enriched both the nations that controlled it and the producers in the colonies who employed it. The scale of the trade was so large that it had a demographic impact upon both the Old World and the New World while creating ideologies and inequalities that have endured until the present.

It was this period that created modern ideas of race, in which social class and standing were mapped onto skin color. This was not a long-standing tradition in European history. The Romans had not placed much importance on skin color, and while they practiced slavery, it was in no way defined by race. The demographic changes created by the slave trade brought peoples together from diverse regions of the globe. This provided a useful tool for economic elites, who could determine a person's social role by their physical appearance. The challenge, of course, was that from the start, mixing took place, and binary categories of race became complicated. Different imperial powers adopted varied approaches to assigning racial identities and social roles, which meant that the idea of race in Brazil was quite different from that in the United States, although both shared the

> The same historical event can seem very different based on your cultural or national perspective. Can you identify three events or trends in this chapter that would be perceived differently by two groups?

brutality of slavery. But it was in this period that conceptions of race appeared that continue to shape social and political issues in North and South America and Europe. Even at the time, there were some individuals who questioned both these categories and slavery itself. But the wealth created by slavery was so central to European empires that economic interests outweighed moral concerns.

Besides the wealth created by the slave trade, the conquest of the New World also enabled Europeans to exploit new agricultural and mineral resources. After silver was discovered at Potosi, Bolivia—an old Incan mining site—in the 1540s, Spain had access to perhaps the greatest single source of mineral wealth in the world. There were also new crops that were introduced into Europe that would put an end to the cycle of famine so common in the late Middle Ages (despite counterexamples, such as the Irish potato famine of the mid-nineteenth century). Alfred Crosby (1972, 64–121) has written about the process of biological imperialism, by which European countries exported new crops to the Americas. By this term, Crosby referred to the practice by which Europeans replaced native plants and animals with crops and domestic animals from the Old World to transform the environment in a manner that suited their economic needs. There are many examples of this process. Sugar came to define Brazilian society throughout the colonial period, but important new crops—chilies, tomatoes, corn, squash, and many others—brought about an agricultural revolution in Europe. As Crosby has argued, these crops led to a demographic explosion in Europe and the Old World, as the food supply increased dramatically. This demographic change created a "surplus population" in Europe, which enabled large populations of European descent to travel and settle in the Americas (165–207). Within Europe, the population increase, the precious metals, the slave economy, and the trade networks that came with the conquest of the New World fed rapid technological advances and the expansion of European power into new regions (Abu-Lughod 1993, 18).

Europe did not confine its ambitions to the Americas. The Dutch founded the Dutch East India Company in 1602 and came to control Indonesia; Dutch ambitions in Brazil were overcome by warfare between 1630 and 1654. In 1788 the British claimed Australia. Although they fought in the New World, the Portuguese and Dutch both expanded their holdings in Africa. In the nineteenth century, European powers competed to acquire colonies in Africa in a process in which the division of vast stretches of African territory was made in conference rooms in Europe.

Even regions that had been wealthier or more technologically advanced than Europe in the fourteenth century were vulnerable. The Ottoman Empire waned, and by the early twentieth century, most of the Islamic world had come under European rule. Even China, which was once the wealthiest and most populous nation on earth, lost control of territories (Hong Kong and Macao) or had areas carved up into "spheres of influence." This phrase recognized the particular areas that European countries tended to dominate, even if they did not formally control them. Although European states engaged in frequent warfare during the region's imperial expansion, this was tempered by diplomatic efforts to define these spheres of influence. This project began as early as the Treaty of Tordesillas in 1494, under which the pope used his authority to divide all newly discovered lands between the Portuguese and Spanish. European states later brokered similar arrangements in Africa, Asia, and the Middle East to avoid inter-European conflict while also expanding their control around the globe. During much of the nineteenth and early twentieth centuries, different areas of the globe either came to be directly under European control or had their destinies defined indirectly through such spheres of influence.

The Legacy of Empire

The Age of Empire would have a profound impact upon the globe, in part because European empires proved to be surprisingly enduring. The Portuguese, who had begun this expansion in the fifteenth century, did not lose their African possessions until the 1970s. While a history of this period is far too complex to detail in this brief chapter, it marked the onset of ideas and markets that continue to shape our world. This section will focus on its legacies. One of the most important legacies is the creation of diasporas—populations outside of their homelands who still retain emotional and cultural connections to their places of origin. As this chapter has discussed, the slave trade brought millions of Africans across the Atlantic. Sections of Africa were devastated and depopulated by the trade, as one West African state after another fell to the Portuguese and other nations. The entire demography of other regions, such as the Caribbean, was remade. Of course, the slave trade was not the only great population movement during this period. The nineteenth century saw large population movements from Europe to the Americas, Australia, New Zealand, South Africa, and other colonies. While some people went looking for more opportunities, many others—such as the Irish in the aftermath of the Great Famine or Russian Jews fleeing violence—sought to escape dangers in the Old World. These diasporas profoundly shaped identities and nationalities from Australia to North America. These movements have parallels in the current era, as poverty and demographic growth in Africa and political instability in the Middle East lead large masses of people to migrate to Europe. In many respects, this current moment represents an inversion of the trends of the previous century.

At the same time, this earlier period saw the creation of colonial relations, in which imperial powers established and governed the economies of their colonies to the advantage of the mother country. For example, the Caribbean islands were devoted to monocrop agriculture that created wealth for a small European population on the islands in addition to the governments of France, Spain, Holland, and England. Trade within this system was carefully controlled so as to discourage the development of manufacturing within the colonies, which might allow the periphery to compete with the center. Colonies were also able to trade only with their mother countries and not with other European powers. In all respects, the economies—and even the ecologies—of the colonies were defined to benefit the metropole. While imperialism came to an end with the collapse of Portuguese rule in Africa in the 1970s, many of these colonial relationships continue to have a legacy in the present. Anyone who has traveled through the vast sugar fields of Brazil or Cuba can see the enduring markets that were created during the Age of Imperialism, as well as their social legacy.

The Age of Empire also gave birth to the identities that ultimately destroyed the imperial system. The inequality of colonial relations created resentments in Latin America and the United States that led to revolution. Colonial censors from Brazil to Mexico sought to limit the spread of nationalist ideals that could challenge imperial authority. But the idea of the nation-state, which was born in Europe, over time spread throughout the colonies, so that the period from 1776 to the 1970s marked the edge of Europe's expansion.

The Rise of Nationalism

In a sense, this period witnessed a struggle between two ideas. On the one hand, European imperialism had continued a process of globalization that may have stretched back to the Islamic flowering that preceded it. On the other hand, the Age of Empire also witnessed the rise of the idea of the nation-state. In 1648 the Peace of Westphalia ended the Thirty Years' War in the region that would later become Germany. The key idea of the two treaties that ended this religious war was that each "prince" had the right to decide the public religion of his own people, while people who practiced other Christian beliefs could still practice their religion in private. At the same time, it was a clear principle of this understanding that states should refrain from interfering in each other's affairs, which is central to the modern idea of national sovereignty. At its core, national sovereignty defines a world in which peoples receive their legal identities through their citizenship in nations. These nation-states, in turn, have the right to govern themselves independently and determine their internal affairs.

Of course, as Europeans adopted this idea and it became an increasingly powerful tool, they did not wish to extend sovereignty to their colonies. And nation making was a violent and contradictory affair, which was often founded upon myth making and exclusion (Anderson 1983). Even the concept of nationalism is difficult to define, despite the intense hold that it gained among millions of people. Nonetheless, the concept of nationhood spread from Europe to the rest of the globe and provided the foundation for our modern international system.

The tension between the ideals of nationhood and empire first became apparent in the Americas, where the United States achieved independence in 1783. In 1804 Haiti claimed independence as part of the only successful slave rebellion in history. Most of Latin America achieved independence by the 1820s. In other areas, such as Canada and Australia, colonies gradually took a peaceful path to nationhood. These two contradictory processes existed side by side, so that even as much of the New World gained independence in the nineteenth century, most of Africa and Asia witnessed the rapid expansion of European empires.

This tension between nationalist ideals and imperialist reality did not exist only on the periphery of empires. The contradiction between the two helped to lead Europe into two devastating world wars in the twentieth century. Newer nations that were late to imperial expansion sought what they argued to be their rightful place on the world stage. To mobilize their peoples, all nations—even in the staunchly anti-nationalist Soviet Union—turned to nationalism. Other empires, such as that of Austro-Hungary, were overwhelmed by the rising tide of nationalism and fractured into multiple nation-states. In the aftermath of the Second World War, many European nations lacked the resources or popular will to maintain an empire. Within Europe, the idea of nationalism was discredited, and sympathy grew among elites for a pan-European vision that would culminate in the creation of the European Union (EU).

In Africa, Asia, and elsewhere, the rising power of nationalism made empires increasingly untenable. In some cases, European nations gave up their empire with a minimum of resistance, as the British did in India. In other cases, such as the French in Algeria and Vietnam, European forces fought on until they were overrun or bankrupted. But the result was the same. The first great wave of nationalist movements took place in the late eighteenth and early nineteenth centuries and freed most of the Americas from European control. The second great wave, after the end of World War II in 1945, saw colonies in the Caribbean, Africa, Asia, and the Pacific gain their independence.

Within Europe itself, the continent was divided, and power passed to two external powers—a fact that demonstrates the degree to which European power was eclipsed. The United States and the Soviet Union dominated the international system. The key line between these two powers was drawn in the heart of Germany, where the Berlin Wall represented the greatest division in the international order. While nations could declare their neutrality in the political, economic, and ideological struggle between these states, it proved difficult to avoid taking sides given the blandishments that each offered. The major European powers, such as England, France, and Germany, feared they could no longer define a conflict that might culminate in the destruction of Europe. The age of European dominance had passed. But the tension endured between the nation-state and global forces.

Imperialism's Collapse and the Cold War

In many respects, from the late eighteenth century onward, the Age of Empire was defined by the tension between imperialism and nationalism. In contrast, after World War II, global political affairs were dominated by the struggle between the Soviet Union and its clients and the United States and its allies. The United States depicted itself as leading an alliance of democratic countries against the totalitarian Soviet bloc. But in practice, it proved quite willing to ally itself with brutally repressive regimes in Latin America, Indonesia, and Africa—provided that they had clear anti-Communist credentials. The Soviet Union depicted itself as the standard bearer of anti-colonialism, but its invasions of Hungary, Czechoslovakia, and Afghanistan showed it had much in common with the nineteenth-century Russian Empire. In theory, China and the Soviet Union were close allies as the world's great Communist powers. In practice, the two sparred over their contested borders, while in the 1970s China drew closer to the United States. Despite these contradictions, both sides sought to maintain alliances, cultivate clients, and punish those nations that aligned with the opposing side.

For more than four decades, this great contest between two global ideologies subordinated all other questions. In other words, the two Great Powers (a Great Power is a state so influential that it is able to help define the international system) viewed all international issues through the lens of the Cold War, often to the great frustration of countries—the nonaligned nations—that did not want to take part in this contest. Because this competition was viewed as a zero-sum game, a win by one side was necessarily a loss for the other. This led to terrible errors, such as the U.S. intervention in Vietnam, and near disasters, such as the Cuban Missile Crisis. But the Cold War also had positive impacts, such as freezing ethnic and nationalist struggles in Yugoslavia, despite the brutality and violence that characterized Soviet rule. The system was also predictable, and it could be assumed that both sides were rational. With time, both sides had invested so much in infrastructure, ideology, and energy in the contest that its end appeared unthinkable. Therefore, it came as a great shock when the Soviet Union collapsed with stunning speed in 1991.

One of the great tasks of the so-called post–Cold War era was formulating a new framework to understand international affairs. For a brief period, authors presented one argument after another. Some proposed that the future would be one of unstoppable democratization—which would be positive but quite boring (Fukuyama 1989). Others foresaw a future defined by clashes between major world civilizations (Huntington 1993). No one framework can capture all the tensions and movements in any historical period. With time, however, it became clear that the Cold War had obscured a contradiction between the expansion of the nation-states and the rising power of globalization. As imperialism ended, the number of nation-states climbed rapidly. At the same moment, however, the institutions that shaped globalization were founded, and the nation-state faced new challenges to its authority.

Globalization

At the broadest level, globalization refers to the rise of sociopolitical and economic networks that dominate local and regional interactions. Manfred Steger (2003, 13) refers to a "multidimensional set of social processes that create, multiply, stretch, and intensify worldwide social interdependencies and exchanges while at the same time fostering in people a growing awareness of deepening connections between the local and the distant." The strength of this definition is that it describes globalization as a process that takes place not only at the level of the state related to trade or politics but also at the level of people's daily lives, which includes culture and identity.

Globalization is not a new phenomenon, and dating its onset is difficult. As we have described already, the period of Islamic expansion (the seventh through seventeenth centuries) had witnessed a period of cultural flowering accompanied by technological, agricultural, and economic exchange that in many respects looks like an early period of globalization. Certainly, the expansion of European empires created global networks that stretched from remote Pacific Islands to West Africa. New technologies, from the development of the telegraph to the rise of steam-powered trains, have been connecting peoples since the nineteenth century. Nonetheless, the period of globalization that began after the Cold War has accelerated the manner in which the global impedes on the local to a degree unknown in earlier eras. While new technologies are important to this process, it could not have taken place without an institutional context, which was deliberately created under the leadership of the United States after World War II. These institutions, collectively called the Bretton Woods System, are fundamental to understanding globalization. Their influence is a key factor that helps to explain why the current period of globalization differs from that of the past.

In 1944 it appeared inevitable that Germany, Japan, and their Axis counterparts would be defeated. It was also clear that Europe would be devastated and that the Soviet Union would be a Great Power. The old order was discredited by the Depression and the war, and there was an opportunity to rethink the world's financial architecture. In 1944 the United States convened a meeting in Bretton Woods, New Hampshire, which created three key institutions. The first was the International Monetary Fund

(IMF). The U.S. dollar became the world's global currency, and the U.S. dollar was backed by gold. The idea was to avoid currency crises, which could bankrupt a nation's industries overnight. For example, during Mexico's financial crisis in 1994, the price of a U.S. dollar rose so quickly that Mexican corporations proved incapable of repaying their debts, while U.S. firms could not sell their goods in Mexico. The IMF was designed to address these crises, and although the world no longer has a system of fixed exchange rates and global currencies are no longer pegged to the dollar, the IMF remains a powerful financial actor. Far better known than the IMF, however, is the International Bank for Reconstruction and Development, commonly referred to as the World Bank. Although its creators designed it to help Europe recover from World War II, its mission changed in the 1950s to focus on development. The World Bank loaned funds to developing countries at low interest rates. The idea was that the infrastructure and projects that the bank funded would prove to be so economically beneficial that the countries could use their growth to repay the costs of the loan.

The final institution in the Bretton Woods System was the General Agreement on Tariffs and Trade (GATT), which began life as a trade agreement between twenty-three nations. The original goal of this agreement was to reduce tariffs (taxes on trade) in the belief that all members of the agreement would benefit if global trade expanded. This was based on the idea of comparative advantage; that is, if each nation specialized in producing the goods to which it was most suited (so that Canada did not grow bananas, and Ghana did not produce ice wine), the total wealth of the world would increase. In order to accomplish this, member nations of GATT had to agree that if they gave a tariff break to one member, they would give the same reduction in tariffs to all. In 1995 GATT changed into a new and more powerful institution: the World Trade Organization (WTO). This body can monitor the trade in ideas as well as in goods. The WTO is also extremely controversial. Like all Bretton Woods institutions, the manner in which the WTO is portrayed depends very much on how the author or speaker views globalization. Chapters 4 and 5 explore this in more detail.

In any case, all observers would agree that the Bretton Woods System created the basic architecture for globalization. The era after World War II saw the integration of the global economy in a manner that was different from earlier eras. Transnational corporations emerged that were so large they rivaled the economic scale of small nation-states. With time, some increasingly lost their identities as corporations located in particular countries. New technologies emerged that dramatically dropped the price of transportation, shipping, and communication. With these changes, global capital became increasingly mobile. People no longer invested in companies abroad but rather in indexes and commodity markets. Money moved with amazing speed. So did people.

Shifting forms of production and trade helped to create economic diasporas, ranging from Indians employed in the Gulf states to the millions of Turks living throughout the European Union. While diasporas are an ancient phenomenon, the numbers and diversity of population movements after World War II are striking, as Seyla Benhabib has suggested: "It is estimated that whereas in 1910 roughly 33 million individuals lived as migrants in countries other than their own, by the year 2000 that number had reached 175 million. Strikingly, more than half the increase of migrants from 1910 to 2000 occurred in the last three decades of the twentieth century, between 1965 and 2000" (2008, 45).

These demographic changes do not mean that older ideologies and inequalities have vanished. For example, many "third-party nationals" lack citizenship rights, despite the fact that they may live for decades in other nations (Benhabib 2008, 51). This is the situation, for example, for some North Africans living in France or Germany. In part, these challenges may exist because of cultural ideals created during the Age of Empire and the way these ideals are now interpreted in an era with a mass media culture, as will be discussed in the chapter on cultural globalization. Jane Rhodes argues that the global media has contributed to a backlash against these migrants, as well as the propagation of racist ideas: "The era of globalization has with it a backlash culture, in which racial ideologies allow us to keep ourselves separate and apart from those we perceive to be a threat. Global media has played a significant role in disseminating racial ideas" (2008, 29–30). From this perspective, globalization has not ended old ideologies that disenfranchised certain groups but rather propagated these problems, and the global media has not broken down old barriers but merely reframed old ideologies.

The Enduring Importance of the Nation-State

Globalization now pressures the nation-state to a new degree. From the late 1940s to 1991, the Cold War limited the impact of globalization. The expansion of markets and commerce did not take place in the Soviet Union. But the Chinese adoption of capitalism in the 1980s and the collapse of the Soviet Union in 1991 removed this constraint on globalization. With the exception of a handful of states, such as North Korea, few nations were able to reject globalization entirely. In the 1990s some authors argued that this trend made the nation-state increasingly irrelevant in international affairs. For example, Arjun Appadurai (1996, 19) wrote:

> I did not begin to write this book with the crisis of the nation-state as my principal concern. But in the six years over which the chapters were written, I have come to be convinced that the nation-state, as a complex political form, is on its last legs. . . . Nation-states, for all their important differences (and only a fool would conflate Sri Lanka with Great Britain), make sense only as parts of a system. This system (even when seen as a system of differences) appears poorly equipped to deal with the interlinked diasporas of people and images that mark the here and now. Nation-states, as units in a complex interactive system, are not very likely to be the long-term arbiters of the relationship between globality and modernity.

There are many well-known arguments supporting this perspective. With the rise of global markets, no nation is immune from financial shocks, capital flows, and currency crises. In order to be attractive to international financial institutions, nations must accede to global norms in finance. Institutions such as the World Bank place clear expectations around loans that may limit national sovereignty. Transnational corporations may make huge investments in countries and gain great political influence as a result. Nations are no longer able to easily control information, given the rise of the Internet and social marketing platforms. The global media can bring intense pressure to bear on particular nations. The rise of global travel means that diseases can spread with unprecedented rapidity, and responses to pandemics must be coordinated to be effective. Similarly, many international problems—from drugs to nuclear proliferation—can be addressed only at the supranational level. Demographic trends, such as the aging populations of Europe and Japan, may create economic pressures to increase immigration. New peoples, however, retain old identities, which may be perceived as a challenge to the nation-state and make increased immigration politically unacceptable. The rise of the EU and new political blocs can challenge how nations define their innate character. The global media—films, the Internet, and television—may spread a common culture among youth globally, which challenges traditional cultures.

There are many examples of nation-states in crisis. In the developing world, there are many areas that either never successfully created a strong

> Meet with one or two other members of your class. As a group, decide on the single most important historical question that this chapter did not cover. Why was this particular question or material critical?

nation-state (Somalia) or nearly collapsed under the weight of ethnic hatreds (Syria). But nation-states in developed countries are also experiencing crises (Appadurai 1996, 142–43). Within Spain, the Basques and other cultures long suppressed by Francisco Franco—the nation's dictator from 1936 to 1975—are asserting their right to autonomy. In the United Kingdom, the Brexit referendum led to a prolonged period of political uncertainty and even the possibility that Scotland might secede. These may not be isolated instances but rather examples of a larger process.

Is the nation-state increasingly irrelevant in global affairs? Our argument in this text is that the situation is more complex. Even though nation-states are engaged in a complicated interplay with new actors, they nevertheless remain powerful agents. It is true that the nation-state system faces significant challenges, but that is true of every form of political organization in any period. With globalization, supranational entities (such as the World Bank, transnational corporations, and the media) may challenge nation-states. But the idea of the nation-state remains important even in regions where the concept is the weakest.

Nation-states remain critical to understanding supranational phenomena, such as terrorism. September 11 could not have taken place without the structure of globalization, which permitted the movement of people and resources globally to make the attacks possible. The identities and alliances that the movement used also relied on an earlier period of Islamic globalization. But that does not mean that terrorism can be understood or addressed outside the context of the nation-state. Although Al-Qaida is a global organization, it needed a base in Afghanistan that was safe from attack to coordinate, train, and plan for September 11. It is for this reason and others that in many ways, Great Powers such as the United States are preoccupied both with the problem of "state making" and with potential allies and enemies in the Islamic world. In all supranational issues, states are still relevant actors, despite transnational threats like terrorism.

In politics, economics, and culture, nation-states remain powerful agents that do not just react to global trends but to some extent limit the power of globalization itself. From a global perspective, there is a contradiction between the mass movements of people and funds and the growing power of nationalism and populism. Regional conflicts or violence (such as in Syria, Afghanistan, and Central America) and population growth (such as in Africa) are driving large numbers of people to cross national borders, not only for security but also for economic opportunity. At the same time, there is a global political turn to populism and nationalism, in which political parties and governments call for the enforcement of their borders. This growing nativist sentiment is also fueled by economic inequalities in North America, Europe, and some Asian states.

A number of factors have driven economic inequality, including the financialization of global markets, the premium placed upon higher education in the labor market, and the decline of manufacturing in many developed states. In Great Britain, for example, during the 1980s and 1990s the financial industry created a wealth of highly paid jobs in London, while manufacturing jobs declined in other areas, such as northern England. While there may have been overall economic growth, in northern England people perceived that the benefits of this growth went disproportionately to a small, educated elite. Of course, there is an ideological aspect to understanding this process. People on the political left have blamed economic inequality on the rise of neoliberalism since the 1980s, arguing that it has undermined the social safety net, lowered taxes on the wealthy, and prioritized the needs of corporations over people (Giroux 2015; Labonté and Stuckler 2016).

On the other hand, some scholars point to Europe, where they suggest that excessive regulation and hiring protections have made it too difficult to hire people. Conservative thinkers have long blamed this regulation for staggeringly high rates of youth unemployment (Lazear 1990; Blanchard and Landier 2002). In 2018 youth unemployment rates exceeded 30 percent in Spain, reached 28.5 percent in Italy, and were over 23 percent in Greece (World Bank 2018). In addition, conservative authors and economists suggest that innovation has been stifled not only by this labor market regulation but also by high taxes, which has led to "Eurosclerosis." Europe's share of the global economy has been declining for decades (Emmanouilidis 2016, 85). Conservative authors suggest that only labor market deregulation and lower taxes can change this trend.

Whichever argument you believe, there is a consensus in many historically developed countries that there is growing income inequality and that the middle class has faced great pressure. People feel insecure, including in developed nations such as in Europe: "As a result, more and more

Europeans feel a sense of insecurity and anxiety. Citizens fear that living standards in Europe will drop and that the European social model will be increasingly challenged" (Emmanouilidis 2016, 92–93). These fears have fueled populism and increased the resentment toward immigrants who arrive searching for opportunity. People look to the nation-states to enforce their borders and to limit the power of economic elites, whom they believe may have little allegiance to the nations in which they live. According to Dani Rodrik, the experience of globalization may shape the form of populism that appears in different countries:

> I will suggest that these different reactions are related to the forms in which globalization shocks make themselves felt in society. It is easier for populist politicians to mobilize along ethno-national/cultural cleavages when the globalization shock becomes salient in the form of immigration and refugees. That is largely the story of advanced countries in Europe. On the other hand, it is easier to mobilize along income/social class lines when the globalization shock takes the form mainly of trade, finance, and foreign investment. That in turn is the case with southern Europe and Latin America. The US, where arguably both types of shocks have become highly salient recently, has produced populists of both stripes (Bernie Sanders and Donald Trump). While many social and political factors foster populism and nationalism, economic globalization—and the resistance to it—is also essential to understanding this phenomenon. (2018, 13)

In the current climate, the dominant tension is that between globalization and the nation-state.

Conclusion

World history matters in international studies because without it we cannot understand the international system—including the origins of the nation-state and globalization, two key forces in current international affairs. Ironically, European empires helped to create the nationalist sentiments that destroyed them. They united diverse peoples in the colonies, alienated this populace by ignoring their political and economic interests, provided the ideology of nationalism, and created a global structure in which nations aspired to statehood. Nation-states now dominate the international system, despite the current period of globalization. What has changed is that it is now a more complex world order, in part because there are more actors, such as international nongovernmental organizations, the Bretton Woods institutions, the United Nations, and transnational corporations.

Every global trend has its own history, and this is particularly true of economic globalization, which reflects a long series of political and international decisions. While economic globalization can challenge the authority of the nation-state, the global financial system also relies on nation-states to implement the architecture upon which economic globalization relies. In turn, how people view economic globalization often depends on their nation's history. How does the experience of a particular nation—and the memories that its people hold—affect its perspective on international questions? How does your history—both as an individual and within a state—determine what seems important to you?

➤ VOCABULARY

diaspora	populism
IMF	Bretton Woods System
World Bank	national sovereignty
GATT	biological imperialism
spheres of influence	Peace of Westphalia

➤ DISCUSSION AND REFLECTION QUESTIONS

1. *What is the relationship between the emergence of more powerful military armaments and European expansion into the Atlantic?*
2. *What role did African slavery play in the development of North and South America and the Caribbean in the sixteenth and seventeenth centuries?*
3. *What role did New World crops and minerals play in the development of Europe?*
4. *Compare and contrast Dutch, British, and Portuguese expansion in the 1600s.*
5. *How do our present-day conceptualizations of race relate to legacies of empire?*
6. *As individuals left their homelands, new landscapes, demographics, and diasporas were created. What impact might shifting demographics have on nation-state development?*
7. *What are some of the tensions that exist between nationhood and empire?*

8 *Why did the Cold War dominate global relations for more than forty years?*

9 *What underlying frameworks for globalization were created by the development of the Bretton Woods System (World Bank, IMF, GATT)?*

10 *How do the competing forces of globalization and nationalism play out in a region you have studied or are familiar with?*

ACTIVITY 1: ANALYZE Identify one primary colonizing nation and at least five of its colonies. Research when the colonies gained their independence. What relationships still exist between the colonizing nation and its now-independent former colonies? Identify whether these relationships are economic, political, and/or cultural.

ACTIVITY 2: REFLECT Prepare a time line that begins in an era of your choosing. Make sure you cover at least 400 years. On the time line, mark all critical global events that you can think of. Include not only wars and treaties but also other critical events that have occurred in particular regions. Once you have finished, compare your time line with those of two other classmates. What do you notice about the events all of you have chosen? Can you make any generalizations?

ACTIVITY 3: EXTEND History affects not only nation-states and cultures but also individuals and families. Make a list of five key historical events or trends that have shaped your family's history. How did your family's experience of these events shape who you are today? How do they define what you may want for your future and for the future of your family? Then ask one family member or loved one what items would be on his or her list.

References

Abu-Lughod, J. L. 1989. *Before European hegemony: The world system, A.D. 1250–1350*. New York: Oxford University Press.

———. 1993. *The world system in the thirteenth century: Dead-end or precursor? Essays on global and comparative history*. Washington, D.C.: American Historical Association.

Alchon, S. A. 2003. *A pest in the land: New World epidemics in global perspective*. Albuquerque: University of New Mexico Press.

Anderson, B. 1983. *Imagined communities: Reflections on the origin and spread of nationalism*. London: Verso.

Appadurai, A. 1996. *Modernity at large: Cultural dimensions of globalization*. Minneapolis: University of Minnesota Press.

Benhabib, S. 2008. Global citizenship and responsibility. In *Meditations on global citizenship: Macalester Civic Forum*, edited by A. Samatar and A. Latham, 45–62. St. Paul, Minn.: Institute for Global Citizenship.

Blanchard, O., and A. Landier. 2002. The perverse effects of partial labor market reform: Fixed duration contracts in France. *Economic Journal* 112:214–44.

Crosby, A. W. 1972. *The Columbian exchange: Biological and cultural consequences of 1492*. Westport, Conn.: Greenwood Press.

Delpech, T. 2007. *Savage century: Back to barbarism*. Translated by George Holoch. Washington, D.C.: Carnegie Endowment for International Peace.

Diamond, J. 1997. *Guns, germs, and steel: The fates of human societies*. New York: W. W. Norton.

———. 2005. *Collapse: How societies choose to fail or succeed*. New York: Viking.

Eaton, R. M. 1990. *Islamic history as global history: Essays on global and comparative history*. Washington, D.C.: American Historical Association.

Emmanouilidis, J. A. 2016. Europe's role in the twenty-first century. In *The European Union and emerging powers in the 21st century*, edited by T. Renard and S. Biscop, 83–104. New York: Routledge.

Fukuyama, F. 1989. The end of history? *National Interest* 16:3–18.

Giroux, H. A. 2015. *Against the terror of neoliberalism: Politics beyond the age of greed*. New York: Routledge.

Guilmartin, J. F. 1974. *Gunpowder and galleys: Changing technology and Mediterranean warfare at sea in the sixteenth century*. Cambridge: Cambridge University Press.

Huntington, S. P. 1993. The clash of civilizations? *Foreign Affairs* 72 (3): 22–49.

Labonté, R., and D. Stuckler. 2016. The rise of neoliberalism: How bad economics imperils health and what to do about it. *Journal of Epidemiology and Community Health* 70 (3): 312–18.

Lazear E. P. 1990. Job security provisions and employment. *Quarterly Journal of Economics* 105:699–726

Mann, C. C. 2006. *1491: New revelations of the Americas before Columbus*. New York: Vintage Books.

McGhee, R. 1991. *Canada rediscovered*. Ottawa: Canadian Museum of Civilization.

McNeill, W. H. 1989. *The age of gunpowder empires, 1450–1800: Essays on global and comparative history*. Washington, D.C.: American Historical Association.

Pringle, H. 2012. Vikings and Native Americans. *National Geographic*. November. Retrieved December 26, 2013, from http://ngm.nationalgeographic.com/2012/11/vikings-and-indians/pringle-text.

Rhodes, J. 2008. Race matters. *Macalester Civic Forum* 1 (Spring): 27–33.

Rodrik, D. 2018. Populism and the economics of globalization. *Journal of International Business Policy* 1 (1–2): 12–33.

Rosen, W. 2007. *Justinian's flea: Plague, empire, and the birth of Europe*. New York: Viking Adult.

Schledermann, P. 2000. Ellesmere: Vikings in the far north. In *Vikings: The North Atlantic saga,* edited by W. W. Fitzhugh and E. I. Ward, 248–56. Washington, D.C.: Smithsonian Institution Press.

Seaver, K. 2000. Unanswered questions. In *Vikings: The North Atlantic saga,* edited by W. W. Fitzhugh and E. I. Ward, 270–79. Washington, D.C.: Smithsonian Institution Press.

Steger, M. 2003. *Globalization: A very short introduction.* Oxford: Oxford University Press.

Sutherland, P. D. 2000. The Norse and native North Americans. In *Vikings: The North Atlantic saga,* edited by W. W. Fitzhugh and E. I. Ward, 238–47. Washington, D.C.: Smithsonian Institution Press.

Tuchman, B. W. 1978. *A distant mirror: The calamitous 14th century.* New York: Ballantine Books.

World Bank. 2018. Unemployment, youth total (% of total labor force ages 15–24) (modeled ILO estimate). September. International Labour Organization, ILOSTAT database. Retrieved April 3, 2019, from https://data.worldbank.org/indicator/SL.UEM.1524.ZS.

THREE **Economic Globalization**

➤ SYNOPSIS

Economic globalization is a dominant force in the world today. For many, competition on the global economic market among nation-states defines globalization. For others, emerging technological collaboration among international and multinational corporations and production networks defines economic globalization (Baldwin 2016).

In this chapter, we explore the origins of the World Bank, the International Monetary Fund, and the World Trade Organization and the degrees to which decisions made in these organizations control the world economic scene. The development of the dominant neoliberal approach to economic decisions is examined through the vehicles of the Washington Consensus and the Augmented Washington Consensus. The shifting power of Brazil, Russia, India, China, and South Africa is discussed, as is the emergence of the Industrializing Six (Baldwin 2016). The chapter also examines the financial crisis in Greece from an initial (2008) and current perspective.

➤ SCAFFOLDING

As you read through this chapter, think about how you would answer each of the questions below.

What are three dimensions of global economics or finance that you are comfortable discussing with a friend? How likely are you to have such a discussion? Why or why not?

How can you be aware of your attitude toward fields of study that you might not know anything about in the same way that you are aware of the information you may need to learn?

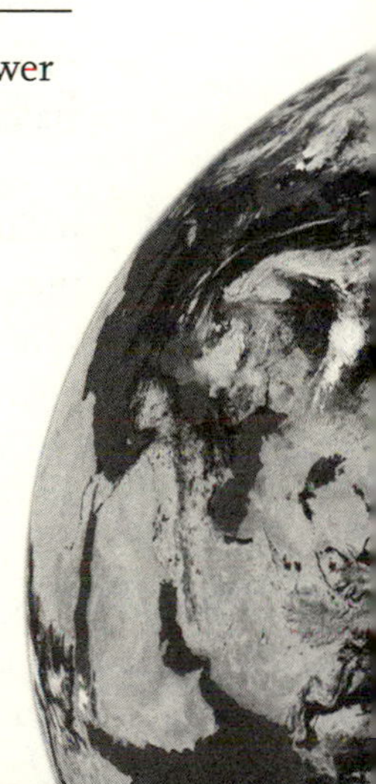

Why are neoliberal economic perspectives so frequently used to determine measures of economic stability?

➤ CORE CONCEPTS

What is conditionality? What is the relationship between structural adjustment programs, conditionality, and poverty reduction strategies for the World Bank and the IMF?

What macroeconomic functions were initially allocated to the IMF, and what microeconomic functions were allocated to the World Bank? Why have these functions and institutions in effect switched roles?

What is financialization, and how is it affecting twenty-first-century economic flows?

Globalization means many things to many people. In *A Brief History of Globalization*, Alex MacGillivray (2006) identifies more than 5,000 books in print with titles linked to globalization. For many, the term itself conveys images of hegemony—that is, economic and political dominance by rich nations over smaller nations. For others, the power of connectivity and information exchange cancel out any negatives that may exist in the equation. Globalization is about patterns of connectedness and patterns of inequality. Because people, goods and services, and information flow differently in the twenty-first century than in the past, landscapes have shifted (Appadurai 1996). Some authors have suggested that we now see a compression of time and space: financial transactions occur transnationally by electronic means, virtual communities are created across traditional boundaries, and information travels faster and more powerfully than ever before via the Internet (Harvey 1989). All over the world, citizens now expect change to occur quickly and in a similar manner in different nation-states. Richard Baldwin suggests that the role of information technology is critical to what he calls a third stage of globalization. He argues that nation-state competitiveness is no longer the key to economic advancement: "The boundaries of competitiveness are controlled by firms who run international production networks" (2016, 12).

In this chapter, building on information that you were introduced to in chapter 2, we explore the mobility of capital, ideas, and power. We then examine how context and localization interact with these forces. We look at the advantages and disadvantages of globalization through the lens of multiple disciplines in order to see how scholars from various perspectives have identified globalization as both a demon and a darling. The global financial meltdown of 2008 and its legacy a decade later provide examples of how context, locale, and the regulatory abilities of key actors—such as the Economic Monetary Union of the European Union—can lead to crisis and inequality.

What is economic globalization? For economist Paul Krugman and entrepreneur George Soros, globalization is a phenomenon intimately linked to trade among nations and various financial markets. Soros (2002) also notes the importance of multinational corporations in this picture. We see that transactions among nation-states may be superseded by transnational transactions dominated by intergovernmental organizations, global movements, or collaboration among civil-society organizations (Global Policy Forum 2008). Parag Khanna and Alpo Rusi (2008) suggest that globalization also has a strong regional dimension. Jan Scholte (2005, 2) sees this regional power of globalization as something that draws power away from the nation-state. Neither individual nation-states nor multinational corporations function independently in our time-space-compressed world. The economic pillars of the Bretton Woods System (along with national and multinational financial institutions) work almost like a lock and dam system: nations and companies navigate waters that are determined by larger global structures.

Economic Globalization

Chapter 2 introduced you to the economic giants of globalization: the Bretton Woods System (the World Bank, the International Monetary Fund, and the General Agreement on Tariffs and Trade) and the World Trade Organization (the former General Agreement on Tariffs and Trade). We explore them in more detail here because the economic world as we know it continues to operate within the parameters shaped by these institutions. At the end of World War II, politicians tried to determine the advantages and disadvantages of a global political entity, ultimately resulting in the shift from President Woodrow Wilson's League of Nations to the charter for the United Nations. At the same time, financiers were discussing the need to create some type of global financial entity, particularly one that could assist countries with what MacGillivray terms "temporary balance of payment problems" (2006, 210).

In 1944 a meeting with representatives from forty-four nations was held at Bretton Woods, New Hampshire, in the Mount Washington Hotel. The representatives were charged with finding ways to assist global trade by helping stabilize the global economy. It was at this meeting that both the World Bank (initially the International Bank for Reconstruction and Development) and the International Monetary Fund were established. The U.S. representative was Harry Dexter, and the United Kingdom representative was Lord John Maynard Keynes, who argued for a global currency called "bancor." This idea was rejected, and the U.S. dollar became the world currency for the monetary system that followed. It was intended that the two organizations would identify and implement procedures for a system of convertible currencies tied to a gold standard, set at $35.00 per ounce. At the time, 70 percent of the world's gold reserves rested in the United States, thus tying the gold standard to the dollar, a process termed "pegging." At the time of the 1944 meeting, it was clear that the Allies would win the war and soon face the challenge of rebuilding a Europe that had been burned and shattered by the conflict. Many senior U.S. officials also believed that one of the origins of the war had been the trade blocs of the 1930s and the political tensions these blocs created. For these reasons, the delegates wanted to create a global lending institution and a means to break down trade barriers. They succeeded in these two goals, but not without costs to the autonomy and social sectors of the countries receiving assistance.

The global lending institutions became the World Bank and the IMF. The solution to trade barriers emerged in the form of the General Agreement on Tariffs and Trade; this agreement became the World Trade Organization. All of these organizations are transnational, even though many argue that rich Western nations continue to dominate and drive policy formulation within them (Scholte 2005). Nation-states were and continue to be the intended recipients of decisions made by the World Bank, the IMF, and the WTO. This triumvirate of economic globalization began in response to the needs of individual nation-states to have access to the power, cash, and influence that came from collaboration with other nations. We now look in more detail at these institutions in order to better comprehend their functions.

The World Bank and the International Monetary Fund

Originally created to help Europe recover from World War II, the World Bank later turned its focus to helping the developing world (the Global

South). Making low-interest loans to countries to support development projects, the World Bank lends at lower rates than those of commercial banks. Its initial charge was to focus on microeconomic dimensions of recovery within a country, including its fiscal policy decisions. Microeconomic challenges typically focus on things like expenditures, tax reform, and regulation of products and services (Thimann 2015, 159). Within one developing country, a microeconomic focus might include issues related to environmental regulation, such as "public disclosure and voluntary programs to address industrial pollution, programs that inform households about environmental risks," and budget dimensions of paying for environmental services (Vincent 2010, 221). Its typical loans were initially designed to increase infrastructure capacity and were often for very large and visible projects such as dams, power plants, and the like. These loans came with conditions imposed on them; the actual term "conditionality" refers specifically to "the conditions that international lenders imposed in return for their assistance" (Broad 2002, 9). According to the IMF website (2009), these conditions are set in order to "restore or maintain balance of payments viability and macroeconomic stability, while setting the stage for sustained, high-quality growth." There are typically three key dimensions to these conditions: privatization, deregulation, and implementation of austerity measures that decrease the size of the government's public-sector spending on social services and education. These are usually very specific measures to address how an agent or individual organization within a country can affect change.

Examples of privatization include electricity in El Salvador and jute production in Bangladesh. Karen Hansen-Kuhn and Steve Hellinger (1999) suggest these have both failed. Other typical privatization examples include industries such as telecommunications, systems such as banking, and products such as oil and gas. Deregulation removes policies that create trade barriers and competitive pricing. These policies may relate to any aspect of society. For the original fifteen members of the EU, energy deregulation for products such as electricity and natural gas was consistent. Another example involves the crafting of waivers to permit international organizations interested in mining in Haiti to skirt restrictions. Julie Lévesque (2013) observes that private ownership of mines is prohibited in the Haitian constitution. Additionally, drilling can occur only with a signed mining convention. Yet deregulation can occur subtly and for individual corporations. For example, Lévesque indicates that "U.S. Newmont mining got a 'waiver' to the current Haiti law without the approval of even the puppet Haiti legislature." Deregulation can often seem appealing to individuals struggling to create new businesses; however, consumer choice does not always benefit all members of a community.

Austerity measures typically decrease the size of the government's public-sector spending on social services and education. One example is the frequent freezing of salaries of public-sector employees; this occurred routinely throughout the EU countries of Greece, Portugal, and Spain in 2008. Yet another is legislation passed in September 2012 in Greece to allow the government to completely close a subset of universities.

The IMF was established to create stable exchange rates by pegging currencies to the U.S. dollar, which in turn was pegged to the price of gold until 1971. Roughly thirty years after the IMF's inception, though, the currency would be unfrozen from its link to gold and floated. This floating was seen as necessary, but many felt this instability would affect the ability of global businesses to trade. The IMF continues to make loans to countries facing currency crises. Its primary role is intended to focus on macroeconomic issues. According to Joseph Stiglitz, these include a "*country's* [emphasis added] budget deficit, its monetary policy, its inflation, its trade deficit [and] its borrowing from abroad" (2002, 14). Countries that join the IMF are assigned a type of quota based on their global economic position. The balance of loans received must be repaid within five years.

The original distinction between the World Bank's focus on microeconomic policy and the IMF's focus on macroeconomic policy has gradually eroded. Stiglitz suggests that the IMF has come to dominate both microeconomic and macroeconomic decisions. Both organizations have crafted conditions for loans to be given. The conditions are sometimes termed the "Washington Consensus." Economist John Williamson coined this phrase in 1989 to characterize the recommendations made by the IMF, the World Bank, the U.S. Treasury, and other financial institutions based in Washington, D.C. At the time, the recommendations articulated were intended to help Latin America pull out of the economic crises of that decade. The phrase "Washington Consensus" has come to mean more than what Williamson originally intended, but for our purposes, it is sufficient to know this consensus refers to ten economic-policy recommendations—basically, conditions to be followed in order to qualify for loans. The Washington Consensus policies are detailed in Table 1, along with what economist Dani Rodrik calls an "Augmented Washington Consensus" (Global Trade Negotiations home page 2008).

Table 1 Original Washington Consensus and Augmented Washington Consensus

Original Washington Consensus	Augmented Washington Consensus
Fiscal discipline	Corporate governance
A redirection of public expenditures toward fields offering high economic returns and potential to improve income distribution (e.g., primary health care, primary education)	Anticorruption
Tax reform	Flexible labor markets
Interest rate liberalization	WTO agreements
A competitive exchange rate	Financial codes and standards
Trade liberalization	"Prudent" capital-account opening
Liberalization of inflows of foreign direct investment	Nonintermediate exchange rate regimes
Privatization	Independent central banks and inflation targeting
Deregulation (to abolish barriers to entry and exit)	Social safety nets
Secure property rights	Targeted poverty reduction

Source: Dani Rodrik, http://www.cid.harvard.edu/search.html. Retrieved July 5, 2010. Used with permission.

These conditions have become part of a package called structural adjustment programs. As you can see from the table, these conditions are designed to shift economic and social structures in the countries receiving loans. Over a period of time, these structural adjustment programs have become quite controversial, as the austerity measures they have created in various nations have had very strong effects on social programs and policies therein. In 2002 the World Bank and the IMF shifted to different terminology: Poverty Reduction Strategy Papers. These papers have also been aligned with the United Nations' Millennium Development Goals, which will be discussed in chapter 6.

General Agreement on Tariffs and Trade and the World Trade Organization

The General Agreement on Tariffs and Trade was created in 1947 to encourage countries to reduce their taxes on imports. It was the third aspect of policy/institution development to come out of Bretton Woods. The goal was to create an international forum based on membership that would both promote free trade among its member nations and provide a forum for dispute resolution (GATT 2008). The purpose of GATT—a treaty agreement and not an organization—was ostensibly to reduce tariffs as well as other types of trade restrictions and subsidies favoring one nation over another. There were seven rounds of negotiations under the treaty. One of the key agreements to emerge from the last GATT round in 1994 was the Agreement on Agriculture; it focused on the three main areas of the agreement: market access, export competition, and domestic support (Ostry 2004, 280).

Nations made substantial achievements at this last meeting. In addition to the agricultural dimensions discussed above, participants agreed to the reductions of tariffs, export subsidies, and various other import limits over the twenty-year period that followed. In addition, substantial progress was made in the area of intellectual property rights—patents, trademarks, and copyrights. Work was also begun to bring a level of enforcement of international trade law to the service sector. Finally, nations began to discuss a way to revise how disputes were settled through GATT. The last phase focused more narrowly on dimensions also central to the WTO: further elements of intellectual property rights and agriculture.

In 1995 GATT was replaced by the WTO, which is a much more powerful body in that it also covers intellectual property and services. Its membership is composed of 159 nation-states, and there are 25 other nations serving as "observers" (these figures are accurate as of 2013). It has assumed the functions of GATT, along with another agreement focusing on services called the General Agreement on Trade in Services. The mechanism within the WTO that allows sanctions to be leveled against particular nation-states for violating global trade rules is called the Dispute Settlement Body (DSB). Within this process, if a country is found to have violated a particular rule, there is only one way to escape the sanctions meted out: all members of the DSB must oppose the imposition of the sanctions. Wayne Ellwood (2003, 34) acknowledges the complete unlikelihood of this happening. Another somewhat slippery dimension of the DSB process is that if one country

Table 2 Comparison of GATT and WTO

GATT	WTO
A set of rules, a multilateral agreement • No institutional foundation • A small associated secretariat	A permanent institution with its own secretariat
GATT provisions were applied on a provisional basis	WTO commitments are full and permanent
GATT rules applied to trade in merchandise goods	WTO covers trade in services and trade-related aspects of intellectual property
Not all agreements were multilateral	Almost all agreements are multilateral and involve commitments for the entire membership
System is subject to blockages by countries	WTO disputes system is less susceptible to blockages

Sources: K. Choi, "The Roots of the WTO," retrieved November 26, 2008, from www.econ.iastate.edu/classes/econ355/choi/wtoroots.htm; and WTO website (www.wto.org), retrieved 2008.

believes something it is doing within its own borders—that is, some type of domestic policy—is necessary and appropriate, any WTO member can argue that the policy could be linked to the trade process. Thus, it could be potentially linked to a dispute and sent to the DSB.

The WTO replaced GATT for all intents and purposes. Table 2 details the differences between them, while Figure 1 details the structure of the WTO. A full analysis of the WTO organizational chart is beyond the scope of this chapter, but a deeper look at a key dispute and how the DSB has resolved it to date may give you a better understanding of the ins and outs of this central arm of the WTO. Trade issues related to the marketing of particular foods are adjudicated first under regional trade organizations, but if disputes occur, they are then adjudicated by the WTO. One such dispute involved sugar.

In April 2016, Brazil filed a complaint against Thailand with the DSB alleging that the Thai government's quota system for sugar functioned as a type of export subsidy. Twelve days after the suit was filed, the EU joined in Brazil's dispute suggesting that the Thai subsidies would also affect the EU's ability to export sugar. An examination of the WTO website in

All WTO members may participate in all councils, committees, etc., except Appellate Body, Dispute Settlement panels, Textiles Monitoring Body, and plurilateral committees.

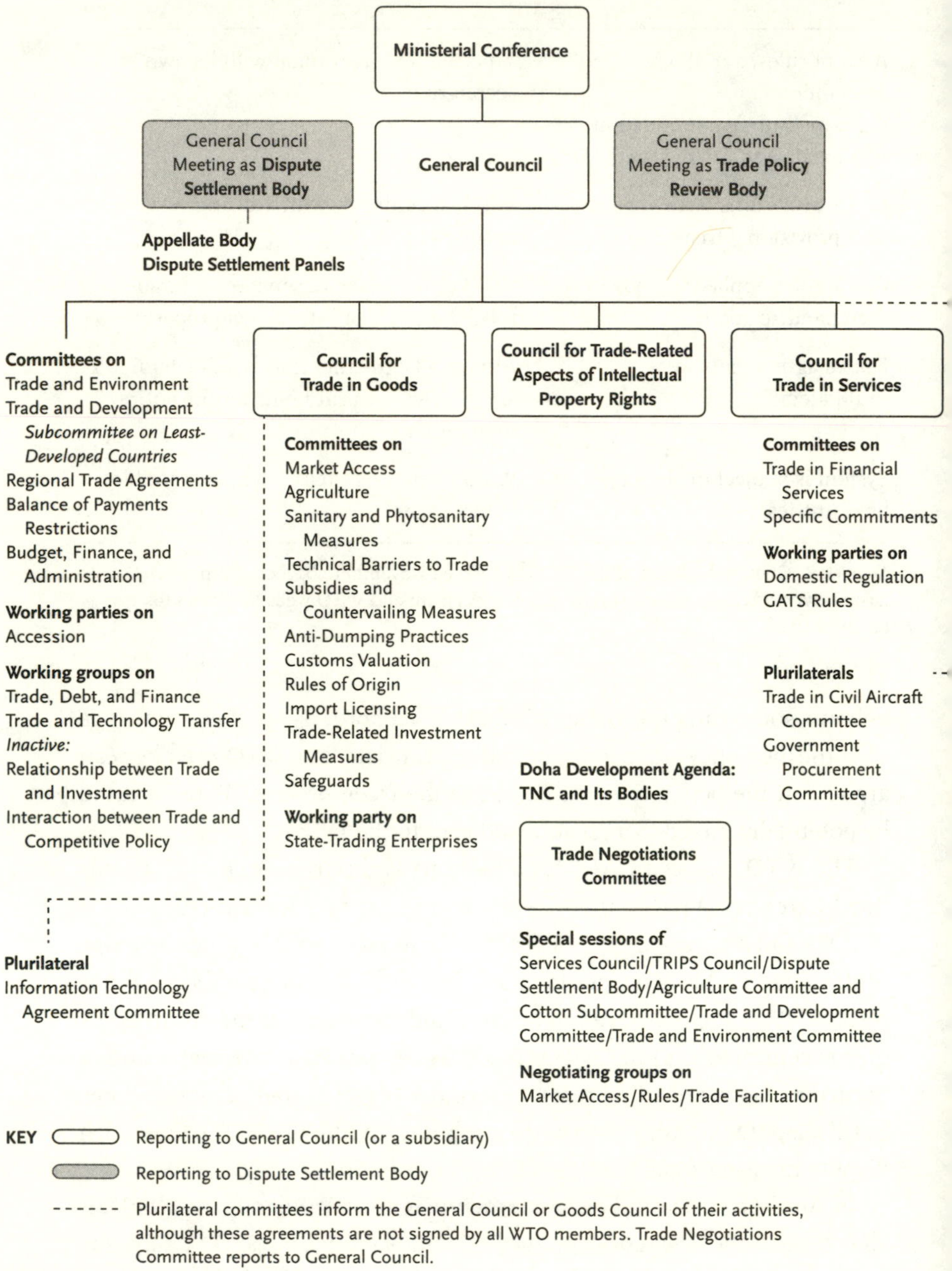

The General Council also meets as the Trade Policy Review Body and Dispute Settlement Body.

Figure 1 WTO Structure

February 2019 did not indicate the dispute had been resolved. However, in June 2018, Brazil suspended its complaint because Thailand removed the government price support and agreed to do three things: "float sugar prices, abolish sugar quotas, and designate reserve stocks only sufficient for domestic consumption (Brazil halts . . ., 2018)."

This example has given you a sense of just how prolonged and complicated both the original disputes and their settlements can be. What is important to notice is that numerous countries have been involved in the dispute. The WTO has crafted a structure to resolve these disputes. The structure is complicated but consistent. The cross-border territories of sugar-producing and sugar-consuming regions ultimately replace the particular countries themselves in the adjudication. The WTO has thus succeeded in the original goals of GATT: to create both a membership-based international forum that would promote free trade and a forum for dispute resolution. While the latter appears to be a neutral policy, it is clear that all free trade–based initiatives are grounded in the neoliberal perspective framed by the Washington Consensus.

The World Bank, the IMF, GATT, and the WTO are powerful multinational forces. They have served as gatekeeping devices for the mobility of capital and ideas and have imprinted the global landscape of the twenty-first century. Sadly, not all nations have been equally represented: more-powerful nations have been more successful than less-powerful nations in using these institutions to resolve disputes and plan for their economic futures. Now that you are familiar with the basic organization of the World Bank, the IMF, and GATT/WTO, we will examine how scholars with competing ideologies characterize the work of these institutions.

Perspectives on the World Bank, the IMF, and GATT/WTO

The economic policy conditions characterized above as the Washington Consensus are a set of market policies that depend on three things: privatization, liberalization, and deregulation. Within the general purview of lending policies of the World Bank and the IMF, these three dimensions can be characterized as "economism" and "marketism" (Scholte 2005). These are all part of a neoliberal economic policy. Jan Scholte, professor and director of the Centre for the Study of Globalisation and Regionalisation in the United Kingdom at the University of Warwick, characterizes this policy in the following way:

> Neoliberalism focuses not just on economics, but also on economics of a particular kind, namely laissez-faire market economics. In a word, from a neoliberal perspective, the global economy should be a free and open market. Production, exchange, and consumption of resources should unfold through forces of supply and demand, as they emerge from the uninhibited interactions of a multitude of firms and households in the private sector. . . . Multilateral institutions, national governments, and local authorities exist to provide regulatory frameworks that maximize the efficiency of global markets, for example, by securing property rights and enforcing legal contracts. (2005, 8)

Scholte suggests that this dominant policy, enforced through the actions of the World Bank, the IMF, and GATT/WTO, has not truly helped arbitrate global inequality. He argues that in the areas of human security, social justice, and democracy, neoliberal economic policies have been ineffective and in fact have "increased destitution" (2005, 11). He looks at markers of poverty in the Soviet bloc between 1989 and 1996 and describes an increase from 14 million to 147 million people living in poverty. He sees increases in global unemployment as contributing to declining global human security and also argues that when the market meets the environment, the environment loses: "[Neoliberalism] affirms—implicitly if not explicitly—that conflicts between market efficiency and ecological integrity should be settled in favour of the former" (12).

In a paper exploring causes of poverty titled "Poverty and Activism: The Heart of Global Civil Society," coauthored with five other colleagues, Scholte states, "They lack the resources, opportunities and *participatory* avenues in collective decision making that would enable them to overcome their poverty. Their poverty is reproduced over and over again through obstacles actually constructed as a *consequence* of modernity; they are the victims not of a timeless condition of poverty but of an ongoing and renewable process of impoverishment" (Seckinelgin et al. 2009).

In like manner, former Nobel Laureate and World Bank senior economist Joseph Stiglitz also sees the downside of these institutions and their practices. Stiglitz is unhappy with both the IMF and the World Bank. He argues quite convincingly that many of the IMF policies, in spite of their original intents, have actually contributed to instability. He describes in detail the importance of sequencing trade, capital market liberalization, and privatization and suggests that the IMF made frequent mistakes in this area. Stiglitz goes on to stress the costs of ignoring or placing inadequate emphasis on particular local social contexts when decisions were made and submits that "forcing liberalization before safety nets were put in place, before there was an adequate regulatory framework," problematized much of the IMF's work (2002, 73). Besides sequencing and the IMF, he also criticizes the inflexibility of conditionality on the part of the World Bank—"the conditions that international lenders imposed in return for their assistance" (9).

Like Stiglitz, entrepreneur George Soros finds specific faults with aspects of the IMF: "We can identify two major deficiencies or, more exactly, asymmetries in the way the IMF has been operating until recently. One is a disparity between crisis prevention and crisis intervention; the other is a disparity in the treatment of lenders and borrowers" (2002, 13). He goes on to suggest that "the general principles that structural reforms in the IMF ought to follow are clear. There ought to be a better balance between crisis prevention and intervention and a better balance between offering incentives to countries that follow sound policies and penalizing those that do not. The two objectives are connected: it is only by offering incentives that the IMF can exert stronger influence on the economic policies of individual countries prior to a country turning to the IMF in a crisis" (134). He is optimistic that these are true changes that can be implemented.

Princeton philosophy professor Peter Singer has written extensively about the ethics of globalization (2002) and argues that those opposed to WTO policies and those supporting them rarely engage in functional dialogues. Those on the left frequently point out the inattention the WTO pays on a global level to worker rights or to the environment. Those on the far right criticize the WTO for its attempts to reign in state sovereignty (Top 10 reasons . . ., 2019). Singer suggests that both sides could reach a third space in dialogue if the Left saw greater protection of people and environment through consistent global policies and the Right were to recognize that some loss of national sovereignty could be countered with an increased say in global economic decisions. Singer criticizes economists in general, even while acknowledging that some individuals have gone too far in taking the Big Three (the World Bank, the IMF, GATT/WTO) to task. He has also criticized the WTO street protesters.

Private financial institutions make up the final pillar of economic globalization. Their activities funding trade and intellectual property development, serving direct foreign investment, and managing portfolio investments helped push the world to the fiscal ruin of 2008. Activities that would not have been generally funded in the 1990s suddenly fell into the laps of private banks. Real estate transactions and junk-bond risks that were not originally the purview of private banks became funded activities arbitrarily approved without strategic oversight, often in countries whose cultures had not previously supported activities such as sovereign bond sales and other government borrowings. The lives of individuals in places like Greece were forever altered by these activities and even a decade later suffer the costs of these decisions. It is important to understand that structural adjustment programs alone cannot account for how nation-states deal with economic crises. Private banks have now shifted approved investments and divestments in countries subject to IMF and EU monitoring.

In 2002, 50 of the top 100 global economies were companies, not countries: "The combined annual revenues of the biggest 200 corporations are greater than those of 182 nation-states that contain 80 percent of the world's populations" (Ellwood 2003, 55). In 2019–20, the top country economies were the United States, China, Japan, Germany, and the UK, followed by India and France. For some scholars, China has already overtaken the United States (Focus Economics 2018). The top multinational company economies in 2013 were Royal Dutch Shell, Walmart, Exxon Mobil, Sinopec Group, China National Petroleum, State Grid, Toyota Motor, Volkswagen, and Total (Fortune Global 500 Companies 2013). We see, then, an interweaving of nation-state economies with multinational corporate economies and nationalized company economies. This complicated list of players and places affects the balance of economic decisions made around the world.

What does all this mean in terms of our focus on economics as a pillar of globalization? First, the neoliberal policies of the Bretton Woods institutions dominate the process of economic globalization. Knowledge of these institutions is necessary, though not alone sufficient, to gain a broad understanding of the flows of capital and economic globalization. Second, globalization includes the integration of financial markets that started after the end of the Bretton Woods monetary system in 1971 and the liberalization of capital flows that followed afterward. First came the integration of financial markets among the industrialized capitalist giants of the Global North in the 1970s, followed by the entrance of emerging market economies into this picture during the 1980s and 1990s. Finally, it is important to keep in mind that transnational economic flows of capital are governed by international financial institutions. Some examples include the European Investment Bank, the Islamic Development Bank, and the Inter-American Development Bank.

BRICS

Researchers have addressed the compression of time and space that has occurred with shifts in technology (Harvey 1989; May and Thrift 2001). Brazil, Russia, India, China, and South Africa have increased their roles as resource providers and service providers because of globalization. Transactions can be managed quicker than ever before due to technological innovation. Over the last fifteen years, four of these economic powerhouses have attracted a great deal of international attention: Brazil, Russia, India, and China. In 2010 South Africa joined these nations by mutual agreement, which created a new bloc: the BRICS. South Africa was asked to join primarily for its ability to "improve access to 1 billion consumers on the continent and mineral resources including oil and platinum" (Seria 2010). All of these economies have engaged in the types of reforms that allow them to play increasing global leadership roles. By 2017 the GDP of all BRICS states amounted to approximately US$18.25 trillion (Statista 2019). McKinley (2018) suggests that the BRICS have been key leaders of global per capita growth in the last decade. While there is diversity in the strengths of each of these nations, we can see one pattern: Brazil, Russia, and South Africa are likely to continue as resource providers, while China and India will continue to deliver services and manufactured goods (O'Neill 2007). The ability of these economies to put pressure on the United States and various trading blocs will increase in the next few decades, as will their ability to promote greater intellectual collaboration "managing ongoing transnational expert networks" (Katada, Roberts, and Armijo 2017, 407). At the present time, there is no political organization representing the interests of these five nations, nor is there anticipation that this is likely to occur; numerous scholars, however, have suggested that the countries function as a type of club (Cooper 2016; Katada, Roberts, and Armijo 2017). At a July 2014 summit, all five countries created the New Development Bank. Saori Katada, Cynthia Roberts, and Leslie Armijo call four primary activities of BRICS either successful or on their way to success: (1) pressuring the IMF and World Bank to reform lending practices in a more equitable manner; (2) influencing markets to push back "against pressure from dominant states to employ their market-based financial or monetary power for political ends"; (3) creating new banks (New Development Bank and China's Asian Infrastructure Investment Bank) and "contingent reserve arrangements"; and (4) challenging the U.S. dollar as the dominant international currency, working

Joseph Stiglitz (2006, 285) recommends that the world consider a new global social contract in which "developed countries . . . compensate developing countries for their environmental services, both in preservation of biodiversity and contribution to global warming through carbon sequestration" (pumping CO_2 underground and capping it so that it remains out of the atmosphere). How realistic does this suggestion seem to you?

to bring the Chinese renminbi into play for international transactions (2017, 407).

Yet another dimension of these nations' economic presence is the regional role they each will play in the next fifty years. The languages used in Russia (Russian), India (Hindi), and China (Chinese) will be dominant regional languages over the coming half century (Graddol 1996). Media programming and delivery of goods and services at a regional level will be through these languages. South Africa remains an English-using multilingual nation. Thus, language will not be an issue for South Africa, but we can anticipate an increase in English-language transactions throughout the southern region of Africa in the next fifty years. How Brazil will deal with its regional power, and the implications of Brazil's rise for the use of Portuguese versus Spanish and English, remains to be seen. Nevertheless, the increasing regional power of each of these countries, coupled with their global influence, means that the rest of the world would do well to familiarize itself with their nation-state traits. Additionally, it will be important to notice the type of pressure BRICS can put upon organizations such as the World Bank to behave differently and to represent needs of the Global South more equitably and to recognize that the individual nation-states represented in BRICS do not always support each other's policies in non-economic contexts. For example, neither Brazil nor India agreed with Russia's re-annexation of the Crimean Peninsula.

Other nations with important roles to play in the emerging global economy include what Baldwin terms the Industrializing Six: China (discussed above), South Korea, India, Poland, Indonesia, and Thailand. Most of these countries have both profited from and been hampered by conditions imposed upon them by the World Bank and the IMF as they have sought to grow their economies. In the long run, it appears that the conditions imposed have ultimately contributed to their growth potential in spite of social and environmental issues that remain unresolved. We can see, then, that the landscape of actors on the world stage has shifted and continues to shift. The Global North will no longer have a monopoly on determining economic policies of the future. Relationships are complicated among Global North and Global South nations and multinational companies; among Bretton Woods institutions, other international financial institutions, and national and regional financial institutions; and among local communities interacting with all of these institutions. Some authors suggest there is a kind of continuum between the global and the local (Friedman 2007).

Political Globalization

We began this chapter by examining economic patterns of connectedness and patterns of inequality across the globe. Having outlined the economic scaffolding of these patterns, it is now possible to explore the role that politics has played in the mobility of capital, ideas, and power. This interlinking of economics and politics is sometimes overwhelming. The next chapter explores political globalization in its own right, but the brief comments below provide a segue into the fuller discussion in chapter 4.

As you saw in the history chapter, it is generally agreed that it was after the Peace of Westphalia, a treaty-like document signed in 1648, that "the constitutional foundations for the emerging state system" were created (Cutler 2001, 134). These state systems protected citizens, negotiated bilateral agreements, and have most recently served as the recipients of international lending funds. A. Claire Cutler stresses the power of the nation-state: "For most of the history of modern international law, states have been regarded as the sole legitimate subjects" (135). One situation where we see nation-states affecting economic globalization is when sanctions are imposed. While these may be more far-reaching than nation-state only, two examples serve as illustrations. Randall Newnham (2013) contrasts Russian energy sanctions versus incentives in its relationship with Ukraine, suggesting that the Yushchenko government failed once Russia introduced sanctions. At this time and with the arrival of Viktor Yanukovych on the scene, Russia then lowered energy prices. Newnham maintains that even moderate sanctions can bring about regime change. He uses the example of sanctions against Iran, stating, "Sanctions do not have to force the country to collapse: they just have to cause enough economic 'pain' to force the Islamic hard-liners to lose elections" (121). In contrast to Newnham, Abdol Majid Cheraghali suggests that in spite of dire health issues caused by sanctions against Iran, "Iran's political leadership has withstood the economic sanctions over [the] last decade, [and] it is clear that sanctions have not achieved their stated political . . . objectives" (2013, 3). Sanctions are tools that play a role in the complicated world of economic globalization and should be examined when relevant to particular nation-state crises.

However, the reach of the nation-state is decreasing in comparison to the reach of various other organizations. When this happens, social fragmentation can happen. Breakdowns in civil society occur, and the question becomes, how can globalization have a positive effect at the local level when this kind of disintegration is transpiring? One answer is that regional organizations, as well as international economic agencies, can provide elements of stability to compensate. Yet some might argue that it is precisely these agencies that are maintaining the breakdowns; structural adjustment programs in particular chip away at national social budgets—including education, health, and welfare.

As states become less effective as key governing agents, other agents, such as the European Union, grow in scope. Global movements of civil society organizations begin to collaborate and use technology to communicate more efficiently, and transnational corporations work around the nation-state (Global Policy Forum 2008). Within the EU in particular, we see how mobility of capital, ideas, and power have all occurred. However, political globalization does not mean political homogeneity, nor does it mean global control. It does mean movement beyond the nation-state—and collaboration when possible.

With respect to social organizations, the Global Policy Forum sees clear places in the future for global movements, such as those associated with the environment, to pull civic society organizations within particular countries together to create partnerships with allies in other countries. The forum sees the power of such movements to engage in what it terms "direct lobbying," which involves "circumventing the nation-state" (Global Policy Forum 2008). The forum's perspective is important because it is a consultative organization to the UN with a fourfold mission: monitoring, advocacy, education, and activism.

Another kind of global force is the transnational corporation. These corporations have mobility of capital and power and work this mobility to their advantage. One aspect of the declining power of the nation-state and the increasing power of transnational corporations is that the transnational corporations are generally private, and as such they are neither responsible to a particular state nor subject to international organizations such as the UN. Jonathan Charney (1983, 55), cited in Cutler (2001, 142), observes the benefits that transnational organizations derive from being neither fish nor fowl: "[Their] international non-status immunizes them from direct accountability to international legal norms and permits them to use sympathetic national governments to parry outside efforts to mold their behavior." This immunity allows transnational companies to move capital in ways governments are unable to do. These companies can also collaborate with other transnational entities.

Thus political globalization involves control systems that move beyond the nation-state. In addition to the forces of transnational corporations, other systems that move beyond the nation-state include regional free-trade associations, nongovernmental organizations, and associations like the United Nations, which has a mission statement that includes peacekeeping, policy assessment and implementation regarding refugees and displaced persons, and the management of information systems through its UNESCO arm.

Roles for regional organizations loom larger than those of individual nation-states. Regional organizations may center on particular commodities—oil, coffee, tea, even bananas. In these cases, it is not government officials who play key negotiating roles but rather business and labor representatives who make decisions, frequently independently of their government representatives (Cutler 2001). Regional organizations may also focus on general promises of trade and defense, such as NATO, Mercosur, the Asia-Pacific Economic Cooperation, and the Association of Southeast Asian Nations. These organizations are working with both economic and political dimensions of globalization. At the regional level, in addition to organizations, particular nation-states can galvanize support for the resolution of structural problems. Australia, for example, sees itself playing a leadership role in the Pacific, collaborating with "Pacific island neighbours to fight poverty in our own region" (Rudd 2008, 64). Kevin Rudd sees Pacific Rim collaboration as central to "the best regional economic, political, and security architecture for 2020 and beyond" (2008, 64). As you will see in the next chapter, political globalization is a complicated, multilayered process. Many scholars believe that there is frequently a gap between economic and political globalization. Hopefully, this last section has demonstrated the commonalities. In the future, closing this gap will likely remain a critical task for global leaders.

We have examined the historical roots of economic globalization, linked it to political globalization, and looked at the ways various types of organizations at different levels affect how individual countries participate in

> The Maastricht criteria—typically termed "convergence criteria"—emerged from the 1992 negotiations and are intended to determine whether an EU member can adopt the euro. The criteria are composed of a nation's inflation rates, its government financial situation calculated as a function of annual government deficit and government debt, its currency exchange rate, and its long-term interest rates.

the globalization process. Within the private business community, there are also competing ideologies that determine how various products are marketed, how companies link their producers and consumers, and how they make decisions about giving back to communities. It now becomes possible to look in more detail at the eurozone and how the financial crisis beginning in 2007–8 deeply affected Greece—a eurozone country—and pitted nation-states in the EU against each other.

Case Study: Greece

On February 7, 1992, a "Treaty on European Union" was passed in Maastricht, the Netherlands. This treaty established both the European Union and the European Monetary Union. The EU currently has twenty-eight sovereign member states. Eighteen of these members use the euro as currency (Austria, Belgium, Cyprus, Estonia, Finland, France, Germany, Greece, Ireland, Italy, Latvia, Luxembourg, Malta, the Netherlands, Portugal, Slovakia, Slovenia, and Spain), while ten do not. Those who do not either "opted out" early on in the Maastricht negotiations (Denmark and the UK) or still need to meet certain "convergence criteria" (see the sidebar above). The EU official website (http://europa.eu/index_en.htm) contains a variety of position papers and clearly documents the growth and development of the European Union, including current membership policies and issues (see European Commission 2013). Your increasing knowledge of the fiscal stakes for the world as viewed through the lenses of both the EU and individual member nations is imperative for your understanding of both economic and political globalization. The Greek government's views on what is needed for economic recovery do not match the views of the European Union, yet the power of the EU and its fiscal counterpart, the EMU, have held sway since 2008 regarding what Greece needs to do to be an effective player in the EU and recover from its collapse.

Pillar Structure of the European Union

Common Foreign and Security Policy (governed by three supranational institutions: the Commission, the European Parliament, and the European Court of Justice)

European Community (EC)

Justice and Home Affairs (JHA)

In 2007 banks in the United States began to play different roles in the management of real estate speculation than they had earlier, which made them vulnerable to a real estate bubble. On September 15, 2008, Lehman Brothers declared bankruptcy and AIG (at the time the largest insurance company globally) collapsed. These two events are generally considered markers of the beginning of a global recession that still continues (Ferguson 2012).

Charles Ferguson (2012) works up to this marker, describing a long period of fiscal deregulation beginning in the early 1980s in the United States. He traces how the continuation of deregulation into the 1990s resulted in the merger of a large number of multinational firms, allowing groups that were formally forbidden from collaborating to unite. In particular, the passing of the Gramm-Leach-Bliley Act facilitated merger processes among insurance companies, brokerage firms, and banks. Bankers were able to speculate on derivatives (see sidebar) in a manner not permitted earlier. While some saw this as an example of fiscal innovation, others saw it as the beginning of a "securitization food chain" (Ferguson 2012), by which derivatives became increasingly unregulated. An early proposal in May 1998 to regulate derivatives was unsuccessful, as Senator Phil Gramm and others pushed through legislation to exempt derivatives from such oversight. By 2000 all commodity-futures derivatives regulation was banned. Ferguson suggests that the ultimate result was that individuals who made loans were not responsible for the success or failure of the loans. Lenders then sold mortgages to investment banks, which created collateralized debt that was sold to investors; this process is termed "credit default swap." Mortgage loans quadrupled. Credit default swaps began to increase; AIG's "credit default book grew from about $100 billion in 2002 to more than $500 billion in 2007" (Lenzner, 2008).

The fallout from these activities affected the EMU in a drastic way. The

A derivative is "a security whose price is dependent upon or derived from one or more underlying assets. The derivative itself is merely a contract between two or more parties. Its value is determined by fluctuations in the underlying asset [such as a bond]. Futures contracts, forward contracts, options, and swaps are the most common types of derivatives" (www.investopedia.com).

crisis stemmed from the fact that some European countries violated the principles of the Stability and Growth Pact (SGP) of 2005. Between 2008 and 2010, the economic health of Greece, Spain, and Portugal bandied about like loose luggage in the hold of a plane: wild careens from one side to the other caused the "plane" to take drastic measures to stay the course. In 2011 reforms of the SGP were implemented. These reforms are often called the "six-pack." They addressed gaps and weaknesses in the framework identified during the recent economic financial crisis. These reforms significantly strengthened both the fiscal surveillance and enforcement provisions of the SGP by adding an expenditure benchmark to review countries' fiscal positions, operationalizing the treaty's debt criterion, introducing an early and gradual system of financial sanctions for eurozone member states, and requiring new minimum standards for national budgetary frameworks (B. Yesilada, personal communication, January 2, 2014).

As an EU member, Greece was directly pulled into implementing austerity measures on numerous occasions, in particular in 2010, 2012, and 2015. Private financial institutions played governing roles in both the country's fall and recovery. As you read the quote below about events, try to imagine several levels of action within a matrix: multiple nation-states, multiple financial structures, public and private entities, and the general population in any given country. A principle to remember is that when austerity measures are imposed on a country to assist it in financial recovery, there are drastic differences in how particular citizens are impacted. A nation could begin to recover while individual citizens' lives remain in chaos.

This is how Costas Lapavitsas and his colleagues at the School of African and Oriental Studies at the University of London summarized the onset of the Great Recession:

> The collapse of Lehman Brothers in 2008 [in the United States] led to a major financial crisis that ushered in a global recession; the result

> Financialization is "the increasing role of financial motives, financial markets, financial actors, and financial institutions in the operation of domestic and international economies" (Epstein 2005, 3).

> was rising fiscal deficits for several leading countries of the world economy. For countries in the eurozone periphery, already deeply indebted after years of weakening competitiveness relative to the eurozone core, fiscal deficits led to restricted access to international bond markets. Peripheral states were threatened with insolvency, posing a risk to the European banks that were among the major lenders to the periphery. To rescue the banks, the eurozone had to bail out peripheral states. But bailouts were accompanied by austerity that induced deep recessions and rendered it hard to remain in the monetary unions, particularly for Greece. (2012, ix)

We see above the use of the terms "eurozone core" and "eurozone periphery." As will be explored in more detail in chapter 6, core nations use resources from periphery countries in ways that are frequently not sustainable to the periphery. In this case, Lapavitsas and his colleagues are suggesting that weaker EU states fiscally threatened to upend the stability of the more powerful core states. As a result, core states such as Germany took the lead in advocating austerity measures as required by the EU's SGP criteria. As we have seen in other settings with World Bank and IMF conditionality, these measures have typically taken away social programs in order to fund outside debt payment.

Greece's fiscal crisis began in 2009, when its deficit reached 15 percent, well exceeding the amount allowed under the EU's SGP criteria. Its international debt rating was downgraded. Index Mundi identifies three primary causes for this: "deteriorating public finances, inaccurate and misreported statistics, and consistent underperformance on reforms." Austerity measures were immediately implemented but proved inadequate for recovery. Since 2010, both the IMF and the EU have imposed three more rounds of austerity measures along with two bailouts—the first in 2010 for US$147 billion and the second in October 2011 for $169 billion. These measures caused and continue to cause social unrest, with closures of schools, public television, and multiple universities, including the venerated Athens University. Greece remains trapped in an austerity recovery program that looks to be interminable in spite of moderate measures of recovery. George Pagoulatos (2017, 6) summarizes the current state of Greece's economy: "Between 2009 and 2016 real wages fell by a yearly average of 3.1%, pensions have been cut 11 times since 2010; unemployment persists at 24%, with youth unemployment at 46%; 36% of the population is at risk of poverty or social exclusion; 450,000 Greeks have migrated abroad since 2008."

Lapavitsas (2012) contrasts the lived experiences of people in high management positions with the experiences of common individuals, whose lives were permanently altered after multiple government and financial institutions abandoned their clients. Scholars, physicians, and researchers who have revisited what happened in Greece over the past decade find higher rates of suicide, general malaise, and a sense of despair (Economou et al. 2011) Lapavitsas suggests that if peripheral economies in the EU are to survive, these nonindustry individuals must be allowed to play leadership roles in the resolution of crises. He lays out an admittedly Marxist economic resolution to the problems facing Greece, calling for a three-phased solution: default, debt renegotiation, and exit. While acknowledging risks to the whole eurozone with such a solution, he states, "Peripheral countries have no obligation to accept austerity for the indefinite future in order to rescue the eurozone. Moreover, if the eurozone collapsed under the weight of its own sins, the opportunity would arise to put relations among the people of Europe on a different basis. Solidarity and equality among European people are certainly possible, but they require grassroots initiatives. The eurozone in its present form is a barrier to this development" (2012, 128). Lapavitsas (2019) revisited the exit recommendations to either default on the debt or to leave the European union, a move called "Grexit."

Sets of criteria established in 2011 termed the "Euro-Plus Pact" attempt to manage deficits in particular member states, provide a level of sanctions if institutions do not meet their deficit targets, and ultimately enforce and fine countries that fail to measure up. This has led to agonizing on the part of many EU members on whether to remain in the eurozone using the euro as currency or to remain in the EU and *not* use the euro as currency. Within the next decade, other periphery eurozone nations will continue to face crises, much as Spain, Portugal, and even Ireland have. It remains to be seen whether traditional neoliberal solutions to debt will have any impact on the lives of individuals in these countries. In like manner, Marxist economic promises of greater attention to daily conditions of workers, and decisions to permit those most affected by austerity measures to have greater control over which measures are implemented, are likely to remain utopian. The European Union and all its members will play for high stakes in the economic globalization scene.

Conclusion

The scholars, entrepreneurs, and policy makers we have introduced to you in this chapter also have visions for our globalized world. Most have outlined roles for multinational organizations at the international or regional level to both craft and implement policy. Entrepreneur George Soros has called for a complementary organization to the WTO in order to resolve issues the WTO has been unable to resolve. He believes it is critically important to do four things: "contain the instability of financial markets; correct the built-in bias in our existing international trade and financial institutions that favors the developed countries that largely control them; complement the WTO with similarly powerful international institutions devoted to other social goals such as poverty reduction and the provision of public goods on a global scale; and improve the quality of public life in countries suffering from corrupt, repressive, or incompetent governments" (2002, 8). Ellwood also pushes the notion of creating another type of global financial authority, even while reforming the Bretton Woods institutions. He suggests that only by "increasing citizen participation" (2003, 108) and "honoring the earth" (2003, 118) will it be possible to undo some of the damage that has been caused by conditionality. In the next chapter, we continue to explore transborder flows, focusing on the history and distinguishing features of political globalization.

➤ VOCABULARY

- Big Three
- privatization
- liberalization
- deregulation
- neoliberal economic policy
- Augmented Washington Consensus
- Poverty Reduction Strategy Papers
- gold standard
- Dispute Settlement Body
- Washington Consensus
- BRICS
- Industrializing Six
- financialization
- derivatives
- Stability and Growth Pact criteria

➤ DISCUSSION AND REFLECTION QUESTIONS

1 *Identify three dimensions of economic aspects of globalization.*
2 *What were the initial hopes for the World Bank and the International Monetary Fund?*
3 *What are three differences between the Washington Consensus and the Augmented Washington Consensus?*
4 *What is the relationship between structural adjustment programs and the Poverty Reduction Strategy Papers?*
5 *Why is it so difficult to escape sanctions meted out by the Dispute Settlement Body?*
6 *What are some of the criticisms that have been leveled against neoliberal economic policies?*
7 *What can we expect in the future from BRICS?*
8 *If you were able to make policy recommendations to manage economic reforms at a global level and maintain social programs within a developing nation qualifying for assistance from the Bretton Woods institutions, what would two of your top priorities be?*
9 *How can you account for the kinds of intellectual and policy changes people like Joseph Stiglitz have made over the course of their careers?*
10 *How has the private sector in banking along with derivative speculation changed the fiscal stability of periphery nations in the eurozone?*

ACTIVITY 1: ANALYZE This chapter defined globalization and looked in some detail at the extended debate regarding sugar in the WTO and ultimately its Dispute Settlement Body. Go online and conduct a search to find one other major dispute currently under consideration at the WTO. Track the amount of time the dispute has been going on and its primary actors. Identify how you would resolve the dispute if the ultimate decision were in your hands.

ACTIVITY 2: REFLECT Lapavitsas and colleagues (2012) suggest that acceptance of austerity principles and neoliberal recommendations on the part of many countries in the eurozone has resulted in measurable temporary fixes but long-term chaos as well. Choose one country—Iceland, Greece, Portugal, or Spain. Identify one austerity principle they were asked to follow. Then, using a newspaper database such as the *New York Times Index*, search for economic stories about that country and identify whether the austerity measures taken are addressed in the article and what the principle followed was. Can you identify the ideological stance of the author regarding these activities?

ACTIVITY 3: EXTEND Some of you may not have a strong recollection of the 2008 financial crisis, but someone in your family likely does. Ask a relative what he or she remembers. If you were outside the United States at this time, ask a few trusted individuals who were in the country what they recall. Contrast what you were told with what you have read about the current economic globalization context. Think about how something like Britain's relationship to the European Union or Venezuela's dive into collapse may be linked to one part of your life. Write about how these circumstances and the difficulties they caused are linked to your current life. Writing about difficult subjects may help you put them on a better shelf in your mind.

References

Appadurai, A. 1996. *Modernity at large: Cultural dimensions of globalization.* Minneapolis: University of Minnesota Press.

Baldwin, R. 2016. *The great convergence.* Cambridge: Belknap Press/Harvard University Press.

Brazil halts its petition for a panel on a WTO dispute against Thailand. 2018. *Sugar Asia Magazine* [June 26]. Retrieved November 5, 2019, from http://sugar-asia.com/brazil-halts-its-petition-for-a-panel-on-a-wto-dispute-against-thailand/.

Broad, R., ed. 2002. *Global backlash: Citizen initiatives for a just world economy.* Lanham, Md.: Roman and Littlefield.

Brown, T. 2013. *Contestation, confusion, and corruption: Market-based land reform in Zambia.* Retrieved December 18, 2013, from www.theidlgroup.com/ . . . /market_based_land_reform_zambia.pdf.

Cerny, P. 1995. Globalization and the changing logic of collective action. *International Organization* 49 (4): 595–625.

Charney, J. 1983. Transnational corporations and developing public international law. *Duke Law Journal* 4 (September): 748–88.

Cheraghali, A. M. 2013. Impacts of international sanctions on Iranian pharmaceutical market. *DARU Journal of Pharmaceutical Sciences* 21:64. Retrieved March 10, 2019, from http://www.darujps.com/content/21/1/64.

Chin, P. 1997. Cheddi Jagan, Michael Manley and the history of U.S. intervention in the Caribbean. *Workers World*, April 3. Retrieved November 26, 2008, from http://www.hartford-hwp.com/archives/43/034.html.

Choi, K. 2008. The roots of the WTO. Retrieved November 26, 2008, from www.econ.iastate.edu/classes/econ355/choi/wtoroots.htm.

Cooper, A. 2016. *BRICS: A very short introduction*. Oxford: Oxford University Press.

Cox, R. 1996. A perspective on globalization. In *Globalization: Critical reflections*, edited by J. Mittelman, 22–30. Boulder, Colo.: Lynne Rienner.

Cutler, A. C. 2001. Critical reflections on the Westphalian assumptions of international law and organization: A crisis of legitimacy. *Review of International Studies* 27:133–50.

Economou, M., M. Madianos, C. Theleritis, L. Peppou, and C. Stefanis. 2011. Increased suicidality amid economic crisis in Greece. *The Lancet* 378 (9801): 1459.

Ellwood, W. 2003. *The no-nonsense guide to globalization*. Toronto: New Internationalist Publications.

Epstein, G. 2005. *Financialization and the world economy*. Northampton, Mass.: Edward Elgar.

European Commission. 2013. *Economic and monetary union and the euro*. Luxembourg: Publications Office of the European Union. Retrieved December 20, 2013, from europa.eu/pol/ . . . /economic_and_monetary_union_and_the_euro_en.pdf. doi:10.2775/37006.

Ferguson, C. 2012. *Inside job: The financiers who pulled off the heist of the century*. Oxford: Oneworld Publications.

Focus Economics. 2018. The world's top 10 largest economies. Blog post. Retrieved July 19, 2019, from https://www.focus-economics.com/blog/the-largest-economies-in-the-world.

Fortune Global 500 Companies. 2013. Retrieved December 18, 2013, from http://money.cnn.com/magazines/fortune/global500/.

Friedman, T. 2007. *The world is flat: A brief history of the 21st century*. New York: Picador/Farrar, Straus and Giroux.

GATT. n.d. CIESIN thematic guides. Retrieved November 23, 2008, from http:// www.Ciesin.orgTG/PI/TRADE/gatt.html.

Global Fund. 2008. International financing institution: About the Global Fund. Retrieved December 5, 2008, from http://www.theglobalfund.org/en/ifi/.

Global Policy Forum. 2008. www.globalpolicy.org/globaliz/politics/index.htm.

Global Trade Negotiations home page. Retrieved January 18, 2008, from http://www.cid.harvard.edu/cidtrade/issues/Washington.html.

Graddol, D. 1996. The future of English. Retrieved December 18, 2013, from www.britishcouncil.org/learning-elt-future.pdf.

Handa, S., and D. King. 1997. Structural adjustment policies, income distribution, and poverty: A review of the Jamaican experience. *World Development* 25 (6): 915–30.

Hansen-Kuhn, K., and S. Hellinger. 1999. SAPS link sharpens debt-relief debate. Retrieved as pdf on January 25, 2010, from http://www.developmentgap.org/worldbank_imf/saps_link_sharpens_debtrelief_debate.pdf (Third World Network; developmentgap.com).

Harvey, D. 1989. *The condition of post-modernity: An inquiry into the origins of culture change.* Cambridge: Blackwell.

Iceland Economic Profile. 2013. Retrieved December 20, 2013, from www.indexmundi.com/iceland/economy/profile.html.

IMF. 2019. IMF conditionality. Retrieved November 26, 2008, from http://www.imf.org/external/np/exr/facts/conditio.htm.

IMF website. n.d. Retrieved January 17, 2009, from http://www.imf.org/external/index.htm.

Index Mundi, Greece Economic Profile. 2013. Retrieved December 20, 2013, from www.indexmundi.com/greece/economy/profile.html.

International networks archive: Remapping our world. n.d. Retrieved December 3, 2008, from http://www.princeton.edu/~ina/infographics/index.html.

Katada, S., C. Roberts, and L. Armijo. 2017. The varieties of collective financial statecraft: The BRICS and China. *Political Science Quarterly* 132 (3): 403–33. doi: 10.10002/polq.12656.

Khanna, P., and A. Rusi. 2008. Europe's century. *The Guardian.* Retrieved January 17, 2009, from www.globalpolicy.org/nations/sovereign/integrate/2008/0617khanna.htm.

Kikeri, S., and A. Kolo. 2005. *Privatization: Trends and recent developments.* World Bank Policy Research Working Paper 3765, November. Retrieved February 26, 2019, from documents.worldbank.org/curated/en/802811468138570860/pdf/wps3765.pdf.

Krugman, P. 2004. *The great unraveling: Losing our way in the new century.* London: Penguin.

Lapavitsas, C., A. Kaltenbrunner, G. Labrinidis, D. Lindo, J. Meadway, J. Michell, J. P. Painceira, E. Pires, J. Powell, A Stenfors, N. Teles, and L. Vatikiotis. 2012. *Crisis in the Eurozone.* London: Verso.

Lapavitsas, C. 2019. Political economy of the Greek crisis. *Review of Radical Political Economics* 51 (1): 31–51.

Lévesque, J. 2013. Haiti "reconstruction": Luxury hotels, sweat shops and deregulation for the foreign corporate elite. *Global Research*, August 16. Retrieved December 18, 2013, from http://www.globalresearch.ca/haiti-reconstruction-luxury-hotels-sweat-shops-and-deregulation-for-the-foreign-corporate-elite/5344546.

Lenzner, R. 2008. Why wasn't AIG hedged? Forbes [28 September]. Retrieved November 5, 2019, from https://www.forbes.com/2008/09/28/croesus-aig-credit-biz-cx_rl_0928croesus.html#7127df34d634.

Lynam, J. 2013. Iceland's "tenacity" lifts economy out of crisis. January 7. Retrieved December 28, 2013, from http://www.bbc.co.uk/news/world-europe-20936685.

MacGillivray, A. 2006. *A brief history of globalization*. London: Robinson.

May, J., and N. Thrift. 2001. Introduction. In *TimeSpace: Geographies of temporality*, 1–46. New York: Routledge.

McKinley, T. 2018. BRICS to play a leading role in driving future economic growth. Retrieved November 5, 2019, from https://www.ineteconomics.org/perspectives/blog/brics-to-play-a-leading-role-in-driving-future-global-economic-growth.

Newnham, R. 2013. Pipeline politics: Russian energy sanctions and the 2010 Ukrainian elections. *Journal of Eurasian Studies* 4:115–22.

O'Neill, J. 2007. BRICS and beyond. Retrieved December 18, 2013, from http://www.goldmansachs.com/our-thinking/archive/BRICs-and-Beyond.html.

Ostry, S. 2004. The future of the world trading system: Beyond Doha. In *Hard choices, soft law: Voluntary standards in global trade, environment and social governance*, ed. J. Kirkton and M. Trebilcock, 270–87. Burlington, VT: Ashgate.

Pagoulatos, G. 2017. Greece: Searching for light at the end of the tunnel. *Intereconomics* 52 (2): 66–67. http://dx.doi.org/10.1007/s10272-017-0646-y.

Riley, C., and I. Sherman. World's largest economies. CNN Money, 2013. Retrieved December 18, 2013, from http://money.cnn.com/news/economy/world_economies_gdp/.

Roberts, C., L. Armijo, and S. Katada. 2018. *The BRICS and collective financial statecraft*. Oxford: Oxford University Press.

Rudd, K. 2008. Large issues and medium powers. *The world in 2009 (The economist)*, 64.

Scholte, J. 2005. *The sources of neoliberal globalization: Overarching concerns*. Programme Paper Number 8 (October). United Nations Research Institute for Social Development.

Seckinelgin, H., J. Scholte, A. Kumar, M. Kaldor, M. Glasius, and H. Anheier. 2009. *Poverty and activism: The heart of global civil society*. Retrieved January 1, 2014, from http://www.opendemocracy.net/authors/jan-aart-scholte.

Segal, S., and D. Gestel. 2018. *The economic effect of sanctions on Iran*. Retrieved February 26, 2019, from https://www.csis.org/analysis/economic-impact-iran-sanctions.

Seria, N. 2010. South Africa is asked to join as a BRIC member to boost emerging markets. *Bloomberg*, December 24. Retrieved January 1, 2014, from http:// www.bloomberg.com/news/2010–12–24/south-africa-asked-to-join-bric-to-boost-cooperation-with-emerging-markets.html.

Singer, P. 2002. *One world: The ethics of globalization*. New Haven, Conn.: Yale University Press.

Soros, G. 2002. *On globalization*. New York: Public Affairs.

Statista. 2019. Gross domestic product (GDP) of the BRIC countries from 2014 to 2024 (in billion U.S. dollars). Retrieved February 26, 2019, from https://www.statista.com/statistics/254281/gdp-of-the-bric-countries/.

Steger, M. 2003. *Globalization: A very short introduction*. Oxford: Oxford University Press.

Stiglitz, J. 2002. *Globalization and its discontents.* London: W. W. Norton.

———. 2006. *Making globalization work.* New York: W. W. Norton.

Top 10 reasons to oppose the WTO criticism. Retrieved November 5, 2019, from https://www.wto.org/english/thewto_e/minist_e/min99_e/english/misinf_e/09sov_e.htm.

Thimann, C. 2015. The microeconomic dimensions of the eurozone crisis and why European politics cannot solve them. *Journal of Economic Perspectives* 29 (3): 141–64.

UN Millennium Goals. 2007. Retrieved January 17, 2009, from www.un.org/millenniumgoals/pdf/mdg2007.pdf.

Vincent, J. 2010. Microeconomic analysis of innovative environmental programs in developing countries. *Review of Environmental Economics and Policy* 4 (2): 221–33. https://doi.org/10.1093/reep/req011.

Vousinas, Georgios. 2015. *The Greek debt crisis: Like the enigma of Sphinx. An estimation of the probability of default.* [May 1.] Retrieved from SSRN: https://ssrn.com/abstract=3186430 or http://dx.doi.org/10.2139/ssrn.3186430.

WTO. n.d. DS 27: European communities—regime for the importation, sale and distribution of bananas. Retrieved July 6, 2010, from http://www.wto.org/english/tratop_e /dispu_e/cases_e/ds27_e.htm.

———. n.d. The multilateral trading system: 50 years of achievement. GATT slideshow. Retrieved January 1, 2014, from http://www.wto.org /english/thewto_e/minist_e/min98_e/slide_e/slide_list.htm.

———. n.d. WTO membership in brief. Retrieved December 18, 2013, from www.wto.org/english/thewto_e/acc_e/members_brief_e.doc.

WTO website. n.d. Retrieved January 17, 2009, from www.wto.org.

FOUR **Political Globalization**

➤ **SYNOPSIS**

After World War II the world witnessed a steady movement to political integration through the rise of alliances, ideals, and organizations greater than the nation-state, from the United Nations to the International Court of Justice (ICJ), the European Union to the Association of Southeast Asian Nations (ASEAN). With the end of the Cold War, authoritarian regimes collapsed in Asia, Eastern Europe, and Latin America. Democratization seemed to be the most important political force after the millennium. The rise of the World Wide Web seemed to make it impossible to control information. Globally, the nation-state seemed to be declining as the main actor in global affairs.

After 2015, however, a rising tide of nationalist and populist leaders and ideologies reversed this trend. The long civil wars in Afghanistan and Syria and the near-collapse of the Libyan state led to a flood of refugees into Italy and Greece. When German chancellor Angela Merkel unilaterally decided to admit a million refugees into Europe in 2015 without prior consultation with other European states, it not only resulted in the decline of her political power but also sparked the rise of nationalist and populist leaders throughout the continent. In June 2016, a slim majority (52 percent) of British citizens voted to leave the European Union, perhaps the most powerful supranational organization on the planet. From the Philippines to Brazil, one nationalist and populist leader after another rose to power.

Old political rules no longer seemed to apply; traditional alliances frayed. Russia's intervention in Ukraine in 2014 showed that international organizations could not stop conflict even in Europe. After 2016, U.S. president Donald Trump questioned the value of the North Atlantic Treaty Organization

(NATO). Even the Web seemed to be splintering into three main blocs: one dominated by China, with tight restrictions; one in Europe, where citizens had a "right to be forgotten"; and one in the United States, with few restrictions on information monitoring or sales (*New York Times* Editorial Board 2018). During crises, some nations shut down the Internet entirely. No longer did democratization or the free flow of information seem to be inevitable. The most powerful rising power, China, is an authoritarian state.

Political globalization may seem like a topic distant from your life. But if you live in Britain and have not been following the debate about Brexit, fundamental changes could take place that could deeply affect you without your understanding what they are. For people living in Asia, the decisions taken by ASEAN have a deep impact on students' lives, such as the establishment of English as a common language of study. The current tension between centralizing trends, on the one hand, and the rise of nationalism and populism, on the other, shapes political debates in every region of the globe. In this chapter we will examine these conflicts—between national identity and integration, populism and cosmopolitanism—which define how economic and cultural globalization take place.

➤ SCAFFOLDING

As you read through this chapter, think about how you would answer each of the questions below.

What did you already know about the League of Nations and the United Nations and the issues that surround them?

How do the institutions and trends described in this chapter relate to those discussed in the economic globalization chapter?

What other institutions or examples of political globalization might this chapter have discussed?

Why do you believe populism and nationalism have acquired such political power globally?

➤ CORE CONCEPTS

Because political globalization is as powerful a force as economic globalization, the two movements must be discussed together.

Democratization arguably represented the most powerful trend associated with political globalization in the early twenty-first century. Currently, populist leaders with authoritarian leanings have risen to power in both developed and developing nations in most major world regions.

Although the nation-state remains the most powerful actor in most situations, the rise of new institutions and beliefs challenges its influence. In some cases, new political organizations—such as the European Union—are even assuming aspects of sovereignty. This has sparked a popular backlash within many nation-states.

When people think of globalization, many of them associate it with the economic trends that are integrating the world's economies. If they think of political institutions, they likely focus on those discussed in the last chapter, which have their roots in the Bretton Woods System and focus on economic policy. But these institutions represent only part of the international forces that are reshaping the global order. Dramatic changes are also taking place in the realm of politics. Some political organizations have emerged that hold great power. After World War II, the founding of both the United Nations and the International Court of Justice meant that even leaders of nation-states had to fear facing justice if they committed war crimes or genocide. Other new political actors appeared that were both influential and complex, particularly when they entered into alliances with other groups to achieve their goals. For example, new transnational organizations (such as Greenpeace, Oxfam, and Amnesty International) established alliances with grassroots organizations (Indigenous rights groups or local environmental movements) to block initiatives from organizations such as the World Bank. Such coalitions have defeated powerful nation-states, including the United States. Although the nation-state remains the fundamental unit in international affairs, other political actors have constrained its power, although not without a popular response.

A decade ago the rise of the European Union, the integration fostered by NAFTA, and increasing migration seemed to fundamentally undermine the power of nation-states. Over the last decade, however, populism and nationalism have emerged as powerful forces. In Europe, the British people voted to leave the EU in a move known as Brexit. There has been a powerful backlash against migrants and refugees both in North America and in Europe. Even such long-standing supranational organizations as

NATO are facing serious political challenges. Globally, there has been a wave of populist or authoritarian victors in national elections who have come to power based on nationalist rhetoric, which decries international organizations, treaties, and rules. In many respects, these movements can be understood as a global backlash against political globalization. To understand these trends, one needs to understand the historical context that shaped many of the players and rules in the international system.

The Legacy of World War I

The roots of political globalization, like those of economic globalization, lay in a terrible conflict. In 1914 Europe exploded into a war that probably no Great Power wanted. Historians have long debated the reasons for this war—with explanations that have emphasized imperial rivalry, rampant nationalism, and train schedules—but the origins of the conflict are so complex that this issue is still contested. For five years, millions of men fought and died in trenches that stretched across Europe on two fronts, from northern France to modern Turkey. For much of this time, the opposing sides were trapped in a stalemate, which each sought to break with weapons that ranged from mustard gas to underground tunnels that were packed with explosives and then detonated. In the end, the conflict destroyed three Great Powers—the Austro-Hungarian, Russian, and Ottoman Empires—and the belligerents achieved nothing positive to balance the suffering inflicted by the war. The complexity and devastation of the war left many shattered veterans wondering what they had fought for.

After the war, Woodrow Wilson, the American president, was determined to create a new order based on his ideals so that such a disaster could never happen again. Wilson, the founder of modern liberalism, believed that new organizations were needed to prevent wars of aggression, to permit the territories once governed by Germany and the Ottoman Empire to achieve sovereignty, and to adjudicate disputes that might lead to war. Wilson told the American people that new organizations and the rule of law—a body of international practices and rules that would resolve disputes—could control the passions and the grievances that led the Old World into conflagration. His allies, France and England, had not fought the war intending to relinquish their empires or create a new national order. But they could not ignore the United States, which had brought the manpower and the money that had tipped the balance to their side.

As a result, the first part of the Treaty of Versailles, which officially ended the war in 1919, contained language describing a new international organization called the League of Nations. Wilson himself suffered a severe stroke in 1919 in the midst of a struggle to persuade the U.S. Senate to join this new body. The United States never joined, and many historians have argued that this fact fatally weakened the league. Another challenge was that Germany was not permitted to join until 1926 (Kennedy 2006, 13). Still, during the 1920s, the League of Nations appeared to be effective, as did the Permanent Court of International Justice, which the league created in 1923. But, faced with the rising power of fascism and without U.S. participation, the league failed to confront the Japanese invasion of Manchuria in 1931 and the Italian invasion of Ethiopia in 1935 (both inspired by imperialist aims), as well as German rearmament. The league's charter contained flaws, which perhaps gave small states too much power and failed to oblige members to act (Sobel 1994, 180). Despite Wilson's vision, the League of Nations could not prevent another conflagration. The postwar period proved to be an interregnum in what came to be a single European civil war, so that "the war to end all wars" (World War I) was soon followed by a second.

The United Nations

In 1939 the Second World War began and lasted six long years before the final defeat of Nazi Germany and Imperial Japan. At this point in 1945, many people believed that a new League of Nations was needed more than ever because they were determined not to repeat the mistakes that made the war possible. (For an in-depth discussion of the creation of the United Nations, see Kennedy 2006, 4–47; and Hurd 2007, 84–91). For this reason, at the war's end, the victors extinguished the old League of Nations and created the United Nations to take its place, with the intent of learning from the league's failure. In April and June 1945, forty-six nations from around the world gathered in San Francisco to create this organization. The meetings saw heated debates, in part because the wartime alliance among the Allies was ending and the first shadows of the Cold War had crept into the meeting rooms. But there were also many serious questions to be answered. As Stephen Schlesinger has argued, it is not true that the UN was "born out of a gentle, idealistic vision of a global body, a sort of immaculate conception. In fact, the U.N. Charter was a meticulously crafted, power-oriented document carefully molded by hard-nosed drafters to conform to the global realities of 1945" (1997, 48). It divided the UN into two bodies. The fifteen-member Security Council addressed critical issues and had five permanent members: China, France, Great Britain, the Soviet Union, and the United States, which were the Great Powers of the time. As global power balances shifted, this choice of nations appeared increasingly anachronistic. In contrast, most nations were confined to the General Assembly, which could make recommendations to the Security Council, write reports, and approve the budget but did not address key issues of peace and security or send troops into an active war zone.

It could be argued that the UN is not democratic. But it could not have been created without the participation of the Great Powers. The United States' decision not to participate in the League of Nations had helped to doom it. If the UN was to avoid being stillborn, it needed to have the support of each of these major nations, even at the cost of inequality. This inequality might appear to be mitigated by the fact that there are fifteen members of the Security Council, of which ten are nonpermanent members from the General Assembly. But these nations soon rotate off the Security Council, and none of them has the power of veto. It was the latter power that gave the permanent members the "ability to decide on U.N. intervention, determine who leads the organization, block U.N. Charter amendments, and so forth" (Schlesinger 1997, 49; see also Hurd 2007, 93–96). While many smaller states had opposed this arrangement, they failed to overcome the position of the Great Powers. With this assurance, the U.S. Senate was willing to ratify the treaty, and the Soviet Union was willing to join.

The UN has not achieved all that was promised at its creation in 1945. There is no denying its failures. It did not stop the Rwandan genocide of 1994, and it needed U.S. leadership to be effective in Bosnia (Shawcross 2000, 124–92). In the case of Kosovo, the United States ultimately ended the fighting in 1999 without the UN. In addition, the UN has often failed to enforce its decisions. It also has a long-standing reputation for being bureaucratic, ineffective, and corrupt. The wide diversity of membership within the UN has often made it difficult to reach consensus on even the most important issues, which at times has caused even the secretary general to express frustration with the organization (Anonymous 2005). The United States invaded Iraq without the support of the UN, despite UN Resolution 1441, which required Iraq to meet its obligations to disarm (Glennon 2003, 18; Hurd 2007, 124–28). The UN has failed to act to end the civil war in Syria, which began as part of the Arab Spring; it has also proved unable to stop Russia from intervening in Ukraine. While its fellow

Traffic circle in Vietnam (Used with permission of the photographer, Christina Caponi)

organizations, such as the World Health Organization (WHO), the UN Refugee Agency, and the World Food Programme, have been recognized for their achievements, the United Nations is often condemned for the crises it has failed to avert.

Despite these failings, the UN also has a long list of major achievements, from helping to end apartheid in South Africa to moderating crises during the Cold War (Schlesinger 1997, 51). It is a cliché to say that nations do not appreciate the UN until there is a crisis. Cynics can claim that the UN resolves problems only when it is in the interest of Great Powers to see them fixed. But as World War I showed, it is possible for nations to slide into war; not every conflict begins through a rational calculation of interests. The UN has provided a forum that has allowed major countries to extricate themselves from hostilities, such as the Suez Crisis in 1956. By providing nations with a face-saving means to avoid conflict, fact finders with a way of determining the truth of events, and peacekeepers with the power to separate rival forces, the UN decreases the likelihood of unintended wars. The UN also possesses moral authority. Perhaps no other power had the legitimacy, for example, to end the violence in East Timor after that nation voted for independence from Indonesia in 1999. The U.S. and NATO air campaign could defeat the Serbs militarily in Kosovo in 1999, but the United States and NATO then needed a UN mandate to send in peacekeepers.

Through its role in peacekeeping, the UN has separated many aggrieved parties and laid the groundwork for a settlement of international disputes, despite the questions that sometimes come regarding the legitimacy of its operations (Hurd 2007, 125). The UN also plays a key role in organizing relief after international disasters. This could be clearly seen after the 2010 earthquake in Haiti, after which the UN's World Food Programme began food distribution on a massive scale. Moreover, some of its components—such as the WHO—have achieved stunning successes, such as eliminating smallpox and polio. Because of its legitimacy, the WHO is able to do work in key areas that are not accessible to other organizations. The truly dangerous flaws of the UN lie less in its unending bureaucracy than in the extent to which it froze the global balance of power in 1945.

UN Reform

The Security Council is at the core of the United Nations, and its nature is defined by its history. (For a discussion of the Security Council's role, see

Hurd 2007, 111–36.) At the end of World War II, the five Great Powers dominated international affairs. Few scholars or diplomats foresaw that the Age of Empire had ended and that in the space of roughly two decades, both Great Britain and France would lose their empires. Both nations underwent a relative economic decline. They remained wealthy states but were no longer central to global affairs. People at the time could see that both Germany and Japan were key global powers, but the victors of World War II excluded them from the Security Council because of their responsibility for the war that had just finished. While this may have made sense at the time, did that make sense a generation later? Two generations later? Germany and Japan now have great influence on the council, but their exclusion still seems an anomaly (Hurd 2007, 118).

This imbalance between power relations on the Security Council, and the power of the global system today, has raised the question of whether the UN Security Council faces a crisis of legitimacy (Efstathopoulos 2016, 429). The challenge, however, remains choosing which countries to serve on the council, as every possible choice (Brazil, India) can lead to a protest from a neighbor (Argentina, Pakistan). Other nations that do not have great power within the UN system claim that they should be chosen as representatives of their region. For example, South Africa claims that it should be added to the Security Council as a representative of Africa (Efstathopoulos 2016, 430). Yet other nations, such as Nigeria, are also advocating playing such a role (Africa News Service 2017). While there is near unanimity that the current system does not adequately represent global power structures, there is no consensus regarding what changes to make. And there remains a serious discrepancy between the makeup of the Security Council and global power relations now.

This problem is only likely to increase with time. If current trends continue, most of the world's economic growth over the next forty years will likely take place outside of the United States and Europe. Asia and Latin America have the most dynamic economies, while Africa will see the greatest population increase among the continents. As is common in international affairs, governance systems are created within a historical context, which pertains to that specific time and environment. These systems need the capacity to adapt if they are not to become obsolete as the context changes. But the UN charter did not create a clear process to determine the manner in which new states would be made permanent members of the Security Council. The UN charter can be changed only with the approval of the Security Council, which means that the five permanent members have veto power over any new additions to this body. This reality, and competition among neighbors, has meant that no new nation has ever become a new permanent member (Luck 2003, 15).

The danger of this situation is that the UN was created to reflect the balance of global power because, without this representation, it would not be effective—a lesson learned from the League of Nations. With each passing year, economic and demographic changes reshape the balance of power, so that the existing makeup of the Security Council seems increasingly out of date, especially in contrast to other organizations that have expanded or adapted. As nations rallied to address the economic crisis of 2009, it was the G20 that drew media attention because the old G8 nations no longer had the influence needed to resolve global problems (Goldstone 2010, 41). A similar evolution could not take place within the United Nations. Resolving this problem would entail revising the UN charter to create a clear process for both adding and removing powers: "International institutions will not retain their legitimacy if they exclude the world's fastest growing and most economically dynamic powers" (41). This problem, however, shows few signs of resolution. (For a contrary view to the above argument, see Hurd 2007, 123.) While this challenge has remained unresolved, the UN has helped to weave a new set of political ties around the globe. This can clearly be seen in the case of the International Court of Justice, which has contributed to the growing importance of international law—another concept important to Woodrow Wilson.

The International Court of Justice

While the UN has many responsibilities—including coordinating disaster relief, peacekeeping, and monitoring elections—few aspects of its work have been as important as the administration of international justice and arbitration of disputes. This was clear immediately at the end of World War II, when the victors decided to try war criminals at the Nuremberg trials, named for the city in Germany in which they were held. Rather than being immediately executed, those responsible for the Holocaust, ethnic cleansing, and the war were tried in a court in which they had counsel and genuine trials. The idea of international justice was to be central to the new world order. For this reason, the new International Court of Justice, the main judicial organization of the UN, had a broad range of responsibilities. For example, countries could agree to submit boundary disputes and other arguments to the court for a binding settlement. Aggrieved parties could also take their disputes to the court for resolution. The ICJ was intended to provide judicial support to the Security Council to avoid and resolve international conflict.

The ICJ has not always succeeded. During the Cold War, the court was incapable of imposing its rulings on the superpowers. For example, in the 1980s the United States refused to recognize a court ruling that condemned it for planting sea mines in Nicaraguan ports. This substantially weakened the court. While the Soviet Union worried that the ICJ was initially weighted in favor of democracies, the United States eventually came to fear its judicial independence (Posner 2004). There has always been a tension between the ability of Great Powers to veto decisions that they oppose within the UN Security Council and their potential vulnerability within the ICJ. Justices were theoretically impartial—that is, they were not supposed to vote based on their national origin. For this reason, the United States' acceptance of the court and its authority has been conditional in a number of manners. For instance, when the United States became party to the Genocide Convention, it did so with a reservation: "Before any dispute in which the United States is a party may be submitted to the jurisdiction of the International Court of Justice under this article, the specific consent of the United States is required in each case" (Jennings 1995, 495–96). In other words, the United States could be brought to court only with its own consent.

On the surface, the Genocide Convention—which forbade the destruction of a people either through killing, the prevention of birth, or the removal of children—would seem uncontroversial. But the United States was concerned about how the convention might be interpreted. For similar reasons, after the creation of the International Criminal Court in 2002, the United States made it clear that it would not ratify this document, even though it had been a signatory (Mayerfield 2003). Ironically, at the same time that the United States regularly qualifies—or even rejects—the authority of the ICJ, it also claims special authority in establishing customary international law (Heller 2018).

While it is logical for any nation-state to not wish to submit itself to the authority of an outside power, states also pay a price when they do not participate in such institutions. In the case of major powers on the Security Council, however, bodies such as the ICJ have limited power. This is true as well for other agreements such as the Paris Agreement on climate change. Although every nation on the planet had signed this agreement, the United States unilaterally withdrew from the accord on June 1, 2017.

The reality is that such agreements and UN bodies have much more power over smaller states than over Great Powers, and the power of ideas—such as human rights—can be as important as international law.

The Rise of Human Rights as a Doctrine

Human rights are those claims and protections that people have because they are part of humanity, independent from their citizenship in a particular state. Historically, in Western culture, these claims came not from one's nationality but rather from one's religion; this was also the case in many other civilizations, such as the Islamic world. During the French Enlightenment of the eighteenth century, however, secular and humanist philosophers began to claim that people had the right to protection based on reason and not religion. The first great human rights battle was against slavery, which ended in the Western Hemisphere with its abolition in Cuba in 1886 and Brazil in 1888. This rights campaign was the model for many that followed. But it was the horrific events of the twentieth century, from the mass killing of Armenian civilians by Turkey during World War I to the Holocaust, that led to the creation of the UN Commission on Human Rights in 1946. Eleanor Roosevelt, the widow of U.S. president Franklin D. Roosevelt, subsequently campaigned for the UN Declaration of Human Rights, which the General Assembly passed in 1948. Some idea of its moral force can be gleaned from the fact that no nation opposed it, although Saudi Arabia, South Africa, and the Soviet Union abstained from the vote. (For a good overview of the history of human rights, see Lauren 1998.)

On the surface, it would seem that both this declaration and the UN proved to be failures because they could not prevent many of the terrible human rights tragedies of the twentieth century. Because of their political power, the Soviet Union and China were able to ignore the UN Declaration of Human Rights as they committed terrible human rights violations. Likewise, the United States shielded authoritarian states in Latin America and elsewhere from UN action during the Cold War. The United States did so in part because it had created many authoritarian regimes as a bulwark against Communism and to serve its business interests, as was the case with the Somoza family in Nicaragua. Yet, the power of human rights has grown as a political ideal, and violating these norms has carried a high political and personal cost for authoritarian leaders and their governments. For example, historian John Lewis Gaddis (2005, 190–94) has argued that the Helsinki Accords, passed in 1975, were fundamental to undermining the Soviet Union's legitimacy. This agreement among almost every state in Europe, as well as Canada and the United States, committed all the signatories to respect human rights and self-determination of peoples. With the end of the Cold War, the United States withdrew its support from authoritarian governments in Latin America, which fell like dominoes in part because they appeared illegitimate in the eyes of both their own people and the international community, given their terrible human rights violations. South Africa found it impossible to face sanctions and international condemnation in order to maintain apartheid, which denied rights to citizens based on race. The UN and the United States intervened to end ethnic cleansing and violence in the former Yugoslavia in the 1990s.

States can still violate human rights if they are willing to pay a political price, as nations such as Burma, China, and Syria have shown. But those who suffer have long memories, and many authoritarian leaders must worry that in their retirement, a warrant will be issued for their arrest, and they may be brought before the International Criminal Court in The Hague. This serves as a check on behavior. The proliferation of nongovernmental organizations (NGOs), such as Amnesty International, has brought publicity to human rights violations, as has the development of global media. Nations that are willing to isolate themselves, such as North Korea and Burma (with the 2016 Royhingya expulsion), are able to continue to violate human rights. But these states still pay both a political and an economic cost. No nations look to them as models. States that violate human rights lose the moral authority to serve as international leaders. The price that the United States has paid for both the use of torture at Abu Ghraib prison in Iraq and waterboarding and other abuses at Guantanamo Bay detention camp in Cuba has been high in terms of its international leadership.

Still, human rights are not uncontested as a doctrine, as the work of Shashi Tharoor (1999) makes clear. Critics ask, who defines what is a human right? The idea itself, they argue, is based on an essentialist vision of human nature—that is, the idea that we are all fundamentally the same. But what an urban Western citizen in Amsterdam may perceive to be a human right may be very different from what a rural religious person in Indonesia believes one to be. In this circumstance, who decides? Is female genital cutting an age-old cultural practice or a human rights violation? Is it acceptable to change practices in the name of human rights if that means fundamental changes to a culture will follow? What rights are universally recognized? Those of women? Sexual minorities? How are these decisions made? If it is the West that imposes its vision of human rights upon developing nations through the World Bank or other institutions, do human rights come with a cultural and political agenda? Can they be viewed as an aspect of neocolonialism? What about human rights that are not recognized in all Western nations? Is housing or health care a human right? Clothing? Equal pay for equal work (see United Nations 1948, Articles 23:2 and 25:1)? These economic rights are not recognized as such in the United States and many European nations. Critics therefore argue that the concept of human rights is an arbitrary one that is used by powerful Western nations to impose their cultural values on others, while they at the same time disregard those rights that they find inconvenient. The United States continues to use capital punishment, even though some other nations find this barbaric. From this perspective, Western nations focus on the rights of the individual rather than on collective rights, giving too much weight to the concept of rights and not enough to the notion of responsibilities. Can the idea of human rights undermine the collective responsibilities that hold a society together?

As Tharoor (1999) notes, there are powerful counterarguments in the UN Declaration of Human Rights to these critiques that emphasize the involvement of developing countries and the fact that many different religions and philosophies share common ideals. No culture exists in a vacuum, and all change through time. Who speaks for a culture? Would not the oppressed oppose slavery and women support their own rights? The concept of human rights is powerful, one that holds intellectual rigor. It is because of this power that authoritarian states feel the need to voice critiques. But this criticism has neither weakened the idea of human rights as an international ideal nor undermined the influence of groups that advocate for them. Indeed, one of the trends of political globalization is the continuing spread not only of this intellectual construct but also of democracy.

Democratization

At a surface level, democracy is relatively easy to define: it is a system in which the vote of the majority of the population determines the government. Yet this apparent simplicity is problematic, because the idea of democracy contains a number of tensions or questions. Is a system democratic if there is extreme economic inequality, which gives political power to a small elite? How must the will of the majority be balanced against the rights of the minority? What if a democratic state engages in imperial projects that oppress other peoples or nations, as was the case with ancient Athens? And to what extent must democracy reflect local cultures and traditions? Is true democracy procedural, or is there more to meeting the standard of being a real democracy, such as the existence of a civic culture? These contradictions and issues have become increasingly important as the twentieth century witnessed a slow but powerful trend toward the rise of democracy.

Between 1964 and 1973, one Latin American government after another fell to military rule, and such regimes were also common in Africa and Asia. But the 1980s were known as the "lost decade" in Latin America. A combination of factors undermined the legitimacy of military governments there, including poor economic performance, terrible human rights abuses, and the lack of a convincing ideology. Throughout the 1980s, many nations in the region returned to democracy. This trend has shown few signs of reversing. With the end of the Cold War in 1991, the United States no longer had an intellectual justification to prop up authoritarian rulers in Latin America (this was not the case in the Middle East), which likely accelerated the decline in military rule throughout the region. But this trend was not confined to Latin America. Globally, traditional authoritarian regimes in many areas lost their intellectual legitimacy and collapsed with sometimes shocking speed.

Asia witnessed an impressive trend toward democratization, as Junhan Lee has described: "In this region between 1986 and 1999, Bangladesh, Indonesia, Mongolia, Nepal, Pakistan, the Philippines, South Korea, Taiwan, and Thailand all embraced genuine transitions to democracy" (2002, 821). Obviously, these transitions occurred in nations with widely different cultures and population sizes. Surprisingly, there seems to be little correlation between the level of these nations' economic development and their turn to democratization. Rather, a wave of mass political protests inspired the collapse of authoritarian rule among diverse nations (823–25).

A similar trend took place in Europe and the former Soviet Union after the end of the Cold War. One Eastern European country after another, from Poland to Bulgaria, emerged as a democracy. Russia itself turned to democracy, although it still has strong authoritarian tendencies. Some former states within the former Soviet Union did turn to authoritarian rule. But these states have proved to be vulnerable to democratic currents. In 2005–6 the "Orange Revolution" brought President Viktor Yushchenko to power in Ukraine in the nation's first free and fair elections. The promise of this revolution, however, was undermined by oligarchical power and political corruption, as well as by divisions between the pro-European West and the pro-Russian East. In Russia, the success of the Orange Revolution in Ukraine was denounced as being the result of a movement funded and inspired by the West (Herd 2005, 15). Russia has also sought to reclaim territory inhabited by ethnic Russians, such as by the seizure of the Crimea from Ukraine in the spring of 2014. President Vladimir Putin's government is increasingly intolerant of artistic, political, and social dissent, and he has sought to bolster authoritarian leaders in its zones of influence. This combination of Russian influence and internal weaknesses has challenged newly democratic states bordering Russia, from Ukraine to Georgia.

It is also important to distinguish between these democratic revolutions from below and the effort of outside powers to impose democracy on other nations by military means. There are examples where this has succeeded, as was the case with Germany and Japan after World War II. Overall, however, the United States has a lengthy historical record of using democracy as a justification for invasions and regime change. The record in the Caribbean and Latin America—Cuba, Haiti, and Nicaragua, among many others—has shown that these regimes lack legitimacy and seldom endure. Despite this fact, the United States has used "democracy" as a basis to legitimate its interventions in Afghanistan and Iraq. It is too soon to know the long-term effects of these invasions. But the general phenomenon of democratization is quite separate from the United States' military activities, particularly in the Middle East. At this time, the trend toward democracy is receding globally, which marks a sharp reversal from the situation at the start of the Arab Spring.

In late 2010, the Arab Spring began in Tunisia, where a young man set himself on fire to protest his perceived mistreatment by a government official. These actions started a wave of protest throughout the region, where people resented authoritarian and corrupt governments, serious economic difficulties, and a lack of opportunity for youth. In Tunisia, the government fell with little violence. In Libya, it took a civil war to overthrow Muammar el-Qadaffi, after which the country was divided among competing warlords and factions. In Egypt, the military overthrew the nation's leadership twice. In Yemen, street protests and urban warfare ultimately led to a transition in government, although there was only one candidate in the February 2012 election. The country then slid into a civil war, in which neighboring states—such as Saudi Arabia—intervened, which caused a humanitarian crisis so severe that there was an epidemic of cholera and risk of a severe famine. In Syria, protests were met with violence, which quickly escalated into a brutal ongoing civil war, which has caused massive destruction, refugee flows, and an epic loss of human life. President Bashar al-Assad's authoritarian regime came to the brink of collapse in 2015, before a Russian intervention—along with support from Iran and Hezbollah—turned around the war. Throughout the region, it has been easier to overthrow isolated leaders than to establish meaningful democratic societies. The many defeats that democratization efforts faced in the Middle East proved to be a harbinger of future political trends.

Globalism versus Globalization

At the same time that the earlier trend toward democratization weakened, there was a powerful backlash against globalization. This trend was reflected in a rhetorical change in how globalization was described by its opponents, who adopted the term "globalism." There are many different definitions of globalization, but it is generally understood as the flows of people, ideas, culture, funds, and biology at a global scale, which connects disparate parts of the globe. Globalism is often (not always) defined as the policy and ideas of those people/nations that support globalization, which is frequently equated with neoliberalism. Globalism is sometimes a politically loaded term, because it is frequently used by those who oppose globalization to critique the policies of elites that favor financial and political globalization. It is also a more complicated term to define than globalization, because different groups use the word in varied ways.

Before his inauguration, Trump's spokesperson Hope Hicks described globalism in this way: "An economic and political ideology which puts allegiance to international institutions ahead of the nation-state; seeks the unrestricted movement of goods, labor and people across borders; and rejects the principle that the citizens of a country are entitled to preference for jobs and other economic considerations as a virtue of their citizenship" (qtd. in Stack 2016). What is core to most definitions of globalism is the idea that globalization takes place because of the policies of elites, who act based on their economic self-interests and who lack any sense of national allegiance.

The term "globalism" became increasingly common because of a populist and nationalist wave in the West. Liam Stack (2016) described the term in an article titled "Globalism: A Far-Right Conspiracy Theory Buoyed by

Trump." He explored how the word became a favorite of conspiracy theorists and right-wing firebrands. While these figures (such as Alex Jones) might appear to be so extreme as to be marginal, they successfully drew upon a populist backlash to globalization that was expressed on social media, YouTube, and Reddit. This rhetoric reflected a shared sense among the public in many nations that their current political system did not capture the needs of working-class and middle-class people, either economically or culturally. This sentiment became much more powerful after the global financial crisis of 2008. The term "globalism" is also associated with anti-immigrant rhetoric, which suggests that globalists are facilitating an invasion of migrants who undermine nations' culture and security. One common theme of this rhetoric is that the masses are powerless, while elites beholden to special interests (such as bankers and the über-wealthy) craft policies that undermine the public's core values, not only economically but also culturally.

Globalism is very different from concepts such as global citizenship, which start from the perspective that all people share common responsibilities to others, regardless of nationality. Instead, globalism begins with the premise that the nation-state owes its primary duty to its own citizens, so any assistance or support for people elsewhere may represent a betrayal of the government's responsibility to its own populace. Among populists, globalism is often rhetorically associated with treason. Global citizenship was a much more powerful concept before 9/11. But as populist and nationalist sentiment waxed after the 2008 financial crisis, globalism has become a formidable rhetorical tool that politicians often use in campaign rallies or social media. This can be seen in the developing world (the Philippines and Brazil) but also in wealthy nations (Hungary and the United States).

Regional Organizations: The European Union

This current trend is drastically different from the one after World War II, which was dominated by a profound distrust of nationalism, as well as the belief that only new organizations could prevent war. For this reason nations sometimes voluntarily gave up some aspects of their power, either to regional organizations or military alliances. Perhaps the most dramatic example of this trend was the rise of the European Union. In the aftermath of World War II, many Europeans blamed unrestrained nationalism for the horrible conflict. In order to create new bonds across national lines and rebuild trade among shattered economies, six nations came together to form the European Coal and Steel Community. Since that time, a series of agreements (such as the Treaty of Rome and the Merger Treaty) have steadily deepened the significance of participating in this evolving body, while it has rapidly broadened to include new members. The Maastricht Treaty of February 1992 formally established the European Union, while in 2004 ten new countries—most of them in Eastern Europe—joined this body. By this point, the EU had become the world's largest economy and a political force, despite its internal divisions and political disputes.

The EU by this time had twenty-eight members, of which eighteen had adopted a common currency called the euro. Such monetary union requires a nation to give up a considerable amount of authority. Until 2008, the EU appeared to be a dramatic success. It had helped to ensure income equality among its members through transfers to low-income countries, which enabled nations such as Ireland to make dramatic and rapid economic progress. With the Schengen Agreement, EU citizens can travel freely across national borders without passports. There was unprecedented European labor mobility. But its successes extended beyond economics and into politics. For example, the European Union also has judicial power and has overturned national legislation that it believed violated EU law. The European Parliament sometimes inflames nationalist sentiments with regulations and directives that speak to the most daily aspects of citizens' lives, such as the food they eat. On a more important scale, nations that wish to join the EU must agree to the Copenhagen criteria, which have significantly changed some countries' behavior. Most observers would agree that this union has brought major benefits. Since the EU's founding, there has never been a war between any of its members. From this perspective, it has clearly achieved the goals for which it was founded.

At the same time, the perception of the EU has changed since the financial crisis of 2008. Youth unemployment rates in southern Europe are horrific. Greece has suffered an economic depression so severe that the government is kept from collapse only by infusions of cash from the EU, which has required the financial power of Germany to implement it. For many Greeks, however, the austerity programs enacted at the EU's insistence have failed to bring prosperity. While the Germans tire of supporting Greece, the Greeks resent the extreme austerity that their nation has had to bear. Of all regional associations globally, the EU is the most economically and politically integrated—a remarkable achievement in the aftermath of World War II. The crisis since 2008, however, has caused economic difficulties so severe that they have undermined the attractiveness of this model.

In addition to the economic crisis, the rise of populist and nationalist forces since 2010 has meant that the eurozone has entered into an ongoing crisis. This one was exacerbated by German chancellor Angela Merkel's decision to welcome migrants and refugees in 2015. Merkel acted in part because of the emergency caused by the Syrian Civil War. Since the onset of this complex struggle to overthrow President Assad in March 2011, perhaps 4 million Syrians had become refugees. In Merkel's eyes, Europe had a moral duty to help people displaced by terror and war. The leaders of other European states—as well as some German citizens—resented that this decision was made without prior consultation. To leaders of small Eastern European states, this looked like an example of neocolonialism. A political leader in Berlin made a decision that brought a million migrants and refugees to Europe, so that people entered, crossed, or settled in Europeans' lands without first seeking a consensus or vote from other European states. There are few issues more central to the idea of sovereignty than the ability to control borders. At a stroke, Merkel's decision seemed not only to undermine European nations' ability to control their integrity but also to reveal the impotence of small states within Europe. This fostered a region-wide rise of nationalism, which sometimes was accompanied by both populism and fearmongering.

In his work Richard Ruiz looks at how linguistic and ethnic minorities are problematized (1984). From an intercultural communication perspective, this mind-set depicts anyone we do not know as a possible threat until proved otherwise. Milton Bennett characterizes this as one stage, "Defense," in his Developmental Model of Intercultural Sensitivity (2017). Most frequently, political policy makers work from constituents' desires and their own ideological groundings. What this means in practice is exactly what we have seen in global dealings with others. A policy of gatekeeping assumes anyone new is a threat. Europe is dealing with a large influx of both political refugees (as defined by the UN High Commissioner for Refugees) and individuals fleeing their home countries due to economic or physical conditions, some willing to risk all because they feel there is nothing else for them in their home countries. Whether we examine more liberal strategies in Germany now challenged by the Right or more restrictive policies in Denmark, it is clear that at the present time, individuals who are perceived as "different" are not to be trusted; rather, they are to be feared. Most recently in Denmark, we have seen legislation aimed at controlling residents of "ghetto neighborhoods" (Barry and Sorenson 2018). Infants and toddlers are restricted to Danish crèche and daycare situations with required hours away from the home to better socialize the children as "good Danes." The current populist backlash against European institutions sometimes defines all refugees and migrants as "invaders," inherently dangerous to the states and peoples whose societies they enter. As such, the issue of migration has now become expressed politically through the rhetoric of fear.

Populism, Nationalism, and Brexit

While the specific motivations of nationalist movements may differ globally, one common thread is their reliance upon populist rhetoric. Populism is a political ideology that claims that strong leaders are needed to defend the masses against the will of the elites. Because this rhetoric argues that the existing system has been corrupted by the special interests of the elites, populist politicians appeal to the masses to overturn existing institutions, laws, and traditions. There are populist leaders on all ends of the political spectrum, from Nicolás Maduro Moros in Venezuela to President Trump in the United States. Populist rhetoric and nationalist appeals were so powerful in 2016 that they led Britain to vote to leave the European Union.

This British referendum on June 23, 2016, resulted in a narrow victory for the "leave" option, which shocked many observers. A number of leading economists, artists, and intellectuals had spoken out in favor of Britain remaining in the European Union (Coleman 2016, 681). On the "remain" side, many of the arguments (Menon and Salter 2016, 1307) focused on the economic benefits that Britain received, particularly in the economically distressed north, which received disproportionately more EU funds (Coleman 2016, 682). In contrast, those who favored Britain's departure focused on the question of sovereignty, and in particular Britain's ability to control immigration.

In the end, 51.9 percent of British citizens voted to leave the EU. Those who voted to leave were more likely to be working-class, older, and living in poorer areas. Those who voted to remain were more likely to live in cosmopolitan areas such as London and typically were younger, better educated, and financially well-off (Menon and Salter 2016, 1311–12). There were also geographical divisions: "All of Scotland voted Remain, but in England, every region apart from London voted Leave" (1312). The referendum saw extremely high turnout, which revealed that the nation was bitterly divided.

But why did the "leave" camp win? As Coleman observes, the referendum was shaped by the fact that after 2004, a flood of emigrants from Eastern Europe had entered the United Kingdom (2016, 682). Indeed, one-third of new births in Britain had at least one immigrant parent (684). This immigration drove rapid and sustained population growth, which Brexit's supporters perceive to be straining social services, such as housing. At the same time, demographers predict that the percentage of people in Britain who will be white will fall to a minority by the late 2060s (688). Merkel's 2015 decision to open Germany's frontiers (and in effect Europe's) encouraged critics to say that Britain was losing control of its borders. This narrative was strengthened by the extensive British media coverage of the thousands of asylum seekers (mostly from Asia, the Middle East, and South Asia) who camped near French ports such as Calais to seek entrance to Britain by smuggling themselves on the "Chunnel" train or trucks (Castle and Breeden 2015).

Critics questioned whether the nation's heritage would be the same if the majority of the population were no longer descended from people who were ethnically British or if the nation continued a policy of multiculturalism. Those who favored departing Europe believed that their country could not adequately limit immigration within the EU. They also argued that urban elites did not have to pay the social costs that immigration entailed—such as greater pressure on subsidized housing—that the working class did. In their eyes, Britain was governed by a wealthy British class that was beholden to the banks and finance industry, which was more concerned with flows of capital than flows of people. Even during the referendum campaign, those in the "remain" camp began to realize that their focus on economics was proving to be less powerful than the discourse on immigration (Menon and Salter 2016, 1309–10). Of course, the fact that the opposition was headed by the Labour leader Jeremy Corbyn was also a factor, as he failed to campaign vigorously for the "remain" camp (1311).

Those who favored remaining in the EU resented that a narrow majority was changing the nation's future; they also believed that their opponents were poorly educated, were voting against their own economic interests, and were perhaps influenced by either outright racism or excessive nationalism. The rhetoric in favor of Brexit made the referendum one defined by populism. As of this writing, it is unclear what the future holds for Britain. As Anand Menon and John-Paul Salter have described, since it joined the EU in 1973 Britain has often been described as an "awkward partner"

(2016, 1298). At the same time, Britain was frequently an effective actor within the EU and, over more than thirty years, became deeply integrated into its political and economic structures. Whatever ultimately proves to be Britain's fate, it is clear that old political arrangements are endangered by populist sentiments and movements. Nor is the EU the only such alliance threatened by populist leaders and trends.

NATO and a Potential European Army

The North Atlantic Treaty Organization is an alliance of the United States, Canada, and twenty-seven European countries, which holds that aggression on any one of these nations will be treated as an attack upon all. It was originally founded in 1949, when Western Europe was economically weak, devastated by war, and menaced by the Soviet Union. Throughout the Cold War, NATO served to prevent an invasion launched by the Warsaw Pact, a military alliance founded in 1955, which united the Soviet Union and its Eastern European allies. With the collapse of the Soviet Union in 1991, however, the clear rationale for NATO's existence evaporated. There was no longer an obvious peer competitor to the United States, and an invasion from a destitute Russia seemed fanciful.

As a result, NATO states began to sharply cut their defense spending as part of the so-called peace dividend. Nations wanted to invest their funds in social goods, not weaponry. Conscription was seldom popular, and European nations phased it out as it no longer seemed necessary. The extent of the cuts was striking, despite the expansion of the EU itself: "Thus, while the number of member states in Europe almost doubled between 1989–2014, the combined military spending of the twenty-six European member-states of NATO in 2014 was 20 percent less than the combined military spending of the fourteen European member states of the Alliance at the end of the Cold War" (Raitasalo 2018).

The United States, the world's dominant power, had a global vision and did not make parallel cuts to its armed forces but became increasingly resentful as European spending on armed forces continued to decrease. Some U.S. political leaders felt that Europe was acting as a "free rider" within the alliance (Raitasalo 2018) in that it was enjoying the security benefits that the United States provided without appropriately contributing to its costs. As Russia began a comprehensive military reform after the millennium and massive energy sales restocked Russian coffers, the threat posed by Russia no longer appeared theoretical. Donald Trump came into the U.S. presidency determined to push European nations to spend more on defense and to publicly question the value of NATO.

There were valid points to this criticism, because European allies did contribute far less than the United States to NATO's forces: "Recently published NATO defense statistics reveal the poor state of European defense capabilities and spending. Only four out of 26 European NATO member-states spend the minimum level needed to train and equip a credible fighting force—namely 2 percent of annual GDP" (Raitasalo 2015). Not only did European states lack military capability, but also polls indicated that in Europe people would be very unwilling to go to war even if Russia attacked another European state (Raitasalo 2015). Europeans, in turn, perceived that they were being bullied by the United States. The Russian intervention in Ukraine in 2014, rearmament, and war games all combined to lead Europe to question the extent to which it should rely on the United States.

These trends resulted in a major change in how European nations viewed their own defense. After French president Emmanuel Macron called for the creation of a European army in 2018—"We have to protect ourselves with respect to China, Russia and even the United States of America" (Meichtry and Norman 2018)—Chancellor Angela Merkel of Germany supported the idea in an address to the European Parliament in Strasbourg (Bennhold and Erlanger 2018). Merkel made it very clear in this speech that Europeans could no longer rely on the United States: "The days where we can unconditionally rely on others are gone. That means that we Europeans should take our fate more into our own hands if we want to survive as a European community" (Bennhold and Erlanger 2018).

This idea was not received warmly by some American commentators, who stated that Europeans were too divided and too reluctant to spend on defense. They also suggested that such a step would be inefficient (Schmitt 2018). On his official Twitter account, President Trump wrote, "Emmanuel Macron suggests building its own army to protect Europe against the U.S., China and Russia. But it was Germany in World Wars One & Two–How did that work out for France? They were starting to learn German in Paris before the U.S. came along. Pay for NATO or not!" (Trump 2018). Any sustained effort to create a European army would take decades to fully realize. If fully realized, however, this development would create a new global military power and contribute to a more multipolar world. Even the fact that this idea was seriously discussed by elites on two continents demonstrated how deeply transatlantic ties had frayed and how the political ground rules had changed from previous decades.

BRICS and ASEAN

It is important to note that this move toward populism and fragmentation is not defining political relationships globally. BRICS is a coalition of newly powerful economies, made up of Brazil, Russia, India, China, and South Africa. While the relationships between the members is at times contested (for instance, China and India have a border dispute), these nations have impressive economic and demographic clout. Over the last decade these five countries have sought to forge deeper relationships, such as enabling a new means for financial transfers to take place among these nations outside the existing architecture. These nations have also worked to create a BRICS contingent reserve system, which would strengthen their financial autonomy in relation to the International Monetary Fund, as well as a New Development Bank. Even though the five nations have deep cultural and political divisions, they have proved to be able to act as a united front against the Bretton Woods System.

While the European Union has staggered from one crisis to the next, its counterpart in the Pacific has thrived. The Association of Southeast Asian Nations is a regional organization of ten countries. Although it was founded in 1961, it truly became politically influential only after the millennium. In December 2008 the member states' representatives signed a charter, which was designed to create a political bloc as well as an economic union. Since this period, the union has made remarkable progress, particularly toward the goal of creating the ASEAN Economic Community, or AEC. While people typically think of the European Union as the best example of a political and economic community, it may be that ASEAN could be an equally significant model. Despite the rise of populism in some of its membership (such as the Philippines), ASEAN's influence continues to grow. In sum, populism and nationalism are powerful forces that challenge political globalization in the West, while in Southeast Asia the trend toward integration remains uninterrupted and even seems to be accelerating.

Conclusion

Imagine that you are a refugee who has set out in a small and rusty boat with other refugees from the coast of Libya. It is nighttime, and you are straining your eyes to see the coastline. The boat is not seaworthy, and you have spent days wondering if one large wave might swamp it. Next to you is a member of a Norwegian human rights group who met your boat as it approached the coast and brought life jackets and medicine aboard. Both you and the Norwegian believe in human rights and international law, key aspects of political globalization, and the rights of all the refugees on board to have a hearing and to seek a new and safe home.

Then there is a light in the darkness. Your boat has been spotted by an Italian frigate that is patrolling off of Sicily. In a few minutes a small rubber craft approaches your vessel, which is soon boarded by armed troops in uniform. It is difficult to understand what they are saying, but it is clear to you that the Norwegian seems to be in some legal difficulty for his role in helping the refugees. Worse, your boat is being turned back.

In this scenario, all the different actors believe that they are acting morally. The refugees believe in their right under international law to seek refuge; the NGO member from Norway believes in the power of human rights; the sailors on the Italian frigate believe that they are tasked with defending their nation's sovereignty and upholding the rule of law regarding how people may enter their country. At issue is the concept of political globalization and the extent to which certain laws or beliefs may trump the power of states. The individuals in this scenario have to reconcile their personal morals, national law, and international human rights.

Globally, the world is experiencing a trend toward populism and nationalism that seems as powerful as the rise of democratization after the fall of the Berlin Wall. In many regions different groups now struggle to define the relative power of nation-states versus other organizations. Ten years ago, scholars needed to argue that the nation-state was still relevant in global affairs; now the power of nationalism is challenging even such immense organizations as the European Union. In other areas, such as Southeast Asia, new political associations continue to gain power. While most people think of economics and markets when they hear the term "globalization," some of the bitterest debates around this term take place in the political sphere.

➤ VOCABULARY

League of Nations
NATO
Warsaw Pact
Security Council
General Assembly
Helsinki Accords
democratization
International Court of Justice
Syrian Civil War
globalism
populism
Brexit

➤ DISCUSSION AND REFLECTION QUESTIONS

1 *What global events did the League of Nations fail to confront?*

2 *Identify a critical difference between the structure of the UN Security Council and the UN General Assembly.*

3 *What are some criticisms that have been leveled against the UN?*

4 *The International Court of Justice is part of the UN. What is its primary charge, and what are some weaknesses of the court vis-à-vis its authority and the authority of individual nation-states?*

5 *Although it is possible for nation-states to violate human rights, globalization has allowed checks on leaders' behavior as never before. What are some examples of these checks?*

6 *How does culture impact our understanding of human rights? Are certain human rights universal?*

7 *What twentieth-century phenomena have contributed to democratization processes around the globe? How does the general phenomenon of democratization differ from the U.S. approach to democratization?*

8 *What are some examples of regional political organizations? What are some of their strengths and weaknesses?*

ACTIVITY 1: ANALYZE Go to the main UNICEF website (http://www.unicef.org/crc/index_framework.html) and examine one of the following pdf documents listed there. Choose one dimension of the document and, in a one-page reflection, discuss how it is linked to a global issue that is important to you.

1 Universal Declaration of Human Rights

2 International Covenant on Civil and Political Rights

3 International Covenant on Economic, Social, and Cultural Rights

4 Convention on the Rights of the Child

5 Convention on the Elimination of All Forms of Discrimination against Women

6 Convention on the Elimination of All Forms of Racial Discrimination

7 Convention against Torture and Other Cruel, Inhuman, or Degrading Treatment or Punishment

ACTIVITY 2: REFLECT Mercosur, also known as the Southern Common Market, is the largest trading bloc in South America. Investigate which countries make up Mercosur's sovereign member states and identify their working languages and current leaders. What do you imagine three critical issues to be for this organization and its members?

ACTIVITY 3: EXTEND Ten countries make up the Association of Southeast Asian Nations. Within these countries more than 1,000 languages are spoken. In 2009, ASEAN established English as its sole working language. Most of the member nations now require their citizens to learn both their national language and English. Imagine that you are friends with a person from an ASEAN nation. Picture a conversation with this friend where you point out the advantages of English being the working language while your friend points out disadvantages. On a sheet of paper, create a force field analysis: on one side list the advantages of this language choice and on the other side the disadvantages. Ultimately, is it more of an advantage or a disadvantage that English is so powerful for your friend and his or her country (see Kirkpatrick 2012)?

References

Africa News Service. 2017. Nigeria says UN Security Council composition outdated, demands reform. September 27. Retrieved November 28, 2018, from http://link.galegroup.com/apps/doc/A506743424/STND?u=s1185784&sid=STND&xid=8efef67c.

Angie, A. 2002. Colonialism and the birth of international institutions: Sovereignty, economy, and the mandate system of the League of Nations. *International Law and Politics* 34:513–633.

Anonymous. 2001. NATO's purpose after the Cold War. Retrieved February 11, 2010, from www.brookings.edu/fp/projects/nato/reportch1.pdf.

Anonymous. 2005. Better than nothing: United Nations reform. *The Economist* *376* (September): 54.

Barry, E., and M. Sorenson. 2018. In Denmark, harsh new laws for immigrant "ghettos." *New York Times*, July 1. Retrieved January 13, 2018, from https://www.nytimes.com/2018/07/01/world/europe/denmark-immigrant-ghettos.html.

Bennett, M. 2017. Developmental Model of Intercultural Sensitivity. Retrieved July 4, 2019, from https://www.researchgate.net/publication/318430742_Developmental_Model_of_Intercultural_Sensitivity.

Bennhold, K., and S. Erlanger. 2018. Merkel joins Macron in calling for a European Army "one day." *New York Times*, November 13. Retrieved from https://www.nytimes.com/2018/11/13/world/europe/merkel-macron-european-army.html.

Borgerson, S. 2013. The coming Arctic boom. *Foreign Affairs 92* (July/August): 76–89.

Breuss, F. 2010. Globalization, EU enlargement, and income distribution. *International Journal of Public Policy 6* (1): 16–34.

Brown, D., and J. Fox. 1999. *Transnational civil society coalitions and the World Bank: Lessons from project and policy influence campaigns.* Boston: Hauser Center for Nonprofit Organizations and the Kennedy School of Government, Harvard University.

Carr, E. H. (1939) 2001. *The twenty years' crisis.* Introduction by Michael Carr. New York: Palgrave.

Castle, S., and A. Breeden. 2015. Britain and France scramble as channel becomes choke point in migration crisis. *New York Times*, July 29. Retrieved July 31, 2015, from https://www.nytimes.com/2015/07/30/world/europe/britain-and-france-scramble-as-channel-crossing-attempts-by-migrants-continue.html.

Coleman, D. 2016. A demographic rationale for Brexit. *Population and Development Review 42* (4): 681–92. doi:10.1111/padr.12014.

Dupuy, P. M. 1999. The danger of fragmentation or unification of the international legal system and the international court of justice. *International Law and Politics 31*:791–807.

Eaton, K. 2003. Restoration or transformation: "Trapos" versus NGOs in the democratization of the Philippines. *Journal of Asian Studies 62* (2): 469–96.

Efstathopoulos, C. 2016. South Africa's reform diplomacy and the legitimacy of the UN Security Council. *Politikon 43* (3): 429–50.

Gaddis, J. L. 2005. *The Cold War: A new history.* New York: Penguin.

Glennon, M. J. 2003. Why the Security Council failed. *Foreign Affairs 82* (3): 16–35.

Goldstone, J. 2010. The new population bomb: The four megatrends that will change our world. *Foreign Affairs 89* (1): 31–43.

Goodritch, L. M. 1947. League of Nations to United Nations. *International Organization 1* (1): 3–21.

Gowland Debbas, V. 1994. The relationship between the International Court of Justice and the Security Council in the light of the Lockerbie case. *American Journal of International Law 88* (4): 843–67.

Heller, K. 2018. Specially-affected states and the formation of custom. *American Journal of International Law 112* (2): 191–243.

Herd, G. P. 2005. Russia and the Orange Revolution: Response, rhetoric, reality? *Quarterly Journal* (Summer): 15–28.

Hurd, I. 2007. *After anarchy: Legitimacy and power in the United Nations' Security Council.* Princeton: Princeton University Press.

Jennings, R. 1995. The International Court of Justice after fifty years. *American Journal of International Law 89* (3): 493–505.

Kennedy, P. 2006. *The parliament of man: The past, present, and future of the United Nations.* New York: Vintage.

Kirkpatrick, A. 2012. English in ASEAN: Implications for regional multilingualism. *Journal of Multilingual and Multicultural Development 33* (4): 1–14.

Lauren, P. G. 1998. *The evolution of international human rights: Visions seen.* Philadelphia: University of Pennsylvania Press.

Lee, J. 2002. Primary causes of Asian democratization: Dispelling conventional myths. *Asian Survey 42* (6): 821–37.

Luck, E. 2003. Reforming the United Nations: Lessons from a history in progress. Edited by J. Krasno. United Nations Occasional Papers.

Mayerfield, J. 2003. Who shall be judge? The United States, the International Criminal Court, and the global enforcement of human rights. *Human Rights Quarterly* 25:93–129.

Meichtry, S., and L. Norman. 2018. France's Macron calls for creating a "European army"; French president sharply criticizes Europe's military reliance on the U.S., days before President Trump is to visit. *Wall Street Journal,* November 6. Retrieved July 4, 2019, from http://stats.lib.pdx.edu/proxy.php?url+http://search.proquest.com.proxlib.pdx.edu.

Menon, A., and J. Salter. 2016. Brexit: Initial reflections. *International Affairs 92* (6): 1297–1318.

New York Times Editorial Board. 2018. There may soon be three Internets. America's won't necessarily be the best. *New York Times,* October 15. Retrieved November 26, 2018, from https://www.nytimes.com/2018/10/15/opinion/internet-google-china-balkanization.html.

Orbie, J., and L. Tortell, eds. 2008. *The European Union and the social dimension of globalization: How the EU influences the world.* New York: Routledge.

Posner, E. 2004. *The decline of the International Court of Justice.* John M. Olin Economics and Working Paper Series, December.

Raitasalo, J. 2015. NATO is not a real military actor. *War on the Rocks,* Blog. July 2. Retrieved December 11, 2018, from https://warontherocks.com/2015/07/nato-is-not-a-real-military-actor.

———. 2018. Uneven burden-sharing isn't NATO's biggest problem. *National Interest,* October 11. Retrieved December 11, 2018, from https://nationalinterest.org/feature/uneven-burden-sharing-isn%E2%80%99t-nato%E2%80%99s-biggest-problem-33196.

Ruíz, R. 1984. Orientations in language planning. *NABE Journal 8* (2): 15–34. doi: 10.1080/08855072.1984.10668464.

Schlesinger, S. 1997. Can the United Nations reform? *World Policy Journal 14* (3): 47–52.

Schmitt, G. J. 2018. "European Army" is not a serious suggestion. American Enterprise Institute, December 10. Retrieved from https://www.aei.org/publication/european-army-is-not-a-serious-suggestion/.

Shawcross, W. 2000. *Deliver us from evil: Peacekeepers, warlords, and a world of endless conflict.* New York: Simon and Schuster.

Sobel, R. 1994. The League of Nations Covenant and the United Nations Charter. *Constitutional Political Economy 5* (2): 173–92.

Stack, L. 2016. Globalism: A far-right conspiracy theory buoyed by Trump. *New York Times,* November 14. Retrieved July 4, 2019, from https://www.nytimes.com/2016/11/15/us/politics/globalism-right-trump.html?searchResultPosition=1.

Tharoor, S. 1999. Are human rights universal? *World Policy Journal 16* (4): 1–6. Retrieved January 25, 2010, from http://www.worldpolicy.org/journal/tharoor.html.

Trump, D. 2018. Emmanuel Macron suggests . . . Twitter post, November 13. @realDonald Trump.

United Nations. 1948. Universal Declaration of Human Rights. Retrieved January 25, 2010, from http://www.un.org/en/documents/udhr/.

Way, L. 2009. Debating the color revolutions: A reply to my critics. *Journal of Democracy 20* (1): 90–97.

Weiss, T. G., D. Forsythe, R. Coate, and K. Pease. 2007. *The United Nations and changing world politics.* 5th ed. Boulder, Colo.: Westview Press.

FIVE Cultural Globalization

SYNOPSIS

This chapter examines flows of people and information in the age of globalization. Voluntary and involuntary movements of individuals account for shifting demographics within countries; refugees and even international students dramatically shift economic and social bases of the new places they call home. Technology and media have created fusions of information and art that move far beyond the nation-state. Political activism on the part of citizens and scholars in particular nations is both aided and suppressed by emerging technologies.

SCAFFOLDING

As you read through this chapter, think about how you would answer each of the questions below.

Can you compare what is important to you with what may be important to individuals living in another country—in particular, a university student, a government official, and a young child attending elementary school in a rural area?

How does your sense of yourself—your identity—shift when you are in different contexts with different people?

What are the advantages and disadvantages of calculating the fiscal contributions that international students make to a state or province's economy?

Do you foresee changes in how nations regard the inflow of refugees, undocumented workers, and international students?

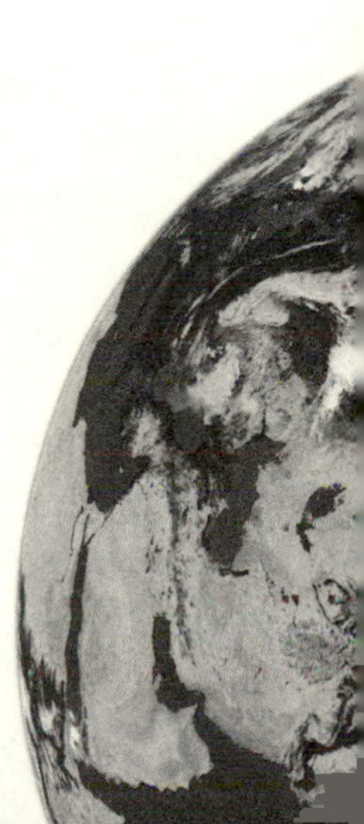

Why do you think the fine arts are sometimes forgotten in studies of globalization?

➤ CORE CONCEPTS

What is the relationship among technology, ideology, people, and finance in a globalizing world?

What flows of people may be important to track in the future?

How can access to the Internet, television, and radio broadcasts impact how people move forward in their lives?

In the previous chapters, we focused on the economics and politics of globalization. However, the patterns of change that have come with greater financial connectedness have also deeply affected societies and individuals throughout the world. Cultural globalization is just as critical a component of the globalization phenomenon as economic and political globalization. People have left their homelands voluntarily and involuntarily, for brief periods of time or for good. They have transformed the landscapes they have joined even as many of them have attempted to remain connected to their homelands via media, the Internet, and other electronic and social-networking technologies. In this chapter, we explore how shifts in demography have ultimately affected cultures and created wholly new social landscapes. Nation-states and individuals have been transformed by these changes.

We begin by focusing on the elements and processes that explain, provide gatekeeping for, and promote movement across national boundaries. These cultural flows involve "contacts between people and their cultures—their ideals, their values, their way of life—[all of which] have been growing and deepening in unprecedented ways" (*UN Human Development Report* 1999, 30). At the same time, we continue with the notion that the nation-state is no longer the sole base for relations. Instead, we return to the global-local continuum, described by Alex MacGillivray as "a tense dynamic between local identity and global ambition, whether in religion, art, film, music, or football" (2006, 9). In this chapter, we look at how individuals move within real spaces and virtual spaces and how key parts of identities adjust to this space and context variation.

In order for you to recognize how these shifting communities and landscapes affect your own spaces—literal and virtual—we ask, What do global citizens need to know about transcultural flows? We will answer this by looking at "the ways in which cultural forms move, change, and are re-used to fashion new identities in diverse contexts" (Pennycook 2007, 6). Scholar Kwame Anthony Appiah introduced one lens from which to view these shifts, cosmopolitanism (2006). The key dimensions he laid out within the concept are, first, that we do not live in a vacuum—we have obligations to others (xv), and second, that "we take seriously the value not just of human life but of particular human lives" (xv). The notion of global citizenship in his work comes from the legacy of Enlightenment scholar Immanuel Kant. Appiah's work and that of scholars over the next decade capture how culture contact has pulled many out of isolated and sometimes defensive spaces and into more receptive spaces where art and literature in particular meld with traditions from many places. Pheng Cheah builds on Appiah's original work characterizing cosmopolitanism as

> syntheses of three different arguments. . . . First it is suggested that cultural and political solidarity and political agency can no longer be restricted to the sovereign nation-state. . . . Second, the various material networks of globalization are said to have formed a world that is interconnected enough to generate political institutions and non-governmental organizations that have a global reach in their regulatory functions as well as global forms of mass-based political consciousness or popular feelings of belonging to a shared world. Third, this new cosmopolitan consciousness is characterized as a more expansive form of solidarity that is attuned to democratic principles and human interests without the restriction of territorial borders. (2006, 491)

As with any powerful theory, over time the theory gets pushed, tugged, and pulled into adapted versions. Most recently, however, some critical scholars have observed that this working definition may be accurate for middle-class members of societies and particular individuals who are white but not for people of color and individuals whose social membership is more vulnerable, such as refugees and undocumented laborers (Das Gupta 2006). Vulnerable social membership does not hang solely on race; other factors like class privilege can account for the gatekeeping that occurs when individuals from different cultures interact. Vulnerable individuals, like the dispossessed peasants originally presented as "subalterns" in Antonio Gramsci's early twentieth-century *Prison Notebooks*, do not have the same agency as those in positions of power in their nation-states. Drawing upon Gramsci's original notion of the "subaltern" (1930, 2011), Sonita Sarker looks at what she terms "subalternity," defining it as "processes of systematic and systemic disempowerment and contestations that are enacted through identities which are positioned materially within and across structures of power and displacement" (2016, 819). As individuals leave their home countries, either forcibly or voluntarily, the spaces they occupy in the places they resettle often do not accord them the agency they possessed in their countries of origin.

In this millennium, flows of people and information are changing the landscape of our world at a pace exponentially greater than that of past centuries. When confronting difference, it is important to identify these shifts as a means to avoid lapsing into a state of fear. As individual members of our communities, we cannot control the flow of people and information across nation-states. A far more productive response is to take full advantage of the richness of cross-cultural mobility by recognizing the natural forces that push people out of one country or region and into another. In looking at flows of people and information, one can get a more organic sense of how these flows work together by imagining a multidimensional figure with a number of facets. This knowledge, in turn, allows a deeper analysis and understanding of how globalization has remastered the earth's landscape. In a now-classic text on globalization titled *Modernity at Large: Cultural Dimensions of Globalization* (1996), anthropologist Arjun Appadurai offers a way to explore the transcultural flows that have contributed to the fragmentation of people and information by examining relationships among what he defines as ethnoscapes, mediascapes, technoscapes, financescapes, and ideoscapes.

As the terms suggest, they relate to how people in movement interact with media and technology in evolution. Financescapes are the "very complex fiscal and investment flows that link [various] economies through a global grid of currency speculation and capital transfer" (Appadurai 1996, 34). Ideoscapes relate to how ideologies and theories are interpreted in particular nation-states and by individuals. An example might be the phrase "loyal citizen." Its meaning would vary greatly from country to country, and behaviors seen as tolerable in one context might be seen as threatening government security in another.

Imagine a kaleidoscope in which a slight turn of the lens changes the entire picture: a number of forces are shaping how we engage with each other in ways that are more complicated than ever before. Appadurai sug-

"Justice for Migrants" wall mural, Oaxaca, Mexico (Used with permission of the photographer, Margaret Everett)

gests that there may also be "disjunctures" among the various scapes. In contrast to the smooth framing of contrasting flecks of color within one turn of the kaleidoscope lens, Appadurai acknowledges that when one scape comes in contact with another, it is not necessarily smooth. Andres Tapias (2008) goes further, arguing that the "global demographic tsunami caused by tectonic shifts in labor" we experienced in the last century will reappear in new and unpredictable ways. Just as a prism or a kaleidoscope never shows the same picture twice, the elaborate interaction of flows of people and information that shape these scapes will create constantly shifting realities for all of us living in the twenty-first century. As members of the global community, we need to become familiar with who and what has accounted for this tsunami.

The economic and political forces explored in the previous chapters have focused on empire, colonialism, and industrialization. Here we look at what Monisha Das Gupta characterizes as multiple flows affecting nation-states and individuals: "Global migration, transnationalism, border controls, neoliberal reform, and economic deregulation are not just reified structural forces operating . . . at the macro level. They also leave their traces in lived experiences, erupting dramatically at crisis-ridden encounters" (2006, 3).

Flows of People

The shifting demographics of the world's population occur both intentionally and unintentionally; political events both internal and international often provoke movement, and natural events often result in either temporary or permanent shifts. Many individuals *choose* to move from one place to another, crossing borders intentionally. These individuals fall into two categories: immigrants and sojourners. Immigrants are individuals who have willingly and legally left their home countries to work and live in a new country, either for an extended period of time or permanently. Unlike refugees, who face a documented fear of persecution or even death if they remain in their home countries, immigrants most often move for economic or family-reunification purposes. They arrive in their new countries with travel documents that indicate they have come legally. In some cases, they must possess a certain amount of money or a certain skill set. This is often the case if the receiving country has granted them immigrant status in order to receive an infusion of monetary investment in the private financial infrastructure or to make up for a shortage of skilled workers, particularly scientists or engineers.

Some international students remain in the country in which they have gone to school. Most, however, return to their home country or perhaps settle in a third country. Students who temporarily live in a place to receive an education are part of a group of individuals known as sojourners. International students have been the subject of much study and speculation, but they form an almost invisible presence in the globalization kaleidoscope. They are in classes next to you, yet perhaps you have never thought of the role your fellow students are playing in Tapias's "global tsunami." Stephen Heyneman (2003) notes that in many countries, international-education flow can actually be tabulated like other commodities. This includes not only students going from one country to another but also students studying in a virtual environment, paying one country to take courses online while living in another country. In addition, the export of textbooks and materials, as well as tests such as the Test of English as a Foreign Language or International English Language Testing System, often involves the exchange of currency across borders.

During the 2016–17 school year, 1,078,822 international students came to the United States; the countries that sent the most students were China, India, South Korea, Saudi Arabia, and Canada (Zong and Batalova 2018). The landscapes of U.S. campuses have thus shifted substantially in the past few years. In some cases, more than 10 percent of the student body is composed of international students. The presence of international students, however, does not necessarily guarantee a globalized education experience for anyone. Milton Bennett argues that simply being in a new country or being in a contact zone with someone from another place is no guarantee of any substantial intercultural contact taking place (personal communication, 2002). We also know, however, that without contact, there is no possibility for personal change. By extension, shifting the demographics of the people within your place of study increases the probability that your college experience will be different from that of your peers on campuses with fewer international students.

In his vision of European higher education, Jan Figel suggests "it should be the norm—rather than the exception—for university students to undertake a period of study or a work placement in another country of the European Union" (2008). Academic institutions outside Europe, Figel hopes, would emulate European outcomes for their own educational planning:

"There is a lot of interest from outside Europe for the European Qualifications Framework, which could inspire policy makers across the globe" (2008).

There is no question that immigrants are becoming increasingly important to the international economy, to the extent that they are impacting the evolution of the English language globally. One example can be found in the approximately 10 percent of international students who become permanent residents and remain in the United States as immigrants after their studies (Rosenzweig 2006). Southeast Asian students graduating in fields such as engineering have suddenly found themselves listening to the English spoken by their Indian engineering colleagues in a U.S. setting. Korean, Chinese, or Japanese students often have little experience listening to Indian English accents, and, in like manner, they have little experience adjusting their accents to be more understandable to their Indian colleagues. Globally, interactions in English between individuals whose first language is not English will continue to become more prevalent than interactions between individuals whose first language is English (Hahn-Steichen 2008).

While the flows of international students are an important international force, they are also impacted by political and natural situations. For example, in the late 1970s, Iranian students made up the largest international student population in U.S. universities. Soon after the Iranian Islamic Revolution in 1979, Nigerian students dominated the U.S. higher education population. At the present time, in both the United States and Canada, students from Asian and South Asian countries like China, Korea, Japan, Taiwan, Indonesia, and India dominate the landscape. With the advent of the Islamic Revolution, many Iranian students were unable or did not choose to go home, and the anticipated return on the home country's investment did not occur. In the mid-1980s, the Malaysian government sent thousands of students to English-speaking nations as part of a human development campaign, most of them going to the United States.

In 2018, Saudi Arabia pulled more than 7,000 students studying in Canadian institutions of higher education from the country due to a perceived insult related to human rights in Saudi Arabia. U.S. institutions of higher education such as Portland State scrambled to get students into U.S. schools, bypassing application fees (KATU News 2018). Yet travel bans for students coming from countries such as Iran, Yemen, and Libya have sent a global message that the United States is a less welcoming space than before for international students, and they are turning to Canada,

Australia, and the UK in great numbers even as the overall international student population in the United States has dropped roughly 7 percent (Zong and Batalova 2018).

These sometimes capricious and often unpredictable pressures can create difficulties for universities that welcome large numbers of international students. When global health scares occur, student flows change. With the advent of the SARS virus in 2002–3, for example, the University of California, Berkeley; the University of Minnesota; and Syracuse University closed their campus-based intensive English programs due to a lack of students—specifically Chinese students, who had represented the bulk of those enrolling in these programs but were banned from entering the United States. Though not a light decision, programs that had been in existence for decades ceased. In the summer of 2009, numerous overseas programs prevented U.S. students from going to their expected destinations due to fears of the H1N1 (swine flu) virus. Those that did let students travel frequently found them quarantined in hotels in places like Korea and China instead of experiencing a season of tourist explorations.

Traditionally, study abroad is promoted as both a long- and short-term investment for the growth of students and the communities they interact with. When student flows change drastically in the short term, we need to expect long-term consequences. Certainly, no treaties are signed, but overseas study is often a first contact, and from such contacts, later contacts emerge. It is these later contacts that can permanently shift landscapes within and across borders. This is not to say that landscapes (and Appadurai's other scapes) are not changed by temporary flows, but permanent shifts occur more frequently with involuntary flows of people. We turn now to these involuntary flows, looking at the example of refugees and internally displaced peoples.

People who do not *choose* to move from one place to another, particularly from a homeland to a new space, include refugees and internally displaced persons. The United Nations High Commissioner for Refugees (UNHCR) crafted a convention in 1951 that is still in place. Article I defines a refugee as "a person who is outside his or her country of nationality or habitual residence who has a well-founded fear of persecution because of his or her race, religion, nationality, membership of a particular social group or political opinion; and is unable or unwilling to avail himself or herself of the protection of that country, or to return there, for fear of persecution" (UNHCR Self-Study Module 2 2005). Current scholars and researchers look at how the term has been twisted and augmented, noting that often individuals can self-select to present themselves this way sometimes to garner empathy or even the opposite as well—that anyone not fitting a particular script of who belongs in the neighborhood can suddenly be othered by being called a refugee (Ramanathan 2013; Ludwig 2016). In all cases we see the power of public and private discourse to control how we perceive and interact with others. This discourse may or may not be accurate.

As of September 2018, the UNHCR placed the total number of refugees worldwide at 25.4 million. In addition, the UNHCR calculated 40 million internally displaced people, displaced most frequently by domestic and international wars, insurrections, and natural disasters. Such people have fewer resources to draw upon than those identified as refugees, in spite of danger and sordid conditions that occur in many of the refugee camps that are set up. In terms of receiving countries, the top receiving nations were Iran, Lebanon, Pakistan, and Uganda, all hosting 1 to 1.5 million refugees each. Topping this list was Turkey with 3.5 million refugees.

Refugees are forced to create new lives and, to varying degrees, new identities. Because many of them remain for extended periods of time in refugee camps, they are literally caught in a kind of third space, neither here nor there. Victor Turner (1967) refers to this state as one of liminality. A liminal person is usually in a less-than-defined space for a temporary period of time, frequently in a socially created transition, such as between the teens and adulthood in age or between civilian status and fully enlisted status in the military. Remaining in a liminal space for an extended length of time stresses the body, soul, and ultimately the social bonds that have created community. Refugees and immigrants do not expect to return to their homes of origin; they are expected to shift their identities in some fashion to better accommodate a new culture for the long term and frequently must use the private sector as the space to maintain home language and home culture attitudes, behaviors, and beliefs. In some cases, these individuals develop a strong, grounded, bicultural or multicultural identity. In other instances, they develop what Peter Adler (1998) terms a "multiphrenic" identity, shape-shifting in a manner that causes long-term stress and potential disability.

Multiphrenic means "many shapes." If you imagine what happens to someone going in and out of various conceptualizations of self, you can see why this is problematic. In the *Star Trek: Deep Space Nine* series, the security officer Odo is able to assume any shape he wants; this is good for a security officer but not for an individual seeking a stable, avowed identity. In the story arc of the series, Odo is constantly searching for his place and his people. Much like Odo, people who assume different identities for different contexts can be constantly living in a liminal space, where they remain uncertain of who they truly are.

When individuals or policy makers consistently refer to "the refugee crisis," this collocation takes on a life of its own (Ansems de Vries and Guild 2018). Once individuals in a receiving nation hear the term "refugee," they immediately associate it with a "problem." Leonie Ansems de Vries and Elspeth Guild (2018) maintain that by continuing to use the phrase "refugee crisis" we invite a link to the notion of a threat. They suggest that solutions to threats are "crisis-led policymaking at odds with democratic principles" (3). These practices "constitute a politics of exhaustion" (3). Critical theorists argue that when issues of race, ethnicity, and class are conflated, nonwhite refugees on their paths to citizenship are frequently perceived as "dis-citizens"—that is, these individuals are inconsistently othered at rates that white middle-class refugees are not (Das Gupta 2006; Ramanathan 2013). Policies dictate that all are equal, but some are more equal than others.

Current U.S. refugee policy contrasts sharply with that of Canada. Between November 2015 and February 2016, roughly 26,000 Syrian refugees were resettled in Canada. By 2018 roughly 54,560 Syrian refugees had been resettled (Foley, Bose, and Grigri 2018). Canada chose to proactively craft an alternative assessment of credentials of prospective Syrian refugees with only partial documentation (Loo 2016). In the United States, in spite of clearly documented vetting procedures Syrian, Libyan, Yemeni, Somali, Venezuelan, North Korean, and Iranian refugees are refused entry (Davis 2018). Note the way World Education Services outlines the Canadian approach to assessment in their document *A Way Forward for Refugees* (2018, 24):

> WES intends to offer this service [alternative credentials assessment] to refugees from countries other than Syria. WES has already begun researching countries in distress and conflict to better understand the criteria by which it can serve refugees from those countries. Many of these refugees have been in Canada for years and have not been eligible for a WES report. This research involves understanding not only the flow of refugees over time to determine the need for services, but the nature of the disruption to institutions, the integrity of the educational system during conflict, and other considerations. WES is committed to rolling out this service to refugees from other countries based on this research, in ways still under consideration.

Multiple scholars have explored both demographic and social causes of anti-immigrant sentiment, daring open boat flights across the Mediterranean on the part of would-be refugees, and policy implications for the future (Czaika and Di Lillo 2018; Etling, Backeberg, and Tholen 2018; Baldwin-Edwards, Blitz, and Crawley 2019). Mathias Czaika and Armando Di Lillo (2018) detail more than ten possible causes of anti-immigrant sentiments in Europe. (Activity 3 at the end of this chapter lists them.) The International Organization for Migration recorded the deaths of more than 3,770 people crossing the Mediterranean in 2015. In addition to those deaths, other scholars note the dangers presented to would-be refugees. Martin Baldwin-Edwards, Brad Blitz, and Heaven Crawley note specifically what has happened in Libya: "In the case of Libya, the main transit country of the central Mediterranean route, the experiences of refugees and other migrants have been increasingly well-documented with widely reported incidents of kidnapping, forced labour, torture and death" (2018, 9).

Another group of individuals, temporary asylees, are those who intended to stay in a new place for a brief period of time due to something like a natural disaster but are subsequently unable to return home. This would include people displaced by hurricanes or tsunamis who expect to return home after a period of rebuilding, only to find that their homes have been completely destroyed. In some cases, they are assigned "temporary asylum status" or "temporary protected status" by the UN and allowed to settle for an indeterminate but not indefinite period of time in a country that agrees to temporarily accept them. Sadly, in December 2017, the Trump administration abruptly announced it was canceling temporary protected status for roughly 60,000 Haitians, 195,000 Salvadorans, and 2,500 Nicaraguans (Schepers 2018) in spite of the fact that the conditions that originally caused their exodus have not resolved. Refugees, internally displaced people, and individuals with temporary protected status do not possess equal status with members of the dominant culture that they come in contact with. When they move from their home space to another, they are typically treated differently from the general population. In some cases, they are isolated not only from their countrymen but also from their new hosts. Many refugee camps are walled off or sealed by barbed wire to prevent culture contact between those in the camps and those outside the camps.

The UNHCR and a variety of global organizations closely track the global situation of refugees and internally displaced persons. Videos are available on YouTube, officially posted by the UNHCR. Reuters has an

Alert Net (www.alertnet.org) with working pages detailing country profiles, offering ways that individuals can help and providing research tools for practitioners, much as the UNHCR site does. Because the issue of refugees is such a large and dramatic problem, it is difficult to summarize information on refugees into a concise form. What is central to our discussion at this point is the knowledge that the number of refugees and displaced peoples is not likely to decline in the near future. In spite of the likely increase, some nation-states have suddenly lowered their annual refugee quotas. The United States has shifted from a peak of over 100,000 annually during the Obama administration to 30,000 for the year 2019 in the Trump administration (Lind 2018). When nation-states suddenly decrease the numbers of refugees accepted, pressure mounts on other countries to make up the difference. The responsible resettlement of these individuals will continue to fall within the purview of international organizations, national governments, and private aid organizations.

Diasporas and culture mixing have profoundly shifted our landscapes, both real and imagined. Ten percent of the population growth in Europe is driven by migration (Tapias 2008). In 1950, 90 percent of the U.S. population was white, but by 2040, only 50 percent of the population will be. The United States is at the halfway point: 40 percent of U.S. citizens age ten years or younger are racial minorities. As various authors look at the power of migration to cause these shifts in peoplescapes, many focus on the stress that exists between former systems and patterns and newer systems and patterns. May Joseph looks at what she terms "nomadic identities," suggesting that the "large-scale displacement of people from the rural to the urban or across nations has heightened the precariousness of arbitrary boundaries while fueling the contemporary identifications with ossified national identities" (1999, 154).

In other words, the mixing of the various types of individuals described above into what were formerly not pan-ethnic spaces is changing who interacts with whom and for what purposes. Appadurai's ethnoscapes are changing, just as the notion of who is cosmopolitan is changing. Even as the kaleidoscope picture shifts with a twist of the wrist, linkages between people change. Many strive to recreate a narrowly defined ethnic community in the new locations that they have migrated to. Others use global flows of information, discussed below, to stay in touch with their former homelands. Still others use the intercultural contact to fuse new identities and new friendships and, ultimately, to establish more connections with more kinds of people in more places than ever before. In all cases, there is often stress in change—whether at the personal level or the societal level. Globalization, for all its positive aspects, takes a toll. For some, the separation and trauma entailed may never resolve. In the next section, we explore how various kinds of information assist individuals and societies in making connections—again, for better or for worse.

Flows of Information

At one point in time, only smoke, drums, and carrier pigeons could cross borders without control. Over time, radio and television waves were included. Now we have information flows via fiber-optic cables and wireless Internet. In the future, there will be forms of communication that we cannot now imagine. Appadurai's mediascapes will change just as ethnoscapes have changed. Alastair Pennycook reminds us that all media serve as vehicles "enabling immense and complex flows of people, signs, sounds, images across multiple borders in multiple directions" (2007, 25). Much of the information is regulated, but much is also pirated. Films cross borders without permission; pirated versions of DVDs are available at a fraction of the real non-pirated cost. Identities are brokered and maintained via these technological connections. In this section, we explore the forces responsible for these flows.

Music

Pennycook (2007) draws on work by John Connell and Chris Gibson, who suggest that "music nourishes imagined communities, traces links to distant and past places, and emphasizes that all human cultures have musical traditions, however differently these have been valued" (2003, 271). Individuals who are no longer physically at home can recreate their sense of space through links to their traditional music via electronic sources or gatherings of individuals in new spaces. In addition, global connections have allowed people around the world easy access to the musical traditions of those in other areas. A brief review of just one music catalog by Putamayo reveals scores of albums showcasing music from around the world, as well as "third culture" or "fusion" music, made when musicians from different contexts come in contact with each other to create completely new forms. Afropop is an example of such a fusion form. Other music forms such as hip-hop have allowed both endangered and dying languages to be recorded. Chi Luu (2015) suggests that rap can be found in "all major languages." One example is Aymara rap from Bolivia. One of Wayna Rap's pieces is titled "Contaminacion Acustica." Young Aymara speakers can make culture and identity connections in the twenty-first century with this music even as the number of Aymara speakers decreases.

This transcultural flow of information has accomplished three things: individuals in the diaspora have been able to remain connected to the music of their own culture; new music has been created as a function of contact; and local and sometimes dying languages have emerged in new music forms and are thus maintained. Connell and Gibson reflect on the ability of music to play an active role in how people interpret the world around them, going so far as to suggest that music can even play a role in flattening diversity insofar as it becomes omnipresent (2003, 270). Pennycook sees hip-hop as a way for the global to shape the local and vice versa. As he submits, "If English can be used to express local cultural practices, can such practices include more recently localized forms such as hip-hop?" (2006, 5). The transcultural flow of hip-hop allows it to move among and beyond nations. The website Nip Hop profiles the top ten Japanese rap groups (Nip Hop, 2019). An exploration of the music of these groups reveals both a fusion of East and West in a singular contact zone. Pennycook examines the Japanese site Nip Hop (2004) and its characterization of the hybridity that occurs when a language and hip-hop enter a singular contact zone: "Hip hop is a culture without a nation. Hip hop culture is international. Each country has its own spin on hip hop. . . . Japanese Hip Hop has its own culture but a culture that has many similar aspects of Hip Hop around the world. These aspects include the DJ, MC, dancers, and urban artists (taggers, spray paint art)."

The Internet and Radio

Perhaps the two key changes in terms of mediascapes that have occurred in the past decade are the ways the Internet and radio have, first, created sociopolitical venues for information to leave countries cracking down on dissidents and attempting to severely restrict access to information and, second, established powerful virtual connections for diasporic communities. Lisa Taraki cites what she terms "the excessive charms of the Internet." Taraki argues that, at least in the Middle East, "Internet-based resources vastly expand individuals' abilities to access greater social information, for example, the importance of blogs . . . from which we can presumably better understand the subjectivities of middle-class intellectuals and other cultural workers or identify the burning public issues as seen by citizens of the region. . . . The same applies to the veritable explosion of Internet sites featuring videos, fatwa forums, celebrity gossip, and myriad other issues of the day" (2007, 529). Blogging has become an essential way for citizens in various countries to express themselves in forums safer than face-to-face speech; it serves a key role in freedom of expression and civil society.

Unfortunately, terrible risks can come to those living in regimes where free speech is highly regulated. Female bloggers Nouf Abdelaziz al-Jerawi and Eman al-Nafjan, founder of the blog *Saudi Women*, were both arrested in the summer of 2018 and have not been heard from since (Reporters without Borders 2018a, 2018b). Canadian government criticisms of Saudi Arabia's human rights record resulted in the termination of studies in Canada for more than 7,000 Saudi students in August 2018. Iran was known as a nation with one of the highest numbers of bloggers in the world (Alavi 2005), yet as of 2017, more than 360 individuals have been jailed there for blogging (Zamaneh Media 2017). A 2014 YouTube video details what has happened there (Global Voice 2014).

Taraki notes two other dimensions of the Internet that are related to knowledge exchange. One is that academic scholarship can go on in spite of problems such as mail strikes. The second is that the Internet permits a "vastly enhanced ability of . . . scholars to act as public intellectuals, that is to invoke their scholarly responsibility and/or authority to express themselves on issues of public concern" (2007, 528). For many of us who live in less censored or more stable societies, it is difficult to imagine what it is like to work as a scholar but not have the freedom to interact with colleagues around the world. For most scholars in the West, speaking out entails less risk than in many other places. In terms of leadership on these "issues of public concern," Daoud Kuttab further comments on the role that Internet-streamed radio has played in allowing traditional radio to thrive while also subverting national restrictions on print media: "Perhaps the most important lesson on the AmmanNet experience is that the creation and success of an Internet radio station in a country [Jordan] of state-run monopolies offers a major forum for activists, liberal politicians, and government officials as they help their press reform and push to allow terrestrial radio to broadcast with freedom" (2007, 535). This dimension links mediascapes with ideoscapes.

Returning again to the link between ethnoscapes and mediascapes, we see that Internet-streamed radio allows individuals around the world to access local programs in a variety of languages. As with satellite dishes, this ability to connect in a specific language with a particular radio station halfway around the world is often very empowering. Globalization in this case has pulled together the best of what is local and what is global. Non-Internet community radio programming in various languages allows members of the diaspora to remain connected to their languages and culture. In the future, we can expect these various forms of social networking to continue to create and maintain transcultural flows and to provide voices for dissidence as well.

Film, Television, and Satellite Programming

Film, television, and satellite programming provide another means to cross borders virtually. As competing sites such as the famed Bollywood in India have given Hollywood a run for its money, we can see shifts in financescapes. Again, the kaleidoscope lens has shifted. Films have long been understood to be carriers of culture and to provide opportunities for outside individuals to come to know and understand more about the values, attitudes, and beliefs of the home culture represented in a particular film. In some cases, especially those films exported by the United States and other English-speaking nations, there is some question as to how the power of the visual pulls viewers into either a love or a hate relationship with what Braj Kachru (1988) terms "Inner Circle" English and culture and what is perceived as its hegemony. Inner Circle countries are those where English is spoken as a native language, including the United States, Canada, Great Britain, Australia, and New Zealand. Kachru argues in all of his work that English can belong to all who use it and that the distribution of English-language films moving throughout the world does not necessarily imply an overt or covert agenda of cultural imperialism (1988). Films invite viewers into an imagined contact zone. They provide one set of lenses from which to view the human condition. But context and the interaction of particular viewers with particular films are the true determinants of cultural flows. Perhaps one of the most powerful aspects of general film distribution all over the world is the degree to which films can be viewed multilingually, particularly in DVD formats. While U.S. retail giants such as Best Buy and Target have ceased to carry CDs, the industry does not see an imminent death of CDs or DVDs (Newman 2018).

Television broadcasting reaches around the globe. In places like the United States, Great Britain, and Italy, viewers watch an average of twenty-seven to twenty-eight hours of television per week (NationMaster Media

Satellite antennas in Morocco (Used with permission of the photographer, Aomar Boum)

Statistics n.d.). In many situations, individuals who are no longer living in their native countries access television in their home languages, via either local programming or satellite programming. For example, Anastasia Panagakos found that in the Greek immigrant population that she surveyed in Calgary, Canada, "viewing Greek television from satellite dishes was strongly favored by the first generation. . . . Over 54% of first-generation [Greek] immigrants were viewers." She goes on to characterize the power of the activity: "Watching satellite television is a prestige-generating activity and has the ability to intensify preexisting or generate new discourses on homeland activities" (2003, 210).

Karim H. Karim looks at the economic power of broadcasting to and for ethnic communities: "The growing ethnic-based commercial broadcasting infrastructure is integral to the increasingly global ethnic economy" (1998, 8). Numerous scholars routinely examine the effects of satellite programming in various languages around the world, noting how both diasporic populations and local populations are affected (see Panagakos 2003; Georgiou 2006; Jeffres 2000; and Karim 1998). Media studies throughout the world introduce students to the role of global television programming and the power of digital satellite broadcasting systems. Panagakos sees the power of both media and information technologies in the maintenance and negotiation of identity building on the part of immigrants. She states that mass "computer-mediated technologies can create new spaces for identity formation" (2003, 203). She goes on to characterize these technologies as a "forum for expressing and cultivating [ethnicities in the diaspora]" (207). In like manner, Indigenous groups have been able to use various media sources to maintain local language and identity (Couldry 2003).

The Written Word

Poetry and fiction provide yet another glimpse into transcultural flows of information. What does it mean to be comfortable writing in a language other than one's own? In most of the previous chapters, we have drawn primarily on various social science and environmental science disciplines to present information. Here, we see the power of literature to capture feelings of displacement in a manner accessible to those of us who have not been displaced. Senayon Olaoluwa suggests that the theme of exile "occupies a conspicuous place in poetic exploration in particular and literary expression in general" (2007, 223). Iranian American Ahmad Naderpoor looks at longing and exile in his poem "Shards of Memories":

Oh land of my birth
Oh land whose shards hold memories for me
I'm caught in thoughts of you
absent and homesick
A homesickness like a candle, burning from the inside.
My homeland, I can't deny you
for you are the truth and undeniable
Tossed into the fire of my heavy heart. (2010)

Olaoluwa (2007) sees the poet as a medium, able to capture the experiences of those described in the section above on flows of people. The descriptions describe states of mind, behavior, and, most important, emotions, something less frequently captured in the other disciplines we have drawn from throughout this text. In like manner, poets who have not left their homelands can capture historical pain experienced by ancestors. Korean American poet Suji Kwock Kim, in her 2003 collection, *Notes from the Divided Country*, includes a poem titled "Borderlands." In the poem, dedicated to her Korean grandmother who lived in Korea at the time of the Japanese occupation, Kim creates a painful landscape: "We tried to escape across the frozen Yalu, to Ch'ientao or Harbin / I saw the Japanese soldiers shoot" (20). The poet goes on to create a question in her grandmother's mind as to why she survived.

Individuals who indicate they have multiethnic identities draw frequently on their own personal border crossings around the world (compare Japanese American poet David Mura and Chinese Singaporean Edwin Thumboo). The anguish of transferring from writing in one's mother tongue to writing in a second tongue also poignantly reflects the affective dimensions of border crossings (Li 2007; Jin 2008). In addition, perspectives on universal processes such as attending school, interacting with members of new groups, discovering oneself, and even encountering war, racism, and prejudice provide us with ways of comparing border crossings (Adiele and Frosch 2007).

The genre of fiction provides yet another dimension of border crossing. There is a plethora of writing from contact zones—immigrants as protagonists in numerous novels socialized into new lives, trying to retain shards of the old while exploring the new. One large volume of such fiction focuses on Pakistani, Sri Lankan, and Indian immigrants settling in the United States and Great Britain. Among the writers are Jumpha Lahiri, B. Mukerjee, and Bharti Kirchner. While some of these stories might question exactly how a homeland long abandoned or never seen must look, others reflect the power of multicultural individuals able to evoke imagined communities all over the globe.

How does this information connect to the other parts of the chapter that have been exploring flows of information in a less personal way? First, the field of international studies has room for scholars of the heart—those who explore affective dimensions of crossing borders. Second, work in identity theory, critical theory, and diaspora studies is often centered in scholarship in humanities—literature, film studies, and culture studies. Examinations of positive and negative dimensions of globalization as discussed in chapters 3 and 4 frequently find their way into literature. Authors such as Nigerians Ken Saro-Wiwa and Chinua Achebe draw on globalization and colonialism themes. As you begin to work your way around the map of international studies, literature and culture studies may become part of your program choices.

Conclusion

In this chapter, we have examined flows of people and information in ways that transcend traditional border crossings and have looked at how changes in places cause deep identity shifts for individuals. At the same time, landscapes at the local and national levels have shifted, changing the ways schools deliver education and community governments deal equitably (or not) with individuals who speak different languages and do not resemble their neighbors physically. The lives of individuals who have involuntarily left their homelands are infinitely more stressful than the lives of those who have left voluntarily (Berry 2006). Like a kaleidoscope, the frames created by the intersections of these individuals with those who have never left home or even encountered people different from them are complicated. Cross-cultural communication scholars suggest that intercultural competence is an integral component of successful interactions in contact zones. These zones will continue to increase—in real time and space as well as virtually. In like manner, media and technology have outlined new relations for students, scholars, and others seeking connection.

Communities are formed by individuals. With increasing person-to-person contact around the globe comes an increasing responsibility to connect in an ethical manner. While what Mitchell Hammer terms “mono-cultural mindsets” are quite functional for individuals who will never leave their home cultures, they are not functional for those who interact face-to-face or virtually with individuals from other cultures (personal communication, October 10, 2009). Some level of intercultural competence is necessary for these individuals. Hammer defines intercultural competence as "the capability to shift cultural perspective and adapt behavior to cultural differences and commonality" (2008). Unless we are able to walk in the shoes of people who are different from those who live in our immediate neighborhood or our country of origin or who communicate with us from afar via technology, we will experience fear, a lack of safety, and an unwillingness to engage in making connections. Without the warp and woof of these connections, our world as we know it will unravel. As global citizens, we can keep this fabric from unraveling, serving as edge walkers, gatekeepers, and the thread that joins various human and technological forces together. Your ability to perceive differences in perspectives, to be curious about what accounts for successful movement in and out of particular cultures, and to tolerate the ambiguity that arises when individuals with strong differences come in contact with each other will allow you to play a facilitative role in how people relate to one another. The following chapter on development will revisit economic, political, and cultural dimensions of globalization as they relate to particular nation-states and provide a more extended description of one setting in Nepal where shifts in culturescapes and financescapes have caused more harm than good.

➤ VOCABULARY

sojourner
liminal person
nomadic identity
diaspora
UNHCR
immigrant
multiphrenic identity

➤ DISCUSSION AND REFLECTION QUESTIONS

1 What do you understand about Appadurai's terms "ethnoscapes," "mediascapes," "technoscapes," "financescapes," and "ideoscapes"? How do these compare to the notion of "landscapes," and why might they be important for understanding transcultural flows?

2 Have you found yourself in the cosmopolitan space Appiah describes? How?

3 How could someone acquire a "nomadic identity," and how does this compare with a traditional identity?

4 What role can music genres such as hip-hop play when they are imported into local languages?

5 What do you think Connell and Gibson (2003, 270) mean when they say, "Popular music has the ability to mediate social knowledge, reinforce (or challenge) ideological constructions of contemporary (or past) life, and be an agent of hegemony"?

6 How can new technologies change the ways people develop their notions of "homeland" and create new spaces for identity formation?

7 How can literature help us to understand refugee and immigrant feelings of exile and displacement?

8 What is intercultural competence?

ACTIVITY 1: ANALYZE Find a community radio station that is broadcasting in your city or town. Examine its program guide. Are there various programs broadcasting in different languages? If so, try listening briefly to one or two of them. Can you hear English mixed with the other language? In linguistics, this can be one of three processes: language borrowing, language (or code) mixing, or code-switching. Language borrowing refers to a word or short phrase from English entering into the other language; language mixing is the introduction of longer, complete phrases from English into the other language; and finally, code-switching involves including whole clauses or sentences from English in the other language. In all of these cases, we recognize evidence of contact. As we have seen over and over in this chapter, new kinds of scapes, both imagined and real, are being created with the assistance of various media. At the same time, these media allow for maintenance of the local landscape as well.

ACTIVITY 2: REFLECT Look at the following list of causes of anti-immigrant sentiments outlined by Czaika and Di Lillo:

> Non-economic explanations emphasize socio-cultural factors, mainly reflecting nativist mind-sets and a high degree of national identification with a strong desire for ethnically homogenous societies. Hostility to newcomers has been associated with, for instance, an isolationist mentality, pessimistic evaluations of the current and future state of the economy, and feeling of alienation

> from mainstream social and political institutions, racial or cultural prejudice, beliefs about the size of the immigrant population, cultural and national identities, and a general disposition to trust in other people, threats to in-group resources and threats to the shared customs and traditions of the society, perceived cultural threats especially with regard to the English language, or stereotypical beliefs about the work and intelligence of other groups. (2018, 3)

In a conversation with a friend, explore whether you have heard such sentiments expressed by anyone around you: friend, family member, work associate, or person on the street. Try to identify where these ideas have originated: in fear, in lived experiences, or in historical memory (that is, you have heard older individuals both expressing and teaching these sentiments).

ACTIVITY 3: EXTEND Identify one of the larger immigrant populations in your community and investigate one of the neighborhoods in your city with a high immigrant population. Document the linguistic landscape with a camera or smartphone. Choose one or two retail streets in the community and take pictures of a bilingual sign. Identify whether both languages are presented equally on the sign or whether English or the other language appears dominant.

References

A Way Forward for Refugees. 2018. World Education Services. Retrieved November 7, 2019, from https://knowledge.wes.org/rs/317-CTM-316/images/report-way-forward-refugees-full.pdf.

Adiele, F., and M. Frosch. 2007. *Coming of age around the world: A multicultural anthology*. New York: New Press.

Adler, P. 1998. Beyond cultural identity: Reflections on multiculturalism. In *Basic concepts of intercultural communication*, edited by M. Bennett, 225–46. Yarmouth, Maine: Intercultural Press.

Alavi, N. 2005. *We are Iran*. London: Portobello Books.

Ansems de Vries, L., and E. Guild. 2018. Seeking refuge in Europe: Spaces of transit and the violence of migration management. *Journal of Ethnic and Migration Studies* 45 (12): 2156–66. doi: https://doi.org/10.1080/1369183X.2018.1468308.

Appadurai, A. 1996. *Modernity at large: Cultural dimensions of globalization*. Minneapolis: University of Minnesota Press.

Appiah, K. A. 2006. *Cosmopolitanism: Ethics in a world of strangers.* New York: W. W. Norton.

Baldwin-Edwards, M., B. Blitz, and H. Crawley. 2019. The politics of evidence-based policy in Europe's "migration crisis." *Journal of Ethnic and Migration Studies* 45 (12): 2139–55. doi: https://doi.org/10.1080/1369183X.2018.1468307: 1–18.

Benhabib, S. 2004. *The rights of others: Aliens, residents, and citizens.* Cambridge: Cambridge University Press.

Bernhard, L., and D. Kaufmann. 2018. Coping with the asylum challenge: Tightening and streamlining policies in Western Europe. *Journal of Ethnic and Migration Studies* 44 (15): 2506–23. doi: 10.1080/1369183X.2018.1433996: 1–18.

Berry, J. K. 2006. Acculturative stress. In *Handbook of multicultural perspectives on stress and coping,* edited by P. Wong and L. Wong, 287–98. New York: Springer.

Cheah, P. 2006. Cospomolitanism. *Theory, Culture and Society* 23 (2–3): 486–96.

Connell, J., and C. Gibson. 2003. *SoundTracks: Popular music, identity, and place.* London: Routledge.

Couldry, N. 2003. *Media rituals: A critical approach.* London: Routledge.

Czaika, M., and A. Di Lillo. 2018. The geography of anti-immigrant attitudes across Europe, 2002–2014. *Journal of Ethnic and Migration Studies* 44 (15): 2453–79. doi: 10.1080/1369183X.2018.1427564.

Das Gupta, M. 2006. *Unruly immigrants: Rights, activism, and transnational South Asian politics in the United States.* Durham: Duke University Press.

Davis, J. 2018. Trump to cap refugees allowed into US at 30,000, a record low. *New York Times,* September 17. Retrieved October 1, 2018, from https://www.nytimes.com/2018/09/17/us/politics/trump-refugees-historic-cuts.html.

Ephron, D. 2007. Arab bloggers face unwanted attention: Government clampdown. *Newsweek,* June 11.

Etling, A., L. Backeberg, and J. Tholen. 2018. The political dimensions of young people's migration intentions: Evidence from the Arab Mediterranean region. *Journal of Ethnic and Migration Studies.* doi: 10.1080/1369183X.2018.1485093.

Feuerherm, E., and R. Roumani. 2016. The journey to U.S. citizenship: Developing a participatory curriculum for Iraqi refugees. In *Language, immigration and naturalization: Legal and linguistic issues,* edited by A. Loring and V. Ramanathan, 56–76. Bristol, UK: Multilingual Matters.

Figel, J. 2008. Promoting understanding and dialogue. NAFSA Conference session: International student and scholar mobility: Programs, trends, challenges and impact. Washington, D.C., May 27. Retrieved October 18, 2008, from www.eurunion.org/en/index2.php?option=com_content and task.

Foley, B., P. Bose, and L. Grigri. Syrian refugee resettlement in Canada. PR9: Technical Report. University of Vermont. doi: 10.13140/RG.2.2.32164.17282.

Friedman, T. 2007. *The world is flat: A brief history of the 21st century.* New York: Picador/Farrar, Straus and Giroux.

Georgiou, M. 2006. Diasporic communities on-line: A bottom-up experience of transnationalism. In *Ideologies of the Internet*, eds. K. Sarikakis and D. Thussu, 131–45. Cresskill, NJ: Hampton Press.

Giddens, A. 1999. *Runaway world: How globalisation is reshaping our lives*. London: Profile Books.

Global Voice. 2014. GV face: Whatever happened to Iran's bloggers? YouTube. Retrieved October 1, 2018, from https://www.youtube.com/watch?reload=9&v=AZbeUNLDqss.

Gopal, P. 2008. Foreign investors love U.S. real estate. *Business Week*, January 27. Retrieved July 5, 2010, from http://www.businessweek.com/the_thread/hotproperty/archives/2008/01/foreign_investors_love_us_real_estate.html.

Gramsci, A. (1930) 2011. *Prison notebooks*, 1–3. New York: Columbia University Press.

Hahn-Steichen, H. 2008. Speaking and listening exercises for high-tech work environments. Unpublished master's project, Portland State University.

Hammer, M. 2008. IDI guided development: Building intercultural competence. Conference plenary, First Annual IDI Conference. Minneapolis, October 3.

Harpaz, Y. 2018. Compensatory citizenship: Dual nationality as a strategy of global upward mobility. *Journal of Ethnic and Migration Studies* 45 (6): 897–916. doi: 10.1080/1369183X.2018.1440486.

Heyneman, S. 2000. Educational qualifications: The economic and trade issues. *Assessment in Education* 7 (3): 417–38.

———. 2003. International education: A retrospective. *Peabody Journal of Education* 78 (1): 33–53.

Hutnyk, I. 2000. *Critique of exotica: Music, politics, and the culture industry*. London: Pluto Press.

International Organization for Migration. 2016. IOM counts 3771 migrant fatalities in Mediterranean in 2015. Retrieved September 2, 2018, from https://www.iom.int/news/iom-counts-3771-migrant-fatalities-mediterranean-2015.

International Student Infographics. 2016–17. Retrieved September 30, 2018, from https://www.iie.org/en/Research-and-Insights/Open-Doors/Fact-Sheets-and-Infographics/Infographics.

Jeffres, L. 2000. Ethnicity and ethnic media use. *Communication Research* 27 (9): 496–535.

Jin, H. 2008. *The writer as migrant*. Chicago: University of Chicago Press.

Joseph, M. 1999. *Nomadic identities: The performance of citizenship*. Minneapolis: University of Minnesota Press.

Kachru, B. 1988. Teaching world Englishes. *ERIC/CLL News Bulletin* 12 (1): 1–8.

Karim, K. H. 1998. From ethnic media to global media: Transnational communication networks among diasporic communities. Paper presented to the International Comparative Research Group: Strategic Research and Analysis/Canadian Heritage, June. Retrieved December 20, 2008, from http://www.transcomm.ox.ac.uk/working%20papers/karim.pdf.

KATU News 2018. PSU eases admissions for Saudi students ejected from Canada. *KATU News*, August 13. Retrieved July 5, 2019, from https://katu.com/news/local/psu-eases-admissions-for-saudi-students-ejected-from-canada.

Kim, S. K. 2003. *Borderlands: For my grandmother.* Retrieved July 17, 2010, from http://www.griffinpoetryprize.com/see_hear_poetry.php?t=26.

———. 2003. *Notes from the divided country: Poems.* Baton Rouge: Louisiana State University Press.

Kuttab, D. 2007. Pensée 3: New media in the Arab world. *International Journal of Middle East Studies* 39 (4): 534–35.

Latane, B. 1996. Dynamic social impact: The creation of culture by communication. *Journal of Communication* 46 (4): 13–25.

Li, J. G. 2007. Subterranean geography: A learner's experience of searching for identity and voice through poetic language. Master's thesis, Portland State University.

Lind, D. 2018. Trump slashed refugee levels this year. *Vox*, September 18. Retrieved July 5, 2019, from https://www.vox.com/2018/9/17/17871874/refugee-news-record-history-asylum.

Loo, B. 2016. *Recognizing refugee credentials: Practical tips for credential assessment.* NY: World Education Services.

Ludwig, B. 2016. The different meanings of the word refugee. In *Refugee resettlement in the US: Language, policy, pedagogy*, edited by E. Feuerherm and V. Ramanathan, 35–54. Bristol, UK: Multingual Matters.

Luu, C. 2015. Word to your mother (tongue): Can hip-hop save endangered languages? Retrieved October 1, 2018, from https://daily.jstor.org/word-mother-tongue-can-hip-hop-save-endangered-languages/.

MacGillivray, A. 2006. *A brief history of globalization.* London: Robinson.

Massachusetts Institute of Technology. 2008. The human cost of the war in Iraq. Retrieved December 20, 2008, from mit.edu/humancostiraq/.

Naderpoor, A. 2010. Shards of memories. Translated by K. Brown. Unpublished poem, reprinted with permission of the author.

NationMaster Media Statistics. n.d. Retrieved December 21, 2008, from www.nationmaster.com/graph/med_tel_vie-media-television-viewing.

Newman, J. 2018. The CD business isn't dying—it's just evolving. Retrieved October 1 from https://www.fastcompany.com/40532455/the-cd-business-isnt-dying-its-just-evolving.

Nip Hop. 2004. Retrieved November 10, 2008, from http://www.gijigaijin.dreamstation.com/Introduction.html. Website no longer available.

Nip-hop music. 2019. Retrieved November 7, 2019, from https://www.last.fm/tag/nip-hop/artists.

Norman, K. 2018. Inclusion, exclusion, or indifference? Redefining migrant and refugee host state engagement options in Mediterranean "transit" countries. *Journal of Ethnic and Migration Studies* 45 (1): 42–60. doi: 10.1080/1369183X.2018.143996.

Notar, B. 2008. Producing cosmopolitanism at the borderlands: Lonely planeteers and "local" cosmopolitans in Southwest China. *Anthropological Quarterly 81* (3): 615–50.

Olaoluwa, S. 2007. From the local to the global: A critical survey of exile experience in recent African poetry. *Nebula 4* (2): 223–50.

Panagakos, A. 2003. Downloading new identities: Ethnicity, technology, and media in the global Greek village. *Identities 10* (2): 201–19.

Pennycook, A. 2006. *Global Englishes and transcultural flows.* London: Routledge.

Pepper, D. 2008. Aftermath of a revolt: Myanmar's lost year. *New York Times,* October 5.

Pratt, M. 1992. *Imperial eyes: Travel writing and transculturation.* London: Routledge.

Project Atlas (Institute for International Education). n.d. Retrieved November 27, 2013, from http://www.iie.org/Research-and-Publications/Project-Atlas.

Ramanathan, V. 2013. *Language policies and (dis)citizenship.* Bristol, UK: Multilingual Matters.

Reporters without Borders. 2018a. Human rights blogger arrested in Saudi Arabia. June 13. Retrieved September 2, 2018, from https://rsf.org/en/news/human-rights-blogger-arrested-saudi-arabia.

———. 2018b. Une blogeuse saodienne arretee pour ses ecrits sur les droits des femmes. May 23. Retrieved September 2, 2018, from https://rsf.org/fr/actualites/une-blogueuse-saoudienne-arretee-pour-ses-ecrits-sur-les-droits-des-femmes.

Rosenzweig, M. 2006. Global wage differences and international student flows. Retrieved October 18, 2008, from http://muse.jhu.edu/journals/brookings_trade_forum/v2006/2006.1r.

Ruiz, N., and A. Budiman. 2018a. Foreign students who stayed and worked in the US under OPT after graduation by metro area, 2004–2016 (Appendix D: Additional tables). Retrieved August 23, 2018, from http://www.pewglobal.org/2018/05/10/appendix-d-additional-tables-foreign-graduate.

———. 2018b. Number of foreign college students staying and working in US after graduation surges. May 10. Retrieved August 23, 2018, from http://www.pewglobal.org/2018/05/10/number-of-foreign-students-staying-and-working-in-US-after-graduation-surges.

Sarker, S. 2016. A position embedded in identity: Subalternity in neoliberal globalization. *Cultural Studies 30* (5): 816–36.

Savicki, V., ed. 2008. *Developing intercultural competence and transformation.* Sterling, Va.: Stylus.

Schepers, E. 2018. Trump to cancel Temporary Protected Status for Salvadoran immigrants. Retrieved September 2, 2018, from https://www.peoplesworld.org/article/trump-to-cancel-temporary-protected-status-for-salvadoran-immigrants/.

Scheuerman, W. 2014. Cosmopolitanism and the world state. *Review of International Studies 4*:419–41.

Soboleva, V. 2007. UNHCR struggles to find solutions for Afghan asylum seekers in Russia. UNHCR, April 17. Retrieved December 21, 2008, from http://www.alertnet.org/thenews/newsdesk/UNHCR/3f794231487ec6d67485b8bf144f455e.htm.

Tapias, A. 2008. Global diversity and intercultural competence development. Conference plenary, First Annual IDI Conference. Minneapolis, October 3.

Taraki, L. 2007. The excessive charms of the Internet. *International Journal of Middle East Studies* 39:528–30.

Turner, V. 1967. Betwixt and between: The liminal period in rites de passage. In *The forest of symbols: Aspects of Ndembau ritual*, 93–111. Ithaca: Cornell University Press.

UNHCR. 2012. Displacement: The new 21st century challenge. UNHCR Global Trends 2012. Retrieved November 30, 2013, from http://www.unhcr.org/cgi-bin/texis/vtx/home/opendocPDFViewer.html?docid=51bacbof9&query=2012%20number%20of%20refugees%20worldwide.

———. 2018. Figures at a glance. Retrieved September 2, 2018, from http://www.unhcr.org/en-us/figures-at-a-glance.html.

UNHCR Self-Study Module 2. 2005. Refugee status determination: Identifying who is a refugee. Legal Publications, September 1. Retrieved September 6, 2009, from http://www.unhcr.org/cgi-bin/texis/vtx/search?page=search&docid=4314.

UN Human Development Report. 1999. New York: Oxford University Press.

Wahlbeck, O. 1998. Transnationalism and diasporas: The Kurdish example. Paper presented at the International Sociological Association XIV World Congress of Sociology, Montreal, Canada (Research Committee 31, Sociology of Migration), July 26–August 1.

Wayna Rap. *Contaminacion Acustica*. Retrieved November 7, 2019, from https://www.youtube.com/watch?v=iKkeyMmoZ2w.

Yu, H. 2009. Global migrants and the new Pacific Canada. *International Journal* 64 (4): 1011–28.

Zamaneh Media. 2017. Imprisoned bloggers in Iran. Medium, August 11. Retrieved October 1, 2018, from https://medium.com/iff-community.../imprisoned-bloggers-in-Iran-3dc957919b4.

Zong, J., and J. Batalova. 2018. International students in the US. *Migration Policy Institute Spotlight*, May 9. Retrieved July 5, 2019, from https://www.migrationpolicy.org/article/international-students-united-states.

Zuberi, N. 2001. *Sounds English: Transnational popular music*. Urbana: University of Illinois Press.

SIX Development

SYNOPSIS

This chapter explores the historical origins of development strategies, as well as the ideological underpinnings of competing frameworks. It compares the UN Millennium Development Goals with goals within the 2017 *Sustainable Development Goals Report*. The advantages and disadvantages of microfinance as a development strategy are examined, as are prior global debt reduction models. Finally, we look to Nepal for a case study that illustrates the nature of competing development sources in a nation where a disaster affected 25 percent of the population.

SCAFFOLDING

As you read through this chapter, think about how you would answer each of the questions below.

What terms have you typically used to distinguish the countries of the Global North from those of the Global South?

Can you think of advantages or disadvantages to using particular terms?

How might the past three chapters on globalization relate to the concept of development?

What academic or intellectual barriers may prevent you as a reader from accessing information about both development theories and practices around the world?

➤ **CORE CONCEPTS**

How do the concepts of modernity and industrialization represent targets of development?

How do either dependency theory or world-systems theory compare and contrast with modernization theory?

How can local context promote the creation of development theories that represent powerful alternatives to theories brought in from the outside?

The focus of this chapter is development, which can be thought of as a partner of, or bookend to, globalization. Just as positive and negative aspects of globalization underlie much current work in international studies, the relationship between "those who have" and "those who have significantly less" has captured the attention of social scientists since the late 1940s, particularly in the fields of economics, political science, sociology, geography, and anthropology. Now, however, researchers argue that this arbitrary split does not adequately account for context and local situations. In the twentieth and twenty-first centuries, disciplines such as ecology, environmental studies, and education have joined the debates. In this chapter, we examine various definitions of development and look at how the interactions of individual nation-states in relation to development historically have become intertwined with those of nongovernmental organizations (NGOs) and multinational organizations.

What Is Development?

Gustavo Esteva (1992) suggests that U.S. president Harry Truman first introduced the present-day vision of development in his 1949 inaugural address. Within Truman's concept of the "Fair Deal" was an obligation to share new industrial and scientific achievements with less-privileged regions. At its earliest, then, the term "development" incorporated a kind of dichotomizing, a dimension of "othering" that created poles or ideological camps: "developed" was contrasted with "underdeveloped," or sometimes "undeveloped." Later on, the labeling branched into "developed" versus "less developed." In each of these cases, the positive anchor "developed" was the starting point for defining its opposite; in other words, the notions of undeveloped, underdeveloped, and less developed could exist only in relationship to the concept of developed. Later on, the dichotomies became less transparent, such as in the terms "First World" and "Third World." The invisibility of countries behind the Iron Curtain, the so-called Second World countries, was a product of the West's relationship to these countries following World War II. Eventually, weaknesses in the bipolar framework caused us to create a Fourth World category. In the early 1970s, West German chancellor Willy Brandt proposed the terms "Global North" and "Global South." In a type of magic that still puzzles the best cartographers, the Global North includes Australia and New Zealand. In fact, we have yet to find expressive yet neutral terms to describe "those who have" and "those who have less." In the same way, we have been unable to find ways to characterize certain areas that do not force a comparison with other areas.

For more than half a century, various scholars have searched for necessary and sufficient measures of development to create a type of index, while others have criticized the inflexibility of such an approach in accommodating particular contexts. The initial measures chosen were tied to economic indicators: national gross domestic product and per capita income. Later measures have included literacy rates, maternal and infant death rates, life expectancy, and now even HIV infection rates. As we will see later in the chapter, certain scholars have pushed practitioners hard to establish measures that are more holistic and include the actual quality of life.

The UN proposed a grounding set of eight broad-based Millennium Development Goals, which were adopted by the UN General Assembly in a resolution on September 8, 2000:

1. Eradicate extreme poverty and hunger.
2. Achieve universal primary education.
3. Promote gender equality and empower women.
4. Reduce child mortality.
5. Improve maternal health.
6. Combat HIV/AIDS, malaria, and other diseases.
7. Ensure environmental sustainability.
8. Develop a global partnership for development.

Since 2000, the UN has issued annual *Millennium Development Goals Reports* documenting the progress made in achieving these eight goals. Evident in these goals, the original resolution, and the subsequent annual

Boy at irrigation line in Morocco (Used with permission of the photographer, Aomar Boum)

reports is a broad-based and contextualized focus on holistic dimensions of development. The 2017 *Sustainable Development Goals Report* moves beyond these original goals, concentrating more on a sustainable development agenda outlined in the UN's 2030 Agenda for Sustainable Development. Rather than eight broad areas, there are now seventeen goals/targets:

No poverty
Zero hunger
Good health / well-being
Quality education
Gender equality
Clean water/sanitation
Affordable and clean energy
Decent work and economic growth
Industry, innovation, and infrastructure
Reduced inequalities
Sustainable cities and communities
Responsible consumption and production
Climate action
Life below water
Life on land
Peace, justice, and strong institutions
Partnerships for the goals

These updated goals reveal a greater level of integration than the original goals. For example, the goal of life below water identifies problems with overfishing and pollution but also goes so far as to recommend multinational collaboration in better managing the creation of biodiversity sites. The report also builds in more data (than that provided in the annual goals report) that is easily accessible (UN 2017). At each juncture that development decisions are proposed, it is appropriate to identify the ideological underpinnings and to recognize that theoretical approaches are most often grounded in a historical and political context. As we will see below, this is absolutely the case for development theories.

Economic and Political Theories of Development from a Historical Perspective

Scholars such as Michael Cowen and Robert Shenton (2010) look as far back as 1937 as an anchor point for discussions about development and underdevelopment. They also acknowledge, however, that most scholars start their analysis from Esteva's 1992 work. World War II and the rapid industrialization that followed it shaped how early economists framed the development dilemma. The issues that scholars and policy makers saw as important at that time ranged from identifying deep-seated roots of economic and political development to linking these roots to social change, self-governance, and the degree to which governments need to craft individual development opportunities for all their citizens. These areas of focus drew on the nation-state as the unit of analysis. However, the Marshall Plan and other plans moved beyond single nation-state assistance, often demonstrating both multilateral and multiorganizational assistance (Bryant and White 1982, 3). Western economists and economic planners conceived these recovery plans; the ideologies they drew from came out of their own cultural frameworks and the intellectual ideas that were dominant from the 1930s into the 1950s. One powerful theory that emerged during this time and fully evolved between 1950 and 1970 was modernization theory.

Modernization Theory

Modernization theory—also known as modernity theory—traces its roots back to the economic perspective of Walter Rostow (1959). Rostow proposed a now-classic model of economic growth in which a society moves through five distinct stages: (1) traditional society, (2) preconditions for takeoff, (3) takeoff, (4) drive to maturity, and (5) age of high mass consumption. His description of how a nation-state becomes modern was first anchored in economics. However, Western political scientists, sociologists, and even education policy planners educated in the era when this theory was most prevalent adapted it to their own fields. Modernization theory is a neo-evolutionary theory in that it supposes that all nation-states will follow through from one stage to the next in a linear fashion. It is a somewhat inflexible model that cannot be adjusted for particular contexts.

Rostow's five-stage theory was clearly tied to an assumption that "West was best," and his ideas had a deep impact on development scholars in the 1960s and 1970s. One of the early architects was sociologist Alex Inkeles, who, with coauthor David Horton Smith, wrote *Becoming Modern: Individual Change in Six Developing Countries* (1974), an exploration of the economic, political, and social dimensions of modernity. In the book, Inkeles and Smith offer a profile of a modern society as one that assumes a level of social organization above that of tribes and is inhabited by individuals who "can keep to fixed schedules, observe abstract rules, [and] make judgments on the basis of objective evidence" (4). Inkeles and Smith's language defines modern society as the industrialized society of the West. The indices of modern economic development are posited as factors indicating the status of societal development. Actual quality of life and dimensions of equality among citizens are not discussed. In addition to measures outlined above, these indices include productivity per person, level of literacy, level of nutrition, and breadth of infrastructure (Rogers 1976).

Inkeles looked both at modern society and at the modern person, suggesting that modernity may take on somewhat different forms because of "local conditions, the history of a given culture, and the period when it was introduced" (Inkeles and Smith 1974, 16). This focus on individual aspects of development singles out the work of Inkeles from that of his well-known contemporaries, among them Samuel Huntington.

As economists were making their mark in planning for modern societies, the discipline of political economics began to emerge. Political economists urged the inclusion of "the context of political reality" (Bryant and White 1982, 10) and recommended that growth be separated from development. The subfield of development economics also emerged. The modernization model is sometimes called the developmental model or the "benign" model. It posits that education makes a direct contribution to both economic output and social stability. Critics of the model, such as Martin Carnoy (1974), suggest that this same education is also used as a means to institutionalize control, maintain income structure, and socialize the dependence of one class on another. An outgrowth of this work is the acculturation view, in which societies that adopt the markers of development begin to more closely resemble model industrialized nations (Frank 1970, 2002). Frequently, an investment in human capital characterizes the impetus for these changes. Frederick Harbison and Charles Myers (1964, 1965) suggest that human resource development is the first step in raising the GDP of a country and that an investment in education for all will shift the speed and efficacy of development.

In the 1980s, examples of the acculturation view, or human capital approach, could be seen throughout the world. The Malaysian government began a massive higher education investment that sent hundreds of students out of the country to the United States, the United Kingdom, and Australia for undergraduate and graduate education. Students received full scholarships but were obliged to repay them with a minimum of ten years of government service or through a reimbursement of the monetary investment. Majors were determined before students left Malaysia. Malaysian students of Indian or Chinese origin were not offered these scholarships, which were reserved for the *bumiputra*, or "children of the soil" (native Malays), and other Indigenous groups.

Following the work of these early modernists, scholars began writing about the human costs of development as defined by the West. Coralie Bryant and Louise White (1982) call this focus on human and ethical dimensions "humanist views." These views move between dependency theory and, ultimately, world-systems theory. A chief architect in this arena was philosopher Denis Goulet, who argued that all development policy "contains an implicit ethical strategy" (1971, 118). He went on to identify three core values: "life sustenance for all, optimum esteem, and freedom" (118). Policy recommendations made by scholars and practitioners with a humanist perspective frequently looked at broad-based human rights alongside traditional markers of development.

In the late 1980s, many scholars of development moved into systems theory. While it is beyond the scope of this chapter to expand on the notions of this theory in detail, what you need to remember is that systems theorists identify lists of dimensions, principles, and other elements; model how one element is connected to another; and provide elaborate discussions of how elements function together within a system. There is an underlying belief in systems theory that it is actually possible for experts to truly identify all dimensions of a particular problem. Unfortunately, it is often the case that such identification is highly Western-centric.

Like modernization theory, systems theory was refined by Western scholars in developed nations who explored applications to less-developed nations. The grounding principles provided by modernization theory are still evident in systems theory. They include the following:

1. Modernization is possible; there is optimism that change can come about.
2. A particular region can change rapidly with the right incentives and inputs.
3. Some level of abandoning traditional social and political institutions is necessary.
4. Structures successful in modern nations should be adopted by modernizing nations.
5. Foreign expertise will be required to help implement change.

6 Foreign investment is uniformly positive and should be accepted without restriction.

The last three principles imply a uniform recipe for development no matter what the context. They suggest that a developing nation will be unsuccessful if it does not adapt Western recommendations based on ideologies developed at Bretton Woods. Outside assistance is deemed paramount. These three principles, in particular, greatly disturbed anthropologists and other social scientists working in Latin America. Dependency theory was developed as a direct rejoinder to modernization theory.

Dependency Theory

Even as American and European social scientists attached themselves to indices of development, a group of anthropologists in Latin America were refining quite another set of theories they had been working on for decades. However, it was not until the early 1980s that their works on dependency theory were translated into English. Raul Prebisch, Andre Gunter Frank, and Fernando Henrique Cardoso, among others, have all actively contributed to theory building in this arena. For the dependency theorists, a dependency on the West—and in particular on "core" countries—keeps nations from developing to their true potential. These scholars termed developing nations "periphery" countries, which provide raw goods and services to their core partners but remain in a state of dependency (and, most often, poverty). The terms "core" and "periphery" are replaced by some dependency theorists by "metropolitan" and "satellite." External factors determine the degree to which a country can develop. These factors can be multinational corporations, as well as development financiers like the World Bank, the International Monetary Fund, and even international commodity markets.

Infrastructure and other internal elements were rarely identified as items that prevented development. Within the dependency theory model, educational systems based on Western capitalist models fostered continuation of a status quo in which elites in the periphery countries carried out the management functions of companies in the host countries. The language of dependency theorists often reflects a focus on class and strong criticism of capitalism.

We see that dependency theorists wish to redress the inequality among nations and to find remedies to increase the ability of less powerful nations to make decisions that are not dependent on First World nations. The basic tenets of dependency theory are these:

1. Developing nations must follow their own paths to industrialization; their history and context prevent them from industrializing in an identical manner to the United States and Europe.
2. The state must play a key role in development, particularly with respect to critical industries like steel and petroleum.
3. The state must enact large tariffs in order to protect domestic industries from foreign competition until they are stable.
4. Foreign investments must be severely restricted or strategically managed.
5. Any development plans enacted must be clearly in the national interest.
6. Investment in agriculture, particularly as a monocrop export, should be discouraged.
7. The core/periphery relationship must shift to a more equal relationship.

Reflected in all of these principles is a grounding within the nation-state. Dependency theorists do not believe that assistance can come only from outside the country. They find that dependence on external, powerful nations keeps countries from truly developing. They are supportive of nationalizing energy and mineral-exploration companies. Early attempts in Iran in the 1950s to nationalize the oil industry, as well as the policies of late Venezuelan president Hugo Chávez, are examples of development decisions that fall more closely within the parameters of dependency theory.

Bryant and White suggest that "dependency theorists insist upon going behind events and leaders to determine the use and abuse of power, whose interests are being served, and what alternatives exist" (1982, 12). Many of these scholars grounded their early work in classic Marxism (as distinguished from Marxist-Leninism), drawing in particular on explanations of scarcity. Bryant and White make it quite clear, however, that there is disagreement among Marxist scholars over the role of scarcity in preventing development. As with any theory, there are strong and weak versions. Radical dependency theorists draw consistently from Marxist theory. More moderate dependency theorists are more willing to work with multinational companies and foreign investment as long as the state keeps close tabs on them. Whether these ideas of dependency appeal to you or not, one dimension is relevant for further study: Michael Hamnett, Douglas Porter, Amarjit Singh, and Krishna Kumar (1984) explore how a dependence on the Global North to generate theories that are used around the world is a present-day extension of dependency theory.

Critics of dependency theory often focus on the degree to which external core countries are given all the blame for a lack of development and suggest that this outward focus should also have an internal component. They argue it is somewhat simplistic to assume there are no internal conditions that, by themselves, prevent development. We even see evidence of attempts to include a broad range of factors by one of dependency theory's earliest architects, Fernando Henrique Cardoso, the former president of Brazil. Like Inkeles, Cardoso acknowledges that local context may determine how to resolve dependency issues; for example, one country may need to renegotiate debt, while another may simply need an infusion of resources into the human sector.

Cardoso shifted ideologies drastically following his work as a chief architect of dependency theory. When Cardoso became president of Brazil in 1995, he bowed to conservative fiscal measures to help the country work its way out of debt, choosing more traditional neoliberal strategies to implement. If you hold a particular belief, it is easy to criticize an individual who moves away from it. However, pragmatism often pushes leaders to compromise.

It is important to understand that dependency theory is only one of a handful of development theories that were created outside of the Global North and that there are scholars today who continue to use this theory to account for inequality. For those interested in the study of language as a commodity—assessing, for example, how language can be used as a "carrot" or a "stick" in development—see Robert Phillipson, who uses dependency theory in his book *Linguistic Imperialism* (1992) to provide a fascinating account of how the British Council manipulated English as a commodity throughout Asia.

World-Systems Theory

Immanuel Wallerstein is the chief architect of world-systems theory. His most seminal work in this area occurred between 1974 and 1976. World-systems theory focuses on the nature of inequality but does not use the nation-state as the primary locus of control; nor does it hold up highly industrialized nations as markers of development. This theory outlines the role of labor movements and social democratic movements in redressing inequality. Wallerstein's theory was characterized by Daniel Chirot and Thomas Hall "as a direct attack against Modernization theory" (1982, 81). Ronan Van Rossem (1996) sees it as a powerful theory that can be used to compare development as it occurs in different places. Many scholars characterize world-systems theory as a subset of dependency theory, but others emphasize the depth of its links not only to Marxist economics but also to the social analysis of the French Annales school. Scholar Fernand Braudel (1972–73) distinguishes it from dependency theory. One contribution that is clearly Wallerstein's alone is the concept of "semi-periphery" countries. Semi-periphery countries possess attributes of both core and periphery countries. They are key industrializing nations in the global economy and are located physically between core and periphery countries, thus allowing them to play vital mediating roles (cf What are semi-periphery countries?). Wallerstein suggests the term is critically important and should be used along with the "core" and "periphery" standards of dependency theory explored above. What is perhaps most significant about the world-systems theory is that current political, economic, and social researchers have been able to adapt a number of its tenets to contemporary analysis—both quantitative and qualitative—and avoid many of the commonly denounced weaknesses of dependency theory.

The Present

Since the 1990s, there has been no dominant development paradigm. At the macro level, neoliberal economic policies have governed the allocation of funding for many projects. Former World Bank chief economist Joseph Stiglitz (2003, 74) terms this "market fundamentalism." These policies are those characterized as Washington Consensus policies and described in chapter 3. In a later volume, Stiglitz (2007, 27) summarizes the five key elements of the Washington Consensus strategies for development as "minimizing the role of government, emphasizing privatization, trade and capital market liberalization, and deregulation." Neoliberal prescriptions for development adhere to the five principles listed above, as well as the following: strong promotion of private initiatives for investment and management; privatization of government-owned monopolies for increased efficiency; and adoption of structural adjustment programs. Stiglitz argues that in general, Washington Consensus views and neoliberal views do not adequately emphasize equity, nor do they watch out for the interests of the poorest members of a nation-state. An alternative view would "put more emphasis on employment, social justice, and non-materialistic values such as the preservation of the environment than do those who advocate a minimalist role for government" (28).

José Cuesta suggests that theories of development that focus solely on what he terms either "economicist" or "culturalist" theories are insufficient. He maintains that "less ambitious theories connecting concrete cultural aspects, such as trust and association participation in communities, have more convincingly estimated a significant and positive impact on economic welfare" (2004, ii).

Andrew Natsios looks at the relationship between development strategies and the military. In areas particularly destabilized such as Afghanistan and Iraq, Natsios argues that "the success of military strategy and the success of development policy have become mutually reinforcing. Development cannot effectively take place without the security that armed force provides" (2015, 6). Both realists and neoliberals are supportive of this military-civilian partnership.

Postcolonialism and Feminism in Development Theory

Uma Kothari (2002) suggests that both postcolonialism and feminism have pushed development theorists to think outside the box in order to escape a Northamericentric and Eurocentric focus. While it is beyond the scope of this chapter to delve deeply into postcolonialism and its legacy, it is appropriate to identify key shifts that have occurred in explorations of women in development. Until the 1970s, women were typically invisible in development planning. Scholars separate three historical approaches in development planning: "women in development," "women and development," and "gender and development." The women in development perspective became popular during the time frame of the modernity paradigm discussed above. According to Eva Rathgeber, it "placed primary emphasis on egalitarianism and on the development of strategies and action programs aimed at minimizing the disadvantages of women in the productive sector and ending discrimination against them" (1990, 490). While it pushed for inclusion of women, the approach was trapped in the limitations of modernization theory and was not flexible enough to eventually draw upon more critical perspectives (491).

In the latter half of the 1970s, the women and development approach evolved, drawing more specifically on neo-Marxist and dependency dimensions. Even so, Rathgeber faults the model for neglecting to "undertake a full-scale analysis of the relationship between patriarchy, differing modes of production, and women's subordination and oppression" (1990, 493).

Finally, in the 1980s the gender and development approach emerged. Within this perspective, the agency of women in both productive and reproductive dimensions of their lives is accounted for. The underlying theoretical paradigm has been socialist feminism. Unlike the other two approaches, however, it has been difficult to build into already occurring programs. Rathgeber suggests that "it demands a degree of commitment to structural change and power shifts that is unlikely to be found either in national or in international agencies" (1990, 495).

In summary, the theories of development that have been proposed so far have cracks that prevent them all—even the best-formulated ones—from performing completely as desired. There have been dominant development paradigms over the years, but no individual theory has yet found a corner on the truth. All development strategies are linked to their ideological underpinnings. Modernization theory presumes that all nations must develop in the same manner. Dependency theory concludes that the root causes of underdevelopment are primarily brought about by external forces. Human capital theory presumes that there is room at the top of the economic ladder for all who wish to get there. Neoliberal theory postulates that the free market and fiscal austerity will help any nation out of poverty. Federico Demaria and Ashish Kothari (2017) argue that even sustainable development is an oxymoron and look to move beyond the concept. Your task is to recognize the underpinnings of any development strategy that is proposed. If you find yourself in disagreement with a particular project, ask yourself what underlying tenets have led to it and consider the degree to which you agree with these tenets and why.

None of the theories outlined above has been able to truly ground sustainable development. However, the UN and other global agencies remain committed to the principles, policies, and actions that promote sustainability, as we have seen from the 2017 *Sustainable Development Goals Report*. Development has increasingly come to mean poverty alleviation rather than a broad national project. This is clearly reflected in the UN's goals and the rise of NGOs over the state (Leopoldo Rodriguez, personal communication, January 23, 2019) .

Having focused briefly on common development frameworks, we can now move to a more practical exploration of development. We first explore the relationship of debt to development. We then look at the role of microfinance in development and conclude with a case study from Nepal.

Relationship of Debt to Development

As discussed in chapter 3, structural adjustment programs proposed by the World Bank and the IMF are frequent linchpins in restructuring debt and repayment plans. Such plans generally call for a decrease in spending on the social sector, an increase in foreign investment, and shifts in subsidies. Since the 1980s—generally agreed to be the starting point of the debt crisis—structural adjustment programs have dominated perspectives on debt management. James Hayes-Bohanan (2007) profiles plans from the 1980s by U.S. Treasury secretaries James Baker and Nicolas Brady to manage debt. In 1985 Baker proposed a plan to extend loans to countries that agreed to three conditions: privatization of state enterprise, shifts in subsidies, and opening to foreign investment. Roughly 80 percent of the largest debtor nations complied with the plan. In 1989 Brady proposed that private banks reduce their claims against many less-developed nations and that the IMF and World Bank use new funding to multilateralize the debt. Hayes-Bohanan reiterates that the neoliberal approach discussed by Stiglitz is still another type of structural adjustment. He goes on to explore ways of relieving debt, including debt-equity swaps and debt-for-nature swaps.

One forum that attracted a great deal of attention was Jubilee 2000, a program to forgive or cancel debt among the world's poorest nations. For example, at the G8 meeting in Gleneagle, Scotland, in 2005, a decision was made to grant debt relief to eighteen of the poorest nations in the world: Benin, Bolivia, Burkina Faso, Ethiopia, Ghana, Guyana, Honduras, Madagascar, Mali, Mauritania, Mozambique, Nicaragua, Niger, Rwanda, Senegal, Tanzania, Uganda, and Zambia (Stiglitz 2007, 227, 347).

While there have been additional calls to extend this type of debt forgiveness, much of the impetus behind Jubilee 2000 has subsided. A review of the program's website (http://www.jubileeusa.org) details current efforts and activities. A European perspective on debt is available from EURODAD (http://www.eurodad.org), the European network on debt and development. The four principles it calls for are "a binding set of standards to define and ensure responsible lending and borrowing; an independent and fair procedure for debt resolution, which should assess the legitimacy and the sustainability of countries' debt burdens; a human rights based approach to debt sustainability; and cancellation of unsustainable and unjust debts."

Microfinance

While country-level policies were being designed and implemented at the macro level, solutions to poverty were also being proposed and implemented at local levels. The best known of these is a microfinance model designed by Muhammad Yunus, a Bangladeshi economist honored with the Nobel Peace Prize in 2006 for his design of the Grameen Bank. The descriptive information that follows presents essentially a positive assessment of the model. Lamia Karim (2008) argues that even though the vernacular press in Bangladesh outlines problems with the model, Westerners do not typically access the information. She terms the Grameen Bank "symbolic capital," arguing that its "latest triumph winning the 2006 Nobel Peace Prize . . . operates as a form of governmentality and authorizes what can be said about the Grameen Bank" (2008, 25). Hugh Sinclair (2014) further addresses this. As you read the section below, try to identify positive and negative dimensions of this type of finance.

Yunus opened the Grameen Bank, the first microfinance bank, in Bangladesh in 1983. It was designed to assist poverty-stricken individuals without collateral to acquire very small loans that were typically too small for ordinary banks to deal with. The ordinance that allowed the bank's creation was ratified by the Bangladeshi parliament and stipulated that "the Bank shall provide credit with or without collateral security in cash or in kind, for such term and subject to such conditions as may be prescribed, to landless persons for all types of economic activity, including housing" (Dowla and Barua 2006, 17). Borrowers were able to take out a loan for one year and were required to make weekly payments, typically after the Friday prayer, when they were assembled in a group. The group formation became a key dimension of the Grameen Bank; groups of five individuals with comparable incomes and trust in each other formed the backbone of the lending scheme. These groups were generally made up of women who went through a training process, elected officers, and remained committed to a social charter that specified "Sixteen Decisions" they would abide by. These "decisions" covered dimensions of health, housing, agriculture, and even marriage contracts, all subsumed under four principles: discipline, unity, courage, and hard work (55). This microfinance model has been

> Michael Todaro (1989) suggests that three elements are critical to a development strategy: "life sustenance," "self-esteem," and "freedom from servitude." Think about which one of these three seems the most important to you and why.

duplicated in hundreds of settings around the world. Over the span of one decade, the Grameen Bank's percentage of borrowers moving out of poverty increased roughly 5 percent each year. In 1997 only 15.1 percent of borrowers had moved above the poverty line one year after receiving a loan, while by 2005, 58.5 percent of borrowers were above the poverty line (43). However, as Karim (2008) observes, while lending to women increased repayment, the money frequently ended up in the pockets of men due to domestic gender relations, something that Grameen ignores.

The Grameen Bank uses specific measures to determine changes in poverty levels of its borrowers. They are very functional measures of development and correspond to a large number of the UN Millennium Development Goals (Dowla and Barua 2006, 42). The measures include type of house (tin-roofed), type of sleeping arrangement (cots or beds), water purity, attendance by children at primary school, hygienic latrines, adequate clothing, mosquito netting, fruit trees or gardens for additional income, food security, ability to pay reasonable doctor bills, and a balance in a savings account. It had enough successes for Yunus and others to launch a model termed Grameen II both in Bangladesh and in other countries (Dowla and Barua 2006). It remains to be seen whether this model can better protect women and address true structural inequality.

We now turn to a case study in Lekali, Nepal. It presents both a disaster and a development issue from the perspective of an insider, an individual who found a way to directly assist the community he belonged to. This case study shares his words and demonstrates an example of "human-centered design" (DevExplains 2016) This is a model being used currently in much development work around the world. It involves more direct agency and solicitation of input from those affected by both problems and proposed changes.

Case Study: Lekali, Nepal

On April 25, 2015, an earthquake of 7.8 magnitude struck Nepal. The epicenter was outside of the capital city of Kathmandu and was the largest earthquake to strike there since 1934. More than 8,000 people were killed and 28 million people "were left in need" (Quick Facts, 2015). A quarter of the country's population was rendered vulnerable as a result of displacement and damage to critical infrastructure. As aid agencies rushed in, conflicts among prospective donors, government agencies, and local stakeholders affected the implementation of assistance.

More than sixty countries and the Vatican sent aid in the form of search and rescue teams, financial assistance professional recovery managers, NGO teams, food, and airplanes to evacuate citizens of other countries (McCarthy 2015). Great Britain was the largest bilateral aid donor. Some speculate this may be due to its historic relationship with India and strong connection to Nepal via the Gurkha soldiers and mountaineering (AndrewRusso, personal communication, January 10, 2019). The United States sent roughly $10 million (USD) in aid, Australia AUD$5 million, and China $3.3 million (USD) (McCarthy 2015). (For an infographic on the earthquake that breaks down Great Britain's aid response, see Coughlin 2015.)

Damaged infrastructures made it difficult to deliver aid. As in many recovery missions, competition among donor agencies—international, local, and regional—did not always allow efficient delivery of needed assistance. One small community, Bhirkhune, located twenty-one miles northwest of Kathmandu, worked with individuals to implement a recovery plan. The success of this plan was not originally due to outside NGOs but rather to the personal relationship between a young American, Andrew Russo, MPA, who had been working with a coffee plantation there and a community leader, Mingma Dorji Sherpa, and his family managing the coffee plantation.

The Lekali Coffee Company had headquarters in Kathmandu for the management and marketing of roughly 10,000 pounds of specialty coffee for international consumption (Andrew Russo, personal communication, January 10, 2019). The coffee plantation, a small 3.5-hectare family-owned estate located near the Himalayan slopes, sustained a community of roughly ten full-time employees with a harvest surge upwards of fifty, their families, and villagers in the surrounding areas. Mingma Dorji Sherpa, in a first-person narrative used with his permission, remembers the following from that day:

Map 2 Nepal

Unforgettable 2016 Earth Quake in Nepal: it was right after lunch the huge shaking took place and we knew this was an earthquake, rumbling strange sound everyone in the kitchen we struggle so hard to run out to safe place but our foot hardly move, it was shaking very badly and somehow struggled to come out from the house. We thought the house is going to crumble in a minute and the concrete roof is going to fall over us and we get killed inside. We see our own very structured house dancing, my car parked in the garage moves even the hand brakes are on, the ground shakes and we hear rumbling sound below, shouting, crying from every direction. The ground was boiling underneath which we can feel, we all sat down on the ground in front of the house. The aftershocks was in every 5 to 8 minutes. Our body shakes and not ready to hold your tea cups for many days and months. We can imagine what happen in the Lekali Coffee farmplace and families who lived there and watched their stone-made house crumbled in a minute.

We received a call from Lekali field staff and explained us about the situation: We asked what happen is happened, but what are most needed helps for the people and we prepared everything that our staff has update us. Without any delay back in Kathmandu, we mobilized our resources and we loaded the truck with supplies and relief mate-

> rial right next day to the village. The relief material mainly tents, tarps, plastic rolls, medicines, blankets, mattress, food supplies like rice, lentil, salt, butter, oil, spices, chili powder, sugar and lot many other daily kitchen items enough for all the family for 7 to 10 days.

A documented immediate need was for corrugated metal sheets to serve as temporary roofs at first and as rebuilding material later. The demand far outpaced supply, and Mingma contacted American Andrew Russo, then living in Seattle, for some creative and efficient assistance. Andrew had been working for Caffe Ladro and the Specialty Coffee Association and had already made a visit to Nepal. Additionally, he was in contact with groups of trekkers, particularly a group connected to REI (Recreational Equipment, Inc.) who had used Mingma's trekking company for an expedition in 2013. This set of contacts, along with coffee aficionados attracted to the niche market of high Himalayan coffee, became a funding base. When communities needed immediate funds, Andrew worked to set up a bank account and began asking for assistance on the Lekali website. The overall response raised enough funds for everyone in the village who needed tarps and corrugated sheets; they could come to Katmandhu to the Lekali main office to receive the materials. Mingma continues in his account: "The villager in the coffee area deeply touched by our help and immediate action. We gave them hope and encouraged them not to lose their energy and keep their good spirits high. I think what Andrew and Lekali did was very best. This is what we human around the world should do in the future."

As of December 2018, Lekali Coffee was searching for a new site with better access to water, one that will better meet the needs of a larger number of families. The new site will allow more young people who had previously left the area to remain. Mingma explains:

> Not having the younger people working in their paddies, most of the families left their land not producing any grain or food. Lekali Coffee therefore wanted to come to this area and bring new ideas of growing coffee. Coffee is cash crop for the people in future too, with the knowledge Lekali can be a great help for the whole community and region in future we thought. Site inspection has happened, plans have been made to plant shade trees, develop the irrigation system, prepare the land using organic manure, build the nursery, and establish a good road to the farm.

Check the Lekali website to see what has been completed: https://lekali coffee.com/.

In this brief case study, we see large nation-state-based and private development organizations sweeping in after a major disaster, along with Nepali-based government assistance. However, since 25 percent of the population was affected, local and regional infrastructures were insufficient to actually get the corrugated panels to those who needed them. A partnership of trust and faith allowed Mingma to reach out and Andrew to work to develop a plan for immediate assistance. This local-to-global approach based on the relationship between Mingma and Andrew actually served an entire community better than other forms of assistance.

Conclusion

This chapter has introduced you to various perspectives on what it means for a country to develop and to be developed. We have seen the strengths and weaknesses of most of the models that have captured the attention of the West and have suggested that indicators of development vary from one ideology to the next. There is a question of whether poverty reduction strategies are the same as or should substitute for the notion of development (Rowden 2011). In our earlier chapters on globalization, we looked at policies and institutions that both promote change and sometimes increase inequality between nations. In the case of the development dichotomy, we have suggested that no country or policy has a corner on the truth. It is evident how even the smallest loans can make major differences in the lives of the most impoverished people throughout the world if the money truly goes to them, especially when their dignity is maintained and they are recognized for their strengths. We are connected to everyone around us. Pause now to think of sustainable dimensions of your life in the context of your neighborhood.

➤ VOCABULARY

Jubilee 2000
microfinance
Grameen Bank
core, periphery, and semi-periphery countries
women in development
women and development
gender and development

➤ DISCUSSION AND REFLECTION QUESTIONS

1 *How would you define the following pairs of terms: developed/under-developed; developed/developing; First World/Third World; and Global North/Global South? Which set of terms do you think best describes the world? Why?*

2 *What are Rostow's five stages of modernization?*

3 *What are two positive and two negative dimensions of the modernization questions that early theorists posed?*

4 *Why do you think neoliberal economic principles played such a key role in the global economy and, ultimately, in development practices in the decade of the 1990s?*

5 *What is the significance of the Sixteen Decisions of the Grameen Bank?*

6 *Why is it important to consider ethical dimensions of development decisions?*

7 *How do you perceive the relationship between globalization and development?*

8 *What is the relationship between personal development and community development?*

ACTIVITY 1: ANALYZE Examine the UN 2017 *Sustainable Development Goals Report*. Choose one of the goals that most appeals to you and read the full section in the report. Based on both the text and the infographics on the pages you examine, see if you can then find specific information about one or two countries using any sources available to you. In a brief paragraph, identify what has happened in the countries you have examined regarding the goals. Then identify one electronic means of continuing to follow what is happening there.

ACTIVITY 2: REFLECT Imagine that you are a young development worker employed by a nongovernmental organization in a country of your choice. The development theories your organization is working from to create its action policies are theories you disagree with or find fundamentally flawed. What would you do? What shouldn't you do?

ACTIVITY 3: EXTEND You have been introduced to the notion of microfinance in this chapter. The website Kiva (http://www.kiva.org/) is an interactive site that links potential lenders with entrepreneurs via the Internet. Go to this site and work your way through the introduction and description of its activities. Identify a country and entrepreneur you could imagine yourself partnering with. Identify the amount of money you are willing and able to invest. Now imagine that it is six months after your investment. Write a two-paragraph letter to the individual you have partnered with. Identify three things you would like to know about how his or her project has progressed. Include a message of hope and success for the partner.

References

Braudel, F. 1972–73. *The Mediterranean and the Mediterranean world in the age of Philip II*, 2 vol., trans. Sian Reynolds. London: Collins.

Bryant, C., and L. White. 1982. *Managing development in the Third World.* Boulder, Colo.: Westview Press.

Carnoy, M. 1974. *Education as cultural imperialism.* Boston: D. McKay.

Chirot, D., and T. Hall. 1982. World-system theory. *Annual Review of Sociology* 8:81–106.

Coughlin, R. 2015. Infographic: Nepal earthquake: UK aid response. Retrieved December 11, 2018, from https://www.gov.uk/government/news/nepal-earthquake-uk-aid-response.

Cowen, M., and R. Shenton. 2010. The invention of development. In *Development ethics,* edited by D. Gasper and A. L. St. Clair, 3–22. London: Routledge.

Cuesta, J. 2004. *From economicist to culturalist development theories: How strong is the relation between cultural aspects and economic development?* Working Paper Series No. 400. ORPAS Institute of Social Studies, The Hague–The Netherlands.

Dadzie, K. K. S. 1980. Economic development. *Scientific American* (0036–8733) 243:58.

Demaria, F., and A. Kothari. 2017. The post-development dictionary agenda: Paths to the pluriverse. *Third World Quarterly 38* (12): 2588–99. doi: 1080/01436597.2017.1350821.

DevExplains: What is human-centered design? 2016. YouTube. Retrieved January 2, 2019, from https://www.youtube.com/watch?v=obxtEqM2TQU.

Dowla, A., and D. Barua. 2006. *The poor always pay back: The Grameen II story.* Sterling, Va.: Kumarian Press.

Esteva, G. 1992. *Development. The development dictionary.* New York: Zed Books. Retrieved July 10, 2019, from development-dictionary-n-a-guide-to-knowledge-as-power-2nd-ed-2010-1.pdf.

Frank, A. G. 1970. *Latin America: Underdevelopment or revolution.* New York: Monthly Review Press.

———. 2002. *World accumulation, 1492–1789.* New York: Algora Publishing.

Goulet, D. 1971. *The cruel choice.* New York: Atheneum.

Hamnett, M., D. Porter, A. Singh, and K. Kumar. 1984. *Ethics, politics, and international social science research: From critique to praxis.* Honolulu: University of Hawaii Press.

Harbison, F. H., and C. A. Myers. 1964. *Education, manpower, and economic growth.* New York: McGraw-Hill.

———. 1965. *Manpower and education: Country studies in economic development.* New York: McGraw-Hill.

Hayes-Bohanan, J. 2007. International debt relief. Web page and PowerPoint presentation revised January 2007 from the Earth Sciences and Geography Club Lecture Series presentation "Global recession and the future of debt relief," February 2002. Retrieved July 17, 2010, from http://webhost.bridgew.edu/jhayesboh/debt.htm.

Inkeles, A., and D. H. Smith. 1974. *Becoming modern: Individual change in six developing countries.* Cambridge, Mass.: Harvard University Press.

Jubilee USA Network. n.d. Retrieved November 30, 2007, from http://www.jubileeusa.org/nc/home/front-page-news.html?print=1.

Karim, L. 2008. Demystifying micro-credit: The Grameen Bank, NGOs, and neoliberalism in Bangladesh. *Cultural Dynamics* 20 (5): 5–29.

Kothari, U. 2002. Feminist and postcolonial challenges to development. In *Development theory and practice: Critical perspectives,* edited by U. Kothari and M. Minogue, 35–51. Houndmills, Basingstoke, Hampshire, England: Palgrave.

Martinez-Vela, C. A. 2001. World systems theory. MIT. Retrieved December 21, 2018, from web.mit.edu/esd.83/www/notebook/WorldSystem.pdf.

McCarthy, N. 2015. Infographic: Earthquake funding in Nepal: The top 10 donors. [May 6.] Retrieved January 2, 2019, from https://www.forbes.com/sites/niallmccarthy/2015/05/06/earthquake-funding-in-nepal-the-top-10-donors-infographic/#4ff6dba9650d.

Natsios, A. 2015. *The nine principles of reconstruction and development.* Defense Technical Information Center. ADA486423. Retrieved September 5, 2015, from http://www.dtic.mil/get-tr-doc/pdf?AD=ADA486423.

Ojomo, E. 2017. Obsession with ending poverty is where development is going wrong. *The Guardian,* February 8. Retrieved December 13, 2019, from https://www.theguardian.com/global-development-professionals-network/2017/feb/08/obsession-with-ending-poverty-is-where-development-is-going-wrong.

Phillipson, R. 1992. *Linguistic imperialism.* Oxford: Oxford University Press.

Quick facts: What you need to know about the Nepal earthquake. 2015 [April 26; updated March 14, 2016]. Retrieved November 7, 2019, from https://www.mercycorps.org/articles/nepal/quick-facts-what-you-need-know-about-nepal-earthquake.

Rafferty, J. n.d. Nepal earthquake of 2015. *Encyclopedia Britannica Online*. Retrieved January 2, 2019, from https://www.britannica.com/topic/Nepal-earthquake-of-2015.

Rathgeber, E. 1990. WID, WAD, GAD: Trends in research and practice. *Journal of Developing Areas* 2:489–502.

Rogers, E. M. 1974. Communication in development. *Annals of the American Academy of Political and Social Science* 412:44–54. doi: 10.1177/000271627441200106.

———. 1976. Communication and development: The passing of the dominant paradigm. *Communication Research* 3 (2): 213–40. doi: 10.1177/009365027600300207.

Rostow. W. 1959. The stages of economic growth. *Economic History Review* 12 (1): 1–16.

Rowden, R. 2011. Poverty reduction is not development. *The Guardian*, January 10. Retrieved December 13, 2018, from https://www.theguardian.com/global-development/poverty-matters/2011/jan/10/poverty-reduction-industrialisation.

Sinclair, H. 2014. Does microfinance really help the poor? *The Guardian*, October 8. Retrieved December 21, 2018, from https://www.theguardian.com/global-development-professionals-network/2014/oct/08/developing-countries-informal-economies-microfinance-financial-inclusion.

Stiglitz, J. 2003. *Globalization and its discontents*. New York: W. W. Norton.

———. 2007. *Making globalization work*. New York: W. W. Norton.

Todaro, M. 1989. *Economic development in the Third World*. New York: Longman.

United Nations. 2007a. *Millennium Development Goals Report*. Retrieved November 11, 2007, from http://www.un.org/milleniumgoals.

———. 2017. *Sustainable Development Goals Report 2017*. Retrieved December 12, 2018, from https://unstats.un.org/sdgs/files/report/2017/ TheSustainableDevelopmentGoalsReport2017.pdf.

Van Rossem, R. 1996. The world system paradigm as general theory of development: A cross-national text. *American Sociological Review* 61 (3): 508–27.

What are semi-periphery countries? Retrieved November 8, 2019, from https://www.worldatlas.com/articles/what-are-semi-periphery.html.

World Bank. 2003. *World development report: Making services work for poor people*. Retrieved December 18, 2018, from https://openknowledge.worldbank.org/handle/10986/5985.

Yunus, M. 2008. *Creating a world without poverty*. New York: Public Affairs.

SEVEN **Security**

➤ SYNOPSIS

How policy makers and citizens define security depends upon how they perceive particular threats, the historical context in which they live, and whether they focus on dangers to the nation-state or to the individual. As such, our understanding of the notion of security is framed by our membership in particular communities and ideologies. Some modern scholars have been particularly influential in determining how Western nations define their security. Flash points around the world may cause individual nation-states and global organizations to respond in particular ways to fears of terrorism, nuclear proliferation, and invasion. At the same time, technology is changing security issues, forcing societies to make judgments about privacy, intelligence gathering, and drone strikes.

➤ SCAFFOLDING

As you read through this chapter, think about how you would answer each of the questions below.

Are you familiar with the terms "Realism" or "human security"? In what context did you learn about them?

What do you remember about the development of the nation-state from chapter 2 ("History")?

Why has this chapter incorporated perspectives about the U.S. war with Iraq from Middle East sources? Where would you go to find European, Latin American, Asian, or African perspectives on this issue?

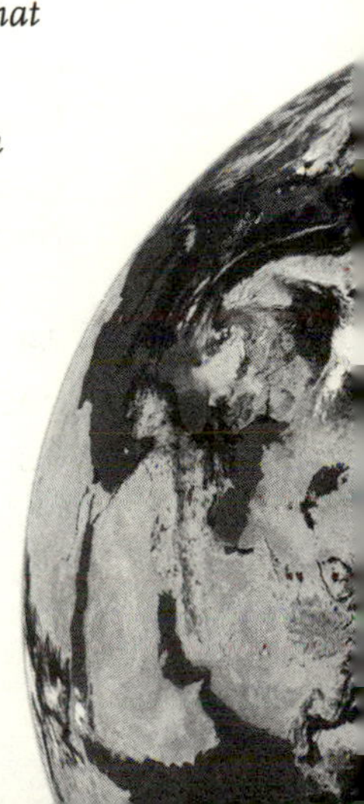

Are you willing to trade your privacy online or during phone calls in return for greater security?

What do you think is the greatest security threat that concerns you personally?

➤ CORE CONCEPTS

How do differing perspectives on the ways nation-states and international governing bodies can keep individuals safe affect policy decisions in times of terror or insecurity?

How have new technologies and globalization changed the threats we face?

How do we balance the need for security against the right to privacy?

The first task of every government is to ensure the security of its citizens from outside threats. Any government that fails in this task faces not only the risk of external takeover but also the loss of legitimacy among its people. But which threats are so important that they are security issues? In France in 1938 or Kuwait in the 1990s, it was easy to define the threat. In other periods, however, nations might discern the danger differently. People in Angola might be extremely concerned about the threat of landmines laid decades before, while someone in Caracas, Venezuela, might be frightened of crime or hunger. Europeans might worry that the National Security Agency of the United States is monitoring their phone calls or e-mail; if they live in the Baltic states or Georgia, they may fear a Russian invasion and believe that the United States is the ally most likely to preserve their independence. For people living on a small Pacific island, the greatest threat to national security might be a rising sea level. For other nations, it might be climate refugees fleeing from environmental change. How people perceive security is defined by the historical and national context. For many years after September 11, 2001, the primary U.S. security threat was terrorism. But with Russian aggression in Ukraine, North Korea's nuclear development, and potential conflicts in the South China Sea, this may no longer be the case. Ultimately, what people fear determines how they define security, and a number of related issues follow from this axiom. Where do citizens look to obtain security? How has the definition of security changed through time? And how do you balance the reality of threats against the importance of human rights?

Security from the Emergence of the Nation-State to Realism

Some scholars would argue that security represents the most basic international issue. It was the central theme of the Greek historian Thucydides, who sought to understand the Peloponnesian War, the greatest conflict of his era. He argued that the war began because of the rising power of Athens, which caused Sparta to act before it could be overwhelmed. His account shaped Western interpretations of international relations for 2,400 years (Monten 2006). In the millennia that followed, a series of thinkers, such as Niccolò di Bernardo dei Machiavelli and Thomas Hobbes, wrestled with the same issues, and their work continues to underpin modern scholarship on international affairs (Sobek 2005). When Renaissance and Enlightenment thinkers in Europe tried to understand the origins of the state, they concluded that its most fundamental reason for existence was to provide security for its citizens from outside threats. People came together and gave up certain freedoms in order to have security from both internal threats, such as criminals, and external threats, such as invasion (Hobbes [1651] 1982). At the same time, these European thinkers lived in a world in which the nation-state system was relatively new. Their work represented an effort to understand an emerging kind of state.

Security was not always defined solely in terms of threats to the nation-state and its sovereignty. In the Middle Ages, political units were defined by dynasties, which meant that people's allegiances could change with a royal marriage. Whether in Angevin England or medieval Italy, political boundaries often did not align with ethnic groups. Authority was frequently fractured or divided. Under the feudal system, a powerful leader could be bound to more than one overlord. People owed political allegiance to their king (or kings), but moral and religious authority was bestowed in a pope. Additionally, there was an ideal of chivalry in which the bond of knighthood appeared more important than those of language or homeland. An English knight probably believed that he had more in common with a Spanish lord than an English peasant. Nationhood did not determine political authority or the role of the state (Rapley 2006, 96–99; see also Ganshof 1971).

This reality began to change in 1648. In that year, the Peace of Westphalia ended the Thirty Years' War in Europe while giving rise to the modern nation-state. As Enlightenment authors sought to explain this new state of affairs, they established ideas that have shaped much subsequent writing on security, which has focused both on the nation-state and issues relevant to the developed world. There are good reasons for this fact. The nation-state system has proved to be an enormously successful construct. As formal empires waned after World War II, all newly freed regions adopted the nation-state system. For this reason, security was defined in terms of the survival of the nation-state and its ability to maintain its sovereignty rather than in terms of the security of its people from violence or death. Internal conflicts and economic issues consequently received little attention as security issues because they rarely threatened the nation-state at the systemic level.

Europe was also the center of global political power for the latter half of the millennium, which meant that security was perceived through the lens of the Great Power competitions, with a focus on armed conflict. When power shifted to the United States and the Soviet Union with the onset of the Cold War, the two parties viewed all security issues in terms of their contest. Because even local conflicts could draw in either power (consider Vietnam or Afghanistan) and potentially escalate to nuclear war, Great Power competition remained the key issue. Security continued to be thought of as a question defined by relationships between states. Scholarship in the field was dominated by a theory called Realism, which reflected this context and remains the dominant paradigm in the field.

Realism

Realism is a complex and rich theoretical perspective that traces its roots back to the work of Thucydides, Machiavelli, and Hobbes (Jackson and Sorenson 1999, 72–76). But the British author E. H. Carr first articulated the theory in the twentieth century, as he sought to explain why Europe was again sliding into a world war in his book *The Twenty Years' Crisis* (Jackson and Sorenson 1999, 41–42). Because of the complexity and depth of this literature, it is difficult to briefly summarize the meaning of Realism, which has developed and evolved over time. Despite its many interpretations, however, Realism as a worldview generally has certain characteristics (68–70). Its proponents typically view security as the key issue in international affairs. They often share a pessimistic view of both human nature and the inevitability of war. Within this theoretical framework, the key factor in international politics is the state. And one of the axioms of Realism is that the international system is anarchic, in the sense that there is no superior power to which an aggrieved nation can appeal. Realists tend to doubt the power of international law or the international community to limit conflict. Although nations may cloak their actions in moral rhetoric, they act based on their national interests, and it is unrealistic to expect them to do otherwise. Realists argue that states therefore have no choice but to engage in the strategies of realpolitik, an approach to diplomacy that emphasizes pragmatic methods to advance national interests, such as alliance formation and power balancing. Any state that fails to do so may be moral, but it may not survive. (For a brief description of Realism, see Sheehan 2005, 5–23.) This theory has evolved considerably through the work of such authors as Hans Morgenthau and Kenneth Waltz, but most of its key ideas have remained intact (Morgenthau 1948; Waltz 1959; Jackson and Sorenson 1999, 51–53, 76–80, 84–89).

This doctrine had been challenged by other theories, such as liberalism, which stresses the importance of international institutions and international law in shaping behavior. This more optimistic vision argues that organizations such as the United Nations could create a new global framework to avoid the devastating warfare of the twentieth century. Progress is possible (Jackson and Sorenson 1999, 108–11). Constructivists, in contrast, argue that the international order is defined by identities that result from history and experience. The international order is not given but rather historically contingent; that is, it could change (238–40). Both theories are more complex than this thumbnail sketch can capture. But they each seek to mount a challenge to Realism, which they argue focuses excessively on conflict and oversimplifies a complex reality.

Other political scientists—such as Robert Keohane and Joseph Nye—have mounted sophisticated critiques of Realism as a doctrine because actors other than states are important in international affairs, nations are interdependent in complex ways, and military force is not always the key factor in international relations (Keohane and Nye 2001, 20–32). But during the Cold War, most policy makers drew heavily on Realism because its emphasis on Great Power politics—the balance of power, alliances, and military strategy—seemed to accord with an era defined by global tension (Sheehan 2005, 6, 23). Then, almost overnight, the Soviet Union collapsed. Some scholars argued that in an era defined by globalization, the meaning of security needed to be rethought. It is not clear, however, that Realism has been superseded as a doctrine.

The End of the Cold War

In the early 1980s, it was difficult to imagine that the Cold War might end. As Philip Gordon notes, the Reagan administration had warned that the United States and its allies were falling behind in the military competition with the Soviets and that vast resources were needed to keep up (2007, 56). Even after the fact, many people could not believe that the Cold War had actually ended (56). The collapse of the Soviet Union brought a period of euphoria in the West. Because global security threats had been viewed in this context, it seemed that the end of this period would eliminate not only the risk of nuclear annihilation but also many of the conflicts between client states. During this time, there was also a wave of democratization, as military regimes collapsed throughout Latin America—in part because the United States no longer bolstered authoritarian governments based on their anti-Communism. But there was also a larger process of democratization taking place, as South Africa ended apartheid and Eastern Europe adopted democracy, as did the Philippines. All of these factors, combined with the rise of the European Union, created a sense of optimism. Francis Fukuyama wrote a much-cited article titled "The End of History?," which proposed that the era of global competition was over, as no great ideological questions remained to be addressed: "We may be witnessing the end of history as such: that is, the endpoint of mankind's ideological evolution and the universalization of Western liberal democracy as the final form of human government" (1989, 4). There was a great deal of discussion of the peace dividend. Military spending fell across the globe.

There was no theoretical framework in place to shape how policy makers interpreted this new era. A new mood of isolationism washed over the United States and, to a lesser extent, Canada and Europe. While developed countries appeared to be transitioning into a more stable future, this was not the case for nations in the Global South, some of which seemed to be sliding into anarchy. There was little concern in rich countries about this, however, because it appeared that Western nations had the security to disengage from poor regions of the world, which might be chaotic or dangerous. In the future, it seemed that the world might divide into two areas, which Max Singer and Aaron Wildavsky called "zones of peace" and "zones of turmoil" (1993, 8). In practice, these zones were defined by their wealth. In the developed world, few ideological questions divided the Great Powers, and ties of democracy mitigated conflict. Political scientists spoke of the democratic peace hypothesis, which states that democracies are less likely to go to war; that if they do go to war, they are less likely to fight other democracies; and that a world with more democracies likely would see less conflict (paraphrasing Mitchell et al. 1999, 771–72; see also Gleditsch and Ward 2000; O'Neal and Russett 1999; and Sheehan 2005, 32–42). In contrast, in the developing world, there appeared to be frequent conflicts over ethnic, nationalist, and resource issues, which had little meaning to key global actors: "While Europe enjoyed what John Gaddis (1986) termed the 'long peace' (the longest period in the post-Westphalia era without a major war among the major powers), conflicts in the Third World inflicted all but 176,000 of the 22 million battle deaths that occurred between 1945 and 1989" (Mason 2003, 19). In the developed world, there was a sense that combat in these areas might entail moral issues but no longer security questions.

The Challenge of Terrorism

Western nations, however, were not impervious to turmoil or violence. In conventional military terms, wealthy nations were untouchable, but rational opponents would not choose to launch a conventional attack. With new technologies such as the Internet, distance seemed to provide less security than in the past. The rise of globalization was fracturing the power of the state and empowering small substate actors—from Aum Shinrikyo, a Japanese cult that launched the sarin nerve gas attacks in Tokyo's subway, to Middle Eastern groups such as Al-Qaida and Hezbollah. While no state was likely to attack the United States, terrorists and other groups were not deterred. Throughout the 1990s and into the new century a series of attacks by terrorists foreshadowed the threat to the United States and Europe, from the failed effort to destroy the World Trade Center in 1992, to the bombing of the USS *Cole* in 2000 off the coast of Yemen. Several large-scale attacks were intercepted before they could be launched against the United States and its allies (9/11 Commission 2004, 59–73, 145–60).

The U.S. government responded to these strikes by using the legal apparatus, working with its partners in the developed world, and launching cruise missiles against terrorist training sites (9/11 Commission 2004, 73–86, 108–43; for why the United States turned from using a legal approach to dealing with terrorism militarily after September 11, 2001, see Shapiro 2007, 10–14). The legal approach was sometimes effective in leading to the arrest and imprisonment of people who carried out attacks. But the perpetrators were often willing to sacrifice their lives, and those who planned, financed, and supported the attacks often remained free overseas. The second attack on New York's World Trade Center took place less than a decade after the first. The United States and other Western nations might have overwhelming military power, but that alone did not isolate them from violence.

Human Security

As scholars, diplomats, and nation-states sought to grapple with this new security context, a new vision of security emerged. At the core of this approach was a new answer to the question "What is security?" The traditional response had been that security came from the nation-state, which held a monopoly on violence that it used not only to maintain internal order but also to protect its citizens from external threats. In this respect, security threats needed to be dealt with through the traditional tools of statecraft, such as alliances, deterrence, and war. But this argument appeared outdated to some scholars, who advanced an ideal called "human security" by arguing that threats should be defined by what endangers not only the state but also the individual. An example might be pandemic flu. A pandemic is an outbreak of an infectious disease that is not confined to a single region of the globe. Such an outbreak could not threaten the state, which would survive even the most devastating pandemic imaginable, but it could take the lives of hundreds of millions of people globally. It needed to be treated with the same seriousness as a potential bioterrorism attack. This represented a different way of looking at international security and how thinkers since the Enlightenment have defined it.

Although its intellectual roots may be traced to before the Cold War, human security first came to prominence after the United Nations Development Programme released a 1994 document titled the *Human Development Report* (Paris 2001, 89; MacFarlane and Khong 2006, 23–142). The document reflected the end of the Cold War and a new international environment in which the rising power of globalization seemed to decrease the importance of nation-states while also increasing the threat posed by nonstate actors such as Al-Qaida (Ripsman and Paul 2004). The growing importance of failed states, organized crime, environmental problems, and infectious disease also led to a reassessment of the security environment (Newman 2001; Axworthy 2004, 348). By shifting the focus from the state to the individual, a new perspective could concentrate resources on the threats killing the most people.

This argument gained traction in part because many small states were dissatisfied with the traditional military approach to security problems. These nations seized upon the idea of human security as a means to not only alleviate human suffering but also create an alternative political order. Their patronage gave great impetus to this new approach: "Among the most vocal promoters of human security are the governments of Canada and Norway, which have taken the lead in establishing a 'human security network' of states and nongovernmental organizations (NGOs) that endorse the concept" (Paris 2001, 87; Owen 2004, 378). Policy makers in these nations (as well as in Japan, Australia, and other Scandinavian nations) often felt that social and economic issues, especially poverty, underlay conflict (Thomas 2001; Kacowicz 2005, 123). An approach that dealt with crises only when they reached the level of open conflict was doomed to a reactive response; it could never take the initiative to prevent emergencies by resolving ethnic disputes, ending political grievances, or preventing economic conflicts (Monaghan 2008, B-8).

Proponents of this approach also argued that traditional Realism was irrelevant to the kind of violence faced by many people living in developing countries. For example, since 1945, most global conflicts had been civil wars, which accounted for most of the world's combat deaths (Mason 2003, 19). Yet traditional Realism gave little thought at all to civil wars or to the state's role as an agent of internal violence (Owen 2004, 375). There seemed to be a split between the widespread violence in the developing world and the focus on Great Power contests. From this perspective, Realism ignored key issues in developing nations, such as land mines, which represented both a security threat and an economic cost in many countries. For this reason, scholars began to question the utility of Realism: "To many, there is little doubt that (in and of itself) the traditional state-based security paradigm is failing in its primary objective—to protect people. Millions a year are killed by communicable disease, civil war, environmental disasters, and famine, none of which fall under the mandate of current security thinking" (374). By the 1990s, the idea of human security emerged as a major challenge to Realism.

One of the strengths of human security is that it recognizes that there can be a linkage between different forms of insecurity, so that threats can spill over from even the most remote regions to the global level. For example, in August 2018 an Ebola outbreak began in the Democratic Republic of the Congo. Even though a highly effective vaccine was available and health workers made Herculean efforts, over 1,700 people had died by July 2019.

Local authorities in the region, riven by warring factions, could not guarantee health workers' safety—the spread of conspiracy theories provoked attacks upon the very people working to vaccinate and protect the populace. Some NGOs even had to withdraw workers for a time, because staff had been killed or wounded. The end result was that many local people were not vaccinated, and some became sick and died. On July 17, 2019, the World Health Organization declared a Public Health Emergency of International Concern, after a case of Ebola appeared in the city of Goma. This particular experience shows that just as health cannot be separated from security, so too security impacts health. The strength of human security as an approach is that it posits that security threats are interrelated, so that one cannot focus only upon nation-states or military forces in isolation.

This new framework did not go unchallenged by realist authors, who argued that globalization had not fundamentally changed security issues and that states remained the key actors in security affairs (Ripsman and Paul 2004). Scholars such as Barry Buzan (2004, 369–70) suggested that the term "human security" was so broad that the phrase had little meaning and practically made every issue a security issue. Roland Paris similarly argued that the term was too vague to be useful to policy makers facing competing demands: "Human security is like 'sustainable development'—everyone is for it, but few people have a clear idea what it means" (Paris 2001, 88). He further suggested that the very vagueness of the concept allows it to unite people with widely different ideas: "The term, in short, appears to be slippery by design" (88; for an overview of the field, see Newman 2001).

Critics argued that this vagueness could be dangerous. For example, AIDS has been depicted as a security threat because it tends to undermine African militaries (which have high rates of HIV infection), which could lead to failed states (Elbe 2006, 121–22). This argument may have been intended to persuade the U.S. government to act by suggesting that this health question had security implications. But this hypothesis also presented a danger, according to Stefan Elbe: if HIV/AIDS became viewed as a military threat, it could then be fought according to the extent the disease impacted U.S. interests (119, 120, 128; see also Peterson 2002–3). This might warp the response to HIV, so that only those aspects of the pandemic that influenced "security" issues would receive attention and funding. What Elbe contended is that HIV was a serious moral issue in itself, regardless of how it impacted the United States.

Critics argue that human security needs boundaries; without them, all issues could become securitized (Shapiro 2007, 113; Owen 2004, 379).

These critics are also concerned that if poverty and development come to be defined as security issues, then militaries from developed nations will become involved in addressing them, which would expand their role in developing countries. If failed or failing states foster terrorism, should the armed forces of developed nations help with state making, or do other agencies have more expertise?

Partly for this reason, the perception of human security has been mixed within developing countries. Some leaders have welcomed a reframing of global priorities to give greater weight to their concerns and justify their requests for more resources. In other nations, leaders have worried that this framework might give European and North American nations the means to involve themselves in issues of national sovereignty: "Even some intended beneficiaries of the approach are skeptical of it. The Group of 77—the coalition of developing countries at the United Nations—tend to be deeply suspicious of human security, seeing it as part of a 'West against the rest' ideological push by countries of the North to impose alien values on the developing world" (Monaghan 2008, B-8). Human security is a concept that is viewed by some developing countries as a potential means of neocolonialism—that is, the maintenance of colonial relations after formal connections are severed. Despite these criticisms, human security has been an innovative area that has led to fresh work on security issues. It is also true that all emerging fields tend to face such ideological debates. Human security continues to attract attention because of rising concerns about organized crime, infectious disease, and the environment.

September 11 and Its Aftermath

These debates about the nature of security became critical after September 11, 2001. In the 1990s political scientist Samuel Huntington had argued that most conflicts took place along the "fault lines" between civilizations. Huntington claimed that wars could take place within a civilization (such as the struggle in the Democratic Republic of the Congo) but that these struggles do not threaten wider conflict. In contrast, conflicts between two civilizations—such as the West and Islam—have far greater potential for violence (Huntington 1996, 254–65). In the aftermath of the September 11 terror attack, the United States found itself in a clash of civilizations as widely debated as it was troubling. How should the United States understand the motivation of the people who attacked it? One study found that "55 percent of Jordanians and 65 percent of Pakistanis held favorable views of Bin Laden," the mastermind of the 9/11 attack (Shore 2006, 5; see also 9/11 Commission 2004, 375). This perspective confused many Americans. Was the United States' position in the Arab-Israeli conflict the determining factor in how the country was perceived abroad? Or did people lash out because the United States supported authoritarian leaders in the Middle East, while the Central Intelligence Agency had a sad history that included the overthrow of Iran's prime minister Mohammed Mossadegh in 1953? Did Islamic extremists associate the United States with globalization, Western secularism, and modernity, which they viewed as threatening? (For the association between the United States and globalization, see Keohane and Nye 2001, 234–35, 250.) Every scholar seemed to have a different opinion. At root was the question of whether it was U.S. actions or U.S. values that caused hostility toward the United States (Holsti 2008, 64). It was critical for U.S. citizens to understand how their nation was viewed in the Middle East.

Despite these debates and questions there was consensus in the West that the main base of Al-Qaida in Afghanistan had to be eliminated. Al-Qaida had found safety under the rule of the Taliban, a fundamentalist movement that had begun among students who promised to end the violence that followed the Soviet-Afghan war. The Taliban sheltered Osama Bin Laden and refused to give him up as the United States demanded in September 2001. In response, the United States joined with the Northern Alliance, whose leader, Ahmed Shah Massoud, had been assassinated by a suicide bomber on September 9, 2001, as Al-Qaida prepared to attack the United States. With support from both British and U.S. airpower, the Northern Alliance overran Taliban forces by December 2001, although Osama Bin Laden escaped U.S. and Afghan troops at the Battle of Tora Bora that same month.

After this invasion, there was a larger debate within the United States about the best means to respond to terrorism. One argument favored a defensive strategy, the broad outlines of which were articulated by the September 11 Commission (9/11 Commission 2004, 380–98; for a summary of the offensive/defensive debate, see Sloan 2005, 6–12). Ian Shapiro (2007), for example, argued that the West should adopt the same strategy of containment that it had followed during the Cold War. Countless authors have written that the "war on terror" is not winnable in a conventional sense. But as Philip Gordon notes, terrorism will not last forever (2007, 54). He suggested investing resources into strengthening the nation's defenses, much as the United States did against the Soviet Union. By securing their ports, tightening airport security, rebuilding public-health infrastructure, and improving intelligence, Western nations could address this threat. The funds needed would be a fraction of what the United States spent on the Iraq invasion: "As one analyst noted in *Mother Jones*, delayed security upgrades for subway and commuter rail systems could be paid for by twenty days' worth of Iraq war spending. Missing explosives screening for all U.S. passenger airlines could be covered by ten days' worth. Overdue security upgrades for 361 American airports could be covered by four days' worth" (Shapiro 2007, 58). The United States and its allies also needed to ensure that the focus on security neither bankrupted the nation nor caused the West to abandon its fundamental values (120).

The counterargument to this position came from neoconservatives such as David Frum (who wrote President George W. Bush's 2002 speech that coined the term "axis of evil") and Richard Perle (2003), as expressed in their book *An End to Evil: How to Win the War on Terror*. It is important to note that the arguments of the neoconservatives were diverse, as there were many different strands within this movement. But some key ideas stand out. The United States was the world's main military power, and conventional force still mattered. The United States needed to use this advantage to change the culture of the Middle East and to foster democracy in the region. At a time of extraordinary threats, neoconservatives suggested, the United States could not be bound by conventional rules. The government could not know when an attack with weapons of mass destruction (WMDs) was imminent (Frum and Perle 2003, 34). WMDs were biological, chemical, or nuclear weapons that were capable of causing immense casualties and could target civilians as readily as soldiers. Given the scale of this threat, old ideas of security did not apply (see Vice President Dick Cheney's comments in Shapiro 2007, 16). Failed states could not be ignored: "There are places where law truly has collapsed and evil has moved to exploit the void: Yemen, Somalia, Sierra Leone" (Frum and Perle 2003, 118). It was better to fight the terrorists abroad rather than face them in the United States' own territory. (For a critique of the "Bush Doctrine," see Shapiro 2007, 15–31.)

These politicians argued that the key was not to try to win an ideological contest but rather to promote democracy—except in places where "Islamists" might win, as in Algeria in 1995 (Frum and Perle 2003, 158–63). Terrorists could not survive without the support of states (231). From this perspective, the war on terror entailed a war on states. And it had to be fought, even if it angered the United Nations or caused the United States to lose support among naive allies (243–50, 270–71). Neoconservative arguments shaped the U.S. government's decision to attack Iraq in the face of widespread international opposition. (For neoconservative arguments regarding Iraq, see Bollyn 2004; and Project for the New American Century 1998.)

The U.S. invasion of Iraq took place without either a UN mandate or the support of the majority of the population of the United States' traditional allies. For example, even though Britain sent troops to fight alongside U.S. soldiers, most British people opposed their country's involvement. Before the invasion, more than 1 million people turned out for an antiwar rally in London (British Broadcasting Corporation 2003). And two contemporaneous polls found, first, that only 9 percent of the Britons polled favored invading Iraq without a supporting UN resolution and, second, that no more than 29 percent of respondents favored the invasion even with UN support (ICM Research 2003a and 2003b). These numbers would probably have been lower in almost any other European country and not dissimilar in many key U.S. ally nations in Asia and the Pacific. The outcome of the war was widely perceived to be a disaster. Although the U.S. quickly overthrew Saddam Hussein, it found no WMDs, and Iraqi society fractured into ethnic conflict. In Britain a subsequent government instituted the Chilcot Inquiry into Britain's involvement in the war, which found that there was no immediate threat from Saddam Hussein and that the invasion was not a last resort (Allen 2016).

In 2014 the terrorist organization Islamic State of Iraq and the Levant (ISIS, also known as Daesh) captured much of western Iraq, including major cities such as Mosul. This city was not retaken by the central Iraqi government until 2017. In 2015 the situation appeared so serious in Iraq that one expert wrote a paper suggesting that the United States might want to permit the country to be decentralized and possibly partitioned into different nations (Khedery 2015). The Iraqi government, at the time of this writing, has managed to beat back ISIS. The caliphate has been defeated on the battlefield, but whether it will survive as a guerrilla movement and terrorist organization is uncertain.

If anything, the situation in Afghanistan is worse. In August 2018 the Taliban launched a major offensive in Afghanistan and temporarily gained control of most of the strategic eastern city of Ghazni. They were soon pushed out, but the government is having difficulty controlling territory, even in major urban areas. As Douglas Wissing has pointed out (Reuters 2017), this is true despite the fact that the United States has committed more development funds to Afghanistan than it did to Europe after World War II through the Marshall Plan, and that in a country with a fraction of Western Europe's postwar population. In March 2018, approximately 15,000 U.S. troops remained in Afghanistan, seventeen years after September 11 (Burns 2018). The neoconservative plan has resulted in an endless war, with no clear exit plan after a generation. Kenneth Pollack (2016, 62) has even stated that the last time the Middle East had seen such turmoil was during the Mongol invasions. While perhaps exaggerated, it captures the sense that the region has faced exceptional turmoil since the millennium.

The Return of a Great Power War?

These regional conflicts continue to draw in outside nations and actors, as has been the case with the Syrian Civil War. This conflict began in 2011 as Arab populations throughout the region rose up against authoritarian rulers. In Syria the government sought to repress these protests with military force, which quickly pushed the country into its most devastating war of the modern era. The conflict quickly became a proxy war, in which the United States, Saudi Arabia, and some Gulf states supported the rebels, while Iran, Russia, and the nonstate actor Hezbollah supported the Syrian regime. By 2015 it appeared that the Syrian government might collapse, but substantial Russian involvement turned the tide of the war. The result has been a conflict that has destroyed cities, killed hundreds of thousands, and displaced millions. It has also led to a massive wave of refugees outside of Syria, seeking safety in Europe. This migration, in turn, has fed populist and nationalist movements within the European Union.

The conflict itself had many roots, including a terrible drought in the countryside. Still, this was perhaps less important than political factors that created an agrarian crisis (Selby 2018). But what was important about this crisis was that it provided a window into the nature of the current global order, in much the same manner that the Spanish Civil War did in the 1930s. At many points it has seemed—such as with the recent Turkish invasion of Kurdish territory in Syria's north—that a broader conflict could emerge from a political miscalculation.

The events in Syria point to the ongoing threat of a war involving Great Powers, but they have been perhaps less surprising than the Russian invasion of Crimea and involvement in eastern Ukraine. During the Cold War the United States and the Soviet Union engaged in many proxy wars in developing countries, but neither engaged in fighting within Europe itself.

It seemed that in Europe, at least, a new liberal order was limiting conflict, with the exception of the Balkan wars in the 1990s. In 2014, however, Russia annexed Crimea, which was only one part of a larger military engagement by Russia in the region. Despite European sanctions and pressure, the low-intensity contest has not ended. This struggle has raised serious questions within Europe about its relative military weaknesses and its belief that war would no longer involve major European states within the continent itself. The old liberal order in international affairs appears to be crumbling. Similarly, new technologies and the fear of terrorism have challenged old liberal beliefs, such as the right to privacy.

Surveillance and Privacy

In the aftermath of September 11, and with the further development of digital globalization, deep concerns about personal-privacy issues began to emerge. Modern technology has made it possible to monitor almost all aspects of a person's life. While most people are familiar with the CIA, before 9/11 far fewer Americans were aware of the National Security Agency (NSA), even though its budget was larger even then (Todd and Bloch 2003, 75). This organization is charged with monitoring communications and electronic surveillance. The scope of its activities is impressive, as Paul Todd and Jonathan Bloch describe. For instance, it routinely monitors international e-mails (43). But this is only the tip of the iceberg. Through a system called Echelon, the United States and its allies "intercept nonencrypted e-mail, fax, and telephone calls carried over the world's telecommunication systems" (44). Software designed in the United States allegedly contains openings that permit intelligence services to view the contents of computers (52). Legislative changes have also increased concerns that oversight over U.S. intelligence agencies has eroded. While there is always a balance between citizen's privacy and national security, the balance has swung decisively away from security.

All of these issues came to a head after Edward Snowden, a contractor for the American corporation Booz Allen Hamilton who had worked for the NSA, leaked information on U.S. intelligence activities in 2013. In particular, Snowden revealed information about the NSA's monitoring of both telephone calls and Internet traffic. Snowden contacted England's *Guardian* newspaper late in 2012 and continued leaking information through his departure from his job in May 2013. When the revelations became public, they created a media firestorm, and Snowden fled abroad to Hong Kong seeking political shelter. He ultimately received asylum in Russia, where he found work as a security official for a Russian social media company. Throughout his extended fight to seek asylum, Snowdon found support from the organization Wikileaks. For the United States, Snowden's revelations were a diplomatic disaster, as Germany was infuriated that President Angela Merkel's phone was monitored, while Brazil was equally angry about the tapping of then president Dilma Rousseff's calls. One of the disturbing aspects about Snowden's revelations was the extent to which people in the private sector have acquired security clearances that allow them access to critical information, seemingly with little oversight. Allegedly, Snowden had misinformation on his résumé, but Booz Allen Hamilton decided to hire him regardless (Reuters 2013). The fact that Snowden, a high school dropout who later acquired a GED, was able to obtain this level of access raised red flags (Reuters 2013). Who else was able to acquire information without proper vetting? To what extent has the privatization of security operations undermined the firewall protection of people's personal information? How has metadata on phone calls and communications been used and why (Landau 2013, 58)?

Snowden's experience also points to the power of nonstate organizations such as Wikileaks, which challenge states' ability to conceal security information. While digital globalization has given the U.S. government unprecedented tools for espionage, it has also allowed individuals within the government—or those who have hacked it—to release stunning amounts of information (Farrell and Finnemore 2013). As a result, not only has the U.S. government lost legitimacy globally, but also its operational effectiveness has diminished. Ultimately, public opinion on Snowden has been divided; a German organization awarded him a "whistleblower" prize, while some Americans view him as a traitor. What is clear is that Snowden has changed the conversation about the balance between security and privacy.

Traditional Security Concerns

Although the war on terror currently shapes most scholarly discussions concerning the meaning of security, traditional security issues have not disappeared. Indeed, it is not clear that Al-Qaida is the main security threat to Western nations. As Thérèse Delpech (2007, 111–75) has outlined, there are multiple flash points around the world and several security threats to world order. A renascent China now threatens to invade Taiwan should the island nation officially declare its independence, a step that would likely lead China into conflict with both the United States and Japan. Recently, China has come into conflict with a number of Southeast Asian states as well as Japan over land claims and sea-rights issues in Pacific waters. In South Asia, India and Pakistan continue their standoff over Kashmir, which brought the two nuclear powers to the brink of conflict in 2001 and 2002 (see Margolis 2002) and caused aerial skirmishes in March 2019. Finally, there now exist a number of "rogue states," which are generally thought of as being countries that fail to adhere to certain key international standards of behavior, of which the most important is probably nuclear nonproliferation (Nincic 2005, 56–58).

The nation that perhaps most embodies this latter security concern is North Korea, which frequently ignores international law and accords. In October 2006 North Korea also declared that it had successfully tested a nuclear weapon. This nuclear test created major concern throughout the region and caused intensive diplomatic pressure. Still, at this writing it appears unlikely that North Korea will abandon its nuclear weaponry. As Lankov has argued, the North Korean regime is made up of "hyper-realists" who are largely immune to popular pressure within the country (2017, 104). North Korea has faced both an economic crisis and a mass famine in the mid-1990s that likely killed "between 600,000 and 1 million" people (Goodkind and West 2001, 220). If such factors did not lead North Korea to change its policies then, diplomatic pressure is unlikely to do so now (Lankov 2017, 106). Indeed, North Korea has perceived its nuclear weapons and arms sales to be key means to ensure the resources that the nation needs to survive.

As Andrei Lankov points out, the Koreans watched how Libya gave up its nuclear program in exchange for better relations with the West, only to be overthrown in 2011; similarly, Ukraine surrendered its nuclear weapons in return for territorial guarantees in the Budapest Protocol of 1994, yet in March 2014 Russia annexed the Crimean Peninsula (2017, 105–6). The North Korean regime also watched the invasion of Iraq—which to their eyes seemed to lack any real connection to 9/11—and believed that this would not have happened if Iraq had nuclear weapons (Chartrand et al. 2017, 36). According to Lankov (2017), the North Korean regime has adopted a realist perspective, which has driven the country's rapid development of both ballistic weapons and nuclear warheads. Despite many U.S. efforts—including by President Donald Trump—to pressure North Korea, many scholars argue that it is highly unlikely that the country will ever give up its nuclear capability (Chartrand et al. 2017, 38), at least as long as U.S. troops remain on the Korean Peninsula (Anderson 2017).

Another country driven by a realist approach to international relations is Russia, which has increasingly preoccupied Western security officials since the annexation of Ukraine. As Niall Ferguson (2017, 76) has noted, Russia has become more aggressive militarily as its economic power has declined. Ferguson has also suggested that Russia has increasingly relied on its cyberforces (78). With the current focus on nonstate actors such as Wikileaks, the hacking group Anonymous, or Snowden's supporters, it is important to remember that cyber-conflict remains firmly part of the traditional realm of interstate conflict. Indeed, Russia has come to adopt hybrid warfare in a manner that blurs many of the old divisions between conventional and nonconventional military action. In this manner, these new tools do not undermine the old international order but rather provide a new venue for security contests. Still, if the most dangerous conflicts—such as in Syria or Ukraine—involve traditional military operations, then as Michael McFaul (2016) has argued the West must focus on long-standing efforts to balance Russian power by policies such as strengthening NATO and countering propaganda. The United States must also strengthen its skills in conventional military areas, which have languished during the counterinsurgency campaigns in Afghanistan and Iraq. In this manner, Realism continues to dominate many discussions about current security issues.

From a European perspective, perhaps the greatest concern is not the rise of Russia but a relative decline in the power and security of the West. As Daniela Schwarzer (2017) has argued, a number of factors have driven this concern. Compared to Asia, Europe has suffered from decades of slow growth, which has meant that its economic power has been in steady decline relative to Asian states such as China, India, and Indonesia (18–19). These trends seem destined to continue for another generation. This economic decline is accompanied by a parallel demographic decline. As a whole, European mothers are having fewer babies, so the population is rapidly aging at the same time that there is a dramatic demographic boom in some Asian states, and above all else in Africa (21–22). Interestingly, China itself will face a demographic decline, which scholars now suggest will have serious economic and social implications by midcentury (Myers, Wu, and Fu 2019). Still, it is Europe that is facing this demographic burden now, with all that entails for its security and economy.

Equally important, with the election of Donald Trump in 2016, Europe began to question the United States' commitment to the region's security. Trump started to pressure European states to increase their military spending and appeared to question the viability of NATO at a time when Europe was divided from within (Brexit) and was facing a resurgent Russia and mass migration (Afghanistan, Iraq, and Syria) from without. Combined, these factors have led to a sense in Europe that the region has to focus on traditional security threats in a manner that it has not since the end of the Cold War. Realism has regained power as an ideological framework.

From an Asian perspective, for some states the main issue is the rise of China. This concern is exacerbated by China's territorial claims in the South China Sea. For a long time, U.S. influence ensured that an invasion of Taiwan remained unlikely and that China could not assert its authority over the sea-lanes of the South China Sea. Based on purchased parity power, however, China has surpassed the United States as the world's largest economy (Desjardins 2015). China also has other strengths, such as its financial reserves, which dwarf those of the United States (Desjardins 2015). While the United States' military remains more powerful than that of China, the Chinese armed forces are rapidly growing in strength. The result is that some of China's neighbors are nervous, which has sparked a maritime arms race as far away as Australia, which is making major investments in its navy.

One measure to judge the extent to which China's neighbors are concerned is the number of nations currently investing in diesel electric submarines, a highly cost-effective and survivable means to ensure sea denial. The combination of competing territorial claims, major military investments by multiple states, and a rapidly rising global power has precedents in global affairs, which make Realism a useful tool to interpret trends in the region. At the same time, Asian nations find China to be a critical trading partner, an important source of development funding and a useful counterbalance to the United States, particularly after the United States decided not to move forward with a trade agreement with the region (Fisher and Carlson 2018). Great Power conflict remains a real possibility, as does the danger of miscalculations leading to the rapid escalation of a seemingly minor skirmish between Great Powers. All security issues ultimately raise the question of fear. On the one hand, there are serious threats to global security, and people are right to be afraid. But how dangerous are these threats to individuals in comparison to the other dangers of daily life? Are security fears manipulated for political ends? And how

Map 3 South China Sea

do we weigh our fear of possible enemy attacks against concerns that we may lose our liberties?

In part, your vision of how you choose to view security will depend on the extent to which you believe new technologies and globalizations have changed the threats that we face. The September 11, 2001, attacks could not have taken place without globalization, which permitted the flow of money, people, and ideologies that underpinned the attack. Similarly, new technologies, some argue, have put unprecedented power into the hands of small groups rather than states. From this perspective, the war against terrorism is the defining security issue of our age. But if you look globally at the security threats that we face, you might argue that the greatest danger remains traditional military conflict between states. In this case, it may be that the older theory of Realism still represents the best framework to understand global affairs. In contrast, proponents of human security might argue that their theory represents the best lens through which to view a multiplicity of security issues, given the complexity of current world affairs. But all of these approaches will need to address how technology is reshaping security issues.

Conclusion

Debates about security may seem abstract or distant from your life. This chapter may seem less accessible than later chapters in this book, in that it is harder to make an emotional connection to this topic. There is a "psychic numbing" that comes with security concerns (Lifton 1993, 82, 208). The threats seem so large, the possibilities so horrific, and the danger so beyond the capacity of ordinary people to absorb that there is a tendency to tune such concerns out. When North Korea tests a nuclear missile, must people in Japan, Guam, or Hawaii fear that they may be on the front line of a potential nuclear war over which they have no power? For someone of Middle Eastern descent, they may experience anxiety every time they pass through the security line at a U.S. airport. But this issue affects everyone, from people who choose not to fly because they are always selected for a search to citizens making judgments about their government's policies during elections.

In times of fear, people turn to the state to protect them. Who defines security issues? Who decides how to respond and how to balance legitimate security needs against human rights? What threats are real, and what responses are excessive? The United States began to use torture (such as waterboarding) on non-American prisoners after 9/11 (Sanos 2009). The United States also has used rendition (a process through which prisoners who are not citizens are sent to other nations for torture) to create a globalized network of terror. We often associate torture with nondemocratic and premodern states, but after 9/11 it was linked to the world's richest democratic country. But there is no legislative framework to define the United States' use of state terror and extrajudicial killing, such as through drone strikes in Middle Eastern countries. Many other Western states have greatly increased the resources and power of their intelligence agencies since 9/11, from New Zealand to Britain. Some Western nations tolerate other countries spying on their own citizens because by sharing information with one another, countries can gain intelligence on domestic targets that their own national intelligence services would be prohibited from targeting. New technologies allow the NSA and equivalent intelligence services to monitor entire populations' texting, Facebook usage, e-mail, and phone calls to create comprehensive information (metadata) on a nation's electronic activities. The United States is not unique in this surveillance.

Countries ceded these powers to their intelligence services—and created a globalized network of intelligence sharing—because there is a real threat from terrorism, as events both before and after 9/11 demonstrated. And terrorism is not the only threat that people face, a fact used by countries to justify such intelligence gathering. For example, technology allows states or criminals to launch cyberattacks on everything from the cloud to financial systems. Of course, people in developing countries might fear other threats. As a citizen, it is important for you to be informed and to be aware of the government's actions. Otherwise, we are working only with the government's definition of security and hoping that it will always make the best choices for us. Every security decision entails high-stakes ethical choices that are so complex that security has remained the most difficult international and moral issue since the time of Thucydides. As such, we all need to be informed about security issues and to think about how these questions affect us. What are you afraid of? How do you want your government to make you more secure? What liberties are you willing to trade in order to have more security? You may or may not agree with the perspective presented in this chapter. How do you think about security in a way that reflects your own values? And how do some approaches to security—such as Realism and human security—highlight or conceal certain issues?

➤ VOCABULARY

psychic numbing
NSA
rogue states
WMDs
liberalism
pandemic
Realism
neoconservatives
human security
realpolitik
zones of peace and zones of turmoil

➤ DISCUSSION AND REFLECTION QUESTIONS

1 *How would you define Realism, the theory that dominated security scholarship from the 1940s until 1991?*

2 *What is a failed state?*

3 *What do some members of the humanitarian-relief community fear will happen if foreign aid is allocated according to security issues?*

4 *What are two central tenets of neoconservative views on the United States and the world?*

5 *What is the relationship between electronic surveillance, human rights, and security?*

6 *What does Delpech mean when she uses the phrase "multiple flash points" regarding threats to world order?*

7 *Why does demography matter when discussing security issues? What demographic trends will shape security issues in the future?*

ACTIVITY 1: ANALYZE The World Economic Forum identified the top ten risks of 2019 in terms of likelihood (Myers and Whiting 2019). In order they are (1) extreme weather, (2) failure of climate-change mitigation and adaptation, (3) major or natural disasters, (4) massive incident of data fraud/theft, (5) large-scale cyberattacks, (6) man-made environmental damage, (7) large-scale involuntary migration, (8) major biodiversity loss and ecosystem collapse, (9) water crises, and (10) asset bubbles in major economy. Make a chart with what you believe are the top five risks listed. Then go to the World Economic Forum website and examine two other lists: "Risks by impact" and "Risks by interconnections." Identify the top five risks in your mind for each of these lists. Finally, add two more columns with five rows each to your original table and fill in your choices. Now that you have listed all these risks and contexts, identify one risk you can help ameliorate or decrease in your lifetime.

ACTIVITY 2: REFLECT Think about contrasts between Realism and human security perspectives. Identify one aspect of each. Stephen Legomsky (2005) suggests that recent U.S. security strategies have increasingly targeted or singled out aliens—immigrants or undocumented workers—through the process of profiling. Does this process strike you as being linked more to the Realism perspective or the human security perspective? Why?

ACTIVITY 3: EXTEND Use the following questions as prompts to help you begin to articulate your personal views on security. What are you afraid of? How do you want your government to make you more secure? What security issues matter most to you? How have you come to hold these beliefs? Write for about twenty minutes, answering each of the four questions.

References

Allen, E. 2016. "Chilcot Inquiry: What is it and what did the Iraq War report say." *The Telegraph*, July 5. Retrieved March 7, 2018, from http://www.telegraph.co.uk/news/2016/06/28/chilcot-inquiry-when-is-the-report-being-published-and-why-has-i/.

Anderson, N. 2017. Explaining North Korea's nuclear ambitions: Power and position on the Korean Peninsula. *Australian Journal of International Affairs* 71 (6): 621–41.

Axworthy, L. 2004. A new scientific field and policy lens. *Security Dialogue* 35:348–49.

Bapat, N. A., D. Ertley, C. Hall, and M. Lancaster. 2007. Perfect allies? The case of Iraq and Al-Quaeda. *International Studies Perspectives* 8:272–86.

Bollyn, C. 2004. America "Pearl Harbored." Retrieved January 26, 2008, from http://www.americanfreepress.net/12_24_02/America_Pearl_Harbored/america_pearl_harbored.html.

Bottici, C., and B. Challand. 2006. Rethinking political myth: The clash of civilizations as a self-fulfilling prophecy. *European Journal of Social Theory* 9:315–36.

British Broadcasting Corporation. 1997. Tourists massacred at temple. BBC News, November 17. Retrieved January 8, 2008, from http://news.bbc.co.uk/2/hi/32179.stm.

———. 2003. Anti-war rally leaves its mark. BBC News, February 19. Retrieved December 24, 2007, from http://news.bbc.co.uk/2/hi/uk_news/2767761.stm.

Broad, W. J., and D. Sanger. 2008. In nuclear net's undoing, a web of shadowy deals. *New York Times*, August 25.

Brunborg, H., and E. Tabeau. 2005. Demography of conflict and violence: An emerging field. *European Journal of Population 21* (2/3): 131–44.

Bueno de Mesquita, B., R. M. Siverson, and G. Woller. 1992. War and the fate of regimes: A comparative analysis. *American Political Science Review 86* (3): 638–46.

Burkeman, O., and J. Borger. 2003. War critics astonished as U.S. hawk admits invasion was illegal. *The Guardian*, November 20. Retrieved January 26, 2008, from http://www.guardian.co.uk/Iraq/Story/0,2763,1089158,00.html.

Burns, R. 2018. 16 years on, US military presence in Afghanistan growing. Boston.com, March 12. Retrieved August 17, 2018, from https://www.boston.com/news/politics/2018/03/12/16-years-on-us-military-presence-in-afghanistan-growing.

Buzan, B. 2004. A reductionist, idealistic notion that adds little analytical value. *Security Dialogue 35*:369–70.

Carr, E. H. (1939) 2001. *The twenty years' crisis*. Introduction by Michael Carr. New York: Palgrave.

Chartrand, P., F. Harvey, É. Tremblay, and E. Ouellet. 2017. North Korea: Perfect harmony between totalitarianism and nuclear capability. *Canadian Military Journal* 17 (3): 29–39.

Delpech, T. 2007. *Savage century: Back to barbarism*. Translated by George Holoch. Washington, D.C.: Carnegie Endowment for International Peace.

Desjardins, J. 2015. China versus the United States: A tale of two economies. *Visual Capitalist* (blog), October 15. Retrieved from http://www.visualcapitalist.com/china-vs-united-states-a-tale-of-two-economies/.

Elbe, S. 2006. Should HIV/AIDS be securitized? The ethical dilemmas of linking HIV/AIDS and security. *International Studies Quarterly* 50 (1): 119–45.

Falkenrath, R., R. D. Newman, and B. A. Thayer. 1998. *America's Achilles' heel: Nuclear, biological, and chemical terrorism and covert attack*. Cambridge, Mass.: MIT Press.

Farrell, H., and M. Finnemore. 2013. The end of hypocrisy: American foreign policy in the age of leaks. *Foreign Affairs* 92 (6): 22–26.

Ferguson, N. 2017. The Russia question: American relations with Moscow have become a geopolitical mess—a mess, very largely, of our own making. *Hoover Digest* 2 (Fall): 76+. Retrieved August 12, 2018, from www.hoover.org/research/russia-question.

Fisher, M., and A. Carlsen. 2018. How the rise of China is challenging longtime American dominance in Asia. *New York Times*, March 16.

Foreign Affairs Canada. 2006. *Human security for an urban century: Local challenges, global perspectives*. Ottawa: Foreign Affairs Canada. Retrieved July 10, 2019, from www.humansecurity-cities.org/page119.htm.

Frum, D., and R. Perle. 2003. *An end to evil: How to win the war on terror*. New York: Random House.

Fukuyama, F. 1989. The end of history? *National Interest* 16:3–18.

Ganshof, F. L. 1971. *The middle ages: A history of international relations*. Translated by Remy Inglis Hall. New York: Harper and Row.

Gleditsch, K. S., and M. D. Ward. 2000. War and peace in space and time: The role of democratization. *International Studies Quarterly* 44 (1): 1–29.

Goldstone, J. A. 2002. Population and security: How demographic change can lead to violent conflict. *Journal of International Affairs* 56 (1): 3–20.

Goodkind, D., and L. West. 2001. The North Korean famine and its demographic impact. *Population and Development Review* 27 (2): 219–38.

Gordon, P. H. 2007. Can the war on terror be won? *Foreign Affairs* 86 (6): 53–66.

Graham, T., Jr. 2004. *Common sense on weapons of mass destruction*. Seattle: University of Washington Press.

Hobbes, T. (1651) 1982. *Leviathan*. Oxford: Blackwell.

Holsti, O. R. 2008. *To see ourselves as others see us: How publics abroad view the United States after 9/11*. Ann Arbor: University of Michigan Press.

Hudson, V. M., and A. Den Boer. 2002. A surplus of men, a deficit of peace: Security and sex ratios in Asia's largest states. *International Security* 26 (4): 5–38.

ICM Research. 2003a. Iraq poll. Retrieved December 24, 2007, from http://www.icmresearch.co.uk/pdfs/2003_february_iraq_britain_decides_iraq_poll.pdf. Website no longer available.

———. 2003b. *Guardian* opinion poll. Retrieved December 24, 2007, from http://www.icmresearch.co.uk/pdfs/2003_february_guardian_february_poll.pdf. Website no longer available.

Jackson, R., and G. Sorenson. 1999. *Introduction to international relations*. New York: Oxford University Press.

Kacowicz, A. M. 2005. Globalization and poverty: Possible links, different explanations. *Whitehead Journal of Diplomacy and International Relations* 6 (2): 111–27.

Keohane, R. O., and J. S. Nye. 2001. *Power and interdependence*. 3rd ed. New York: Longman.

Khedery, A. 2015. Iraq in pieces: Breaking up to stay together. *Foreign Affairs* 94:33–41.

Landau, S. 2013. Making sense from Snowden: What's significant in the NSA surveillance revelations. *IEEE Security and Privacy* 11 (4): 54–63.

Lankov, A. 2017. Why nothing can really be done about North Korea's nuclear program. *Asia Policy* 23 (1): 104–10.

Legomsky, S. 2005. The ethnic and religious profiling of non-citizens: National security and international human rights. *Boston College Third World Law Journal* 25 (1): 1–36.

Lifton, R. J. 1993. *The protean self: Human resilience in an age of fragmentation*. New York: Basic Books.

MacFarlane, S. N., and Y. F. Khong. 2006. *Human security and the UN: A critical history*. Bloomington: Indiana University Press.

Margolis, E. 2002. *War at the top of the world: The struggle for Afghanistan, Kashmir, and Tibet*. New York: Routledge.

Mason, T. D. 2003. Globalization, democratization, and the prospects for civil war in the new millennium. *International Studies Review* 5:19–35.

McFaul, M. A. 2016. Peace as cold as Siberia. *Hoover Digest* 4 (Fall): 110+. Retrieved July 11, 2019, from https://www.hoover.org/research/peace-cold-siberia.

McRae, R. G., and D. Hubert. 2001. *Human security and the new diplomacy: Protecting people, promoting peace.* Montreal: McGill-Queen's University Press.

Mitchell, S., S. McLaughlin, S. Gates, and H. Hegre. 1999. Evolution in democracy-war dynamics. *Journal of Conflict Resolution* 43 (6): 771–92.

Monaghan, P. 2008. Beyond bullets and borders: "Human security" advocates call for a different approach to global problems. *Chronicle of Higher Education* 54 (42, June 27): B-8.

Monten, J. 2006. Thucydides and modern realism. *International Studies Quarterly* 50 (March): 3–26.

Morgenthau, H. J. 1948. *Politics among nations: The struggle for power and peace.* New York: Knopf.

Myers, J., and K. Whiting. 2019. These are the biggest risks facing our world in 2019. World Economic Forum, January 16. Retrieved July 2, 2019, from https://www.weforum.org/agenda/2019/01/these-are-the-biggest-risks-facing-our-world-in-2019/.

Myers, S., J. Wu, and C. Fu. 2019. China's looming crisis: A shrinking population. *New York Times*, January 21. Retrieved April 16, 2019, from https://www.nytimes.com/interactive/2019/01/17/world/asia/china-population-crisis.html.

Naím, M. 2005. *Illicit: How smugglers, traffickers, and copycats are hijacking the global economy.* New York: Doubleday.

Newman, E. 2001. Visions of international studies: Human security and constructivism. *International Studies Perspectives* 2 (3): 239–51.

Nincic, M. 2005. *Renegade regimes: Confronting deviant behavior in world politics.* New York: Columbia University Press.

9/11 Commission. 2004. *The 9/11 Commission report.* New York: W. W. Norton.

Nowosielski, R., dir. 2006. *911: Press for truth.* Documentary film. New York: Banded Artists/Standard Issue Films.

Nye, J. S., Jr., and J. D. Donahue, eds. 2000. *Governance in a globalizing world.* Washington, D.C.: Brookings Institute Press.

O'Neal, J. R., and B. Russett. 1999. The Kantian peace: The pacific benefits of democracy, interdependence, and international organizations, 1885–1992. *World Politics* 52:1–37.

Owen, T. 2004. Human security: Conflict, critique, and consensus; Colloquium remarks and proposal for a threshold-based definition. *Security Dialogue* 35:373–87.

Paris, R. 2001. Human security: Paradigm shift or hot air. *International Security* 26 (Fall): 87–102.

Peterson, S. 2002–3. Epidemic disease and national security. *Security Studies* 12:43–81.

Pollack, K. M. 2016. Fight or flight. *Foreign Affairs* 95 (March): 62–75.

Project for the New American Century. 1998. Letter to president Clinton on Iraq. Retrieved January 26, 2008, from http://www.newamericancentury.org/iraq clintonletter.htm.

Rapley, J. 2006. The new middle ages: Gangsters' paradise. *Foreign Affairs 85* (May–June): 95–104.

Retherford, R., and N. Ogawa. 2005. Japan's baby bust: Causes, implications, and policy responses. *East-West Center Working Paper,* Population and Health Series 118, 1–44.

Reuters. 2013. Booz Allen hired Snowden despite discrepancies in his résumé. *South China Morning Post,* June 22. Retrieved June 22, 2013, from http://www.scmp.com/news/world/article/1266209/booz-allen-hired-snowden-despite-discrepancies-his-resume.

Ripsman, N. M., and T. V. Paul. 2004. Globalization and the national security state: A framework for analysis. *International Studies Review* 7:199–227.

Sanos, P. 2009. *Torture team: Rumsfeld's memo and the betrayal of American values.* New York: Palgrave.

Sarasin, P. 2006. *Anthrax: Bioterror as fact and fantasy.* Translated by Giselle Weiss. Cambridge, Mass.: Harvard University Press.

Schwarzer, D. 2017. Europe, the end of the West and global power shifts. *Global Policy 8* (S4): 18–26.

Selby, J. 2018. Climate change and the Syrian Civil War, part II: The Jazira's agrarian crisis. *Geoforum.* Retrieved from https://doi.org/10.1016/j.geoforum.2018.06.010.

Shanker, T. 2008. Command for Africa established by Pentagon. *New York Times,* October 5, A-5.

Shanker, T., and S. Myers. 2007. Reassessments reflect fear of Taliban rise. *Oregonian,* December 16, A-2.

Shapiro, I. 2007. *Containment: Rebuilding a strategy against global terror.* Princeton: Princeton University Press.

Sheehan, M. 2005. *International security: An analytical survey.* Boulder, Colo.: Lynn Reiner.

Shore, Z. 2006. *Breeding Bin Ladens: America, Islam, and the future of Europe.* Baltimore: Johns Hopkins University Press.

Singer, M., and A. Wildavsky. 1993. *The real world order: Zones of peace, zones of turmoil.* Chatham, N.J.: Chatham House.

Sloan, E. C. 2005. *Security and defense in the terrorist era: Canada and North America.* Montreal: McGill-Queen's University Press.

Sobek, D. 2005. Machiavelli's legacy: Domestic politics and international conflict. *International Studies Quarterly* 49:179–204.

Thomas, C. 2001. Global governance, development, and human security. *Third World Quarterly 22* (January): 159–75.

Thucydides. 1972. *History of the Peloponnesian War.* Translated by R. Warner. Harmondsworth, UK: Penguin.

Todd, P., and J. Bloch. 2003. *Global intelligence: The world's secret services today*. New York: Zed Books.

United Nations Development Programme. 1994. *Human development report*. Oxford: Oxford University Press.

Urdal, H. 2005. People vs. Malthus: Population pressure, environmental degradation, and armed conflict. *Journal of Peace Research* 42 (4): 417–34.

Waltz, K. N. 1959. *Man, the state, and war*. New York: Columbia University Press.

War College. 2017. The case for leaving Afghanistan. Podcast, episode 78, March 9. Retrieved August 17, 2018, from https://soundcloud.com/war_college/the-case-for-leaving.

Ware, H. 2005. Demography, migration, and conflict in the Pacific. *Journal of Peace Research* 42 (4): 435–54.

EIGHT Food

➤ SYNOPSIS

Following a broad introduction to multiple global issues linked to food, this chapter traces historical origins, current concerns, and critical issues associated specifically with chocolate, coffee, and sugar. We examine climate change, child labor, fair trade, genetic modification of crops, industry monitoring, monocropping, worker migration, biopiracy, and slavery. The chapter also discusses various partnerships for the export and marketing of particular products.

➤ SCAFFOLDING

As you read through this chapter, think about how you would answer each of the questions below.

How often do you think about the food choices you make?

Do you know the origins of the food you eat on a regular basis?

How do terms like "commodity speculation," "biopiracy," and "slavery" relate to food, values, and agriculture?

As you read descriptions about causes of food-related issues, think about how the information is presented and supported. Does it seem sufficient?

➤ CORE CONCEPTS

How does a globalized food economy in a time of climate change affect the types of food people consume?

What is a food commodity chain?

How do chocolate, coffee, and sugar provide a way to understand the broader implications of globalization?

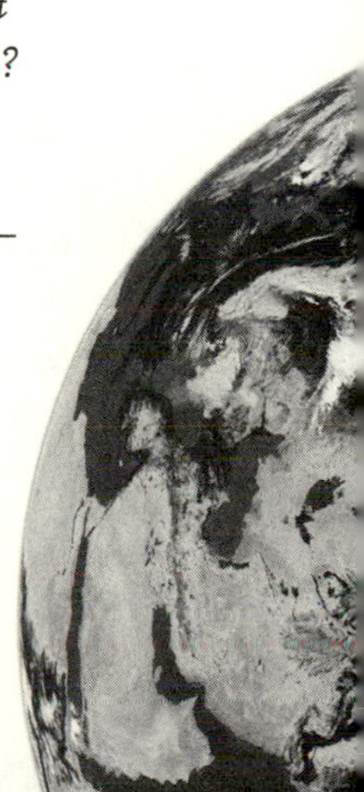

What are some sustainable agricultural choices that could be made to ensure the future viability of access to food and water around the globe?

How does your ability to make informed food choices affect farmers around the globe?

Everyone has to eat. Our connections to our daily bread, rice, tortillas, or chapatis reflect a complicated chain from producer to consumer. Andrew Heintzman and Evan Solomon remind us, "Food lies at the crossroad where global issues meet personal choice, where we all quite literally taste the world around us. Every bit of food connects us, however unconsciously, to systems and debate about fat and famine, mad cows and GMOs [genetically modified organisms], global trade regulations and subsidies, pesticides and collapsing food stocks" (2004, 6). Scientists now believe that climate change will deeply affect the food we consume and crop yields. The United Nations' Intergovernmental Panel on Climate Change recently published a study suggesting that heat waves may harm sensitive crops and that crop production will be reduced by roughly 2 percent per decade, resulting in about a 20 percent reduction by the end of the twenty-first century (Gillis 2013). Crops that grow well in one climate may no longer thrive when even a small change occurs in typical temperatures; coffee and cacao are two such products. Typically, there is an inequality between what the Global North produces and consumes and what the Global South produces and consumes. This leads to more challenges for some than for others. In the Global North, the middle class generally has access to sufficient food to avoid problems of starvation and malnutrition, but for others in the United States today, economic pressures—including shifting gas prices and an unstable economy—have contributed to an increased dependency on local food banks and government support.

Such dependency, however, comes nowhere close to the food issues affecting people in the Global South. In 2016, the following countries spent 40–56 percent of their income on food: Nigeria spent the most (56.4 percent), followed in short order by Kenya (46.7 percent), Cameroon (45.6 percent), Kazakhstan (43.0 percent), Algeria (42.5 percent), the Philippines (42.9 percent), Pakistan (40.9 percent), Guatemala (40.6 percent), and Azerbaijan (40.1 percent) (World Economic Forum 2016). There is also a clear pattern of inequality between where food is produced and where the population is most dense. Erik Millstone and Tim Lang indicate that

In 2015, Rwandans spent an average of 64 percent of their total budget on food. In contrast, in the United States in 2016, Americans spent 9.8 percent of their disposable personal income on food (Hjelm 2015). Can you estimate the percentage of your disposable income that you spend on food?

"chronic under-nutrition is not a consequence of overall scarcity, but of unequal access to land, technology and employment opportunities, coupled with a whole range of socioeconomic and environmental factors" (2008, 20). Some of these factors include inequality in food distribution as described above, competition between biofuel needs and human consumption needs, availability of water, food security, and food contamination. Climate change is also shifting the landscape of what is available to whom. Countries like Saudi Arabia are going as far as the southwestern United States and Ukraine for outsourced crop development (DeNicola et al. 2015). Other structural factors include a shift from producing food locally for local needs to producing export crops for the global market. Michael Pollan describes a global food economy based on inexpensive fuel: "More recently, cheap energy has underwritten a globalized food economy in which it makes (or rather, made) economic sense to catch salmon in Alaska, ship it to China to be filleted and then ship the fillets back to California to be eaten; or one in which California and Mexico can profitably swap tomatoes back and forth across the border; or Denmark and the United States can trade sugar cookies across the Atlantic. About that particular swap the economist Herman Daly once quipped, 'Exchanging recipes would surely be more efficient'" (2008, 14).

If we move to identify the actual cost of producing and marketing food products, it is necessary to look at the carbon and water cost: planting, harvesting, transportation, shipping, and distribution. Another dimension of true cost identification is to look at how a product has been subsidized. In many developed countries, agricultural dimensions of the GATT/TRIPS (Agreement on Trade-Related Aspects of Intellectual Property Rights) provisions allow for heavy subsidizing of foodstuffs. World Bank and IMF conditionality provisions do not permit countries receiving assistance to provide these same subsidies to their own farmers. Increasing privatization of fish-bearing seas via a program called "catch shares" is also driving small fishers out of centuries-old fishing grounds, severely affecting their ability to take care of their families and generate income (van der Voo 2018).

This chapter will not explicitly address more than an introduction to the topic of potable water for consumption and agriculture. No agricultural subject can be understood without knowledge of the role of water in production and how access to water is a local, regional, and global issue. The UN chose not to make water issues part of its individual development goals in its *Millennium Report*. The reason for this is that water underlies all of the goals and issues addressed.

People are extracting water from aquifers more rapidly than it has been possible for them to replenish it, which is causing a major environmental crisis. Saudi Arabia, in particular, has drawn down its water reserves rapidly. It has now chosen to no longer grow wheat. It has also embarked on a comprehensive global strategy to better manage its oil and water resources and outsource food production: "Plans have been made by the Saudi government to rely almost entirely on imported crops from other countries to feed its population of 30 million people. Arrangements are also underway for outsourcing food production to countries such as Sudan and Ukraine and others in South America and Asia, where Saudi Arabia will grow its own food to be exported back to the Kingdom" (DeNicola et al. 2015, 347).

Water depletion is also a major problem in multiple locations including China, India, and the United States. Indeed, researchers anticipate that by 2030, demand will exceed global supply (Michaels 2018). Cape Town, South Africa, has anticipated that "Day Zero," the moment when it does not have the water supply to meet the needs of its population, will occur in 2019 (Michaels 2018). There is no global infrastructure in place to redress water imbalances, nor is there any indication that individual nation-states will do so.

Water raises larger issues of social equity and the ability of people to meet their basic needs. Unfortunately, as we will see in the section of this chapter focusing on the food commodity chains of chocolate, coffee, and sugar, we are not yet moving toward greater equality in access to foodstuffs, nor are we making sustainable plans for how to harvest and market food crops. Forced labor in both the chocolate and sugar industries remains a little-known fact to most consumers. Our ability to redress imbalances due to our global interconnectedness is fueling greater food safety and security issues than ever before.

Before examining any of these products, it is necessary to clarify what is meant by the term "commodity chain." Commodity chains, first defined

Table 3 Global Food Issues

	In This Chapter			On Your Own		
	Cacao/ Cocoa	**Coffee**	**Sugar**	**Quinoa**	**Rice**	**Bananas**
Commodity speculation, global supply and demand		•		•	•	•
Monoculture crops for export	•	•		•		•
Fair labor practices, human trafficking, child labor	•	•	•			
Industry monitoring (private companies, regional cartels)	•	•				
Fair trade	•	•		•		•
Niche marketing	•	•		•		
Sustainable practices	•	•		•		
Worker migration issues			•			
Biopiracy					•	
Shifting consumption patterns			•	•	•	•
Genetic modification issues			•	•	•	•
Private/public/NGO partnerships	•	•		•		
Global/local continuum issues				•		

by Terence Hopkins and Immanuel Wallerstein in 1977, are analyzed by "tak[ing] an ultimate consumable item and trac[ing] back the set of inputs that culminated in this item—the prior transformations, the raw materials, the transportation mechanisms, the labor input into each of the material processes, the food inputs into the labor. This linked set of processes we call a commodity chain" (128). With respect to food products, the commodity chain would begin with the acquisition of seeds and, potentially, fertilizers and chemicals, then move through to harvesting, marketing, and distribution phases.

By looking at what are no doubt some of your favorite foods, it is possible to explore some of the most pressing global issues of the twenty-first century. In each case, we begin with a historical overview of connections between peoples and products, considering both producers and consumers. We examine critical issues with respect to these products, challenging you as a reader to identify your own thoughts about them. Table 3 shows the myriad of issues interconnected with the food products discussed in this chapter. Many of the terms you will see may not be familiar to you. We hope that, by the end of the chapter, this will no longer be the case.

Health claims have been made about the "magic elixir" properties of chocolate and coffee for more than 400 years. While consumers of chocolate and coffee are found all over the world, the central producing region for these products is a belt around the equator. The next forty years of climate change will determine whether this pattern changes.

Chocolate

History

Throughout Mexico and Central America, archaeologists have found ancient remains of cacao trees, as well as vessels with cacao seeds in them. The cacao beans served both as a source for a chocolate beverage believed to have healing properties and as a form of currency. Excavated sites suggest a long link between both consumption and trade use of cacao on the part of cultures such as the Maya and the Olmec. Ruth Lopez (2002) cites historical data confirming cacao trade routes between Costa Rica, Nicaragua, and Mexico that even Columbus was familiar with. Archaeologists also have discovered traces of cacao in sites in El Salvador (A.D. 590), Honduras (2000 B.C.–A.D. 1000), and Guatemala (A.D. 500) (Lopez 2002, 30–45).

In Mexico, legend has it that cacao was a gift from the god Quetzalcoatl. When the explorer Hernán Cortés arrived in Mexico in the early 1500s, some Aztecs may have believed him to be a reincarnation of Quetzalcoatl. In spite of attempts on the part of the Indigenous peoples to welcome him, Cortés was ultimately responsible for the political demise of the Aztec chief Montezuma. In approximately 1528, Cortés returned to Spain, bringing with him Europe's first taste of cocoa, which was reserved for royalty alone.

Jack Weatherford (1989) argues that this is one of the earliest cases of gifts from the Indigenous peoples of the New World to Europe. At the time that the cacao beans made their way to Spain to be processed into cocoa, there were no trade and tariff protections. As we will soon see, the bean's most recent travels now fall under such protections.

By the 1700s, European leaders and members of the Catholic Church were weighing in on the benefits of chocolate. While the Jesuits were much in favor of the product, Lopez suggests the Dominicans strongly criticized its consumption. In London, purveyors of chocolate began to appear. As would later be true in the tea industry, the British government played a role in importing cacao beans by controlling supplies through high tariffs. By the early 1800s, chocolate consumption reached all of England's classes, and by the mid-1800s, recipes for sweet milk chocolate had been developed by the Swiss.

While cacao beans went first from the New World to the Old World, it was Spain that ultimately shipped cacao beans *back* to the Caribbean and South America to become the primary crop of plantations, ultimately staffed by slave labor. While the Spanish went west and the French joined them on the Caribbean islands of Martinique and St. Lucia, the Dutch moved into Indonesia. The British tried briefly to produce cacao in Jamaica, but after an expensive six-year investment, disease killed off almost the entire crop. The British also brought cacao to Sri Lanka (then named Ceylon) to substitute for coffee beans ravaged by disease. Ultimately, however, it was tea that replaced cacao in Sri Lanka. For 250 years, ending around 1850, the plantation system supplied chocolate to consumers throughout Europe and the United States.

It will come as no surprise that the opportunity to consume chocolate was virtually nonexistent for individuals farming the cacao beans. The beans were strictly for export and for the consumption of the non-Indigenous people heading up the plantations. Economic control of the plantations was never in the hands of anyone other than colonizers. For 400 years, single crops, or monocultures, have continued to flourish under the plantation system. However, the failure to maintain a diversity of local food sources along with crops for export comes at an enormous cost, leaving nations without a hedge against disease and major price fluctuations. Time and again, we see the problems that arise when a nation has only one major crop to export or when a critical crop for domestic consumption, such as quinoa, suddenly becomes an export darling and the center of health-food niche marketing.

The Present

There are four primary areas where cacao beans are grown today: the Caribbean, Latin America, West Africa, and Asia (Indonesia and Vietnam). Plantations are displacing small farmers in all these geographic areas, and new plantations are cropping up in Vietnam. Typically, cacao trees have been part of mixed-culture plantings generally grown on small family farms. In 2007 there were more than 5 million family farms producing over 3 million tons of cacao beans; Côte d'Ivoire was the largest producer, followed by Ghana and Indonesia. However, the last decade has brought more large plantations as well as incursions by small farmers into protected forests in both Côte d'Ivoire and Ghana (Solidaridad 2018). The volatility of the cacao market has caused these plantations to reassess production targets, and top-producing nations such as Côte d'Ivoire are actually lowering production goals due to an oversupply of cacao beans on the global market (as detailed below). In Côte d'Ivoire, scientists noted that more than 75 percent of parkland and forest reserves have now been taken over for cocoa production. Political instability close to two decades ago in the form of civil war resulted in warlords giving land parcels to whomever they chose within these protected areas (Cocks and Aboa 2018; Bitty et al. 2015). The largest global chocolate companies are working together to design more effective monitoring schemes to prevent sourcing from these areas, but both pledges and legal moves have not yet been successful. Africa is projected to remain the principal cocoa producer, but with both a glut of cacao beans in 2017 and climate change causing increased biological threats, countries are reassessing their output goals:

> Output in Ivory Coast has risen from 1.6 million tonnes 10 years ago to 2 million tonnes in the 2016–17 season because of higher yields, but global demand has failed to meet supply. The CCC expects production for the 2017–18 season to slip to 1.9 million tonnes, partly because of bad weather.
>
> High-level sources at the CCC said the organisation wants to try to reduce output to between 1.7 million tonnes and 1.8 million tonnes over the next two years, affecting exporters and chocolate makers that also include Ferrero, Cargill, Olam, Cemoi and Cocoa Barry. (Reuters 2018)

Cacao plays a key role in the economies of a number of West African countries. In the case of Côte d'Ivoire, almost a third of their economy is based on cocoa exports (Chanthavong 2002). The fragile nature of global prices of this commodity contributes to what Samlanchith Chanthavong terms "pull" factors supportive of conditions promoting indentured servitude. Cacao-producing nations cannot afford to risk potential market loss and thus are ready to do anything necessary to guarantee appropriate market shares. In 2018, however, a glut of beans caused Côte d'Ivoire to pull back on programs to increase yields. From a high of 2 million tons in 2016–17, it anticipates dropping to roughly 1.7 million tons annually (Sterk 2018).

Predicting prices and export volumes is part of futures forecasting. Forecasting is key to all commodity production. Weather, internal politics, international politics, and international agreements all affect production. As we will see in later discussions of coffee, alternative explanations frequently exist for the apparently arbitrary rise and fall of prices. For example, from 2007 to 2012, there was a 43.5 percent net drop in cocoa production in Malaysia (World Cocoa Foundation 2012). Agricultural decisions to increase land devoted to palm oil production account for much of this change.

Vietnam has now become a key player in the cocoa market. The country is seeing an almost tenfold increase in production, from 5,500 tons in 2011 to a predicted 52,000 tons by 2020. Additionally, Vietnam's cocoa is "clean cocoa" and is UTZ certified, which means that it is in compliance with a 2002 global sustainability protocol for production and product labeling. Some 80 percent of cocoa production in Vietnam is owned by the private U.S. company Cargill. In 2014 Cargill purchased Archer Daniels Midland's global cocoa business for $440 million. The purchase was completed in August 2015 once it cleared the European Commission (Cargill.com 8/3/15, 9/12/14). This added Ambrosia, Merckens, and Schokinag brands to Cargill's stable. During the summer of 2013, Callebaut chocolates (Switzerland) became the world's largest cocoa processor when it purchased the cocoa division of Petra Food. Lina Khan (2013) reports that this means these two companies now control more than 60 percent of global cocoa processing.

Most of the Latin American and Caribbean beans are exported to the U.S. market, while the West African and Indonesian beans are exported to Europe. In all cases, there are large auction houses that sell the beans. Because of the speed and volume of sales, it is sometimes difficult to keep an eye on the origin of the beans, which is important when attempting to guarantee that no forced child labor has been involved in their harvesting and marketing.

Nestlé, Mars, Hershey, Mondelez, and Kraft are the largest manufacturers and marketers of chocolate in the world. These companies are all members of the International Cocoa Initiative and wield a great deal of power in terms of production and marketing policy. In the United States, Hershey and Mars control between two-thirds and three-fourths of the market, while in Europe, Kraft (formerly Cadbury), Nestlé, and Mars account for a similar market share. After a bidding war between Hershey and Kraft, Kraft acquired Cadbury for $19 billion in 2010. Despite promises by Kraft to continue using Fairtrade cocoa beans, within six years of its purchase of Cadbury, Kraft switched its production to Cocoa Life, which does not use Fairtrade beans (Fearn 2016).

Given the example from Vietnam, we can see that full control of production to processing of a significant percentage of cocoa now lies in the hands of large multinational agribusiness firms. Fears for the livelihood of small farmers and niche marketing chocolatiers are increasing (Khan 2013).

Critical Issues

Perhaps the most troubling issue in cacao production is that of child labor. In 2000 the BBC produced an investigative report documenting how tens of thousands of children were taken from countries such as Mali, Burkina Faso, and Togo to work as indentured laborers for ten to fourteen hours per day on cacao farms. Parents were unaware of their children's perilous lives; some thought their children were working as legitimate laborers under controlled conditions, while others thought they were being groomed to head to Europe as sports stars. A 2000 U.S. State Department report estimated that at least 15,000 children from Mali were working on cocoa plantations in Côte d'Ivoire. The price of purchase was US$40 per child. The children worked twelve-hour days for less than $200 per year (Off 2006, 133). In 2002 similar numbers were reported, and the children on these cocoa farms were characterized as slaves (Save the Children Canada 2005). A powerful, richly descriptive account of this servitude is presented in Carol Off's *Bitter Chocolate: Investigating the Dark Side of the World's Most Seductive Sweet* (2006).

The issue of child indentured labor was so critical that beginning in the late 1990s, the Chocolate Manufacturers Association joined with a variety of domestic and international organizations to survey labor practices in West Africa. On October 1, 2001, the Harkin-Engel Act, cosponsored by U.S. senator Tom Harkin and U.S. congressman Eliot Engel, went into effect. The protocol was designed to ensure that by 2005 there would be no child slavery or indentured servitude used in the production of chocolate. Unfortunately, this goal was not achieved; the current goal is now 2025. The International Cocoa Initiative presented some stark facts about the situation: "[A]n estimated 1.5 million children—aged 10 to 17—[are] in child labour in Côte d'Ivoire and Ghana. In Ghana, there were 668,000 children . . . in child labour (including 632,000 performing hazardous tasks) out of the 708,000 children working in cocoa between August 2016 and August 2017. In Côte d'Ivoire, the number of child labourers between October 2016 and November 2017 was found to be 829,000 (including 769,000 working in hazardous conditions) out of the 891,000 working in cocoa production" (International Cocoa Initiative 2018).

Simon Brayn-Smith directs sustainability at Olam Cocoa, the key cacao exporter in Africa. In a confectionery news article, Anthony Myers (2018, 1) details Brayn-Smith's description of Olam's commitment: "Olam is focusing its efforts to eradicate child labour in its supply chain on three key areas: pulling smallholders out of poverty; developing Child Labor Monitoring and Remediation Systems (CLMRS); and harnessing data at farm level from smartphones to identify where vital social infrastructure like schools are lacking alongside details of farmer families."

In addition to Olam, well-known producers such as Mondelez, Nestlé, Cargill, Callebaut, and Tony's Chocolonely have committed to the CLMRS protocol (Myers 2018). Private industry giant Cargill has also committed to eradicate child labor in its supply chain by 2025 (Myers 2018). The chocolate bar you eat to fend off hunger pangs may have been created from labor you would not approve of. How can you tell? For the most part, particularly in the United States, this is very difficult because in the fast-moving auction houses throughout the world, beans from all over the globe frequently get mixed together. One possible choice is to buy organic chocolate. Because no organic cocoa beans come from areas like Côte d'Ivoire—a key site of indentured labor—you can be reasonably sure that by buying organically, you are not supporting an unjust labor practice. Among the companies able to document that no slave labor has been involved in the production of cacao beans in their products are Clif Bar, Cloud Nine, Dagoba Organic Chocolate, Denman Island Chocolate, Gardners Candies, Green and Black's, Kailua Candy Company, Koppers Chocolate, L.A. Burdick Chocolates, Montezuma's Chocolates, Newman's Own Organics, Omanhene Cocoa Bean Company, Rapunzel Pure Organics, and the Endangered Species Chocolate Company (Stop chocolate slavery

2014). An even more active choice is to participate in campaigns to change child labor practices. Equal Exchange is an example of an organization that makes use of a range of strategies from school-based campaigns to petition drives; its efforts are detailed on its website.

In addition to the question of whether indentured labor has been used in the harvesting of cacao is the question of whether fair prices have been paid to the cocoa farmers. Gregory Dicum and Nina Luttinger characterize fair trade as a "market-driven model that redefines the dynamics of the trading system to achieve [the goal of fair trade]. Fair trade relationships are simplified; exploitative middlemen are bypassed as farmer co-ops trade directly with importers in consuming countries. And, crucially, power across the value chain is equalized as growers have access to better market information and credit on fairer terms" (1999, 195). Jane Pettigrew further addresses advantages of fair trade in her discussion of the tea trade (as do Dicum and Luttinger 1999 in their discussion of coffee), reminding her readers that when a fair trade system is put in place, more money is invested in bettering the lives of workers through "pension funds, alternative training opportunities, environmental improvements, and welfare and medical programs" (1997, 46).

A third critical issue is that of agricultural sustainability. The Alliance for Sustainability provides the following definition: "A sustainable agriculture is ecologically sound, economically viable, socially just and humane. For different regions and contexts the exact meaning may vary—in some cases no chemicals are used—in others, a much smaller amount than in conventional agriculture without costs to the ecosystem" (2007). Sustainability practices can increase crop yields and decrease the amounts of fertilizers and pesticides used.

An illustrative case study comes from the Cocoa Project in Vietnam at Nong Lam University (World Cocoa Foundation 2012). Since 1997 the project has been actively committed to strengthening smallholder farmers' ability to grow cacao sustainably. A Field School Method is used, providing farmers with active on-site training on demonstration plots in multiple areas. External development agencies work collaboratively with SUCCESS alliance Vietnam. Tanager (once ACDI/VOCA) is a Washington, D.C.-based agency focusing on four development goals: "catalyzing investment, climate smart agriculture, empowerment and resilience, and institutional strengthening and market systems" (www.acdivoca.org). This Cocoa Project promotes sustainable farming practices and means of controlling pests with minimal chemical investment. Current research work looks at "use of black ants and weaver ants to control *Helopeltis*; use of Vetiver grass to control termites; irrigation systems; incorporation of livestock into the farming system; and fermentation techniques suitable to the local environment" (World Cocoa Foundation 2012).

In addition to international and local development agencies, the confectionery business itself has worked to craft collaborative, sustainable cacao plantations. Belgium's Puratos Grand Place is one group that began an initiative in 2008 called "From Farming to Chocolate." With a goal of promoting on-site harvesting of beans and on-site product production, this program is an example of a win-win situation for farmers and chocolate brokers.

Summary

This section has profiled the history of and current conditions in the trade of cacao beans for the production of cocoa and, ultimately, chocolate. At the present time, niche marketing has allowed for a broad increase in the numbers and types of chocolate bars sold around the world. Recent health advertisements for dark chocolate's antioxidant properties have drawn in a broad base of consumers beyond chocoholics and children. While an examination of health benefits is well beyond this chapter, it is clear that chocolate is here to stay. We turn next to coffee.

Coffee

History

Two accessible publications detail the role of coffee in our lives. Tom Standage (2005) captures coffee's role in relation to five other beverages in his lively romp through the centuries, *A History of the World in Six Glasses*, while Nina Luttinger and Gregory Dicum (2006) provide a more comprehensive account in *The Coffee Book: Anatomy of an Industry from Crop to the Last Drop*, which includes a rich time line detailing events from A.D. 1000 to the present. For our purposes, the following events are of note. History suggests that Avicenna of Bukhara (located in present-day Uzbekistan) was writing about coffee's health benefits in A.D. 1000. Sometime between 1470 and 1499, coffee made its way to Mecca and Medina (Saudi Arabia) from Yemen. Antony Wild (2004) details this, in contrast to descriptions of coffee as first appearing in Ethiopia, which has been proposed in other histories. The first appearance of coffee in Europe seems to have been in Holland around 1616. By the late 1600s, it was the subject of futures speculations in auctions throughout Europe.

As trading and speculation escalated, coffeehouses sprouted up in Venice and England. Fears arose on the part of government officials in England about the role these coffeehouses were playing in promoting opinions that differed from those of the government. Seeking a place to produce coffee that belonged to the empire, the British began coffee cultivation in Sri Lanka around 1658. Europeans strove to gain control of the plants themselves, sending Javanese coffee beans to Holland's botanical gardens in 1706. Some might term this one of the earliest instances of "biopiracy" or "industrial espionage." Biopiracy "refers to the appropriation of the knowledge and genetic resources of farming and indigenous communities by individuals or institutions who seek exclusive monopoly control (patents or intellectual property) over these resources and knowledge" (ETC Group n.d.).

In 1723 France sent coffee seedlings to its colony of Martinique in the Caribbean. In like manner, in 1727 coffee seedlings from French Guyana made their way to Brazil. In 1730 the British joined in, sending seeds from England to Jamaica. Over a ten-year period in Sri Lanka, coffee plants had been slowly dying from *Hemileia vastatrix*, a disease commonly called coffee rust. By 1869 the volume of acreage killed off by coffee rust decimated coffee production and provoked a switch from coffee to tea production, a decision accounting for the first planting of tea seeds in 1867 (Pettigrew 1997).

Between 1727 and 1800, the coffee industry developed to such a degree that Brazil was able to export the product. Its ability to do so was enhanced by two years of abject destruction of coffee plantations and estates in Haiti during the 1791–93 uprisings by the nearly 500,000 African slaves on the island. This caused Haiti to fall from its top position, and it no longer delivered half of the world's coffee supply (Dicum and Luttinger 1999). Over the next thirty-five years, Brazil secured its position as a producer of somewhere between half and three-quarters of the global supply of coffee. This success allowed it to "replicate the policies of the original coffee exporters" and begin "a series of initiatives to create a coffee cartel on a scale that dwarfed anything the Arabs were able to accomplish at the dawn of the original coffee era" (Luttinger and Dicum 2006, 30). By 1906 Brazil was powerful enough to control the global supply and price of coffee in a process termed "valorization," government price control of a commodity. An organization begun first by the growers and later taken over by the government, the Brazilian Instituto de Café was one example of a developing nation crafting a leadership role in commodity control.

Inspired by its neighbor Brazil, Colombia was struck with coffee fever. As thousands of coffee farms began in Colombia, a domestic organization called the Federacion Nacional de Cafeteros (FNC) was created. Luttinger and Dicum contrast the two organizations, characterizing the Colombian FNC as a group that "promoted unrestrained and aggressively expansionist trade in coffee. While the [Brazilian] *instituto* was inward-looking and more concerned with domestic control of supply to established markets, the FNC was resolutely cosmopolitan and sought to stimulate demand—particularly demand for Colombian coffee" (2006, 75–76).

The contrasting approaches of the two organizations came together briefly in 1936, when Brazil and Colombia finally decided to work together to keep the prices of their coffees consistent on the world market. This effort fell apart by June 1937, however, as the FNC once again separated itself from the Colombian government and continued a sort of cowboy-style expansionism. Brazil then dumped much of its coffee supply on the market, and the resultant glut caused the complete collapse of the world market. Luttinger and Dicum characterize the resulting move by Colombia, Brazil, and the United States to create a trilateral agreement as one of the earliest examples of a combined economic and political policy: "The Inter-American Coffee Agreement . . . was a major break with established trade policy that generally favored free international markets. The United States entered into it to support friendly nations in its hemisphere, thereby securing their resistance to Axis overtures during this time of global war" (2006, 79).

Between 1937 and 1962, international players shifted a bit. Instant coffee became important. Central America and Africa joined the playing field. In the years after World War II, the era of the Cold War, the United States was hypervigilant in attempting to keep Communism from crossing into Latin America. The trade relationships with Colombia and Brazil were instrumental in this effort and eventually provided the scaffolding for the creation in 1962 of an International Coffee Agreement (ICA). Like OPEC (the Organization of Petroleum Exporting Countries) today, the ICA was designed to set quotas for production and maintenance of market prices. The stability of this organization invited Central America, Africa, and Indonesia to step up their roles in production. Organizations like the World Bank and the IMF provided start-up monies. However, since the ICA was designed primarily to assist giant producers like Brazil and Colombia, these other geographic areas were forced to sell their beans to countries that were not part of the ICA. For roughly ten years, this "us" and "them" system continued. The types of beans planted in the smaller countries were not carefully monitored by the ICA.

By 1994 the ICA shifted from an agency that designed and enforced policy to one that provided and maintained a database of coffee information to disseminate for trade and marketing purposes. The lack of global policing via an association again put pressure on individual nation-states and multinationals to develop production and marketing plans, often in isolation. In 1997, Vietnam stepped in as a key player, with production rising from zero to more than 1.8 billion pounds in 1997. In spite of unevenness in quality, Vietnamese coffee continued to flood the market, which ultimately impacted global pricing. Luttinger and Dicum (2006) argue convincingly that the role of Structural Adjustment Programs imposed by the World Bank and the IMF essentially rendered ineffective the national coffee boards in Africa, Indonesia, and even Mexico. In terms of patterns, we see the push and pull between independent development and product marketing and large-scale international governmental and multinational corporations. We have looked at costs and benefits of individual nation-states controlling the destiny of their GNP through the single commodity export of cacao; we see this same situation with coffee.

By 1999, a global coffee crisis was triggered by a glut in production and a drop in prices. The year 2001 brought the lowest adjusted prices per pound in the history of coffee production (Luttinger and Dicum 2006). In *The Coffee Book*, Luttinger and Dicum present a list of the world's most coffee-dependent countries in terms of export for 2003. Several of the countries at or near the top of the list, including East Timor, Burundi, Ethiopia, and Rwanda, have also experienced some of the worst political and human-rights crises in recent history. These authors argue that "worldwide, the regime of careless capitalism contributed to one national tragedy after another" (104). Coupled with corruption, these gluts in production and price fluctuations played central roles in the destabilization of these countries.

The Present

Both Arabica and Robusta beans continue to be cultivated around the world. Arabica is the dominant coffee in niche marketing and is considered a high-end coffee. Roughly 70 percent of global production is Arabica (Killeen and Harper 2016). This coffee is grown at higher elevations, typically in the shade. Robusta makes up the other 30 percent of coffee in production. Grown at lower levels in the sun, Robusta is the dominant coffee in mass-market brands (Killeen and Harper 2016). Coffee trends were fairly stable from 2005–6 to 2010–11 (Statista 2019), with a moderate increase beginning in 2013–14 of Robusta sales. Arabica has seen a moderately expanded production from 2017–18 to 2018–19 from 94.88 million sixty-kilo bags to 101 million sixty-kilo bags. Timothy Killeen and Grady Harper see Robusta growing in importance in the next thirty years because of climate change. They suggest Robusta is "genetically adapted to the conditions of warmer lowland landscapes" (2016, 4). A variety of scholars engage in mathematical modeling of both production and consumption. Killeen and Harper predict a brighter future for Robusta than Arabica but acknowledge that research may create more temperature-tolerant hybrid Robusta/Arabica blends in the next thirty years.

As temperatures around the globe rise, "coffee supply chains are likely to experience significant disruption due to climate change over the next forty years [until 2050]" (Killeen and Harper 2016, 22). It may be the case that lands not currently in production will be tapped, particularly in Indonesia, Honduras, and the Andes. Killeen and Harper suggest that deforestation will become a growing public policy and environmental concern if this comes to pass. In 2016, the leading global producers of coffee were Brazil (2,595,000 metric tons);Vietnam (1,650,000 metric tons); Colombia (810,000 metric tons); Indonesia (660,000 metric tons), and Ethiopia (384,000 metric tons) (World Atlas, 2019).

At this point, it becomes useful to revisit the notion of ideologies within arguments, which we first introduced in chapter 1. The information presented to you in this chapter is ultimately a set of facts, woven together with arguments designed by your authors. Perhaps you agree with us; perhaps you disagree with us. Whether or not you agree is not as important as whether you can identify how we have built up rationales for the perspectives presented in this chapter and elsewhere in the book.

Read through the three numbered paragraphs below. They present different perspectives on the demise of Central American coffee production in the early 1980s, moving toward 2018:

1 Green (with Branford) (2013, 23):

Vietnam's rapid rise as a coffee producer in the 1980s created a global glut and a price collapse that ravaged the Latin American coffee industry. Prices are also affected by dumping: when Latin American farmers compete with crops also grown in the rich countries, northern governments rig the rules by pouring subsidies into their agriculture, enabling firms to flood Latin American markets with food exported at below the cost of production.

2 Igami (2012, 11):

The breakdown of the coffee cartel coincided with the emergence of Vietnam as a fringe exporter urged along by foreign aid, government-led migration, and market-oriented reforms. Thus both the cartel's breakdown and Vietnam's expanded exportation represent changes in market structure that are exogenous to the year-on-year price."

3 World Bank (2018):

Vietnam's emergence as a leading exporter of agro-food commodities—for aquatic products, rice, coffee, tea, cashews, black pepper, rubber, and cassava—contributes to its food security and poverty reduction. . . . By 2020, efforts to maximize finance for development are expected to provide 200,000 coffee and rice farmers with higher incomes, as profits are projected to increase by 20 percent. Additional benefits are considerable, including lower-carbon, climate-smart farming for 40,000 hectares for coffee production and 75,000 hectares of rice fields; 17,000 hectares of renewed coffee trees; and increased exports thanks to better quality raw materials. Contract farming will link farmers and agribusinesses to reduce transaction costs, maintain competitiveness, and ultimately increase farmers' revenues. Farmers will also be better organized and attuned to the product requirements of agribusinesses. Going forward, better regulations will incentivize more private capital to invest in coffee and rice value chains.

The perspective in the first quote shows us how someone in Central America might perceive Vietnam's entry into the coffee production market. The second faults not only foreign assistance and promotion by organizations such as the World Bank but also the coffee cartel itself. The last quote, from the World Bank, highlights the positive development aspects of Vietnamese coffee production and lists local production problems but does not address the global relationship among coffee producers. These perspectives are not surprising. We all learn what we are taught, and in general, policy decisions that negatively affect us are not perceived in a positive or even neutral light. In the first quote, we see words like "rig," "dumping," and "ravaged." The second presents a neutral, balanced description of typical development issues. The phrase "changes in market structure that are exogenous to the year-on-year price" reflects traditional academic prose. In the final quote, we see a focus on the good that will come to a particular country, often ignoring effects on others.

Critical Issues

Niche marketing of coffee, tea, and chocolate has increased dramatically. Terms like "organic," "fairly traded," and "80 percent cacao content" help consumers distinguish products that have not been on the market for very long. Nations traditionally seen as key market players are being challenged by newcomers, often with the support of global entities such as the World Bank. Coffee cooperatives in Central and Latin America are now competing for the attention of organizations like Green Mountain Coffee to ensure their continuing existence. Farmers on many of these cooperatives have never actually tasted the coffee produced from the beans they have grown. As some cooperatives live and others die, the World Bank is providing incentives to Vietnam to strengthen its place in the global coffee market. Future coffee marketers will consciously focus on direct trade, taking out the "middleman" (Stanley 2018). There is also a trending suggestion that superfoods will continue to be added to coffee. Thus we will see more products such as mushroom coffee and even the addition of carbonated water to coffee (Stanley 2018). Both environment and politics will affect where coffee is grown and who buys it. To coffee consumers in Finland, the Netherlands, and Austria, the top three consumer nations, coffee will not go away. We may, however, see competition among consumers once the new markets in China and India expand.

Summary

With the products profiled in this chapter so far, we have visited the notions of sustainability, fair trade, fair labor practices, and climate change. In addition to these issues—all of which are linked to the growth and consumption of coffee—we have seen a tighter framing of the relationship between producing and consuming countries. Many authors who examine the commodity of coffee throughout the world today have scrutinized how much money from the sale of a single cup of coffee actually reaches anyone in the producing country. Clearly, the consumer countries have a stronger grip on aspects of the profit margin—from roasting the beans all the way to marketing and sales. Some authors have suggested that a more equitable balance of profit between the bean-producing countries and all others is in order. This brings us back to the issue of commodity and value chains. As with other luxury products such as chocolate, daily choices you make will trickle back to the land of origin. Is your impact positive, negative, or neutral? More important, can you begin to see yourself as a member of a broad global community? The relationship between producing and consuming nations affects the overall health of our planet.

Sugar

We move now to an exploration of the final product of this chapter, the carbohydrate darling of our daily consumption: sugar. Sidney Mintz claims that "since the invention of agriculture [our diets] ha[ve] centered upon a core complex carbohydrate 'fringed' with contrasting tastes and textures to stimulate appetite" (1985, 192). As in the other sections, we begin with a brief historical overview and a discussion of the most critical issues.

Just as with the plantation practices for cocoa and coffee, slave labor ended on sugar plantations in the mid-1800s, but the commodity chains that were developed early on still remain. Because of sugar's link to other products, such as tea and milk chocolate, it is sometimes difficult to see its role in fostering or restricting development. Nevertheless, sugar is clearly at the center of development issues discussed in this and earlier chapters.

Most important is the connection to human servitude: of all the industries profiled here, the sugar industry has enslaved more human beings than any other and accounted for the indentured servitude of hundreds of thousands of others. As we will see in the next few pages, this is perhaps the reason that large, private multinational sugar producers such as Illovo are going to great lengths to distance themselves from such activity, to document their compliance with international business principles, and to actively promote their current approach to employment. Moving forward, we can anticipate further tensions between those enactors of policies allocating sugarcane to biofuel production and those allocating it to food production. Additionally, the rise of genetically modified sugar beets, which account for about half of the sugar produced globally, may prove to be an emerging health issue.

History

While people have been consuming sweet beverages from time immemorial, the earliest documentation of actual production of sugar comes in A.D. 500 (Mintz 1985). After A.D. 700 but before A.D. 1000, sugar made its way to Europe, starting with Spain. As Mintz describes it, with the Arab conquest of Spain came "sugarcane, its cultivation, the art of sugar making, and a taste for this different sweetness" (23). The introduction of sugar to Europe followed the earlier pattern of its introduction throughout Persia, India, and the Arab Mediterranean, where both sugar and the secrets of its production followed the Arab conquest of each area.

People in Western Europe first joined the sugar commodity chain as consumers. However, Mintz describes their subsequent development as controllers of sugar after the Crusades. Both Mintz and J. H. Galloway suggest that declines in population due to the Black Death caused places like Crete and Cyprus to withdraw as sugar producers. Mintz describes the roles that Sicily, Spain, and Morocco played in producing sugar in the 1400s and suggests in no uncertain terms that the links between sugar and slavery began at this time (1985, 28–32). Citing Galloway, he states that "it was the expanded use of slave labor to compensate for plague-connected mortality that initiated the strange and enduring relationship between sugar and slavery" (29).

In the New World, as early as the fifteenth century, African slaves were brought to Brazil to work sugarcane fields: "Between 1450 and 1600 the Portuguese shipped 175,000 slaves from West Africa, transforming what had been a series of regional slave markets into a transatlantic trade where the tickets were one-way" (MacGillivray 2006, 148). Brazil's primary trading partner was Lisbon. Mintz characterizes the sixteenth century as "the Brazilian century for sugar" (1985, 33). The following centuries drew in both British and French colonies in the Caribbean with at least 3.5 million slaves (MacGillivray 2006, 149). In Haiti alone, more than half a million Africans were enslaved as sugar plantation laborers in the late 1700s (West 2007). In the Guianas in 1595, attempts were made to grow sugarcane. Both sugarcane and slaves were brought to Jamestown in the early 1600s, but the cane did not take (Mintz 1985). In 1627, however, Barbados was settled by the British, and within thirty years, noticeable exports of sugar were making their way to Great Britain. Mintz suggests that this seamless link between centers of production and centers of consumption enabled England to be its own commodity chain. In all the settings described above, with the exception of Jamestown, it was slave labor that fueled the successful plantation economies. In like manner, slave labor fueled rum production. Jean West (2007, 3) details what was termed the Triangle Trade: "Sugar stands at the center of the Triangle Trade; it was the engine that drove the African Diaspora. Slaves of the Caribbean sugar plantations produced molasses that was transported to New England for distillation into rum that was shipped to Africa in exchange for the slaves who would endure the final leg of the triangle, the horrific Middle Passage to the sugar islands." These plantation economies "would foster the beginnings of the largest trafficking in human souls the world had seen" (Hohenegger 2006, 102).

Although the slave trade ended in 1807, it was not until thirty to forty years later that slavery was abolished—1838 for the English and 1848 for the French (Mintz 1985, 53). In Haiti, a successful slave rebellion in 1791 led to the country's independence in 1804. In the Caribbean, slave labor shifted to indentured labor (in French, *engagés*). While the title changed, sugar was still being harvested on the backs of unpaid or ill-paid workers unable to leave workplaces of their own free will. Alex MacGillivray argues that the "reliance on cheap sugar . . . created an ethical callousness on the part of consumers towards distant producers that continued long after the abolition of slavery" (2006, 151). This is the same point made by Carol Off (2006) regarding cocoa harvesting in West Africa: when we are geographically separated from the sources of production, it is easy to anesthetize ourselves and ignore the dehumanizing aspects of conditions of harvest and production. Keeping the core countries and their behavior "clean" while restricting "dirty" behavior to the periphery countries allows the core countries to maintain an aura of innocence. For postcolonial theorists, the issue with sugar and other commodities is part of a larger system of neocolonial relationships that define the global structure of power (Fischer-Tene 2010).

The World Wildlife Fund states that "145 million tons of sugars are produced in 121 countries each year" (qtd. in Beaudry 2017). According to the Illovo Sugar website (Czarnikow Sugar), close to 80 percent of the world's sugar production comes from the top ten producers. Sugar is clearly embedded in the food chains of consumers around the world. However, it cannot be called primarily an export crop because roughly 70 percent of sugar produced in any area is sold within its country of origin. Africa's largest private sugar-producing company, Illovo, operates in six countries. It recently became a subsidiary of Associated British Foods.

Among its many sugar products, Illovo produces specialty high-end sugar and sugar syrup in South Africa, Zambia, and Malawi. The specialty sugars produced in Malawi are exported both to the European Union and to the United States, while those produced in Zambia are consumed domestically and exported to the EU. Think for a moment about the geographic location of these three African nations. What may account for where the specialty sugar products are marketed? Consider also the relationship of niche marketing to small farmer subsistence to the privatization of land access with these sugar plantations. Try to predict what future issues might arise in the production of sugar.

Illovo's website lists its commitment to sustainable agricultural practices, including water management. The front page of the website details not only its environmental commitments but also its commitment to greater social equity and poverty reduction (www.illovo.com). This information, featured so prominently on essentially a business website, reinforces the delicate space sugar producers find themselves in. Illovo has chosen to be quite transparent in its description of the water basins it operates in and lists its withdrawals on its website. The company provides specific information about its environmental compliance. This may be because multiple environmental groups, such as the World Wildlife Fund, have observed the toll sugar production takes on biodiversity (Beaudry 2017). Additionally, in response to calls for more transparency and monitoring of labor conditions, companies like Illovo have subscribed to the UN Guiding Principles on Business and Human Rights. Associated British Foods has issued a specific statement on human trafficking and slavery. In it the British company states, "Our new supply chain pillar focuses on international communications and activities around modern slavery risks in the supply chain." (Associated British Foods 2017).

Critical Issues

Some critical issues linked to sugar production are safety, sourcing, work conditions, and genetic modification. The Global Alliance for Sugar Trade Reform and Liberalisation has pushed strongly for the removal of sugar subsidies on the part of the more powerful WTO members. The United States is unlikely to support this; there are serious current concerns about NAFTA and Mexican sugar production. The future of NAFTA at the writing of this chapter is unclear as well.

With respect to indentured servitude, general work conditions, and civil society, various NGOs and alliances continue to present information at world meetings. The popular press routinely notes issues related to worker conditions and debt (Ortiz, 2014). World meetings and local workshops will not change the severity of these conditions without permanent structural changes to the politics and economics of sugar consumption.

Case Study: Land Acquisition by Saudi Arabia and China

As we explore food security and insecurity throughout the world, it is necessary to look not only at arable land but also at the water that reaches this land. Is the water a right or a commodity? Who truly owns underground aquifers and water flowing through watershed systems that run through multiple countries and multiple states? What does it mean to cede land and water rights to a landlord in another country instead of exporting crops as an owner? The case study below addresses some of these dimensions.

Imagine this scenario: you are in a developing country at the mercy of a corrupt government or large private corporation that paints a glowing picture of what your possible life will be like if you sell ancestral land, and there is also pressure from farmers around you to sell. Family farms that were multicropping for domestic and international use may be taken over by large industrial farms with an eye to monoculture. As development worker Jeanne Zoundjihekpon in the video "Land Grabs in Africa Neocolonialism" (2010) states, "To give the land to multinationals—to foreigners—favors industrial-scale farming, so that means single-crop cultivation and that destroys local biodiversity; then [another] danger I think is the question of food sovereignty—see, if small farmers no longer have their own land to produce their own crops, then their control over their food supply is weakened and they have to rely on what the multinationals produce."

But now think about this scenario: a major Middle Eastern oil-producing nation needs land and water to grow crops and chooses to purchase land in your Global North country. It grows wheat and then alfalfa and then hay, all heavy water-grabbing crops, and over time the water table in your state drops. Water rights to your state are trumped by water rights in the states located ahead of you in the riverbed. Is this colonialism/neocolonialism in the Global North? Some would say absolutely; the U.S. states of California and Arizona are currently active participants in this exchange, much to the chagrin of small farmers in these states (Miller 2016).

Without access to accurate information, without curiosity, and without empathy we will be unable to make ethical policy decisions affecting the whole world in the coming century. This case study explores land acquisition (grabs) by foreign companies in two geographic areas: the Horn of Africa and the U.S. Southwest. We argue here that these bilateral and multilateral land deals generally benefit the purchasing nations and rarely benefit the "colonized" nations in the long run. However, these exchanges will only increase. In the first case, China is purchasing land in Ethiopia and Sudan. As we will see below, some scholars argue China's activity is absolutely neocolonial, while others argue that there is in fact no land rush (Liberti 2013). In the second case, Saudi Arabia is purchasing land in California and Arizona to grow crops to feed its citizens and for export. Both China and Saudi Arabia fear they will be unable to feed their people due to loss of arable land. Both countries have purchased large amounts of land in other countries in order to grow crops to ship back to their homelands. This land ownership provides a level of security to the purchasing countries. It does not, however, provide security to the nation-states losing land and water rights. This acquisition is most typically termed "land grab." For Maria Rulli, Antonio Saviori, and Paolo D'Odorico, there is both a narrow definition and a more general one:

> The 2011 Tirana conference of the International Land Coalition defined land grabbing as land acquisitions that are in violation of human rights, without prior consent of the preexisting land users, and with no consideration of the social and environmental impacts. In many cases, land grabbing is not the result of a transparent and democratic decision process. Lack of consultation with local land users, violation of human rights, and social or environmental impacts are, however, difficult to verify. Therefore, here we use a broader definition of land grabbing as the transfer of the right to own or use the land from local communities to foreign investors through large-scale land acquisitions (more than 200 ha[hectares] per deal). (2013, 892)

Some negotiations are private while others are government-supported or brokered. In general, food security in the purchasing country is listed as the most common reason for foreign entities to purchase land in other countries. An emerging issue is also the need to acquire sufficient biofuels—nations striving to move away from fossil fuels are turning to biological alternatives, most frequently soybeans, corn, and sugarcane.

The information typically supportive of such land grabbing suggests that nation-states receive more funds to manage their agriculture plans and as a consequence receive greater "soft" benefits to farming communities such as infrastructure growth—schools, clinics, roads, and the like

(Seo and Rodriguez, 2012, 166). Those critical of such land grabbing look toward the dimensions of neocolonialism and capitalism. In these cases, we have such countries in the Global North as the UK, the United States, and Germany acquiring land in the Global South, as well as South-South deals, for example, China with Sudan and Ethiopia and India with Ethiopia. Sometimes the arable land purchased is tagged as "wasteland" (Seo and Rodriguez 2012), even though vulnerable Indigenous communities may have been not only farming there but also gathering medicines in land that has belonged to them for centuries.

Saudi Arabia was once a net exporter of grains. It has most recently ceased wheat production (2016), with hay and alfalfa to follow (James 2017; Liberti 2013; Slav 2016). This has been due to the severe depletion of underground aquifers. Anticipating food security needs in the future, Saudi Arabia has been slowly buying up land in places that may surprise you, including Ukraine and two spots in the United States: California and Arizona (James 2017; Slav 2016; Miller 2016; Weiser 2016). The total land purchased or leased by Saudi Arabia by 2012 included 1,132,945 hectares (Seo and Rodriguez 2012) in areas requiring heavy irrigation. Depletion of underground aquifers in these areas may deeply affect agricultural productivity. As in the Global South, small farmers selling their land reap short-term benefits as large agribusinesses move in. When large agribusinesses focus on one export crop, whether these businesses are foreign or national, local food supplies may be affected.

The total land purchased or leased globally by China by 2012 was 1,953,527 hectares (Seo and Rodriguez 2012). It has typically purchased land for other agricultural uses than grain production, unlike Saudi Arabia's specific purchase for grain production. China has frequently presented its activities as supportive of development needs of other Global South countries and an example of soft capitalism (Hofman and Ho 2012). In much of the Western press, however, we see the phrase "land grab" associated with China. Other scholars dispute this notion; SIANI (2013) referenced in van Dijk suggests, "There is little evidence to suggest such a pattern of behaviour in the agricultural sector" (2016, 8). Scholars note that China is twelfth on the list of countries acquiring land in parts of Africa (van Dijk 2016) in what amounted in 2018 to roughly 240,000 hectares (Brautigan 2018). What is clear regarding both Saudi Arabia and China is that both countries are looking globally and outside the physical boundaries of their nation-states for long-term land investments. The rationales given for this behavior focus on future food security and future biofuel needs. Both countries are considered part of the Global South. In the case of Saudi Arabia, we see a South country purchasing land throughout countries in the Global North. In the case of China, we see a South country purchasing or long-term leasing land in the Global South. South-South development operations will continue for some time to come. Regarding Saudi Arabia, we would do well to consider the long-term role of water rights and aquifer levels when exploring effects of continued agricultural investment in arid lands. Whether we use the phrase "land acquisition" or "land grab," we see clear evidence of continuing complexity in nation-state relations. For Irna Hofman and Peter Ho, "the phenomenon of world-wide land-based investments is like other processes of globalization likely to feature multiple layers, that constitute a highly complex, and at times, downright contradictory reality" (2012, 22).

Conclusion

Food connects us all on physical, emotional, and economic levels. The commodity chains we have explored in this chapter reflect common relationships between developed and developing nations. We have seen clear examples of the power differentials between multinational corporations, international organizations, and small family farms and cooperatives. From the examples you have read, you should now have a sense of the fragile nature of food on the global commodities market: politics, economics, and weather can wreak havoc on the GNP of smaller nations in a very short period of time.

Perhaps you can now catch a glimpse of the wider world in your coffee cup or in the next chocolate bar you eat. As sustainability becomes more important to everyone, we see that even large multinational companies are making changes in the way they do business (Davis-Peccoud and Duchnowski 2018). We have seen that sustainably produced items may have less of a negative impact on our agricultural future than those produced in a more technological setting.

At the same time, we have observed the complexity of producer/consumer relations over time and the impact of export and import commodities from year to year. Historical patterns of relationship can maintain dependency between exporting and importing nations. In addition, new actors have arrived on the scene, and products once consumed in single areas are being brought to new markets to satisfy newly acquired consumer tastes. Land productivity issues and bilateral relations are also very impor-

> The largest repository of agricultural seeds in the world is in an area of the Arctic owned by Norway. Why do you think the Svalbard Global Seed Vault exists when there are 1,400 seed banks located in other parts of the world?

tant. China has been purchasing land in East Africa. Many characterize these land acquisitions and long-term leases as "land grabs," a type of neo-colonialism that will never benefit small landholders and may ultimately pull arable land out of availability to its citizens.

We have looked primarily at connections between countries but have not examined in detail connections between individuals. Nevertheless, it is important to be aware of the impact our individual choices have on the environment and to notice how global trends in consumption and marketing affect us all. Global issues such as world hunger have clearly been beyond the scope of this chapter. A key point to remember as you consider this chapter is that perhaps the problem of global hunger is due less to production than to food availability in particular areas.

On Your Own

One product not profiled in this chapter is rice. Yet all of the issues we have discussed so far are relevant to the current global production of this food-stuff. On your own, we invite you to explore the links between rice—particularly the jasmine and basmati varieties—and issues such as biopiracy, seed banks, genetically modified foods, and agrobusinesses. The Green Revolution of the 1960s substantially changed producers and consumers forever. Nations such as Iran, once self-sufficient in rice production, became rice importers. High-yield hybrid varieties of rice, complete with their own compatible pesticides, became varieties of choice in numerous Asian nations. Some multinational corporations applied for patents on staples such as basmati and jasmine rice, varieties grown in India and Thailand for centuries. Charges of biopiracy were filed. Cases have been taken to court. Promoters of sustainable agricultural practices go head-to-head on the local level with marketers of less-traditional practices. See what you can discover on your own online and through other resources. As you reflect on foods in your daily life, it is important to recognize the role that food security will play throughout the globe in the coming decades.

In early 2009 a UN-sponsored meeting that focused on the global food crisis was held. It centered on food security and unequal distribution of food. In spite of a commitment on the part of members of the UN Food and Agriculture Organization to try to reduce global hunger levels by 2015, it is believed that at the present rate, it will be 2150 or later until that goal is achieved (IOL 2019).

➤ VOCABULARY

monoculture crops
fair trade
valorization
land grabs
niche marketing
sustainable agriculture
food security
genetically modified (GMO) food

➤ DISCUSSION AND REFLECTION QUESTIONS

1. *How would you characterize the relationship between food production and population density in the world today?*
2. *What is the relationship between food production, biofuels, and water?*
3. *How do fuel prices—both high and low—contribute to our globalized food economy?*
4. *What factors make it difficult to keep track of the origins of cacao beans, and what relationship do these factors have to the use of child labor?*
5. *What recent examples of niche marketing in either cacao/cocoa or coffee are you familiar with?*
6. *How did the IMF and the World Bank shift the world map in terms of coffee production, and how did the activities of these organizations impact national coffee boards around the globe?*
7. *In what ways might the General Agreement on Trade in Services and the protection of intellectual property rights enter into the world of food production and consumption?*
8. *How will water rights, intellectual property rights, and changing climate patterns affect food security in the next ten years?*
9. *What might account for the preponderance of characterizations in the Western press that China is one of the primary land grabbers in Africa?*

ACTIVITY 1: ANALYZE Look again at Table 3 and focus on the columns for quinoa, rice, and bananas, crops not discussed in this chapter. See if you can find details about any of the areas on the matrix that are marked with a •. Create an illustration summarizing your findings.

ACTIVITY 2: REFLECT Choose one of the issues raised in this chapter and think about the information you now have. Look at the continuum below and identify where you are on this spectrum.

1	2	3	4	5	6	7
Identify local/global problems associated with one food issue.	Gather information.	Compare/contrast what you knew initially and what you know now.	How does this relate to your current program of study?	How might you engage in a level of stewardship or activism while in school?	What could you do to parlay your interest into a local or global internship?	What could you do to parlay your internship into a paid position in this arena?

ACTIVITY 3: EXTEND Buy a product discussed in this chapter. Using the packaging information, identify where the product was produced, where it was packaged, and where the packaging came from. How far did the product travel from its harvesting to your door?

References

Alliance for Sustainability. n.d. Retrieved March 29, 2007, from http://www.mnt.org/iasa/susafdef.htm.

Amarasinghe, U., C. Hoanh, D. D'haeze, and T. Hung. 2015. Toward sustainable coffee production in Vietnam: More coffee with less water. *Agricultural Systems 136*:96–105.

Associated British Foods. 2017. Modern slavery and human trafficking statement. Retrieved July 31, 2018, from https://www.illovosugarafrica.com/UserContent/documents/group-gov/2017/abf_modern_slavery_statement_2017.pdf.

Beaudry, F. 2017. Thought company: Sugar produces bitter results for the environment. *Earth Talk*, March 17. Retrieved July 13, 2018, from https://tinyurl.com/y5n9no8p.

Bitty, A. E., S. B. Gonedele, J. C. Koffi Bene, P. Kouass, and W. S. McGraw. 2015. Cocoa farming and primate extirpation inside Côte d'Ivoire's protected areas. *Tropical Conservation Science 8* (1): 95–113. Retrieved June 12, 2018, from www.tropicalconservationscience.org.

Brautigan, D. 2018. US politicians get China in Africa all wrong. *Washington Post*, April 12. https://www.washingtonpost.com/news/theworldpost/wp/2018/04/12/china-africa/?noredirect=on&utm_term=.7f12ef898f58.

Cargill completes acquisition of ADM's global chocolate business, deepening service offering to its customers. 2015 [August 3]. Retrieved November 6, 2019, from Cargill.com.

Cargill to buy ADM's chocolate business. 2014 [September 12]. Retrieved November 6, 2019, from Cargill.com.

Chanthavong, S. 2002. Chocolate and slavery. TED Case Studies 664. Retrieved January 24, 2009, from www.american.edu/ted/chocolate-slave.htm.

Chocolate Manufacturer's Association (Chocolate Council of the National Confectioners Association). n.d. Retrieved January 24, 2009, from http://www.chocolateusa.org/About-Us/.

Cocks, T., and A. Aboa. 2018. Ivory Coast, chocolate giants team up to make cocoa production more sustainable. *Christian Science Monitor*, April 19. Retrieved June 12, 2018, from https://www.csmonitor.com/World/Africa/2018/0419/Ivory-Coast-chocolate-giants-team-up-to-make-cocoa-production-more-sustainable.

Cocoa Market Update. 2012. World Cocoa Foundation. Retrieved November 6, 2019, from www.worldcocoafoundation.org.

Cocoa Market Update. n.d. Retrieved August 30, 2013, from http://www.chocolateusa.org/About-Us/.

Cocoa production under control of foreign companies. 2013. *Saigon GP Daily English Edition*, March 13. Retrieved May 5, 2013, from http://www.saigon-gpdaily.com.vn/Business/2013/3/104360/.

Cohen, L. 2016. As climate change threatens Central American coffee, a cocoa boom is born. Retrieved May 28, 2018, from https://www.reuters.com/article/us-climatechange-cocoa-coffee.

CSR Asia. 2013. *Inclusive business in Asia: A case study of cocoa*. 2013. Retrieved May 28, 2018, from www.csr-asia.com/report/Cocoa_paper.pdf.

Czarnikow Sugar. n.d. https://www.czarnikow.com/.

Daniels, S. 2006. Developing best practice guidelines for sustainable models of cocoa production to maximize their impacts on biodiversity protection [pdf]. World Wildlife Fund Vietnam.

Davis, E. 2016. Sustainable development in Vietnam: The interconnectedness of climate change, socio-economic development, land use, and food security. *Pursuit: The Journal of Undergraduate Research at the University of Tennessee* 7 (1): article 11. Retrieved May 28, 2018, from http://trace.tennessee.edu/pursuit/vol7/iss1/11.

Davis-Peccoud, J., and S. Duchnowski. 2018. Working with suppliers for sustainable food supply chains. *Bain and Company Business Insights*. Retrieved July 13, 2018, from http://www.bain.com/publications/articles/working-with-suppliers-for-sustainable-food-supply-chains.aspx.

DeNicola, E., O. Aburizaiza, A. Siddique, H. Khwaja and D. Carpenter. 2015. Climate change and water scarcity: The case of Saudi Arabia. *Annals of Global Health 81*(3): 342–53.

Dicum, G., and N. Luttinger. 1999. *The coffee book: Anatomy of an industry from crop to the last drop.* New York: New Press.

ETC Group. n.d. Biopiracy. Retrieved January 24, 2009, from https://www.etcgroup.org/content/biopiracy.

Ethical Sugar. 2009. Retrieved September 9, 2009, from http://www.sucreethique.org/Brazilian-seminar-Ethical-Sugar.html.

Fearn, H. 2016. In a final betrayal of the Cadbury brand, Kraft has quietly abandoned its promise to stick with Fairtrade. November 29. Retrieved May 28, 2018, from https://www.independent.co.uk/voices/cadburys-chocolate-fairtrade.

Fischer-Tene, H. 2010. EGO: European History Online: Postcolonial Studies. Retrieved November 7, 2019, from http://ieg-ego.eu/en/threads/theories-and-methods/postcolonial-studies.

Gillis, J. 2013. Climate change seen posing risk to food supplies. *New York Times*, November 1. Retrieved July 10, 2019, from https://archive.nytimes.com/www.nytimes.com/2013/11/02/science/earth/science-panel-warns-of-risks-to-food-supply-from-climate-change.html.

Global Alliance for Sugar Trade Reform and Liberalisation. n.d. Retrieved September 9, 2009, from http://www.globalsugaralliance.org/resources.php?action=displayResources&requestType=News.

Gonzalez-Perez, M.-A., and S. Gutierrez-Viara. 2012. Cooperation in coffee markets: The case of Vietnam and Colombia. *Journal of Agribusiness in Developing and Emerging Economies 2* (1): 57–73.

Green, D. (with S. Branford). 2013. Faces of Latin America. New York: Monthly Review Press.

Group, E. 2008. Do you know what's in your candy? September 8. Retrieved September 9, 2009, from http://www.globalhealingcenter.com/naturalhealth/do-you-know-whats-in-your-candy/.

Guilbert, K. 2017. Falling cocoa prices threaten child labor spike in Ghana, Ivory Coast. Reuters, June 12. Retrieved May 28, 2018, from https://www.reuters.com/article/us-westafrica-cooa-children/.

Ha, D. T., and G. Shively. 2005. Coffee vs. cacao: A case study from the Vietnamese Central Highlands. *Journal of Natural Resources and Life Sciences Education 34*:107–11.

Harkin, Engel: Final report shows that work must continue to eradicate child labor in the cocoa supply chain. 2011. April 4. Retrieved August 30, 2013, from Tom Harkin press release, http://www.harkin.senate.gov/press/release.cfm?i=332330.

Heintzman, A., and E. Solomon, eds. 2004. *Feeding the future: From fat to famine, how to solve the world's food crisis.* Toronto: House of Anansi Press.

Hjelm, L. 2015. *Rwanda 2015: Comprehensive food security and vulnerability analysis.* Retrieved June 24, 2019, from https://documents.wfp.org/stellant

/groups/public/documents/ena/wfp 284395.pdf. [Also available at http://www.wfp.org/food-security, www.statistics.gove.rw].

Hofman, I., and P. Ho. 2012. China's "developmental outsourcing": A critical examination of Chinese global "land grabs" discourse. *Journal of Peasant Studies* 39 (1): 1–48.

Hohenegger, B. 2006. *Liquid jade: The story of tea from East to West.* New York: St. Martin's Press.

Hopkins, T., and I. Wallerstein. 1977. Patterns of development in the modern world system. *Review 1* (Fall): 111–45.

Igami, M. 2012. Oligopoly in international commodity markets: The case of coffee beans. Retrieved July 21, 2018, from https://economics.yale.edu/sites/default/files/igami-120926.pdf.

Illovo Sugar. n.d. www.illovo.com.

International Cocoa Initiative. 2018. Risk of forced labour in cocoa present in both Ghana and Côte d'Ivoire: 2018 Global Slavery Index. July 20. Retrieved July 22, 2019, from https://cocoainitiative.org/news-media-post/finding-on-forced-labour-in-cocoa-in-the-2018-global-slavery-index/.

IOL. 2009. Call for new focus on food security. January 26. Retrieved January 24, 2019, from https://www.iol.co.za/news/world/call-for-new-focus-on-food-security-432378.

Huntington, S. P. 1996. *The clash of civilizations and the remaking of world order.* New York: Touchstone.

James, I. 2017. Booming demand for hay in Asian, Middle East driving agribusiness in the California desert. *Desert Sun*, September 28. Retrieved July 18, 2018, from https://www.desertsun.com/story/news/environment/2017/09/28/booming-demand-hay-asia-middle-east-driving-agribusiness-california-desert/702400001.

Khan, L. 2013. Why so little candy variety? Blame the chocolate oligopoly. Retrieved November 6, 2019, from http://ideas.time.com/2013/11/01/why-so-little-candy-variety-blame-the-chocolate-oligopoly/.

Killeen, T., and G. Harper. 2016. Coffee in the 21st century: Will climate change and increased demand lead to new deforestation? *Conservation International*, April 14.

Land grabs in Africa neo-colonialism. 2010. YouTube. Retrieved July 3, 2018, from https://www.youtube.com/watch?v=GxFTGq94dXs.

LeBaron, G. 2018. *The global business of forced labour: Report of findings.* Sheffield, UK: SPERI and University of Sheffield.

Leissle, K. 2018. *Cocoa.* Cambridge: Polity Press.

Liberti, S. 2013. *Land grabbing: Journeys in the new colonialism.* New York: Verso.

Lopez, R. 2002. *Chocolate: The nature of indulgence.* New York: Harry N. Abrams.

Luttinger, N., and G. Dicum. 2006. *The coffee book: Anatomy of an industry from crop to the last drop.* New York: New Press.

MacGillivray, A. 2006. *A brief history of globalization.* London: Robinson.

Myers, A. 2018. Zero incidents by 2025? How the cocoa industry intends to eradicate child labor from the supply chain [June 14]. Retrieved November 6,

2019, from www.confectionerynews.com/Article/2018/06/14/How-the-cocoa-industry-intends-to-eradicate-child-labor-from-the-supply-chain#.

Michaels, M. 2018. Cape Town is running out of water—I visited and saw what the financial problems of "Day Zero" look like on the ground. *Business Insider*, May 27. Retrieved July 29, 2018, from https://www.businessinsider.com/cape-town-day-zero-photos-inequality-2018-2.

Miller, D. 2016. La Paz County at odds with Saudi Arabian farm. Fox News, February 23. Retrieved July 18, 2018, from http://www.fox10phoenix.com/news/arizona-news.

Millstone, E., and T. Lang. 2008. *The atlas of food: Who eats what, where, and why*. Los Angeles: University of California Press.

Mintz, S. 1985. *Sweetness and power: The place of sugar in modern history*. New York: Viking/Penguin.

Murphy, P. 2013. The ecofeminist subsistence perspective revisited in an age of land grabs and its representations in contemporary literature. *Feminismo/s* 22:205–24.

Nieburg, O. 2015. After the earthquake: Haitian cocoa rep rises on high-end chocolate scene. Confectionery News, February 17. Retrieved June 12, 2018, from https://www.confectionerynews.com/Article/2015/02/17/Haitian-cocoa-a-rising-origin-for-premium-chocolate.

———. 2018. Cocoa child labor lawsuits against Mars and Hershey filed. Confectionary News, February 28. Retrieved May 28, 2018, from https://www.confectionerynews.com/Article/2018/02/28/Cocoa.

Off, C. 2006. *Bitter chocolate: Investigating the dark side of the world's most seductive sweet*. Toronto: Random House Canada.

O'Keefe, B. 2016. Inside big chocolate's child labor problem. *Fortune*, March 1. Retrieved May 28, 2018, from http://fortune.com/big-chocolate-child-labor-problem.

Ortiz, F. 2014. Face of slave labour changing in Brazil. Retrieved November 7, 2019, from http://www.ipsnews.net/2014/04/face-slave-labour-changing-brazil/.

Pettigrew, J. 1997. *The tea companion: A connoisseur's guide*. New York: Macmillan.

Pollan, M. 2008. Farmer in chief. *New York Times Magazine*, October 9. Retrieved October 24, 2008, from http://www.nytimes.com/2008/10/12/magazine/12policy-t.html.

Reuters. 2018. Ivory Coast to reduce cocoa output over next 2 years. Reuters, March 9. Retrieved June 12, 2018, from https://www.reuters.com/article/cocoa-ivorycoast/update-1-ivory-coast-to-reduce-cocoa-output-over-next-two-years-idUSL5N1QR2SJ.

Rulli, M. C., A. Saviori, and P. D'Odorico. 2013. Global land and water grabbing. *PNAS 110* (3): 892–97. Retrieved July 10, 2019, from https://doi.org/10.1073/pnas.1213163110.

Rwanda. n.d. Retrieved June 24, 2019, from https:www1.wfp.org/countries/rwanda.

Save the Children Canada. 2005. Expert forum. Child protection in raw agricultural commodities trade: The case of cocoa. Retrieved January 24, 2009, from http://www.savethechildren.ca/canada/what_we_do/advocate/cocoa.

Seo, K., and N. Rodriguez. 2012. Land grab, food security and climate change: A vicious circle in the Global South. Human and social dimensions of climate change. INTECH. Retrieved July 28, 2018, from https:d-grab-food-security-and-climate-change-a-vicious-circle-in-the-global-south.

Shepherd, B. 2012. A need for new institutions? Bilateral deals over food producing resources and international co-operation on food security. In *New security frontiers: Critical energy and the resource challenge,* edited by S. Krishna-Hensel, 173–97. Burlington, Vt.: Ashgate.

SIANI. 2013. Is China one of the main countries to blame for land grabbing in Africa? Chinese "land grabs" in Africa—the reality behind the news. Retrieved July 18, 2018, from www.momagri.org/UK/focu-on-issues/Is-China-one-of-the-main-countries-to-blame-for-land-grabbing-in africa.

Slav, I. 2016. Saudi Arabia buying up land in the U.S. Southwest to feed its cows. Oil Price.com, April 2. Retrieved July 28, 2018, from https://oilprice.com/Latest-Energy-News/World-News/Saudi-Arabia-Buying-Up-Land-In-The-US-Southwest-To-Feed-Its-Cows.html.

Solidaridad. 2018. Farming families and forests victim of failing cocoa market. *Solidaridad,* April 19. Retrieved June 12, 2019, from https://www.solidaridadnetwork.org/news/farming-families-forests-victim-of-failing-cocoa-market.

Standage, T. 2005. *A history of the world in six glasses.* New York: Walker and Company.

Stanley, C. 2018. 2018 coffee trends: Where is the coffee industry going next? Retrieved July 11, 2018, from https://revelsystems.com/blog/2018/01/20/2018-coffee-trends/.

Statista. 2019. Coffee production worldwide from 2003/04 to 2017/18 (in million 60 kilogram bags). Retrieved July 13, 2019, from https://www.statista.com/statistics/263311/worldwide-production-of-coffee/.

Sterk, R. 2018. Ivory Coast seeks to cut cocoa bean crop. *Food Business News,* March 9. Retrieved June 5, 2018, from https://www.foodbusinessnews.net/articles/11441-ivory-coast-seeks-to-cut-cocoa-bean-crop.

Sudersan, R., and S. Chatterjee. 2001 [June 24]. Stop chocolate slavery. Retrieved November 7, 2019, from http://vision.ucsd.edu/~kbranson/stopchocolateslavery/atasteofslavery.

Tackling Child Labor. 2017. *Nestle cocoa plan.* Retrieved May 28, 2018, from https://www.nestle.com/asset.../nestle-cocoa-plan-child-labour-2017-report.pdf.

Van der Voo, L. 2018. *The fish market: Inside the big-money battle for the ocean and your dinner plate.* New York: St. Martin's Press.

van Dijk, M. 2016. Is China grabbing land in Africa? A literature overview study. Paper presented at the LANDac Conference, infrastructure development session, Utrecht, June 20, 2016.

Vietnam: The next cacao frontier. 2016. Chocolate class: Multimedia essays on chocolate, culture, and the politics of food, February 19. Retrieved May 28, 2018, from https://chocolateclass.wordpresscom/2016/02/19/vietnam-the-next-cacao-frontier.

Voice of Vietnam. 2016a. "From farming to chocolate" model boosts Vietnam's cocoa reputation. *Voice of Vietnam*, December 2. Retrieved July 11, 2018, from http://english.vov.vn/economy/from-framing-chocoate-model-boosts-Vietnam's-cocoa-reputation.

———. 2016b. Vietnam cocoa splashes into organic market. *Voice of Vietnam*, July 8. Retrieved July 11, 2018, from http://english.vov.vn/trade/vietnam-cocoa-splashes-into-organic-market.

Weatherford, J. 1989. *Indian givers*. New York: Crown Publishers.

Weiser, M. 2016. Water-poor Saudi Arabia moves farming venture to drought-stricken California. *The Guardian*, March 8. Retrieved July 11, 2018, from https://www.the guardian.com/sustainable-business/2016/march/08.

West, J. 2007. Sugar and slavery: Molasses to rum to slaves. Slavery in America. Retrieved November 7, 2019, from https://docplayer.net/52934970-Sugar-and-slavery-molasses-to-rum-to-slaves-jean-m-west.html.

Wild, A. 2004. *Coffee: A dark history*. New York: W. W. Norton.

Willow, F. 2018. Does your chocolate come from slaves? Ethical unicorn: Sustainable living and social justice. Retrieved May 28, 2018, from https://ethicalunicorn.com/2018/02/24/does-your-chocolate-come-from-slaves.

World Atlas. 2019. Top coffee producing countries. Retrieved November 6, 2019, from https://www.worlatlas.com/articles/top-coffee-producing-countries.html.

World Bank. 2018. Vietnam: Transforming livelihoods for coffee and rice producers. *World Bank Brief*, May 16. Retrieved July 11, 2018, from http://www.worldbank.org/en/about/partners/brief/vietnam-transforming-livelihoods-for-coffee-and-rice-producers.

World Cocoa Foundation. 2012. Cocoa project in Vietnam (Nong Lam University). Retrieved July 11, 2018, from http://wwww.worldcocoafoundation.org/cocoa-project-in-vietnam.

World Economic Forum. 2016. Which countries spend the most on food? This map will show you. Retrieved June 5, 2018, from https://www.weforum.org/agenda/2016/12/this-map-shows-how-much-each-country-spends-on-food/.

NINE **Health**

SYNOPSIS

This chapter examines the role of health issues in a globalizing world. It explores tensions between science and policy, focusing in depth on AIDS, tuberculosis, and malaria. The chapter also discusses the link between health and other aspects of society, such as food production and environmental conditions. In some cases, diseases are caused by the medical system itself. Additionally, the chapter presents country-specific responses to global pandemics and considers ethical issues related to the control and production of vaccines and medications. As we have seen in prior chapters, nation-states may deal with their own internal health issues very differently from how they address these same issues in a global context.

SCAFFOLDING

As you read through this chapter, think about how you would answer each of the questions below.

How have you viewed global health issues prior to reading this chapter?

What food production and consumption issues seem intimately linked to global health?

CORE CONCEPTS

How do nation-states decide how to take care of their citizens in terms of providing health care for both regular and infectious diseases?

What kinds of factors have contributed to the resurgence of infectious diseases?

What are some potential links between global health, development, demographics, and global organizations such as the World Health Organization?

How does social inequality impact global health, such as for Indigenous peoples?

Chile, Costa Rica, Cyprus, Guadalupe, Hong Kong, Israel, Macau, Malta, Martinique, Singapore, and the United Arab Emirates make up a diverse set of nations and territories. Yet they all have one fact in common: on average their citizens live longer than those of the United States, as do the citizens of many developed countries (United Nations 2006). This truth might be unexpected, given the wide gap between the wealth, power, and technology of these countries and those of the United States. But health inevitably becomes linked to broader issues of politics and policy. This may appear strange, given that in Western culture, our perception of health is defined by medicine, which entails a rigorous process of scientific training for people entering that profession. But health cannot be discussed outside of a social context. While Costa Rica, for example, does not have the United States' wealth or technology, it has found a way to address health issues so as to give its citizens a greater life span on average than U.S. citizens. Health is such a broad topic that it touches most global issues, such as food production, public policy, global equity, and economic growth. Like security, health issues can also be defined in different ways. In the United States and some Latin American nations, illicit drug usage is seen as a security issue that is best fought through the national security apparatus. In other countries, such as the Netherlands, drug usage is thought of mainly as a public-health issue. Both approaches have unintended consequences and problems. How nations perceive health issues depends on their cultural background. These perceptions have profound impacts, in turn, on how governments ensure their citizens' health.

In some sense, the story of medicine and health in the last three decades has been one in which Western medicine has come to understand its limits (Garrett 1994, 30–52). It is important to examine the limits of modern medicine in order to understand the current challenges to global health. Only a few decades ago, it seemed that technological change could manage most health challenges and the future would bring steady progress. The remaining diseases that threatened health would be eliminated, while developing countries would gradually follow the path of Europe and the United States. This vision of health placed great emphasis on medical technology and the ability of the medical profession alone to manage disease. But trends in both infectious and chronic disease now have created a more complex and chaotic vision of the future.

In the 1960s it seemed clear that infectious diseases were on the decline: "In 1969, the U.S. surgeon general, Dr. William H. Stewart, told the nation that it had already seen most of the frontiers in the field of contagious disease. Epidemiology seemed destined to become a scientific backwater" (Karlen 1995, 3). People gradually stopped studying infectious diseases in medical schools because it was perceived to be a dead end, as the famous virologist C. J. Peters described: "For at least twenty years I have heard that the discipline I work in is a dying field and there is no career track. . . . In spite of our optimism (which may be the optimism of the brontosaurus) and deep belief in the need to continue, the number of gray heads around the conference tables is disproportionate" (Peters and Olshaker 1997, ix). Across the developed world, governments made a renewed commitment to fight chronic diseases, which they believed to be the new frontier in medicine (Karlen 1995, 3).

But by the late 1980s, it became clear that this belief needed to be qualified, as a host of new diseases emerged to infect humanity. (For a partial but nonetheless impressive list, see Karlen 1995, 6; Miller 1989, 509; and Ryan 1997, 383–90.) The rise of AIDS and other illnesses pushed infectious disease—now far from a backwater of medicine—into the newspaper headlines. By the 1990s, a plethora of books (Garrett 1994; Karlen 1995; Peters and Olshaker 1997; Ryan 1997) dealt with the threat of emerging infectious diseases. After the terrorist acts of September 11, 2001, and the anthrax attacks that followed, people next worried about the danger posed by bioterrorism. Ken Alibek's revelations about the secret Soviet bioweapons program, combined with the penury of many Russian scientists in the post-Soviet era, magnified these fears (Alibek and Handelman 1999; see also Garrett 2000, 481–545). By 2005 there was global concern about a lethal strain of bird flu (H5N1) that had emerged in South Asia. Government authorities warned that sufficient stockpiles of antivirals did not exist and that in the event of a pandemic it would take at least six months to create enough medications for North Americans, Europeans, and Japanese. In most of the world, neither medications nor drugs would be available. In

2009 the emergence of the novel H1N1 virus (swine flu) showed that even though much work had been done, it would be months before a vaccine against pandemic influenza could be developed. By 2013 global health experts worried about the simultaneous emergence of H7N1 in China and MERS-COV in Saudi Arabia. How could infectious diseases, which had seemed to be fading into a nightmarish past, have returned to pose such a threat?

There were multiple reasons for their revival (Karlen 1995, 215–30). Health conditions are related to food, and some emerging diseases— such as bovine spongiform encephalopathy (also known as mad cow disease) in Britain in the mid-1980s (Ryan 1997, 330–32)—sprang from agricultural practices, like the antibiotic resistance fostered by feeding large quantities of antibiotics to healthy farm animals.

Farm markets also proved to be a new venue for the spread of disease in a globalized world. In November 2002 a new respiratory illness called SARS emerged in southern China. The outbreak likely began in the wild game markets of Guangdong Province, where civet cats were housed in small cages in open-air markets and buyers would come to purchase them as food for meals (M. Murray 2006, 23; M. Davis 2005, 75–76). H7N9 avian influenza in China has been transmitted from poultry to humans both on farms and in live markets. Although Hong Kong implemented a sophisticated system to control live poultry markets after the emergence of H5N1 influenza in 1997 (this strain differs from the H1N1 influenza strain that emerged later in 2009), there remains a significant risk that the virus could begin to spread from this trade. The 1918 influenza pandemic, which killed between 50 million and a 100 million people globally, demonstrated the potential dangers of such an event in a globalized world. The point is that the same food-production methods that have allowed countries to feed ever-growing populations also pose health threats. For instance, the widespread adoption of high-fructose corn syrup in the 1970s was a key step in the ever-widening global diabetes epidemic. Illness and food production are linked.

Modern medicine has also created iatrogenic diseases—that is, diseases created in part by modern medicine itself. One of these diseases might be the human immunodeficiency virus (HIV). HIV is a retrovirus, which is spread through sex, blood, birth, and breastfeeding and is characterized by a long latency period. Although the syndrome that this virus creates, AIDS (acquired immunodeficiency syndrome), was first described in 1981, we know that the virus dates back decades before that. The first blood sample to contain HIV was drawn in 1959 in Zaire, Africa, while molecular geneticists have suggested that the epidemic first began around 1908 in southeastern Cameroon (Quammen 2015, 60, 67). The virus itself is a clear descendent of simian immunodeficiency virus (SIV), a disease that infects primates, such as chimpanzees. SIV has been found in many people who were infected by bites from primates or from nicks on their hands while butchering monkeys or apes for food (68). Although many people must have been infected with SIV historically, the virus did not easily spread from human to human. Then something changed in Central Africa, most likely in the early 1900s.

There have been many debates about what caused SIV in humans to transform to a pathogenic form, but one possible explanation is that its rapid transmission by contaminated needles during mass vaccination campaigns created profound changes to the virus (Quammen 2015, 125–31; Pépin 2011, 4). It may also have been transformed through blood transfusions. As Jacques Pépin (2011, 11) has argued, Ebola itself was often spread through injections when it first emerged in 1976 in Yambuka, Zaire (now the Democratic Republic of the Congo). Tens of millions of people have died of HIV/AIDS, and many millions more are infected. There are now treatments to manage the infection, which are also able to reduce the transmission of the virus. The death rates have plummeted from the 1990s, and there is renewed hope in the field. But the irony is that modern medicine itself may have also helped to start this pandemic, even though the people responsible acted only with the best of intentions. Indeed, Pépin and Labbé (2008) titled a paper on this topic "Noble Goals, Unforeseen Consequences."

Infectious diseases also emerged for natural reasons, the most basic of which is evolution. Antibiotics seemed extremely effective for a decade, but with misuse and time, resistant strains of bacteria began to appear. The routine use of antibiotics in agriculture to promote the rapid growth of livestock has been a serious concern (McKenna 2010, 140–57). The same careless use of medications took place with parasitic diseases such as malaria. Human behavior, such as saving leftover medications to self-treat other illnesses, also likely exacerbated the problem of antibiotic resistance. This situation has created a frightening reality in which diseases that most modern doctors have never seen are now reemerging. Without question, the most worrying example is tuberculosis (TB), which the HIV/AIDS epidemic accelerates. In Russia, one study published in 2017 (Jakimova et al.) found that 14.3 percent of Russian TB patients had extensively drug resistant TB. In some countries of southern Africa, the HIV prevalence is terrifying; in Botswana and Swaziland, over 20 percent of adults had been infected in 2016. People with HIV are especially vulnerable to TB and therefore often transmit it to others. There are now major policy changes taking place regarding how to incentivize pharmaceutical companies to create antibiotics, which tend to be less profitable than other classes of drugs (Shlaes 2018), but such developments take time.

A related issue is that inadequate medical infrastructure has created environments in which people often receive only partial treatment for TB, which has led to a catastrophic rise in the proportion of the disease's strains that are now multidrug resistant. In South Africa, where over 7 million people are HIV positive, this has created a situation in which a new epidemic of drug-resistant TB threatens the country with disaster. This form of tuberculosis has also been found in other nations, such as India and China. As the work of Paul Farmer (2004) has shown, this problem can be addressed through improved policy decisions, even in the slums of Lima or the prisons of Siberia. Yet this task takes a concerted effort at the international level that until now has been lacking. New diseases also continue to emerge because of ongoing changes to the earth's environment, many of which have been caused by humans. This understanding is not new. Indeed, in the 1990s, authors such as Laurie Garrett (1994, 550–91) and Frank Ryan (1997, 318–42) argued that global environmental changes were key factors driving the emergence of dangerous new diseases.

Writing from this perspective, authors portrayed diseases as the emissaries of a wounded Mother Nature, who was reacting against the human populations that harmed her: "It could be argued that viruses have, through the empirics of evolution, become unwitting knights of nature, armed by evolution for furious genomic attack against her transgressors. Although not primarily designed to attack humanity, human exploitation and invasion of every ecological sphere has directed that aggression our way" (Ryan 1997, 320; see also Miller 1989). These authors used multiple examples to support their arguments, from the emergence of a hemorrhagic fever in Argentina that was associated with wheat production (Garrett 1994, 27–28) to the rise of the Oropouche virus on cacao plantations in the Amazon (Ryan 1997, 327). The development of new diseases, they suggested, can be viewed as an environmental response to the damage inflicted by people: "It is significant in this sense that Ebola, Marburg, and HIV all derived from the African rain forest or its hinterland, savannah. When scientists map the epicenters of origin of newly emerging virus infections on the global map, it is clear that interference with the rain forests, and deforestation in particular, is the most dangerous activity with regard to the emergence of epidemic viruses" (Ryan 1997, 321–22). There is almost a religious rhetoric to this argument, though instead of a plague being God's wrath for sin, now nature is defending itself against humanity. Arno Karlen has pointed out how arbitrary these attributions of blame for disease creation are: "Some call AIDS a divine chastisement. So far, at least, they have not similarly blamed Lassa fever, Lyme disease, and legionellosis on the sins of Nigerians, suburbanites, and aging veterans" (1995, 10).

Another perspective is that all environments change, which means that new niches are endlessly created for diseases. This can happen in unexpected ways. For example, although both Garrett (1994, 550–52) and Ryan (1997, 330) have depicted new diseases as emerging because of the environmental damage humans caused in the tropics, both have also discussed the emergence of Lyme disease, a tick-borne disorder that expanded in New England as agricultural land reverted to forest. The extent of the environmental change in the region is striking. Moose have settled regions they had abandoned for hundreds of years. Moises Velasquez-Manoff (2007) has reported that more than a thousand moose inhabit Massachusetts, the "third most densely populated state in the nation, according to the U.S. Census (after New Jersey and Rhode Island)." There are black bears in Connecticut. The change has been striking and positive, but it has also created new opportunities for a disease vector to infect humans with a terrible microbe, as large numbers of deer spread the tick that carries this disease (Karlen 1995, 179; Karlen 2000, 134–44).

The point is that viruses and bacteria are not merely a problem to be conquered; they are an integral part of our environment, from the canopy of the rain forest to the planet's oceans, where they swarm in stunning abundance (Ryan 1997, 338–41). They cannot be eliminated, and no technological fix will ever free us from them. The same agricultural and medical technologies that have improved our lives have also created new opportunities for viruses and bacteria. Equally important, humans also form part of the planet's ecosystem, one characterized by increasingly dense populations. As Karlen's work (1995) has made clear from a historical perspective, the emergence of "crowd" diseases has been intimately connected to the growth of cities, the appearance of new trade routes, and changing levels of human population. Viruses such as measles could spread only once viruses had reached critical densities, associated with the rise of urban living (47–63). Diseases cannot be understood apart from a social and

Medication package inserts vary from country to country, even for an identical drug. The advised dosage, contraindications, and description of the drug's purpose in these inserts may differ. How can you guarantee that you have accurate information for your health purposes when you travel outside of your home country? (Hint: find out what the *Physicians' Desk Reference* is and how it is used.)

global context. This means that diseases are a particular concern in the era of globalization.

As chapter 2 suggested, there is a major debate over when the modern era of globalization began. Some authors suggest that this process truly originated with the European expansion around the globe in the fifteenth century. From this perspective, globalization is a process intimately linked with the spread of disease. The inhabitants of the Americas had no immunity to New World diseases, from smallpox to yellow fever. Tens of millions died; entire peoples disappeared (Alchon 2003; Karlen 1995, 93–110). The process was repeated countless times in North America as Europeans spread to the North and West (Boyd 1999; Hackett 2002). Many times, the disease arrived before the Europeans did (Fenn 2001). The exchange of diseases that began with this process has not ended, as the 2003 SARS outbreak showed. The Zika virus arrived in Brazil in late 2014 and began to cause an epidemic of microcephaly in infants the following year (see the time line in Diniz 2017; see also Smallman 2018). Globalization continues to introduce "new" diseases.

The legacy of colonialism and imperialism also continues to shape the health experiences of Indigenous populations, even in relatively wealthy countries such as Canada and Australia. One cannot understand health apart from its social context. To appreciate how structural inequalities shape global health, one can examine the experiences of Canada's Inuit people and the Aboriginal people of Australia.

In Canada, the original inhabitants of the land are known as the "First Peoples," who make up a little under 4 percent of the population. Many of these First Peoples live on reserves (not "reservations," as in the United States), to which they were confined as first the British Empire and then the Canadian state expanded their sovereignty ever since the defeat of New France. These peoples have faced a long history of land loss, political marginalization, and social discrimination. This has included the experience of the residential schools, during which children were removed from their parents during a period from the 1880s to the 1960s. For a long time the First Peoples were ignored in Canada's national narratives, which stated that the nation had two founding peoples, the English and the French.

Since the 1970s the Canadian government has made some efforts to reverse the harms of the past, such as by trying to resolve outstanding land claims. On April 1, 1999, Canada's Northwest Territories split to create a new territory, Nunavut, which was governed by the Inuit people. This territory is absolutely immense, with over 2 million square kilometers (or over 800,000 square miles) of land and a population of slightly more than 35,000 people. The Inuit now are guaranteed a share of royalties, recognition of their language, and political power. Yet the new territory is also haunted by the sad legacies of colonialism, which can be seen in health indicators, such as the high rate of suicides and the unusual prevalence of tuberculosis.

As was mentioned earlier, TB is a bacterial infection (caused by *Mycobacterium tuberculosis*) that originally came from cattle and then infected human beings. It is spread through the air, particularly on droplets expelled during coughing. Although some people never develop symptoms after infection, others who do gradually lose weight, run a fever, and face increasing difficulty breathing. Although the illness can be treated by antibiotics, such treatment is lengthy. If the treatment is stopped, the bacteria may quickly develop resistance.

In the 1950s the Canadian government resettled Inuit peoples onto Arctic lands so as to better assert its authority over its Arctic territory. At the same time, Inuit people were compelled to change their way of life and settle in Western-style housing in permanent villages. During this period, the government also collected all Inuit with active TB to be sent south for treatment (Møller 2010, 38). According to Kelly Bennet (2016), more than 1,200 First Peoples in the eastern Arctic went to a single sanatorium in the southern city of Hamilton (near Toronto in Ontario) alone. Perhaps 4,500 Inuit were taken from the Arctic as a whole (N. Murray 2017a). One ship, the *C. D. Howe*, was sent throughout the Arctic, where it made stops to pick up all Inuit who had been identified as having active TB (Bennett 2016). There was little choice for the Inuit who departed, and scant communication was provided to their home communities afterward. Some patients never returned to the north, and many Inuit families were never notified where their graves were (N. Murray 2017a). In the context of the residential schools and efforts to destroy Indigenous culture, this experience left the Inuit community with a profound mistrust of the medical system.

TB rates remain astonishingly high in Nunavut. As M. Patterson, Sandy Flinn, and Karen Barker note, the "average annual rate of tuberculosis (TB) among Inuit in Canada is now more than 290 times higher than Canadian born non-Indigenous people" (2018, 82). But many Inuit have been reluctant to be tested because of the fear of stigma, as well as cultural gaps with non-Inuit doctors (the term for non-Inuit in Canada is Qallunaat) who spoke only English or French (Møller 2010, 40). There was also a painful legacy of sexual abuse by Qallunaat teachers and administrators in the north, which has made some Inuit mistrustful of Qallunaat authorities (42). Some Inuit view health care institutions as colonial tools (43).

It is impossible to discuss the high prevalence of TB in the Canadian Arctic without referring to issues related to housing, history, and social inequality. It is also the case that the Canadian government has not adequately prioritized resolving the TB epidemic in the Arctic. One of the terrible aspects of this particular epidemic is that it has especially impacted the young (MacDonald, Hebert, and Stanbrook 2011, 741). Indeed, it was the death of one particular fifteen-year-old woman, Ileen Kooneeliusie, in Qikiqtarjuaq, Nunavut, in January 2017 that brought this issue to national awareness (N. Murray 2017b). The teen was taken to a local health center for difficulty breathing, coughing, and headaches, which had been ongoing for weeks, and sent home with painkillers. She was finally diagnosed too late in the illness to be treated, as the infection had spread to her brain. Despite a Medevac flight south, she died on January 14, 2017. People wondered how it was possible that her illness had not been appropriately diagnosed and treated earlier (N. Murray 2017b). One family doctor wrote an op-ed piece that noted that in Nunavut the incidence rate of TB was the same as in Somalia, a less-developed country (Giles 2018a). In March 2018 the Canadian government launched a $27 million program to fight TB in these northern communities (Giles 2018a). As Sarah Giles suggested (2018b), even these resources were clearly not enough, given the long history of underfunding and the structural inequalities that drove the epidemic.

In Australia, a similar long-standing infection, HTLV-1, has created astounding disparities between Aboriginal and Torres Islander people and the majority society. HTLV is an ancient virus, which most likely came to Australia with the original settlers millennia ago (Cassar et al. 2014, 56). The virus is spread by the same mechanisms as HIV, namely sexual transmission, blood, and breast milk. Because the disease can be transmitted sexually, it is also associated with shame, which has made many patients and communities reluctant to discuss the illness. For some people who are infected it will ultimately lead to terrible health consequences, such as leukemia, kidney failure, or lung disease (Allam 2018b). Although millions of people are infected globally, the highest rates are perhaps in central Australia among Aboriginal peoples, who were the original inhabitants of that nation. Although there is no vaccine, Japan has been able to reduce the transmission of the virus by perhaps 80 percent (Allam 2018b).

In contrast, in Australia there has been no such mass testing and education program, in part because people have argued that there is no cure for the disease. Yet as Ian Mackay (2018) has argued on his blog *Virology Down Under*, it is routine to test for many other diseases for which treatments are not currently available, because patient tracking and epidemiology is a key aspect of public health. Knowing one's health status is also a basic human right. As Mackay further points out, the reason that there is not more testing and health support in affected communities is that most of the people in them are rural, less educated, and Aboriginal. These are also communities that have major social problems, which are often tied to colonial legacies. The end result is that in some Aboriginal communities, prevalence may have reached 40 percent (or more), which is causing protests among doctors (Howard 2018). As a number of researchers wrote in 2016, "Unfortunately, in the quarter-century since HTLV-1 was first shown to be endemic to central Australia, there has been no systematic attempt to provide Indigenous Australians with information about this infection" (Einsiedel et al. 2016, 797). It was this reality that led doctors and health experts from twenty-six different countries in 2018 to write the World Health Organization (WHO)—an agency of the United Nations that seeks to improve global health and provides a venue in which nations can collaborate to improve global health—to say that more had to be done to fight the virus (Allam 2018a).

As has been the case in Canada, there are immense disparities in Australia in the prevalence of a major infectious disease, which has reflected not only socioeconomic inequalities but also a long history of government indifference. These are only two examples—in wealthy, democratic countries—of how social inequalities and discrimination can affect health. While people in wealthier countries may not be aware of these illnesses, in a globalized world infectious diseases do not recognize borders.

These connections are particularly worrisome on a planet that is now mainly urban and where vast populations in the developing world live in squalor without adequate medical care. As Mike Davis's (2005) work illustrates, the world's continued population growth is largely taking place in slum areas of megacities in the developing world, where sewage, water, and health services are lacking. There is a clear connection between global health and development, as the work of Paul Farmer (2007) has shown. A doctor passionately committed to the issue of global health, Farmer has dedicated his life to providing health care in the poorest parts of Haiti, as well as in Peru and Russia. Diseases such as tuberculosis and cholera thrive in areas of social misery, which in turn can be linked to global processes. The spread of AIDS in the Amazon among Indigenous peoples is driven by a frontier environment in which poor young men flood areas claimed by native peoples in order to mine gold for the global market. Social conditions and health are linked. Attempts to alleviate or manage particular diseases are consistently compromised when the structural conditions that allowed them to develop are not ultimately addressed. This was clearly demonstrated in Russia after the collapse of the Soviet Union, as a country that long prided itself on its health system underwent what can only be described as a social collapse. Vaccinations stopped, childhood diseases returned, intravenous drug use skyrocketed, HIV spread rapidly, suicides climbed, alcoholism took off, and life expectancy plummeted. It was not until 2012 that Russia's demographic decline was fully reversed.

The association of development with health is not only a national issue; structural adjustment programs and intellectual property provisions impact health programs and outcomes on a global level. To understand global health, one must talk about the roles of the World Bank and the World Trade Organization, in particular its Agreement on Trade-Related Aspects of Intellectual Property Rights (TRIPS) provision in facilitating or impeding policy creation and implementation. The links between global health and international organizations can be illustrated through the example of HIV. As we have already mentioned, HIV is caused by a virus that has a remarkably long latency period, perhaps ten years on average from infection to the development of AIDS. One of the terrible aspects of this latency period is that it provides a lengthy window in which people can unknowingly spread the virus or in which they must wrestle with the implications of being HIV positive. Globally, tens of millions of people are infected with the virus, and the number continues to climb. The region most impacted by the virus has been sub-Saharan Africa. The educated, urban class—teachers, nurses, doctors, government officials, and other professionals—have been heavily affected, which not only has undermined the region's economies but also its ability to address the crisis. No part of southern African society has escaped the disease's impact, which ranges

"When you have communities living in abject poverty, exposed to all the diseases, the diseases are going to recur and they'll keep on recurring, and we have to turn our attention to that. At this point, I put my money on the bugs" (Dr. Willam Close in Bienstock 2007). If you were in charge of health policy decisions for your country, how would you balance budget allocations for infectious disease prevention with budget allocations for general poverty reduction?

from the growing number of AIDS orphans to the falling rates of school attendance as families spend money on medications and not tuition. The disease has also spread broadly in the former Soviet Union, Eastern Europe, and Southeast Asia. AIDS is a truly global crisis. Sadly, despite long-term and well-funded efforts, the fact that HIV has many different clades (strains) complicates the drive to develop a vaccine. For the time being, we must manage this pandemic without a vaccine.

There is also reason for hope. In 1996 David Ho and other scientists announced that a combination of antiretroviral medications could suppress the level of the virus in the blood to a level so low that it could not be detected. This was not a cure. If the treatment was stopped, the virus returned. And failure to comply with therapy quickly led to drug resistance. But no longer did being HIV positive mean death. Instead, the disease began to change into a chronic condition for many people—though only if they could afford the treatment. In the early years, triple therapy might cost $10,000 to $15,000 annually. Such costs were heavy but perhaps manageable.

In the developing world, however, prevention appeared to be the only hope. The nations of the Global South refused to accept this discrepancy in the availability of treatment. The cost of these medications might be more than $10,000 a year if a pharmaceutical company produced them, but laboratories in Brazil or India could make the same drugs at a cost of $150 to $300 a year. Was it reasonable that tens of millions of people would die when treatments existed that could save them? Beginning in 1996, Brazil moved to make these medications available to everyone who needed them. This program proved to be effective: people wanted to know their status to receive treatment, so they were more likely to be tested for HIV. Mortality rates fell sharply. And the Brazilian government saved money because people did not enter public hospitals for expensive end-of-life care but rather remained employed and paid taxes (Marins 2002; Anonymous 2001, 331–37). The success of the Brazilian effort promised to change the terms of the debate about fighting AIDS in the developing world.

Pharmaceutical companies, however, argued that this policy was dangerous because it would discourage the research needed to produce new HIV/AIDS medications. The U.S. government initially supported this argument and tried to block the production of generic HIV medications by appealing to the TRIPS provisions of the World Trade Organization, which uses an international agreement to defend intellectual property rights. Nonprofit organizations rallied to support the efforts of the developing countries by pointing out that many medications are produced with public funds. Few drugs had been produced for tropical diseases over the course of decades; extracting profits from the developing world would do little to address the diseases in this region, critics suggested. They cited statistics that showed that "90 percent of the global expenditure on medical research is on diseases causing 10 percent of the global burden of disease. Moreover, of 1,223 new drugs developed between 1975 and 1997, only 13 were for the treatment of tropical diseases" (Benatar, Daar, and Singer 2003, 110). The result was a heated battle that the United States gradually realized it could not win (Smallman 2007, 14–15, 92–96). A turning point was the 2001 anthrax attack in the United States, which killed five people and made seventeen ill. The U.S. government debated producing the expensive antibiotic ciprofloxacin as a generic so that it could afford to provide care to all those affected (Bayer has since lost the patent, and the drug is available generically). In this context, it became difficult to deny poor countries access to the medications that could address the AIDS pandemic. With the resolution of this international debate, many developing countries are moving to expand their citizens' access to these medications. By 2012 there was a realization in the medical community that people living with HIV are much less infectious when receiving treatment, which suggested that treatment was part of prevention. At this moment, an old dichotomy disappeared. This knowledge seems likely to reshape all debates about the costs of HIV medications in the future. Global health is shaped not only by microbes but also by international organizations and beliefs.

International factors also shape the discovery of new drugs and the availability of medications to the poor. The majority of the world's medications have been developed from plants, and this remains true even in an era of synthetic chemistry. Much of the knowledge that has permitted the rise of modern medical treatments has roots in Indigenous knowledge, such as the discovery of quinine by Peru's Indigenous peoples, which created the first effective treatment for malaria, and the use of curare, from which a drug was created for use in anesthesia (W. Davis 1997, 209–15, 302, 377). Many communities in the Global South are worried that if they share their knowledge with pharmaceutical companies, the companies will patent the active ingredient in the plant and local producers will no longer be able to sell their products. For people in developing countries, this has been an emotional issue. After the U.S. patent office gave a patent for turmeric to researchers at the University of Mississippi Medical Center in 2005, the Indian government had to fight to prove that Indians had long been aware of the medical benefits of turmeric. They succeeded after a decade-long legal battle (Philip 2010, 250). But with intellectual property law permitting the patenting of life forms, people in developing countries now fear that the TRIPS clause of the WTO could be used to enforce companies' claims to traditional knowledge.

Other issues can be seen through the case of a breakthrough treatment for malaria called *Artemisia annua*, or sweet wormwood. Malaria is one of three infectious diseases that have been responsible for the greatest loss of life in the tropics. Hundreds of millions of people are infected each year, and hundreds of thousands die. With global warming spreading the range of the mosquitoes that serve as the disease's vector and with the malaria parasite's increasing resistance to most drugs used for treatment, the future appears dire. But there is some hope. Sometimes, travelers find effective treatments using local remedies. For example, one student suffered from repeated bouts of malaria while working on volunteer programs in Tanzania, even though she had taken the standard drugs for prophylaxis. It was then that a fellow traveler suggested that she try sweet wormwood, a plant long used by Chinese herbalists to treat diseases, including malaria. She was rapidly cured of her third bout with malaria (Thom 2006).

The student then began to research the history of artemisinin, the drug extracted from sweet wormwood; she soon learned that the plant had been adopted by Chinese doctors who were searching to find a treatment for malaria in the 1960s in order to treat North Vietnamese soldiers infected during the fight against the United States. They isolated the active component in the 1960s, but it took another decade for the medication to become commercially available (Thom 2006, 3). This drug has now become a standard treatment for malaria; the Global Fund for AIDS, Tuberculosis, and Malaria is giving major grants to poor countries to purchase this medication while asking these countries to move away from some older drugs.

The World Health Organization is encouraging countries to adopt this medication, particularly where drug-resistant malaria is a problem (4–5).

The discovery of artemisinin is a triumph that has had both medical and social benefits. It has helped to return malaria to its former status as a treatable disorder and to buy time for the production of other new-generation malaria drugs. But it has also created an industry, because large amounts of sweet wormwood are needed to produce the drug. Rebecca Thom's research found that for this reason, companies made plans to grow large amounts of the plant in East Africa (Thom 2006, 5–6). This story also raises difficult issues: How should Indigenous peoples be compensated for their knowledge and the products they create? What obligations do pharmaceutical companies have either to share their profits or to develop drugs to treat diseases affecting the poor?

The point of this section is not to ascribe major health issues to globalization, which is a two-edged sword. On the one hand, globalization brings structural adjustment plans that can undermine health-care systems, facilitate the rapid spread of new diseases, and permit multinationals to block the production of generic drugs. On the other, globalization also brings the expertise of the WHO to fight disease outbreaks, the work of the United Nations to improve health standards, donations from wealthy nations to fight illness, and the efforts of international NGOs to address health inequities. Nowhere can this dual character of globalization be seen with greater clarity than in the case of HIV in Brazil, discussed above. When Brazil tried to implement a comprehensive program to provide free treatment to those suffering from HIV, it faced a struggle with both the United States and major pharmaceutical companies because of intellectual property issues. Yet this program itself was also made possible by a series of loans from the World Bank. The irony is that the World Bank did not believe that the provision of treatment to people living with HIV was sustainable. But the World Bank's funds helped to create the infrastructure of testing facilities, laboratories, pharmacies, and clinics that made the Brazilian program possible (Smallman 2007, 88–91, 96–97). Health cannot be separated from questions of global governance. Indeed, in some cases, one must wonder whether the current nation-state system provides the best structure to address global health issues.

This issue can be explored through the case of influenza, which raises questions about global health governance and the best way to face an urgent threat to global health. The influenza virus is a very contagious agent that causes a respiratory disease. In the Northern Hemisphere, the flu season usually begins in October and peaks around February. (The Southern Hemisphere's flu season peaks in July or August.) We are all familiar with the flu: the rapid onset of exhaustion, aches, headache, and coughing and heaviness in our chest. For most people, after some time in bed and a little care, the flu quickly passes. But flu is a highly mutagenic (changeable) virus, which sometimes undergoes major changes, in particular when a form adapted to birds enters into humans or other animals. In this case, the world can see a devastating pandemic (see www.pandemicflu.gov). The worst pandemic of the twentieth century struck in 1918, when an avian form of the flu adapted to humans and began to spread rapidly, from the hills of northern India, the country most devastated by the disease, to the trenches of Western Europe during World War I (M. Davis 2005, 26, 32). The origin of the outbreak is still unknown, although some recent scholarship suggests that it began in China. As Alfred Crosby (1990) and Arno Karlen (1995, 145) have pointed out, one of the most unusual aspects of the pandemic is that it has been largely forgotten, not only in the United States and Europe but also globally.

There were also flu pandemics in 1957 and 1968, although neither proved as deadly as the 1918 outbreak. In some respects, little has changed in the intervening decades. We do have some treatments now for the flu. There are currently four drugs used to treat influenza, obtained in most developing countries only with a doctor's prescription. All must be taken shortly after one develops symptoms, and none cures the illness. Instead, they shorten the course of the disease and alleviate suffering. Vaccines are also available, but they currently represent an imperfect means to address this threat. The flu virus mutates rapidly, and there are many different strains, each characterized by different proteins in their outer shell. Every year, scientists scour the planet looking for different forms of the virus. They then have to guess which forms will likely dominate epidemics in the coming winter (for each hemisphere). They come to a consensus on three different forms. It then takes months to grow the virus in chicken eggs, the main means to make most influenza vaccines. But this approach has limitations; sometimes a strain of virus will circulate widely that is not covered by that year's vaccine. The virus also adapts to eggs, which makes it less effective at triggering an immune response in humans, as happened in 2018 with the H3N2 strain. But the greatest risk is that a novel form will appear for which the vaccine developers are completely unprepared.

In 1997 an outbreak of bird flu in Hong Kong sickened eighteen people and killed six. The government killed more than a million chickens in a few days, which stamped out the outbreak (M. Davis 2005, 45–54). But this was not the only appearance of bird flu. In 2009 a new form of influenza, H1N1 (swine flu), emerged in Mexico. This new strain put years of preparation to the test from a completely unexpected virus. In the end, the 2009 pandemic did not come close to resembling that of 1918. But then H7N9 began to circulate in eastern China in 2013 and again raised concerns about the pandemic potential of a new influenza strain.

While health authorities conducted surveillance and took steps to prepare for a possible pandemic after 2009, efforts to fight the flu also raised key moral questions about equity in global public health. European and North American governments collectively spent billions of dollars stockpiling medications, testing vaccines, and encouraging basic research on the flu. At the same time, developing nations struggling to contain bird flu found comparatively little aid forthcoming for tasks such as culling infected flocks. With the emergence of H1N1, developed countries were able to activate preexisting contracts with major vaccine manufacturers, which gave them first access to vaccines. The manufacturers would not take orders from poorer but more populous countries because the companies did not have the capacity to produce such a quantity. This inequality threatened the world's efforts to contain flu pandemics.

Even before the emergence of novel H1N1, developing nations were reluctant to collaborate with First World nations to develop possible vaccines because they knew they were unlikely to benefit from this research in the event of an outbreak. In some cases, developing countries may have sought access to vaccines in the event of an outbreak by offering individual companies access to emerging viral strains. Indonesia, for example, did not want to share strains of the bird flu collected from fatalities because the country wanted guaranteed access to any vaccine developed from this resource. As a result, in 2007 Indonesia temporarily stopped sharing viral samples of avian influenza from human cases with the WHO. It also briefly considered making a proprietary arrangement with a pharmaceutical company, in which Indonesia would share viral samples in exchange for free vaccines. It quickly abandoned this idea after international criticism. But the result of this crisis was a lengthy political struggle that drew in pharmaceutical companies, the World Health Assembly, and the WHO (Smallman 2013). At issue were the terms under which developing countries would share viral samples with the WHO. The United States and other developed countries argued that frontline countries had to share samples as a matter of international law, as governed by the International Health Regulations.

The frontline states argued that this was an example of biopiracy, in which developed countries received material from the WHO without any benefits accruing to the countries that provided the samples. As a result, the WHO made significant changes to its policies, as reflected in its Pandemic Influenza Plan of 2011.

This struggle reflects the deep frustration officials in some developing countries have felt about inequalities in access to health resources and their governments' inability to protect their own people. This issue is not new, and the anger it generates has sometimes proved destructive. Under President Thabo Mbeki, South Africa's health minister Manto Tshabalala-Msimang questioned the value of Western medicines to treat HIV and recommended a dietary regime of garlic, lemon juice, and beet root to treat the virus—at a time when hundreds of thousands of South Africans were dying from the disease (Dugger 2008). South African skeptics doubted that HIV caused AIDS. They said that pharmaceutical companies promoted this idea so that they could sell toxic antiretrovirals to poor Africans for a profit. In this view, racist ideas of Africans' sexuality formed part of a conspiracy to present HIV as the cause of AIDS. One Harvard study found that this tragic argument resulted in the death of 375,000 South Africans who would have lived (or not become infected, in the case of babies) with appropriate medications during the period from 2000 to 2005 (Dugger 2008).

In Afghanistan, Nigeria, and Pakistan, polio has continued to circulate (Nnadi et al. 2017, 190). In part, this reflects the lack of security in these nations that makes vaccination efforts problematic (Verma et al. 2018). In these countries it has often been local religious leaders who have issued directives to people to avoid vaccinations. It is also the case that anti-Western sentiments have driven attacks on vaccinators, which has led to the deaths of multiple health-care workers, many of whom have been women (McGirk 2015). The perceived association of vaccination with Western health actors and values has made polio eradication much more difficult. Globally, health campaigns become embedded in larger issues related to how people in developing nations view their position in the world.

India and other developing nations have seemed inclined to support an Indonesian ideal of "viral sovereignty," which states that a country's right to "control all information on locally discovered viruses should be protected through the same mechanisms that the U.N. Food and Agriculture Organization uses to guarantee poor countries' rights of ownership and patents on the seeds of its indigenous plants" (Holbrooke and Garrett 2008). Rich-

Activities affecting length and severity of epidemics (Rutherford http://www.youtube.com/watch?v=K3P2Aqp5Axs; no longer available):

1. Expenditures on experimental vaccines
2. Stockpiling antivirals that may be outdated when put to use
3. Stockpiling supplies (just in case)
4. Identification of impact of social distancing on overall economy (e.g., school closures)

ard Holbrooke and Laurie Garrett have argued that this idea of sovereignty, as applied to something as denationalized as viruses, could fundamentally undermine efforts to control diseases such as SARS and HIV. Yet the perspective of developing nations regarding influenza is shaped by a belief that the world's effort to fight the disease may not help them.

At its root, this conflict is part of a larger debate concerning what is called global disease governance. At issue are some key questions: Is the nation-state the best framework within which to address global health issues? What role should the WHO play in fighting disease? How can the issues of the Global North and South be reconciled to ensure a collaborative response to illnesses such as influenza? The emergence of new forms of influenza has required global health authorities to propose changes in everything from animal husbandry practices to disease reporting. To accomplish such changes on a scale likely to be successful entails a truly global commitment.

Although people can collaborate to block the spread of disease, their decisions and actions often have the opposite result. As Arno Karlen (1995, 59–60) and others have explained, there is a long association between war and disease that dates back to the disastrous experience of Athens during the Peloponnesian War, as Thucydides described. During the medieval period, armies were more likely to bring death by the diseases they carried, such as typhus, than by the sword (Karlen 1995, 114–15). Even during the U.S. Civil War, more troops died from disease than in combat. Disease can also be much more than an unanticipated consequence of warfare; people have used disease as an instrument of war for almost as long as history. During Pontiac's Rebellion in 1763, Lord Amherst sanctioned the deliberate infection of rebellious tribes by means of smallpox-contaminated blankets, although it is unknown whether his request was acted upon (Fenn

2001, 88–89). There are many other examples of biological warfare. With the development of medical science and humanity's ability to manipulate the genome of disease organisms, there has been growing concern that escalating work on biological warfare could lead to a global disaster. For this reason, the Soviet Union and the United States signed a treaty to ban offensive work with biological warfare agents in 1970 (Mangold and Goldberg 2000, 53–59).

While the United States appears to have lived up to its treaty agreements, we now know that the former Soviet Union has not. Instead, it developed an immense industrial and research capacity with the goal of weaponizing disease strains and developing new means to deliver them, including specially designed intercontinental ballistic missiles. With the defection of Ken Alibek, one of the Soviet scientists charged with developing this weaponry, the West learned the true scale of the Soviet threat (Alibek and Handelman 1999; Mangold and Goldberg 2000, 62–195).

This revelation was especially horrifying because the 1990s saw increasing concerns about the dangers that bioterrorism posed. Unlike nuclear weapons, which might take a large portion of a state's resources to develop, bioterrorism agents could be easily smuggled and dispersed. Of special concern was the collapse of the Soviet military's research apparatus. There were considerable fears that a disgruntled scientist, unpaid for months, might decide to stick a test tube with smallpox into a suitcase and shop it to rogue states or terrorist organizations. A number of examples heightened this concern (Mangold and Goldberg 2000, 335–51). In Oregon in 1984, for instance, followers of Indian spiritualist Bhagwan Shree Rajneesh deliberately laced salad bars at restaurants in The Dalles, Oregon, with salmonella in an effort to sway local elections. The water supply was also infected, and over 700 people fell ill. After Rajneesh was deported, the cult collapsed, but there were many similar groups that worried security analysts. Information grew that different groups were striving to obtain this capability. In particular, the sarin nerve gas attacks in Japanese cities carried out by the Aum Shinrikyo cult served as a warning that there were groups willing to use such weapons to cause the mass deaths of civilians. Aum Shinrikyo also researched biological weapons and carried out an unsuccessful attack on U.S. naval forces with botulinum (Goldberg and Mangold 2000, 340–41). How long would it be before another group had greater success?

On September 11, 2001, the world changed for many Americans as they watched jets slam into the World Trade Center's twin towers. This attack revealed the depth of hatred held toward the country by Al-Qaida, a group that most U.S. citizens had never heard of. On September 25, 2001, the first of a number of letters containing anthrax was received at news outlets. While the total number of deaths was small, it caused immense disruption and showed how easily a biological agent could be dispersed (Rosner and Markowitz 2006, 16–19, 123–28). No suspect was ever arrested, and we still do not know the identity of the attacker, although there are allegations it was a U.S. scientist. In the months that followed, many public-health authorities in the United States mused about the dangers posed by smallpox. This disease had once killed millions before vaccination had eliminated it from the face of the earth. Both the United States and Russia, however, still contained frozen strains of the virus in two special repositories (Karlen 1995, 155). And suspicions existed that some other nations might have smallpox samples, which they had not declared to the WHO.

With the clear threat from bioterrorism, funds poured into basic research and preparedness in this area, which greatly benefited local health departments in many U.S. states (Rosner and Markowitz 2006, 56, 68–69, 73). Project Bioshield, which passed the U.S. Congress in 2004, represented a major investment in the United States' health capacity. At the same time, some public-health officials argued that this distracted from their efforts to deal with other pressing issues, such as the spread of West Nile virus or the fight against drug-resistant tuberculosis (77, 81–92). Part of the challenge was that it proved difficult to evaluate priorities because measuring the threat from bioterrorism was very complicated. If smallpox were reintroduced into humanity, it would represent a global calamity that could kill hundreds of millions of people before a successful medical response. At the same time, the threat was entirely theoretical, since there was not one person ill with smallpox anywhere on the planet (98). Mike Davis has contrasted the funds spent on preparing for bioterrorism with those expended preparing for a flu pandemic (2005, 128). This contrast between the theoretical risks and the immediate costs undermined the federal government's efforts to vaccinate first responders in the United States against smallpox (Rosner and Markowitz 2006, 92–101). In the aftermath of the Iraq War, Americans learned that Iraq had not possessed the weapons of mass destruction that the Bush administration had referred to as a means to justify the invasion, raising questions about whether the administration had exaggerated or even lied about this threat.

There are certainly valid reasons to fear bioterrorism. But millions of people die every year because of the tobacco industry. How should these health challenges be evaluated? Is bioterrorism an ogre that frightens

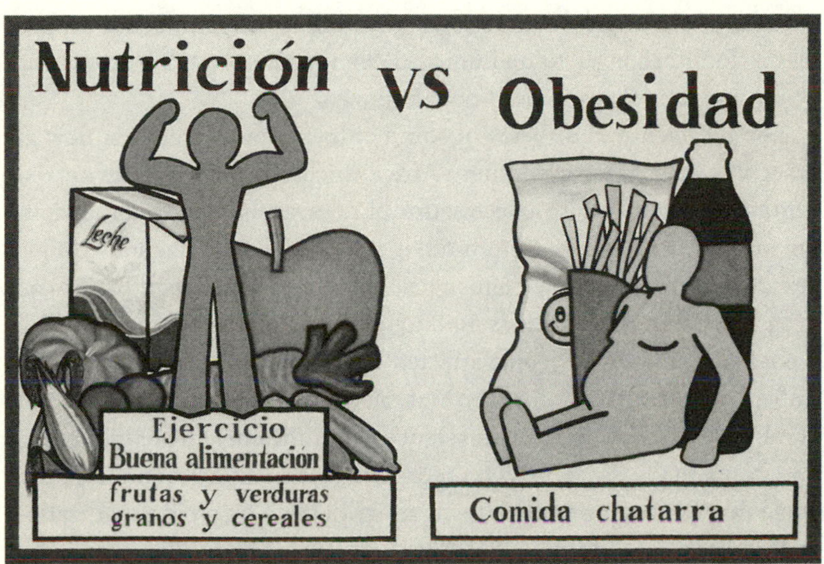

"Nutrition vs. Obesity" wall mural, Oaxaca, Mexico (Used with permission of the photographer, Margaret Everett)

Western society now but will fade from the news in coming years? The global diabetes epidemic provides an example of another health threat that could also justify massive expenditures of money and funds. With changes in diet—in particular a rise in the consumption of sugar and processed food—combined with a decline in physical exercise, diabetes rates have climbed throughout the world. In particular, type 2 diabetes, which usually develops later in life, has been rising at a rapid rate, with most growth taking place in developing countries (Halasey 2016). The largest populations now living with the disease are in China and India (Halasey 2016), and Asia as a whole is the region facing the greatest burden. On a global level, while the death rates for some diseases are falling, such as for cardiovascular diseases, the death rates are climbing for diabetes (Ali et al. 2015, 1444).

Many Indigenous populations have been greatly affected, ranging from the Akimel O'odham in the United States to the native peoples of Oaxaca, Mexico. In some communities, the numbers are frightening: "In the Pacific island of Naura, where diabetes was virtually unknown 50 years ago, it is now present in approximately 40 percent of adults" (Zimmet, Alberti, and Shaw 2001, 784). There are arguments within the scientific community about why these Indigenous populations appear to be more vulnerable to diabetes. Some people contend that there may be a genetic basis, in that populations more exposed to famines conserved genes that in times of plenty proved disastrous (785). But equally important must be the profound changes to traditional diets, the rise of high-fructose corn syrup, and the collapse of traditional lifeways.

The prevalence of diabetes in some of these communities is now approaching that of HIV in southern Africa. Such a high rate carries not only a human burden but also an economic burden, as the weight of managing the disease saps resources from other activities. For Indigenous peoples already juggling multiple challenges, diabetes represents a major cost. Even for major states such as India and China, the expense entailed by the tens of millions of people affected by this disease is daunting (King, Aubert, and Herman 1998, 1416). Most new cases of diabetes will be in the developing world, where the prevalence is significantly higher in the cities (1415, 1417). In this sense, diabetes represents yet another urban health challenge in a developing world already overwhelmed by rapid urbanization. Type 2 diabetes is a largely avoidable disorder that is readily addressed by interventions in diet and exercise (785). How should the world respond to this "disease of development"?

The challenge of chronic disease can be so magnified by development that one might be tempted to question the benefit of economic growth at all. John Bodley captures this perspective well in a description of how "modernization" has impacted health in Pacific island communities, comparing them with the isolated island of Pukapuka.

> Predictably, the population of Pukapuka was characterized by relatively low levels of imported sugar and salt intake, and a presumably related low level of heart disease, high blood pressure, and diabetes. In Rarotonga, where economic success was introducing town life, imported food, and motorcycles, sugar and salt intake nearly tripled, high blood pressure increased approximately ninefold, diabetes increased two- to threefold, and heart disease doubled for men and more than quadrupled for women. Meanwhile, the number of grossly obese women increased more than tenfold. Among the New Zealand Maori, sugar intake was nearly eight times that of the Pukapukans, gout in men was nearly double its rate on Pukapuka, diabetes in men was more than fivefold higher, and heart disease in women had increased more than sixfold. (Bodley 1999, 135)

Obviously, access to Western medicine has also brought great benefits, from childhood vaccines to the antibiotics that quickly cure otherwise deadly infections. But there has been a trade-off.

This complexity makes all health-care decisions challenging. It is difficult to address one health-care issue without addressing others, such as food consumption. Indeed, health care is a holistic topic, because it reflects larger aspects of societal and environmental health. In the Arctic, northern peoples who rely heavily on local game and fish are having serious problems with contamination from pesticides and mercury that come from developed regions. In 2008 there was a major health crisis in China after melamine, a food additive that increases protein levels, was added to infant formula, sickening nearly 300,000 children. This event led to significant changes in China's food safety system (Wu and Chen 2018, 429). The health of people in developed countries is inextricably linked to economic and social issues in places that they will never visit and of which they may not even be aware. Nowhere is this clearer than with food-related issues, which are tightly intertwined with health. Malnutrition increases a population's vulnerability to all diseases and can impact a child's health for life. Efforts to address the challenges of both infectious and chronic diseases entail engaging the food issues discussed in the previous chapter.

Globalization and health issues also are intertwined, as one can see by returning to the history of HIV. Undoubtedly, the movement of HIV has been linked to the flows of people. In the case of South Africa in the 1990s, large numbers of men entered the country from neighboring states to work in the gold and diamond mines, where they were separated from their families, had substantial income, and had ready access to a local population of sex workers. The result was the rapid amplification of HIV, which returned with the migrant laborers to their home countries, facilitating the spread of the disease. In South and Southeast Asia, it was less the voluntary migration of laborers than the human trafficking industry that drove the evolution of the virus, as young women from Nepal to Myanmar were entrapped and traded in a sex trade that stretched over thousands of miles (Beyrer 1998, 128–39). This was paralleled by a trade in opium that was so key to the epidemic's spread that it can be witnessed even on the fundamental level of viral biology by tracing the propagation of viral clades (forms) in the region (Smallman 2007, 213–16).

Mexico has long had a lower rate of HIV than its northern neighbor, but that may change as large numbers of migrant laborers from small rural (and often Indigenous) villages travel north. Young men, freed from the conservative strictures of their home communities, sometimes experiment with sex or drugs and then return home to their wives and families. Oaxaca is a poor state in southern Mexico where far more rural housewives than urban prostitutes are being infected with HIV. Ironically, HIV has also spread among Central American women, who may have entered Mexico on their way to the United States but then became entrapped in Oaxaca and enmeshed in the sex trade (Smallman 2007, 113–64). In other words, HIV itself feeds upon larger structural issues of gender inequality, labor mobility, and human trafficking. While the disease is a biological entity, the epidemic also is a social construct. Without a much-wished-for cure and vaccine, HIV will have to be fought not only by medical means but also by addressing the social ills upon which the disease feeds globally. While this is true for HIV, the same can be said for many other diseases. Within the United States, for example, the documentation status of immigrants is a key variable for their health (McGuire and Georges 2003).

Conclusion

The key argument of this chapter has been that health cannot be narrowly defined in terms of access to Western biomedicine or the scientific knowledge that allows a professional class to treat patients. Instead, health is a complex topic that is intimately related to the most important issues in international studies, from development to the environment, global governance to security. For this reason, health-care decisions cannot be left to health-care professionals alone. Instead, health must be viewed in a social context. Technological developments will not save us from the dilemmas we face. Social and environmental change will continue to create new health issues that will in turn require political and social action to resolve. How do we weigh the potential threat of bioterrorism against the real damage caused by diabetes? How do we ensure that the interests of the Global North and the Global South are reconciled to permit Indigenous knowledge to create new medicines or to combat bird flu? How do questions of food—its production, delivery, and quality—impact global health? How do global food and health issues impact you?

➤ VOCABULARY

Inuit
Nunavut
Aboriginal peoples
SIV
iatrogenic
artemisinin
WHO
SARS
viral sovereignty
TRIPS provisions

➤ DISCUSSION AND REFLECTION QUESTIONS

1 *Why might it be the case that health cannot be discussed outside of its social context?*

2 *What processes have contributed to the link between processed foods and disease?*

3 *How have globalization and the increase in border crossing and migration changed the shape of disease spread?*

4 *How is global climate/environmental change affecting the emergence of new diseases?*

5 *How does globalization introduce new diseases, and what is the most recent example?*

6 *How do structural adjustment programs and intellectual property provisions impact health programs and outcomes on a global level?*

7 *What is the relationship between NGOs, multinational drug companies, and local and regional infrastructures?*

8 *What are the conditions that can cause a public-health issue to become a security issue?*

9 *What are some ways to devise a more equitable resource distribution between "disease darlings" (HIV) and "old stalwarts" (malaria, tuberculosis, etc.)?*

10 *How would you decide how to fund bioterrorism research and relief versus pandemic research and relief?*

ACTIVITY 1: ANALYZE Find three countries with Indigenous peoples and non-Indigenous peoples. Look at the tuberculosis rates for the different populations. Are there differences? If so, what accounts for these different rates?

ACTIVITY 2: REFLECT Examine three blog posts at one of the following blogs: Virology Down Under, Avian Flu Diary, or Antibiotics—The Perfect Storm. How does the content covered connect with the material that you read in this chapter? Can you suggest a public policy recommendation based on these materials?

ACTIVITY 3: EXTEND Think about the health-care experiences of your family and friends. What topics covered in this chapter have been most relevant for them? What seems to be the most pressing health-care issue in your own life? Why?

References

Alchon, S. A. 2003. *A pest in the land: New World epidemics in a global perspective.* Albuquerque: University of New Mexico Press.

Ali, M., L. Jaacks, A. Kowalski, K. Siegel, and M. Ezzati. 2015. Noncommunicable diseases: Three decades of global data show a mixture of increases and decreases in mortality rates. *Health Affairs (Project Hope) 34* (9): 1444–55.

Alibek, K., and S. Handelman. 1999. *BioHazard: The chilling true story of the largest covert biological weapons program in the world—told from the inside by the man who ran it.* New York: Delta.

Allam, L. 2018a. Time to eradicate HTLV-1, World Health Organisation is warned. *The Guardian,* May 11. Retrieved July 10, 2019, from https://www.theguardian.com/australia-news/2018/may/11/time-to-eradicate-htlv-1-world-health-organisation-is-warned.

———. 2018b. What is HTLV-1? The devastating health crisis afflicting central Australia. *The Guardian,* April 24. Retrieved July 10, 2019, from https://www.theguardian.com/australia-news/2018/apr/24/what-is-htlv-1-the-devastating-health-crisis-afflicting-central-australia.

Anonymous. 2001. Brazil fights for affordable drugs against HIV and AIDS. *Revista Panamericana de Salud Pública 9* (May): 5, 331–37.

Associated Press. 2007. Indonesia won't share bird flu virus data. *Globe and Mail,* March 13. Retrieved March 21, 2007, from http://www.theglobeandmail.com/life /article745892.ece.

———. 2008. Pakistan: Polio found in baby. *New York Times,* July 18, A-9.

Benatar, S., A. Daar, and P. Singer. 2003. Global health ethics: The rationale for mutual caring. *International Affairs 79* (1): 107–38.

Bennett, K. 2016. Telling the story of hundreds of Inuit, sick with TB, who were shipped to Hamilton. CBC News, November 9. Retrieved July 10, 2019, from http://www.cbc.ca/news/canada/hamilton/telling-the-story-of-hundreds-of-inuit-sick-with-tb-who-were-shipped-to-hamilton-1.3842103.

Beyrer, C. 1998. *War in the blood: Sex, politics, and AIDS in Southeast Asia.* New York: Zed Books.

Bienstock, Ric Esther, dir. 2007. *Ebola: The plague fighters.* Nova series. WGBH Educational Foundation: WGBH Boston Video.

Bodley, J. H. 1999. *Victims of progress.* 4th ed. Toronto: Mayfield.

Boyd, R. 1999. *The coming of the spirit of pestilence: Introduced infectious diseases and population decline among northwest Indians, 1774–1874.* Vancouver: University of British Columbia Press.

Cassar, O., L. Einsiedel, P. Afonso, and A. Gessain. 2014. HTLV-1 molecular epidemiology in central Australia: Two distinctive HTLV-1 subtype C lineages in Indigenous Australians. *Retrovirology 11* (Suppl. 1): 56.

CIA World Factbook. n.d. HIV/AIDS—adult prevalence rate, 2016. Retrieved July 10, 2019, from https://www.cia.gov/library/publications/the-world-factbook/rankorder/2155rank.html.

Crosby, A. 1990. *America's forgotten pandemic: The influenza of 1918*. New York: Cambridge University Press.

Davis, M. 2005. *The monster at our door: The global threat of avian flu*. New York: New Press.

Davis, W. 1997. One River: Explorations and Discoveries in the Amazon Rainforest. New York City: Simon & Schuster.

Diniz, D. 2017. *Zika: From the Brazilian backlands to global threat*. Translated by D. R. Grosklaus Whitty. London: Zed Books.

Dugger, C. W. 2008. Study cites toll of AIDS policy in South Africa. *New York Times*, November 26. Retrieved November 27, 2008, from www.nytimes.com/2008/11/26/world/Africa/26aids.html.

Einsiedel, L., R. Woodman, M. Flynn, K. Wilson, O. Cassar, and A. Gessain. 2016. Human T-lymphotropic virus type 1 infection in an Indigenous Australian population: Epidemiological insights from a hospital-based cohort study. *BMC Public Health 16*:787–98.

Farmer, P. 2004. *Pathologies of power: Health, human rights, and the new war on the poor*. Berkeley: University of California Press.

———. 2007. Aid, AIDS, and global health. *Foreign Affairs 86* (March/April): 155–59.

Fenn, E. F. 2001. *Pox Americana: The great smallpox epidemic of 1775–1782*. New York: Hill and Wang.

Garrett, L. 1994. *The coming plague: Newly emerging diseases in a world out of balance*. New York: Farrar, Straus and Giroux.

———. 2000. *Betrayal of trust: The collapse of global public health trust*. New York: Hyperion.

———. 2005. The lessons of HIV/AIDS. *Foreign Affairs 84* (July/August): 51–65.

———. 2007. Do no harm: The global health challenge. *Foreign Affairs 86* (January/February): 14–38.

Giles, S. 2018a. Canadians must hold government accountable in Nunavut's tuberculosis outbreak. CBC News, April 25. Retrieved July 10, 2019, from http://www.cbc.ca/news/canada/north/nunavut-tuberculosis-outbreak-1.4633882.

———. 2018b. $27.5M pledged to tame TB in Canada's north may not be nearly enough. CBC News, May 11. Retrieved July 10, 2019, from http://www.cbc.ca/news/canada/north/tb-treatment-costs-in-north-1.4657470.

Hackett, P. 2002. *"A very remarkable sickness": Epidemics in the Petit Nord, 1670–1846*. Winnipeg: University of Manitoba.

Halasey, S. 2016. Diabetes: In search of early intervention: Rising diabetes rates are raising concern on a global scale. *Clinical Lab Products 46* (4): 20.

Holbrooke, R., and L. Garrett. 2008. "Sovereignty" that risks global health. *Washington Post*, August 10. Retrieved August 11, 2008, from www.cfr.org/publication/16927. No longer active.

Hooper, E. 1999. *The river: A journey to the source of HIV and AIDS*. New York: Little, Brown.

Howard, J. 2018. Doctors raise alarm about ancient HTLV-1 virus: "Prevalence is off the charts" in Australia. CNN, May 8. Retrieved July 10, 2019, from https://www.cnn.com/2018/05/07/health/htlv-1-virus-australia-explainer/index.html.

Jakimova, M. A., V. V. Punga, V. V. Testov, and L. I. Rusakova. 2017. XDR-TB prevalence in some regions of the Russian Federation. Retrieved July 10, 2019, from https://www.researchgate.net/publication/321923314_XDR-TB_prevalence_in_some_regions_of_the_Russian_Federation.

Karlen, A. 1995. *Plague's progress: A social history of man and disease*. London: Victor Gollancz.

———. 2000. *Biography of a germ*. New York: Pantheon.

King, H., R. E. Aubert, and W. H. Herman. 1998. Global burden of diabetes, 1995–2025. *Diabetes Care 21* (9): 1414–30.

MacDonald, N., P. C. Hebert, and M. B. Stanbrook. 2011. Tuberculosis in Nunavut: A century of failure. *CMAJ: Canadian Medical Association Journal 183* (7): 741.

Mackay, I. 2018. HTLV-1 in Australia: Don't test, don't find, can't understand. *Virology Down Under* (blog), May 25. http://virologydownunder.com/3896-2/.

Mangold, T., and J. Goldberg. 2000. *Plague wars: The terrifying reality of biological warfare*. New York: St. Martin's Griffin.

Marins, J. R. P. 2002. The Brazilian policy on free and universal access to antiretroviral treatment for people living with HIV and AIDS. PowerPoint presentation, Regional Forum of the Latin American and Caribbean Regional Health Sector Reform, Ocho Rios, S. Ann., Jamaica, February 20.

McGirk, T. 2015. Taliban assassins target Pakistan's polio vaccinators. *National Geographic, 3*. Retrieved July 10, 2019, from http://news.nationalgeographic.com/2015/03/150303-polio-pakistan-islamic-state-refugees-vaccination-health/.

McGuire, S., and J. Georges. 2003. Undocumentedness and liminality as health variables. *Advances in Nursing Science 26* (3): 185–95.

McKenna, M. 2010. *Superbug: The fatal menace of MRSA*. New York: Free Press.

Miller, J. A. 1989. Diseases for our future: Global ecology and emerging viruses. *BioScience 39* (8): 509–17.

Møller, H. 2010. Tuberculosis and colonialism: Current tales about tuberculosis and colonialism in Nunavut. *Journal of Aboriginal Health 6* (1): 38–48.

Murray, M. 2006. The epidemiology of SARS. In *SARS in China: Prelude to pandemic?*, edited by A. Kleinman and J. Watson, 17–30. Stanford: Stanford University Press.

Murray, N. 2017a. "It gave me a sense of closure": Database on Inuit tuberculosis graves offers some answers. CBC News, October 5. Retrieved July 10, 2019, from http://www.cbc.ca/news/canada/north/inuit-tb-database-1.4331163.

———. 2017b. "She was my only girl": Nunavut teen's death sheds light on failures in fighting TB. CBC News, March 23. Retrieved July 10, 2019, from https://www.cbc.ca/news/canada/north/tb-nunavut-teen-death-ileen-kooneeliusie-1.4036205.

Nnadi, C., E. Damisa, L. Esapa, F. Braka, N. Waziri, A. Siddique . . . and U. Adamu. 2017. Continued endemic wild poliovirus transmission in security-compromised areas—Nigeria, 2016. *Morbidity and mortality weekly report 66* (7): 190.

Patterson, M., S. Flinn, and K. Barker. 2018. Addressing tuberculosis among Inuit in Canada. *Canada Communicable Disease Report* 44 (3/4): 82–85.

Pépin, J. 2011. *The origins of AIDS*. New York: Cambridge University Press.

Pépin, J., and A. Labbé. 2008. Noble goals, unforeseen consequences: Control of tropical diseases in colonial Central Africa and the iatrogenic transmission of blood-borne viruses. *Tropical Medicine and International Health 13* (6): 744–53.

Peters, C. J., and M. Olshaker. 1997. *Virus hunter: Thirty years of battling hot viruses around the world*. New York: Anchor Books/Doubleday.

Philip, K. 2010. Producing transnational knowledge, neoliberal identities, and technoscientific practice in India. In *Tactical biopolitics: Art, activism and technoscience*, edited by B. da Costa and K. Philip, 243–67. Cambridge, Mass.: MIT Press.

Quammen, D. 2015. *The chimp and the river: How AIDS emerged from an African forest*. New York: Random House.

Rosner, D., and G. Markowitz. 2006. *Are we ready? Public health since 9/11*. Berkeley: University of California Press.

Ryan, F. 1997. *Virus X: Tracking the new killer plagues*. New York: Little, Brown.

Seidell, J. C. 2000. Obesity, insulin resistance, and diabetes—a worldwide epidemic. *British Journal of Nutrition 83*:5–8.

Shlaes, D. 2018. *Antibiotics—The Perfect Storm* (blog). Retrieved July 10, 2019, from http://antibiotics-theperfectstorm.blogspot.com/.

Smallman, S. 2007. *The AIDS pandemic in Latin America*. Chapel Hill: University of North Carolina Press.

———. 2013. Biopiracy and vaccines: Indonesia and the World Health Organization's new Pandemic Influenza Plan. *Journal of International and Global Studies* 4 (2): 20–36. Retrieved December 28, 2013, from http://www.lindenwood.edu/jigs/.

———. 2018. Conspiracy theories and the Zika epidemic. *Journal of International and Global Studies* 9 (2): 1–13. Retrieved July 10, 2019, from http://www.lindenwood.edu/jigs/.

Thom, R. 2006. *Artemesia annua*: A cure for malaria. March 20. Unpublished student manuscript.

United Nations. 2006. World population prospects: The 2006 revision. Retrieved January 8, 2010, from www.un.org/esa/population/publications/wpp2006_Highlights_rev.pdf.

Velasquez-Manoff, M. 2007. Forests lure moose to Massachusetts. *Christian Science Monitor*, February 14. Retrieved July 21, 2013, from http:www.csmonitor.com/2007/0214/p13s02-sten.htm.

Verma, A. A., M. P. Jimenez, R. H. Tangermann, S. V. Subramanian, and F. Razak. 2018. Insecurity, polio vaccination rates, and polio incidence in northwest Pakistan. *Proceedings of the National Academy of Sciences* 115 (7): 1593–98.

Wines, M. 2007. Virulent TB in South Africa may imperil millions. *New York Times*, January 8. Retrieved July 20, 2013, from http://www.nytimes.com/2007/01/28/world/africa/28tuberculosis?pagewanted=print.

Wu, Y. N., and J. S. Chen. 2018. Food safety monitoring and surveillance in China: Past, present and future. *Food Control* 90:429–39.

Zimmet, P., K. G. Alberti, and J. Shaw. 2001. Global and societal implications of the diabetes epidemic. *Nature* 414 (December 13): 782–86.

TEN Energy

➤ SYNOPSIS

A decade ago, many observers believed that the world was about to reach its peak oil production, after which global oil reserves would taper away. But with the development of hydraulic fracturing (fracking) and increased production of unconventional oil from sources such as Canada's Oil Sands, the global energy picture has changed dramatically. At the same time, the nuclear disaster at the Fukushima power plant in Japan has led nations such as Germany to abandon nuclear energy entirely, while the declining cost of both solar and wind power have made coal and nuclear energy increasingly uncompetitive. As a result, the global energy supply is in a state of rapid change. Solutions to global energy needs in the emerging decades will call for flexibility and creativity—a difficult path within the confines of the nation-state.

➤ SCAFFOLDING

As you read through this chapter, think about how you would answer each of the questions below.

Besides the supply of oil now and in the future, what energy issues do you think about on a weekly basis?

What global health issues are clearly linked to energy extraction?

What economic ideologies have governed much of the Global North's energy strategies in the twentieth and twenty-first centuries?

What incentives do multinational energy companies have to invest in alternative energy sources?

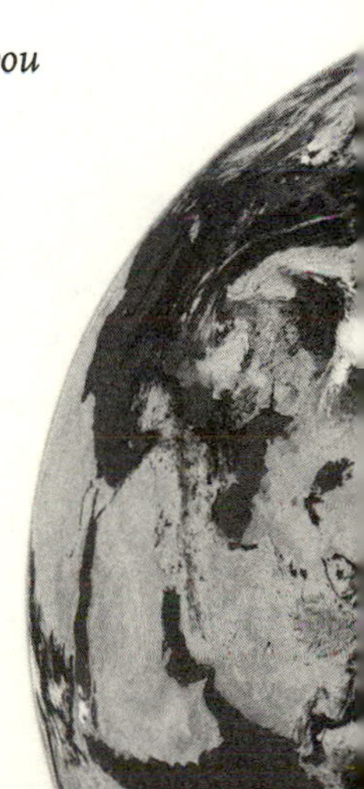

➤ **CORE CONCEPTS**

Why was Hubbert's concept of Peak Oil so central to global energy policies in the past three decades?

How has the rise of unconventional oil and fracking changed the global energy context?

What are advantages and disadvantages of using particular energy sources for our vehicles and for our daily use in other arenas?

The global energy picture is in a state of dramatic change. With the rise of fracking, North America has been able to rapidly increase its production of both oil and natural gas to such an extent that it is nearly independent. The United States will likely see more growth in its oil production than any other country in the next decade and might "double its oil production by 2030" (Wheeling 2019). This change has geopolitical implications, as the Middle East becomes less critical to U.S. foreign policy than in the past. In other parts of the world, the Fukushima nuclear disaster has led countries to reconsider the potential benefits of nuclear power. Germany, for example, has decided to close nuclear plants while at the same time investing heavily in renewable energy. The price of renewable energy has fallen sharply over the last five years (perhaps 50 percent); wind production has significantly increased, while solar is now becoming less expensive than fossil fuels in some countries, such as Australia. The supply of coal is sufficient for centuries, but the industry is in decline because of both environmental concerns and market pressures (Randers 2012, 99; Cockerham 2013). In this context, energy markets are in a state of flux, with larger global changes taking place right now than at any time since the introduction of electricity in the late nineteenth century. The one certainty is that many predictions for our energy future from a decade ago are now badly outdated.

Peak Oil and Fracking

As late as 2010, an introduction to this chapter would have included dramatically different information. At the time, discussions of global energy issues were dominated by the so-called Peak Oil movement, which began as an academic community and morphed into a broad-based popular movement with its own website and conferences (see www.peakoil.com). Amazon and other booksellers were stocked with widely selling works on this topic, such as Kenneth Deffeyes's *Hubbert's Peak* (2001), David Goodstein's *Out of Gas* (2005), and Richard Heinberg's *The Party's Over* (2003). The movement was based on the 1956 prediction of petroleum geologist M. King Hubbert that U.S. oil production would peak in 1970, which was known as Hubbert's Peak. As it happened, his prediction was correct for a period, although U.S. production briefly rebounded after Alaskan oil came online in the late 1970s (Simmons 2005, 45). U.S. oil production then entered into a steady and long decline, despite deep water discoveries in the Gulf of Mexico. Most Peak Oil authors predicted that the world's total production was about to peak (if it had not done so already) and would soon enter a decades-long slide. Their argument was not that there would be a sudden, dramatic falloff in the production of oil but rather that global production of oil would show the same bell-shaped curve that we have seen from many oil-producing states.

The gradual fall in world production would take place at the same time that the emerging economic powers of India and China continued to demand increasing amounts of oil (Simmons 2005, 46). As evidence for this prediction, Peak Oil proponents pointed out that multinational oil companies were not discovering new reserves of oil as quickly as they were pumping petroleum out of the ground (Roberts 2004, 172–73). The future seemed bleak, as the developed nations of Europe, Asia, and North America entered into an intense competition for the remaining oil.

Today, oil is the most important global commodity. When people think of oil, they think of cars and gasoline, because those are the products through which the price of oil most directly and noticeably impacts us. But there are other uses of oil that are just as fundamental. Petroleum is used to create the nitrogen for fertilizers that are a key part of Western agriculture. In particular, corn is a key feedstock in the United States, and no other crop depends as much upon fertilizer. Our industrial economy relies on plastics for everything from children's toys to medicine bottles; these are almost entirely made from petroleum. Heating oil also remains an important energy source in many areas, such as southern Canada and the northeastern United States. Even if we could magically find an alternative source to oil to meet our transportation needs tomorrow, the problem of our dependency on petroleum would remain. This problem is acute in the United States, where it is commonplace to note that the country has 5 percent of the world's population but uses 25 percent (or more) of the world's petroleum. But this issue also worries Europe, as the North Sea fields enter into decline. In Asia both Japan and China are dependent upon imported oil; China is the world's fastest growing superpower and its largest importer of oil. For the emerging economies of Southeast Asia, the question is how they can develop without the energy resources that the West and Japan enjoyed during industrialization.

Given the scale of this problem, as seen from over a decade ago, the Peak Oil movement had an understandable tinge of hysteria. In the fall of 2005, Bryant Urstadt attended the second U.S. Conference on Peak Oil in Ohio, which he later described in an August 2006 article in *Harper's* magazine titled "Imagine There's No Oil: Scenes from a Liberal Apocalypse." The sad message that many members of the Peak Oil community seemed to purvey was not only that the world was running out of oil but also that no good alternative would be found. Indeed, the movement's advocates seemed so determined to envision a future dystopia that Urstadt found himself musing about the historical origins of the movement: "Americans seem born to love the apocalypse, although it jilts us every time. Peak Oil and *Left Behind* are mere froth on a sea of doom-saying that stretches back to the Puritans" (36). But it would have been wrong to view the Peak Oil movement as a purely American group. Rather, it formed part of a larger discussion within the environmental movement, which argued that current practices in developing countries were unsustainable. Skeptics point out that there have been numerous predictions before that the world is about to run out of petroleum, as well as many other commodities. In almost every case, not only have these items continued to be found, but their price has also declined. From this perspective, the Peak Oil movement was made up of a group of people united perhaps less by their fears than by their hopes.

The global energy picture has now changed so dramatically that the website of the Oil Drum announced in the summer of 2013 that it was closing. The site had provided a venue for the Peak Oil community to share information about the coming global collapse, driven by the shortfall of oil production. But the website's editors announced that they could not find quality content any longer. After 2010 it proved increasingly difficult to believe in Peak Oil because U.S. oil production greatly increased with fracking. This term refers to a process by which fluid under high pressure is pumped into petroleum-bearing rocks, which creates fractures to release gas or petroleum. This technology has allowed energy companies to access petroleum resources that were completely inaccessible in the past. Such technological change means that we are unlikely to face any shortage of petroleum in the foreseeable future.

Fracking technology is not new. It was first attempted in 1947, but it became an economically viable technology in the space of a decade. This development has had a dramatic impact on natural gas production in the United States. In the eastern states, such as Pennsylvania, natural gas production has increased so rapidly that the price of natural gas has collapsed. According to some estimates, the nation may now have a century's supply of this fuel. The positive aspect of this change has been that natural gas releases less carbon than most other fossil fuels. Energy companies are building very few new coal plants in the United States: "Coal still accounts for 37 percent of U.S. electricity generation, although its share has dwindled from 50 percent just a few years ago and natural gas is catching up" (Cockerham 2013).

The declining cost of natural gas will also make it more difficult to build new nuclear plants. In the aftermath of the 2011 nuclear disaster at the Fukushima power plant in Japan, that country temporarily closed all fifty-four of its nuclear reactors, while Germany made a strategic decision to move away from nuclear power. So the nuclear energy industry was already under intense pressure globally. China is the main country likely to invest in many reactors, not only because of the cost savings but because nuclear energy avoids air pollution and can cut the country's carbon dioxide emissions (Xu, Kang, and Yuan 2018). Yet even in China there are still concerns about nuclear energy's safety (Huang et al. 2018), although these worries may be outweighed by the belief that the nation needs to end its dependence on coal. With the United States, however, the falling cost of natural gas has also made nuclear power seem increasingly uncompetitive.

The increase in natural gas production has also had an unexpected series of spin-off effects, such as making it cheaper for U.S. manufacturers to make petrochemicals, fertilizers, and other products. In the first decade of the millennium, many U.S. manufacturers had moved overseas where energy was cheaper. With the falling cost of natural gas, many of these same companies are now moving production back to the United States, which has a huge price advantage over almost every country in the world. Steelmakers also use natural gas, which is helping that sector of the economy regain lost ground. This trend is leading to an increase in U.S. manufacturing, an area of the economy that had been in a long decline.

With the growing importance of natural gas in heavy vehicles and the emergence of electric cars, oil is no longer practically alone at the top of transportation fuels (Krauss 2013).

While much of the attention to fracking has focused on natural gas, the technology has also been used to release oil on a scale that would have been unimaginable around 2000. The main state for this production has been Texas, followed closely by North Dakota. For the United States as a whole, domestic oil production is growing, and there are no signs that this increase will stop in the near future. This expansion of production has been so large that it has had geopolitical significance. The United States relies less on the Middle East for oil, while globally, the power of OPEC has declined. One study has found that as the United States has increased production, the global price of oil and OPEC's supplies have declined (Frondel, Horvath, and Vance 2018, 34). The global economy is also now partly shielded from the danger of an oil shock plunging nations into a recession, as happened in 1973 (Krauss 2013). The United States is now arguably the largest oil producer in the world and will likely increase its production relative to Russia and Saudi Arabia (numbers two and three respectively) over the next decade.

These benefits of this growth have also come with significant environmental concerns. Energy companies place chemicals into the water that they push into the rocks. The companies don't like to release information on which chemicals they are using, arguing this is a trade secret and thus proprietary. But communities affected by fracking argue that they have a right to know and worry that these chemicals may be released into the watershed. While research has not yet shown that the chemicals migrate, the time frame to date has been relatively short. How long will these chemicals remain in place? Hundreds of different chemicals are being used, some of which (according to environmental groups) are known toxins or carcinogens. Some companies also have used radioactive tracers to help determine where cracks are moving. There is currently no technology that allows these companies to remove the chemicals or radioactive tracers from the rocks into which they have been injected. In 2005 the U.S. Congress exempted fracking from any regulation under the Safe Drinking Water Act in order to ensure that this industry could continue its rapid development. But environmental groups and some impacted communities argue that there is insufficient regulation of the industry. One recent peer-reviewed study found that in Pennsylvania "the more fracking wells were in a county, the more hospitalizations the county saw for genital and urinary problems like urinary tract infections, kidney infections, and kidney stones" (Marusic 2019).

There is another challenge with fracking, in that it can create earthquakes, although there is little research on this topic. Small earthquakes (4.0 or under on the Richter scale) have been reported in Canada, Japan, and the United States. In this context, the economic benefits of fracking have been matched by significant environmental concerns. In October 2013 France's highest court upheld a ban on fracking (Jolly 2013). There are two major exceptions to Europe's general opposition to the process: Britain views fracking as a possible means to replace its declining oil supply in the North Sea, while Poland sees it as a possible means to end its energy reliance on Russia (Jaspal, Nerlich, and Lemańcyzk 2014, 255, 260). But environmental questions are relevant to all new sources of petroleum because of changes to the source of the global energy supply: "[I]n the aggregate, production capacity growth will occur almost everywhere, bringing about a 'deconventionalization' of oil supplies. During the next decades this will produce an expanding amount of what we define today as 'unconventional oils'—such as U.S. shale/tight oils, Canadian tar sands, Venezuela's extra-heavy oils, and Brazil's pre-salt oils" (Maugeri 2012, 2). Because much of the growth in the world's energy supply is taking place in North America, it is worth discussing trends in this region in detail.

Canada's Oil Sands

Ultimately, the real question may not be "When will the world run out of petroleum?" but rather "How dirty will oil have to become before nations abandon it?" (Randers 2012, 99). Oil production from unconventional sources is increasing not only in the United States but also in Canada, the country that exports the most oil to the United States. Despite Canada's importance as an energy exporter to the United States, for many years it remained practically invisible in policy discussions surrounding petroleum. Canada's role did not attract attention because the country was seen as a politically secure source of supply and also because most of its oil reserves are not in conventional oil but rather in the Oil Sands. These deposits represent a vast petroleum resource. Although there are smaller deposits of Oil Sands in Australia and some other nations, major fields of Oil Sands exist in only two nations: Canada and Venezuela. This particular resource is so distinct that only relatively recently has the International Energy Agency (a Paris-based organization that helps developed states manage energy issues) included it when calculating Canada's reserves. To understand why this is the case, we need to first discuss the nature of the Oil Sands (Smallman 2003).

The oil resources in northern Alberta, Canada, seemed unlikely to create such a stir when they were first discovered. In the late 1700s, European explorers in northern Alberta began to find bitumen (a tarry material from which asphalt is made) along the Peace River. The Oil Sands are mostly sand, mixed together with smaller amounts of water, clay, and bitumen. The sands have an oily feel, and they smell of petroleum (which is an oily fossil fuel made of hydrocarbons). This resource was buried beneath the boreal forest and muskeg over an immense area. People in the industry in Alberta commonly claim that the four main deposits cover an area greater than the state of Florida. The quantity of oil held in these lands is also staggering—by some estimates, more than a trillion barrels of oil. But this resource is produced in an unusual manner: it is not pumped but rather mined. What is distinctive about the process is that the challenge is not finding but rather releasing the oil in an environmentally sound (and fiscally feasible) manner. It is a capital-intensive product.

To compete with nations that can simply pump oil, companies in northern Alberta have turned to immense economies of scale. Outside of Fort McMurray, a boomtown north of Edmonton that houses most of this industry's workers, one can stand at the edge of a pit hundreds of feet deep and stretching almost to the horizon. Vast trucks, each weighing 320 tons, pass along the pit floor and receive the bitumen material dumped into them from gigantic bulldozers. From the pit's rim, despite their immense size, these trucks look like children's toys. Drivers work in shifts twenty-four hours a day throughout the year, despite the frigid Canadian winter. The drivers actually prefer the cold because it makes it easier to drive in the pit. Unless you have seen the scale of this undertaking, it is difficult to imagine. Two tons of sand must be mined in order to create one barrel of oil. The size of Canada's oil production from this industry can be measured in the face of the land and the quantities of earth moved to extract this resource.

The high cost of producing oil from the Oil Sands and the technological challenges of producing oil in this manner explain why for many years this resource was simply not included when calculating the size of oil reserves in Canada or Venezuela. Any estimate of the size of the reserves entailed predicting the future cost of oil. How much oil could be extracted depended upon its price and the technology available to extract it. How, then, could an accurate prediction be made? To create the necessary infrastructure to extract the oil entailed tens of billions of dollars in investment. What would happen if investors poured that money into the industry, only to find that the price of oil collapsed? No investor wanted to commit vast sums if the Saudis might decide to grab for market share and drop the bottom out of oil's price.

Estimates for the size of Alberta's oil recoverable reserves (based on what is economically recoverable, not the total size of the reserves) range from roughly 175 billion barrels to 300 billion barrels, which is larger than the total reserves for Saudi Arabia (if those estimates are to be believed, as Simmons [2005] points out). Yet it is unclear whether this oil will ever be produced, despite the billions of U.S. dollars that have been put into creating an immense infrastructure. The first problem is that fracking has exploded as a technology, which has increased the total oil supply and limited OPEC's ability to raise prices. OPEC is a coalition of major oil producers that have sought to maximize their collective profits from petroleum sales. Yet even they have not been able to counterbalance the new production creating by fracking. Second, the resources represent a stranded asset, as energy companies have faced immense difficulties expanding Canadian pipelines to move their product to market. Of course it is also possible to move crude oil by rail. But in July 2013 a train loaded with oil from North Dakota exploded in Lac-Mégantic, Quebec. The resulting blast and fires killed forty-seven people, and the center of the town was severely damaged. The horrific footage of the disaster made the rail shipment of oil a source of protest throughout North America.

For this reason, Alberta has fought to expand its ability to ship oil by pipeline. As the price of oil has declined since 2014, bringing layoffs and a provincial deficit, the industry and the province have campaigned to expand the Transmountain pipeline. The neighboring province of British Columbia, however, has grave reservations about a pipeline, as Alberta would experience the benefits while B.C. would bear the costs of any leaks or damaged ships. Early in 2018 the interprovincial dispute became so bitter that for two weeks the province of Alberta banned the sale of B.C. wines (CBC News 2018). In addition, while First Nations are not united with regard to pipelines, many bands (the term used in Canada) have opposed any pipelines crossing their traditional territories. In November 2017 the Keystone pipeline leaked approximately 5,000 barrels of bitumen in North Dakota (Griggs 2017). Such examples have fueled ongoing risks about pipelines.

The fundamental issue, however, for the Oil Sands may not be the pipeline policy of B.C. but rather the underlying economics. The fracking revolution has remade the finances of oil. It is true that Canada remains the top oil exporter to the United States. But the financial value of its exports to the United States has declined, which is part of a larger pattern: "Overall, the value of American crude oil imports were down by an average –50.2% from all supplying countries since 2017 when crude oil purchases were valued at $279.5 billion" (Workman 2019) Some critics argue that Alberta has to face the reality that the problem is not the lack of pipelines but rather declining demand (Anderson 2018). In an era that is witnessing fracking, the rise of electric cars, new forms of energy storage, and efforts to decarbonize transportation, can the Oil Sands realistically compete globally?

The Environmental Cost of Alternative Oil Sources

Economic questions aside, there are other serious problems with increasing production from the Oil Sands, which the Canadian government is reluctant to acknowledge or discuss. Environmental groups, however, are working hard to raise awareness about the massive problems associated with this resource. (To learn more, visit http://www.pembina.org/oil-sands; see also Heinberg 2003, 112; Burgess 2004; and Nikiforuk 2008.) In essence, mining this resource has a substantial impact on the land, air, and water. Some useful information has been produced by an environmental organization called the Pembina Institute, which has produced both a book, *Death by a Thousand Cuts* (2006), and an online documentary, *Oil Sands Fever*. According to the Pembina Institute and other critics, mining for the Oil Sands permanently changes the land. In order to gain access to the oil-bearing layer, roughly 75 to 100 feet of topsoil first has to be removed. The scale of this process is difficult to describe. Afterward, the tailings are returned to the land, and it is replanted. One oil company brings visitors to view land reclaimed in this manner, on which it keeps a wood buffalo herd managed by local native peoples. But critics say that it is impossible to restore the wetlands or muskeg to its previous condition. It may appear natural, but the land is not what it once was, in an area of boreal forest famous for its bird life. There are also by-products such as sulfur, vast piles of which accumulate near Fort McMurray. The support infrastructure for the Oil Sands also spreads out deep into the forest; water containment pits, sulfur piles, equipment staging, pipelines, and equipment storage extend beyond the boundaries of the mining areas.

Another problem with the Oil Sands development is its immense demand for water. A newer technology is now available for releasing the petroleum without mining called steam-assisted gravity drainage, or Sag-D. But this requires a steady supply of water, as does the process that extracts petroleum from the sands with conventional mining. According to Andre Plourde (2006) of the University of Alberta, in the latter case, it takes between "2.5 to 4 barrels of water" to extract one barrel of bitumen. The challenge is that after this process, the water is too contaminated with napthenic acids and other toxic chemicals to be returned to the watershed. No one currently has a technology able to process contaminated water on an industrial scale. As a result, it is now dumped into tailings ponds that cover about fifty square kilometers, according to the Pembina Institute. Both fish and birds exposed to this water suffer serious harm.

In the spring of 2008, a flock of at least 500 ducks died after landing in one of the Mildred Lakes Basin tailings ponds, which brought international attention to the issue of water pollution in the Oil Sands development (Witt 2008). The Mildred Lakes Basin is twenty-one kilometers in diameter, and there is no existing technology to clean the waters that it contains (Tait 2008a). This may represent a fundamental physical limit on the ability of this resource to be developed, which no one in the industry or government wishes to face (Nikiforuk 2008, 57–92; for the industry view of the environmental issues related to the Oil Sands, see www.canadaoilsands.ca).

The most serious environmental problem with the Oil Sands is its potential impact upon global warming (Nikiforuk 2008, 117–28). It requires a great deal of energy to mine the sands, to separate the bitumen from the sand itself, and to convert the bitumen into oil. A portion of the oil produced is burned to produce the electricity that provides the steam that companies use to drive this process, or natural gas is employed. As a result, oil from the Oil Sands produces much more carbon dioxide (CO_2) than other sources: "Producing the steam requires burning enough natural gas each day to heat 3 million North American homes. The intensive burning of natural gas is particularly alarming to climatologists because it sends three times more climate-changing greenhouse gases into the atmosphere than drilling for conventional oil" (Witt 2008).

Throughout the planet, there are substantial reserves of unconventional or difficult-to-access oil, which means that the conflicts in Canada may presage debates elsewhere. Currently, many European governments are debating the costs and benefits of fracking. Venezuela has the world's second-largest supply of unconventional petroleum in its Oil Sands, although it has not been developed because of that nation's severe economic and political crisis that began in 2014. Argentina may also have large reserves of shale gas. With global warming, the Arctic Ocean's ice cap is receding and thinning, which will open new undersea areas for oil exploration if the region becomes ice-free during the summer in coming decades. Polar nations are now striving to assert their claim to the Arctic seabed in the hope that this region may contain significant oil reserves. Globally, the world would not appear to be on the verge of running out of oil, as the Peak Oil movement suggested. According to one report produced by Rystad Energy in 2018, the United States may surpass the oil production of Russia and Saudi Arabia combined by 2025 (Anonymous 2019). So the question is, How can the global economy move to more-sustainable resources, or at least to those that do not contribute to climate change?

In this context, what has transpired after recent shale oil discoveries in Australia seems like a cautionary tale. In the South Australia town of Coober Pedy, recent discoveries suggest that there may be over 200 billion barrels of oil, which would make Australia rival Saudi Arabia as an energy producer (CBC News 2013). There is still great uncertainty about the size of the reserve. Yet the company that discovered these funds has filed for bankruptcy, and it seems unlikely that these resources will be developed at current low oil prices (Kurmelovs 2016). What is certain is that people in this remote Australian community live in a climate so hot that the town has houses and other buildings underground. People play golf on a grassless course with glowing balls at night because it is often too hot to play during the day. In 2018 the town was seriously worried about one company's plans to drill for oil that was located under the main aquifer used for the town's water supply (Lysaght 2018). What will the future of Coober Pedy be if its water supply is impacted or temperatures in Australia rise from continued fossil fuel production?

Nuclear Power

One global option for increasing energy resources without a parallel increase in CO_2 emissions is nuclear energy. Although it is a nonrenewable resource, there are substantial supplies of uranium in North America and other world regions to meet global demand. So this is one fuel in which there is no danger of a shortage in the near term. Yet there are substantial challenges for nuclear power, one of which is cost. In January 2019 the Japanese firm Hitachi announced that it would not develop a £13 billion nuclear plant in northern Wales (Jack 2019). The decision to stop work on the project cost the company over £2 billion.

The challenge is that new nuclear plants are extraordinarily expensive to build, often exceed their budget, and then find it difficult to compete with the price of other noncarbon energy sources such as wind. In Pennsylvania, the state legislature is about to debate whether to offer subsidies for nuclear power (including the Three Mile Island Unit 1 reactor). In South Carolina, the state Public Service Commission decided to add two new nuclear reactors (Lacy 2019). In the end, after $9 billion in expenditures, mismanagement and cost overruns doomed the plan. Worse, because of state law the corporation and state-owned utility that were responsible for the fiasco did not have to pay for the costs, which were to be passed on to taxpayers in the state (Lacy 2019). After a new company bought the private corporation that owned the project, it promised to reimburse South Carolina's taxpayers the cost, except for $2.3 billion.

Such examples, critics argue, prove that nuclear plants simply cannot produce energy at a rate that is competitive on the marketplace and without exposing taxpayers to excessive financial risk. According to nuclear energy's supporters, though, these plants provide zero-carbon energy that merits public support (Maykuth 2019). Whatever the outcome of this debate, the massive capital costs to create these plants are making them economically challenging to build. There is currently one nuclear power plant under construction in the United States (at a cost of $28 billion), and the project is facing major issues: "The Vogtle project—which has doubled in price and is running more than five years behind schedule—is critical to the U.S. nuclear industry" (Ryan 2019). Since the Fukushima accident in Japan, the cost of nuclear power has continued to rise significantly, while the cost of renewable power (particularly wind) has dropped dramatically.

Another significant issue with nuclear power is the disposal of radioactive waste. This problem is a serious one, especially given the difficulties that have surrounded the nuclear waste disposal facility at Yucca Mountain in Nevada. There is now a discussion about having local communities in the United States compete for interim storage facilities (Victor, Stetson, and Kern 2019). Internationally, Finland seems to have made the most progress toward the disposal of nuclear waste. Britain and France also have plans for underground disposal. Canada plans to place waste in a location deep underground near Lake Huron. Because any possible leak might contaminate the Great Lakes water system, however, there are concerns on the U.S. side of the border about this solution (McCarthy 2013). But no waste-disposal project has been fully implemented yet, so it remains difficult to assess the options. New reactor designs, such as Terrapower's TWR technology, would significantly reduce waste production by using depleted uranium (Terrapower 2015). This technology, however, is still unproven. At present, it seems that major nations will have to spend hundreds of billions of dollars to dispose of nuclear waste, even if no more is created.

Nuclear power also is associated with security issues, as well as with the risk of a catastrophic accident. Nuclear reactors can create the plutonium for nuclear weaponry, which raises the fear of proliferation; such is the case with Iran's nuclear program. After September 11, 2001, there were also real concerns about the possibility of a terrorist takeover of a reactor facility, as well as the theft of radioactive material to make a "dirty bomb" (Hertsgaard 1999, 151). Still, the major issue with nuclear power is the risk of a catastrophic accident, as happened in both the former Soviet Union at Chernobyl in 1986 and Japan's Fukushima plant after the 2011 earthquake and tsunami. In Japan, the nuclear accident magnified an already terrible crisis in which over 15,000 people died. Now Japan has to rethink its energy future while dealing with nuclear cleanup. Even now, the reactor cores have extremely high levels of radioactivity. There are vast amounts of contaminated water, even after the Japanese energy company Tokyo Electric Power Company dumped some radioactive water deliberately into the ocean in September 2015 (Xinhua News Agency 2018). The future costs of the cleanup are staggering. In the aftermath of the nuclear disaster, Japan temporarily closed its nuclear reactors—although many have now restarted—plunging the entire country into efforts to conserve energy. Although rare, these events have devastating impacts that cross national borders.

It is difficult for national governments to have honest conversations with their people about the risks posed by nuclear energy. For example, as Wolf Richter (2013) has argued, the French government has sought to suppress information about the possible impact of a nuclear disaster in France:

> Catastrophic accidents, like Chernobyl in 1986 or Fukushima No. 1 in 2011, are very rare, we're incessantly told, and their probability of occurring infinitesimal. But when they do occur, they get costly. So costly that the French government, when it came up with cost estimates, kept them secret. But now the report was linked to a French magazine, *Le Journal de Dimanche*. Turns out, the upper end of the cost spectrum of an accident at a single reactor at the plant chosen

> for the study, the plant at Dampierre in the Department of Loiret in north-central France, would amount to over three times the country's GDP. Financially, France would cease to exist as we know it. Hence the need to keep it secret. The study was done in 2007 by the Institute for Radiological Protection and Nuclear Safety (IRSN), a government agency under joint authority of the Ministry of Defense and the Ministry of Environment, Industry, Research, and Health.

Such an accident would also contaminate Belgium, England, Germany, the Netherlands, and Switzerland. At the same time, the experience of past nuclear accidents provides some reassurance. In Chernobyl, scientists are proposing to reduce the size of the 4,000-square-kilometer exclusion zone. And there is evidence that many people affected by the disaster are as much at risk from their fear of radiation as they are from the radiation itself (Gill 2019).

In the aftermath of the Fukushima disaster, Germany committed to phasing out nuclear power. In February 2019 the Spanish government announced plans to close all of its nuclear power plants by 2035, as part of an effort to entirely move the economy to renewable energy by mid-century (Binnie and Stonestreet 2019). Given the risks that this energy supply poses, it is unlikely that any country will turn to nuclear power in a substantial manner in the future. Even China slowed its construction of nuclear power plants after Fukushima and recently canceled the construction of a uranium concentration plant in Guangdong after popular protests (Bradsher 2012; Mullaney 2013). Most energy forecasts predict a declining role for nuclear power in the future (Randers 2012, 114).

Coal

Coal also has a reputation as a "dirty" fuel. In England, when people think of coal, they think of the Industrial Revolution and the vast smokestacks that once covered the countryside. English literature from the Victorian era is filled with descriptions of the environmental damage done by coal—the grime that covered the cities and the yellow "fogs" of London. When an inversion layer covered the city in 1952, at least 4,000 people died from the trapped pollution (Christianson 1999, 150–51). This pushed the British to decide to move away from coal as a fuel source. In countries such as Germany, which historically relied on coal for much of its energy, people think of acid rain and the environmental damage suffered by the Black Forest (Morris 2006, 60–61). In coal-producing regions of the United States, people also think of the damage done to the land by the coal industry—the mountaintops leveled by strip-mining and the tailings dumped down the hillside, where they leach pollutants into the watershed. In West Virginia, coal is more than a business; it is part of the culture. But it is reviled in literature and song, which often describe how miners have lost their lives or suffered. Miners working in the mines face serious risks, including lung damage from the exposure to coal dust. Whole towns have had to be moved to make way for coal. Pollution from coal-fired energy plants in the U.S. Midwest plagues southern Canada and the New England states.

Coal is also a major source of greenhouse gases. Coal-powered plants generally run for more than fifty years. The coal industry often resists updating these plants because it is expensive, and once these plants pay for themselves, they are extremely profitable. For this reason, the industry has a poor environmental reputation, as it consistently has opposed stricter standards for its plants. Coal must be scrubbed in order to reduce pollutants as it is burned. The most serious pollutant is mercury, which contaminates the coal. When the coal is burned, mercury is released into the atmosphere and then returns to earth in rainwater. Chemically, mercury is an element, which means that it cannot be broken down into a safer substance. Once in the environment, it remains there and becomes increasingly concentrated as it moves up the food chain. Mercury causes serious health effects, particularly in prenatal children. It is for this reason that pregnant women are discouraged from eating too much fish: "Mercury acts on the central nervous system and can reduce mental ability, making kids shy, irritable, and slow to learn, and causing tremors and visual disturbances. Children under 7 should not eat more than a single 4-ounce portion of non-migrating fish every seven weeks, while women of childbearing age should eat no more than one 8-ounce portion a month" (Read 2006a). This food source has been contaminated by the coal industry, and all consumers of seafood carry this burden. The scale of the contamination is huge, not only in the inland waters of the United States or Europe but also in the vast waters of the world's oceans. The world will be paying the price of coal as an energy source for generations to come.

China is currently attracting global attention because of the rapid pace with which it is building coal power plants. China has a much larger population than the United States, but its petroleum resources are quite modest. As the nation struggles to fuel its rapid growth, it has turned to coal as a key domestic source of energy, a decision that has global implications. As

Mark Hertsgaard (1999, 164–70) eloquently describes in *Earth Odyssey*, Chinese cities such as Beijing already suffer from serious air pollution from existing power plants (see also Roberts 2004, 143–64). But in the early part of the twenty-first century China was building coal plants at a staggering pace, with serious environmental costs. In October 2013 the city of Harbin had pollution levels so severe that flights had to be canceled, schools were closed, and monitoring stations documented record levels of particulates. More recently the growth rate at which new coal plants are built has slowed in China, or possibly reversed (Lin et al. 2018; Wang and Li 2017). Still, China consumes far more coal than any other nation: "In 2018 the U.S. consumed 691 million tons, down from a 2007 peak, but it's still a heavy user. China is also consuming tons of coal numbering in the billions: 3.82 billion metric tons in 2017" (Lekach 2019).

Elsewhere, coal is waning in importance. In 2019 in Germany a commission announced that by 2038 the nation would cease to produce any energy from coal whatsoever (Rockström and Gaffney 2019). This was a remarkable decision, given that coal was the single largest component of the nation's energy mix. In addition, Germany had already decided to forgo nuclear power, which meant that it had to replace two energy sources. (Rockström and Gaffney 2019). While the decision still needs to be put into law (Deign 2019), German commentators believed that the nation would quickly move to adopt this plan.

In the United States, President Trump came to power in 2016 with a campaign promise to end the "war on coal." Despite this promise, coal's proportion of energy production in the United States has seen a steady decline because of cheap natural gas and the rapidly falling price of wind and solar energy. In the entire country, the only coal power plant to open since 2015 was at the University of Fairbanks, Alaska, near a coal mine, in an area with poor solar resources, inadequate wind, and little access to natural gas (Ryan 2019). If the coal industry is not able to grow production in the United States, where it has experienced unusual political support, its future seems poor.

If not oil and coal, what are the other choices for energy in the present day, and how realistic are they?

Biofuels: Ethanol and Biodiesel

One potential fuel source is ethanol, with which many drivers in the United States are already familiar. Ethanol can be stored in existing gas stations with minimal retrofitting. In theory, it also does not significantly contribute to global warming because—if you do not count the petroleum-based fertilizers used to help grow crops—it is made from plants that draw carbon dioxide out of the air as they grow. An equivalent amount is then released as the fuel is burned. These factors have made ethanol attractive as an alternative. The U.S. Midwest has a vast infrastructure now devoted to ethanol production, upon which both individuals and corporations have come to rely. The corn growers of the Midwest have formed a powerful political lobby. A key presidential primary is held in Iowa every four years. Across the country, politicians have found that supporting ethanol is an easy means to prove their environmental credentials. Biofuels now supply nearly 10 percent of the U.S. oil demand. This has helped to shield the United States from oil shocks (Krauss 2013).

Critics, however, argue that ethanol has been hyped beyond its real potential. Fundamental problems, they maintain, limit its ability to replace oil as a fuel. First, only a small fraction of U.S. service stations carry ethanol, and they are mostly in the Midwest. Even supporters acknowledge that creating enough refineries and infrastructure to replace gasoline would take "hundreds of billions of dollars" (Lashinsky and Schwartz 2006, 78). Second, biofuels require a great deal of land, which means that increasing biofuel production increases the cost of other crops. When the price of corn rises globally to provide fuel, it increases the cost of food in poorer nations such as Mexico. There is a limited supply of farmland, and global population is increasing. Third, despite massive investments in research and development, new technologies such as cellulosic ethanol have not proved to be commercially viable. Producing ethanol at scale from crops such as soybeans would likely entail massive tropical deforestation. For these reasons, biofuels seem unlikely to become key providers of the energy used for transportation, except in niche markets such as Brazil (ethanol from sugarcane) and Indonesia (biofuel from palm oil). Shortly after the millennium there was a great deal of interest and investment in biofuels, but at the time of this writing the tide seems to have turned.

Wind and Solar

While fracking has led to dramatic and unexpected changes in the world's petroleum supply, the falling price of wind and solar energy is leading to equally dramatic changes in renewable energy production. For both resources, technology and cost have limited their adoption for so long that people became cynical that they would ever become viable alternatives. Over the last decade, however, the price of wind power has plummeted, which has meant that in the United States, it is now the single largest source of new electricity capacity: "Today, deployed wind power in the United States has the equivalent generation capacity of about 60 large nuclear reactors. Wind is the first non-hydro energy source to begin to approach the same scale as conventional energy forms like coal, gas and nuclear" (U.S. Department of Energy 2013, 2). The price of wind towers has fallen sharply, while the size of turbines has increased dramatically with new technology. The pace of this change has been breathtaking: "In 2012, the U.S. deployed almost twice as much wind as it did in 2011. In fact, wind accounted for 43 percent of new electrical generation capacity in the U.S.—more than any other source" (3).

Of course, not all parts of the United States have adopted wind power equally quickly. Texas has been the nation's leader in installed wind-power projects, but most of the southeastern states have lagged behind. Still, given the scale of wind as a resource—it could single-handedly supply all of the country's energy needs—wind has a bright future: "With continued technology improvements and policy support, the Department of Energy estimates that as much as 20 percent of U.S. electricity demand could be met by wind power by 2030" (U.S. Department of Energy 2013, 3). While Texas leads the United States, other nations are embracing wind as well. In Britain, there are vast supplies of wind offshore, which has led to the development of major wind projects in the ocean, such as the London Array. Denmark, Germany, Portugal, Spain, and Sweden lead Europe in total wind production, in which they are far ahead of the United States on a per capita basis. In the future, wind is likely to be the most cost-effective option for China and India, so these two countries will likely see rapid growth in this area.

While wind has increasingly come to be seen as a mainstream power supply, solar has only just reached a tipping point, which sets the stage for explosive growth. Of all energy resources, none can compare with solar power in terms of the total supply available: "In a strictly rational world with a long time horizon, people would have aimed directly for the ultimate energy solution, which is the sun. . . . The sun shines thousands of times more energy on planet Earth than we will ever use" (Randers 2012, 105). The price of solar photovoltaic power has fallen with incredible speed, far more rapidly than the decline in the cost of wind (106). In some nations, such as Australia, solar power has already hit price parity with fossil-fuel generation. The cost of solar energy has fallen rapidly in parts of Europe, such as Germany, where its price is half that of the United States. Germany's feed-in tariff (which gives long-term contracts to companies producing renewable energy while paying a higher price) has made it the world leader in solar power. Still, the price of solar energy is falling so quickly in the United States, too, that it will soon be cheaper than other forms of power (U.S. Department of Energy 2013, 4). The great advantage of both wind and solar power is that once the plant is built, there is no expense for the purchase of fuel. This makes these plants financially predictable. As solar becomes less expensive than carbon-based fuels, there will likely be a rapid adoption of solar power by residential users, even in the absence of government subsidies (Randers 2012, 110). The future may have arrived early in Australia, where solar power is becoming so inexpensive that it is beginning to threaten the future of traditional utility companies.

It is important to note that as the supply of electricity from renewable energy increases, other technological changes are eliminating the problem posed by solar energy's variability. In Germany, Ontario, and Wales, companies are building large-scale energy-storage facilities that rely on pumping water from a reservoir to another location above it (pumped hydro-energy storage). This means that power can be released at night from solar energy captured during the day. Other companies have adopted solar technology that generates steam to create power. By storing energy in liquid salt, this heat can be converted into electricity hours after the sun has set. This is not a theoretical technology but one that is now in use in places such as Arizona and California: "When it snowed in Flagstaff, Ariz., recently, thousands of people woke up and turned up their electric heating, and Arizona Public Service saw electricity demand reach a morning peak. To meet the demand, the company used the previous afternoon's sunshine" (Wald 2013a). In this case, the Solana project has a peak capacity of 280 megawatts, so this facility is not a small demonstration project.

At the same time, the rapid adoption of LED lights is reducing the demand for electricity for light, which is a major component of electrical use globally. Finally, electric vehicles have rapidly fallen in cost while improving in quality. Tesla, a new American car company, has created an electric car that has received rave reviews from car enthusiasts, while other electric vehicles have also received positive reviews: "For instance, for three years in a row the Chevy Volt has topped J. D. Power's *APEAL Study on Consumer Satisfaction for Compact Sedans*. And this spring, *Consumer Reports* said that the Tesla Model S was the best car they had ever tested"

(U.S. Department of Energy 2013, 9). As the number of cars produced has increased, the costs have rapidly fallen: "Energy Department models for EV [electric vehicle] battery fabrication costs show that the cost of high volume EV batteries has fallen more than 50 percent in the last four years" (8). In the near future, the costs of electric vehicles look likely to continue a significant decline. All of these changes have meant that many challenges to adopting solar energy have been diminished at the same time that its price has plummeted.

Conclusion

In the first edition of this book, this chapter was dominated by a discussion of oil and what could possibly replace this resource. It has now become clear that oil supplies will not collapse in the coming decades. At the same time, nations such as Germany and Denmark have managed to innovate and decrease their demand for traditional fuels. In this context, what is seen as a resource has changed. Solar energy and wind are now remaking the global energy market in a change that is perhaps driven more by their falling costs than global concerns about climate change. Some fuels, such as coal, that were historically important are declining not because of a diminished supply but rather because of concerns about climate change. Since the nuclear disaster in Japan in 2011, most nations have been reluctant to build new nuclear power plants. But equally significant, the construction of such plants entails companies or nations committing to selling electricity for a certain minimum price for decades. If the price of wind and solar continues to decrease, there is a real risk that these plants would be uneconomical and would chain their owners to inflated costs for a long period. For this reason, some sources of energy that were important at the turn of the millennium may be much less significant in the future: "[T]he world's consumption of fossil fuels will be in steep decline by 2052. The contribution from nuclear will be declining. The real winner will be the new renewables—solar, wind, and biomass—which, along with hydro, will grow from 8 percent of energy use in 2010 to 37 percent in 2050" (Randers 2012, 105). While petroleum will likely remain a critical part of many nations' energy mix, it will no longer be the unique source of energy for transportation.

Obviously, it is difficult to predict the future because innovations—such as the development of fracking and new technologies for the mass storage of electricity—can change global energy markets with astounding speed.

From the perspective of 2050, it will be clear which energy sources will dominate, but we cannot know with certainty now. It is possible, however, to make more or less informed judgments, which accord with personal or national priorities. As you read articles in the press about energy, try to look for the underlying assumptions or beliefs that color their portrayal of the subject. What perspective influences each argument, and how does this influence the information that each author presents? How does an individual's argument embody the perspective of a larger group, either on a national or global level? And what voices and information are missing?

➤ VOCABULARY

Hubbert's Peak	International Energy Agency
Peak Oil	OPEC
petroleum	fracking

➤ DISCUSSION AND REFLECTION QUESTIONS

1 *What is the Peak Oil movement?*

2 *Why is it the case that Canada's role as a U.S. neighbor seems to have made it so invisible in policy discussions regarding petroleum?*

3 *Will there likely be a point in the future when people will decide that the environmental costs are too high to extract oil in areas like the Oil Sands?*

4 *Robert Jay Lifton uses the phrase "psychic numbing" to describe behavior on the part of citizens wherein they seem to ignore nuclear power plants in their midst, or fracking equipment next to their pastures, in order to go about their regular daily routine with a tolerable level of anxiety. Are you aware of any conversations among your friends and family that might be examples of this phenomenon?*

5 *If you had the opportunity to make a policy recommendation to a high-level federal administrator regarding energy policy for the next twenty-five years, what would it be and why?*

ACTIVITY 1: ANALYZE The website Cleantechnica (www.cleantechnica.com) is devoted to news articles that place a positive spin on renewable energy. Spend some time reading articles on the website. What picture do you have of global trends in renewable energy based on this website? What information is missing from this Web page?

ACTIVITY 2: REFLECT Many poets have helped the rest of us remember nuclear meltdown events and their legacies. Silently read a poem of your choice in a small group. To find a poem, conduct a search with the phrase "Fukushima + poems." Then in your small group, identify what struck you the most about the poem you read. With one person as scribe, under the word "Fukushima" write eight words in a column in the middle of a sheet of paper. These words can be from the poem or words you think of triggered by the poem. Now working together, craft sentences that will become part of a group poem. Keep the words from your list in the middle of each sentence. Ingrid Wendt (2003) suggests, "Add words on either side of the list, or . . . leave spaces before and after some words. . . . Writing quickly, spontaneously, often gives a boost to our intuitive sense. When your group is finished, put your names on the bottom and give it a title.

(Chain poem instructions adapted from Ingrid Wendt [2003], https://www.nwp.org/cs/public/print/resource/580.)

ACTIVITY 3: EXTEND Wind-farm developers in eastern Oregon have been forced to drop plans for several wind farms and scale down their plans for a remaining farm on Steens Mountain, which is famous for its natural beauty. Environmentalists oppose this placement because it will detract from the scenic splendor of the site, while wind-power advocates point out that it will bring jobs to an economically depressed area and produce clean, renewable power. If you were living in eastern Oregon—a rural, economically challenged part of the state—how would you respond to this issue?

References

Anderson, M. 2018. Only fantasies, desperation and wishful thinking keep pipeline plans alive. Tyee, February 23. Retrieved January 25, 2019, from https://thetyee.ca/Opinion/2018/02/23/Fantasies-Keep-Pipeline-Plans-Alive/.

Anonymous. 2019. US oil production to surpass Russia, Saudi Arabia combined in 2025. *Oil and Gas Investor*, January 24. Retrieved January 30, 2019, from https://www.oilandgasinvestor.com/us-oil-production-surpass-russia-saudi-arabia-combined-2025-1729286.

Binnie, I., and J. Stonestreet. 2019. Spain plans to close all nuclear plants by 2035. Reuters, February 13. Retrieved February 13, 2019, from https://www.reuters.com/article/us-spain-energy/spain-plans-to-close-all-nuclear-plants-by-2035-idUSKCN1Q212W.

Bradsher, K. 2012. China slows development of nuclear power plants. *New York Times*, October 25. Retrieved October 25, 2013, from http://www.nytimes.com/2012/10 /25/business/global/china-reduces-target-for-construction-nuclear-power-plants.html.

Burgess, P., dir. 2004. *Extreme oil: The wilderness*. DVD. New York: Films for the Humanities.

Cardwell, D. 2013. Unplugging bottlenecks in oil and gas deliveries. *New York Times*, October 8. Retrieved October 25, 2013, from http://www.nytimes.com/2013/10/09/business/energy-environment/unplugging-bottlenecks-in-oil-and-gas-deliveries.html.

CBC News. 2013. Australian shale oil discovery could be larger than Canada's Oil Sands. CBC News, January 24. Retrieved October 10, 2013, from http://www.cbc.ca/news /business/australian-shale-oil-discovery-could-be-larger-than-canada-s-oilsands-1.1320034.

———. 2018. Cheers! B.C. wine industry celebrates end of Alberta ban. CBC News, February 22. Retrieved January 25, 2019, from https://www.cbc.ca/news/canada/british-columbia/b-c-alberta-wine-ban-1.4548341.

Chen, S. 2019. Is China's plan to use a nuclear bomb detonator to release shale gas in earthquake-prone Sichuan crazy or brilliant? *South China Morning Post*, January 27. Retrieved January 30, 2019, from https://www.scmp.com/news/china/science/article/2183466/chinas-plan-use-nuclear-bomb-detonator-release-shale-gas.

Christianson, G. E. 1999. *Greenhouse: The 200-year story of global warming*. New York: Walker and Company.

Cockerham, S. 2013. EPA rule on emissions adds muscle but has a catch. *Oregonian*, September 21, A-3.

Deffeyes, K. S. 2001. *Hubbert's Peak: The impending world oil shortage*. Princeton: Princeton University Press.

Deign, J. 2019. Germany has agreed to phase out coal by 2038. What happens next? Green Tech Media, February 9. Retrieved February 20, 2019, from https://www.greentechmedia.com/articles/read/germany-agreed-to-phase-out-coal-now-what#gs.1VZMSjzq.

Frondel, M., M. Horvath, and C. Vance. 2018. The US fracking boom: Impacts on global oil prices and OPEC. In *International Association for Energy Economics: IAEE Energy Forum* (Second Quarter 2018). Retrieved July 10, 2019, from https://www.iaee.org/en/publications/newsletterdl.aspx?id=466.

Gill, V. 2019. Chernobyl: The end of a three-decade experiment. BBC News, February 14. Retrieved February 15, 2019, from https://bbc.in/2IgpI2P.

Goodstein, D. 2005. *Out of gas: The end of the age of oil*. New York: W. W. Norton.

Griggs, M. 2017. The Keystone pipeline just spilled another 210,000 gallons of oil. *Popular Science*, November 17. Retrieved January 28, 2018, from https://www.popsci.com/keystone-pipeline-leak.

Harrison, P. 2008. Oxfam blames biofuel for rising poverty. *International Herald*, June 26.

Heinberg, R. 2003. *The party's over: Oil, war, and the fate of industrial societies.* Gabriola Island, B.C.: New Society Publishers.

Hertsgaard, M. 1999. *Earth odyssey.* New York: Broadway Books.

Huang, L., R. He, Q. Yang, J. Chen, Y. Zhou, J. K. Hammitt, X. Lu, J. Bi, and Y. Liu. 2018. The changing risk perception towards nuclear power in China after the Fukushima nuclear accident in Japan. *Energy Policy* 120:294–301.

Jack, S. 2019. Nuclear plant in Anglesey suspended by Hitachi. BBC News, January 17. Retrieved January 30, 2019, from https://www.bbc.com/news/business-46900918.

Jaspal, R., B. Nerlich, and S. Lemańcyzk. 2014. Fracking in the Polish press: Geopolitics and national identity. *Energy Policy* 74:253–61.

Jolly, D. 2013. France upholds ban on hydraulic fracturing. *New York Times*, October 11. Retrieved October 15, 2012, from http://www.nytimes.com/2013/10/12/business/international/france-upholds-fracking-ban.html?_r=0.

Kanter, J. 2013. European lawmakers tighten rules on fracking. *New York Times*, October 9. Retrieved October 25, 2013, from http://www.nytimes.com/2013/10/10/business/energy-environment/european-lawmakers-tighten-rules-on-fracking.html.

Krauss, C. 2013. Oil shocks ahead? Probably not. *New York Times*, October 8. Retrieved October 25, 2013, from http://www.nytimes.com/2013/10/09/business/energy-environment/oil-shocks-ahead-probably-not.html.

Kurmelovs, R. 2016. How does a company find an ocean of oil under the Australian desert, then go bankrupt? *Vice News*, June 7. Retrieved January 28, 2018, from https://www.vice.com/en_au/article/wdaz85/link-energy-found-233-billion-barrels-of-oil-in-the-australian-desert-then-went-bust.

Lacy, A. 2019. South Carolina spent $9 billion to dig a hole in the ground and then fill it back in. *The Intercept*, February 6. Retrieved February 11, 2019, from https://theintercept.com/2019/02/06/south-caroline-green-new-deal-south-carolina-nuclear-energy/.

Lashinsky, A., and N. D. Schwartz. 2006. How to beat the high cost of gasoline. *Fortune*, February 6, 74–87.

Lekach, S. 2019. Germany wants to reduce its carbon emissions so it's closing its coal plants. Mashable, January 27. Retrieved February 2, 2019, from https://mashable.com/article/germany-energy-coal-climate-change/#obm6LEj9caOS.

Lin, J., D. Fridley, H. Lu, L. Price, and N. Zhou. 2018. Has coal use peaked in China? Near-term trends in China's coal consumption. *Energy Policy* 123 (C): 208–14.

Lysaght, G. 2018. Oil, gas drilling plan raises concerns for outback Coober Pedy's underground water supply. ABC News, March 1. Retrieved January 29, 2019, from https://www.abc.net.au/news/2018-03-02/coober-pedy-fears-for-water-supply-amid-oil-gas-drilling/9493640.

Marusic, K. 2019. Fracking linked to increased hospitalizations for skin, genital and urinary issues in Pennsylvania. Environmental Health News, March 1. Retrieved March 8, 2019, from https://www.ehn.org/fracking-linked-to

-increased-hospitalizations-for-skin-genital-and-urinary-issues-in -pennsylvania-2630649093.html?fbclid=IwAR1AC-ydOoUGLfgCyxel7 Pv7XW5Re30EZoepSbNVXJ1EFizOsp39c3QGSlU.

Maugeri, L. 2012. Oil—the next revolution: The unprecedented upsurge in oil production and what it means. Discussion paper, June. Cambridge, Mass., Harvard Kennedy School.

Maykuth, A. 2019. Hundreds of Pennsylvania jobs on the line as bailout deadline looms for struggling nuclear plants. *The Inquirer*, January 26. Retrieved January 30, 2019, from http://www.philly.com/business/energy/pennsylvania -nuclear-bailout-aeps-exelon-three-mile-island-20190125.html.

McCarthy, S. 2013. How to deal with tonnes of nuclear waste: Bury the problem. *Globe and Mail*, September 13, A-8–9. .

Morris, C. 2006. *Energy switch: Proven solutions for a renewable future.* Gabriola Island, Canada: New Society Publishers.

Mullaney, G. 2013. After protest, China cancels plans for petroleum plan. *New York Times*, July 13. Retrieved October 25, 2013, from http://www.nytimes .com/2013/07/14/world/asia/china-uranium-plant.html.

New York Times. 2006. Taming king coal. Editorial. November 25, A-14.

Nikiforuk, A. 2008. *Tar sands: Dirty oil and the future of a continent.* Vancouver: Greystone.

Plourde, A. 2006. Canada's oil sands: Potential and challenges. Presentation to the Detroit Association for Business Economics, May 18.

Pratt, L. 1976. *The tar sands: Syncrude and the politics of oil.* Edmonton: Hurtig.

Randers, J. 2012. *2052: A global forecast for the next forty years.* White River Junction, Vt.: Chelsea Green Publishing.

Read, R. 2006a. China's mercury flushes into Oregon's rivers. *Oregonian*, November 24, A-14.

———. 2006b. Our warmer world: China's dirty exports—mercury and soot. *Oregonian*, November 24, A-1.

Richter, W. 2013. France predict[s] cost of a nuclear disaster to be over three times their GDP. Blog post at http://oilprice.com/Alternative-Energy/Nuclear -Power/France-Predict-Cost-of-Nuclear-Disaster-to-be-Over-Three-Times-their -GDP.html. March 14.

Roberts, P. 2004. *The end of oil: On the edge of a perilous new world.* New York: Houghton Mifflin.

Rockström, J., and O. Gaffney. 2019. Breaking Germany's coal addiction. New Europe, February 12. Retrieved February 15, 2019, from https://www .neweurope.eu/article/breaking-germanys-coal-addiction/.

Rohter, L. 2006. With a big boost from sugarcane, Brazil is satisfying its fuel needs. *New York Times*, April 10, A-1.

Romm, J. J. 2005. *The hype about hydrogen: Fact and fiction in the race to save the climate.* Washington, D.C.: Island Press.

Ryan, J. 2019. First U.S. coal plant in years opens where no options exist. *Bloomberg*, February 11. Retrieved February 15, 2019, from https://www

.bloomberg.com/news/articles/2019-02-11/coal-s-final-flicker-1st-new-u-s-plant-since-2015-set-to-open.

Simmons, M. 2005. *Twilight in the desert: The coming Saudi oil shock and the world economy*. Hoboken, N.J.: John Wiley and Sons.

Smallman, S. 2003. Canada's new role in North America's energy security. *Security and Defense Review 3* (2): 247–60.

Tait, C. 2008a. Fort McMurray feels duck glare "unfair." *National Post* (Canada), May 17, FP-5.

———. 2008b. Tailing ponds sticky dilemma. *National Post* (Canada), May 17, FP-5.

Terrapower. 2015. A solution to the nuclear waste problem. Terrapower, October 29. Retrieved January 20, 2019, from https://terrapower.com/updates/a-solution-to-the-nuclear-waste-problem/.

Urstadt, B. 2006. Imagine there's no oil: Scenes from a liberal apocalypse. *Harper's Monthly*, August, 31–40.

U.S. Department of Energy. 2013. Revolution now: The future arrives for four clean energy technologies. September 17. Retrieved July 10, 2019, from https://www.energy.gov/sites/prod/files/2015/11/.../Revolution-Now-11132015.pdf.

Victor, D., D. Stetson, and J. Kern. 2019. Nuclear waste has been piling up across America with nowhere to go. Congress needs to act. *Los Angeles Times*, January 24. Retrieved January 29, 2019, from https://www.latimes.com/opinion/op-ed/la-oe-victor-stetson-kern-san-onofre-20190124-story.html.

Wald, M. 2013a. Arizona utility tries storing solar energy for use in the dark. *New York Times*, October 17. Retrieved July 10, 2019, from http://www.nytimes.com/2013/10/18/business/energy-environment/arizona-utility-tries-storing-solar-energy-for-use-in-the-dark.html?hpw.

———. 2013b. Atomic goal: 800 years of power from waste. *New York Times*, September 24. Retrieved July 10, 2019, from http://www.nytimes.com/2013/09/25 /business/energy-environment/atomic-goal-800-years-of-power-from-waste.html.

———. 2013c. Despite climate concern, study finds fewer carbon capture projects. *New York Times*, October 10. Retrieved July 10, 2019, from http://www.nytimes.com/2013/10/11/science/earth/study-finds-setbacks-in-carbon-capture-projects.html.

Wang, Q., and R. Li. 2017. Decline in China's coal consumption: An evidence of peak coal or a temporary blip? *Energy Policy 108*:696–701. Retrieved July 10, 2019, from https://ideas.repec.org/a/eee/enepol/v108y2017icp696-701.html.

Ward, M. 2013. Study finds setbacks in carbon capture projects. *New York Times*, October 10. Retrieved July 10, 2019, from https://governorswindenergy coalition.org/study-finds-setbacks-in-carbon-capture-projects/.

Wendt, I. 2003. The chain poem, a way of breaking the ice. *The Quarterly 25* (2) [Spring].

Wheeling, K. 2019. U.S. oil production is set to rise as experts say fossil fuels need to be phased out. *Pacific Standard*, January 16. Retrieved January 20, 2019, from https://psmag.com/environment/us-oil-production-is-set-to-rise-as-experts-say-fossil-fuels-need-to-be-phased-out.

Wines, M. 2013. A push away from burning coal as an energy source. *New York Times*, November 14, A-18. Retrieved July 10, 2019, from https://www.nytimes.com/2013/11/15/us/a-push-away-from-burning-coal-as-an-energy-source.html.

Witt, H. 2008. Vast oil sands hide dirty environmental secret. *Oregonian*, November 27, A-21.

Workman, D. 2018. Crude oil imports by country—USA. World's Top Exports, September 16. Retrieved January 25, 2019, from http://www.worldstopexports.com/crude-oil-imports-by-country/.

Xinhua News Agency. 2018. Spotlight: Seven years on, Fukushima nuclear cleanup still long way to go. *Xinhua News Agency*, March 11.

Xu, Y., J. Kang, and J. Yuan. 2018. The prospective of nuclear power in China. *Sustainability* 10 (6): 2086–3007.

ELEVEN **Environment**

➤ SYNOPSIS

This chapter explores the beginning of the environmental movement, its tenets and contributions, and some important criticisms that have been leveled against it. Examples from the Amazon rain forest and the Arctic are presented, along with a case study of how sea level rise will affect Pacific island nations. The chapter will also examine how demographic changes will both cause and reflect climate change. An underlying current within the chapter is the notion that environmental issues reflect globalization perhaps more powerfully than other thematic issues presented in this book.

➤ SCAFFOLDING

As you read through this chapter, think about how you would answer each of the questions below.

How directly do media reports and news items about global warming affect you?

If you were countering general global warming arguments, what would you say?

Given the information in the previous chapter about energy sources and their environmental impact, what are key environmental issues you believe people should be familiar with?

Are the countries that are most affected by global warming those that are most responsible for it?

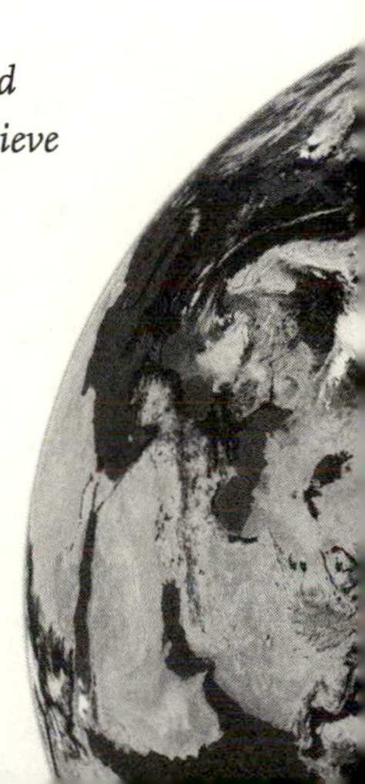

➤ CORE CONCEPTS

Why is the Amazon such an important case study in terms of environment and globalization?

What are some arguments from scholars and practitioners in the Global South regarding how the Global North uses environmental discourse to advance its interests?

How do species extinction and biodiversity loss impact your daily life?

How does the impact on your life compare with the impacts on Indigenous peoples throughout the world?

Perhaps the most surprising fact about the environmental movement is that it was established so recently. The nineteenth century saw individual environmental authors and activists such as Henry David Thoreau and John Muir but not political blocs supporting the cause. Environmentalism became a true movement only in the early twentieth century, and it remained a relatively small subculture until the 1960s. By that time, the impact of DDT; the example of Love Canal; the mercury disaster at Minamata, Japan; the damage to the Great Lakes; the choking smog in cities; and growing worries about nuclear energy combined to create widespread concern about environmental issues in the developed world. Recently, books such as *Fieldnotes from a Catastrophe* (Kolbert 2006) and Jeff Goodell's widely praised work *The Water Will Come* (2017) have brought environmental issues to the forefront of public discourse. The power of the modern environmental movement reflects widespread anxiety about global warming, species loss, and deforestation. And people fear for the future of humanity. The nuclear disaster at Fukushima, Japan, in 2011 created an ongoing release of radioactive water into the North Pacific Ocean that now seems impossible to control. This disaster in particular has led people to think about the limits of technology.

At the same time, there is currently an intellectual backlash against the environmental movement, not only in the United States but also in Europe. In some places, economic interests have influenced governments to conceal information about sea level rise, as has perhaps been the case in North Carolina (Pilkey, Pilkey-Jarvis, and Pilkey 2016, 150–54). There have also been significant investments by industry to fund climate change skeptics (139–54). The entire real estate industry in South Florida is built upon a denial of sea level rise. It is difficult to understand the state of Florida's decision to build the Turkey Point nuclear plant at the water's edge (115–17) or the St. Lucie nuclear plant on Hutchison Island. Denial may be one aspect of the anti-environmental movement, a complex ideology that draws on some unexpected sources (Spotts 2006). It would be unfair to suggest that it is swayed solely by economic influences. For example, a particularly powerful attack on the environmental movement comes from the Global South. One needs to look at the historical and political experience of southern countries in order to understand why their populations might not trust environmental rhetoric. One way of observing this reality is to examine the contested arguments about the future of the Amazon and how this issue is perceived in northern and southern nations. This perspective helps us to examine the interconnections between social and environmental issues in a manner that permits a more critical evaluation of environmental debates.

The Amazon

The Amazon is a powerful symbol for environmental destruction, given the issue of deforestation and species loss. Changes to the forest are so profound that they might have implications for planetary climate. Most works on the Amazon begin by describing the staggering size of the largest tropical rain forest on the planet and the river that gives it its name. If one end of the Amazon River were laid on the coast of Brazil, it would span the Atlantic Ocean and end in Africa. Or if the Amazon River basin were overlaid upon the United States, it would cover most of the country (Hanson 1944, 4). It has "one-fifth of the freshwater flowing off the face of the earth" (N. Smith 1999, 4). Bolivia, Brazil, Colombia, Ecuador, French Guyana, Guyana, Peru, Suriname, and Venezuela all lay claim to parts of the river basin. Marajó Island, in the mouth of the Amazon, is the size of some small European nations. The Amazon has many tributaries that on their own would be major world rivers, such as the Negro. At its mouth, the river is farther across than the distance from France to England. But reading about such statistics and facts, while impressive, is not the same as viewing the river in person. Travelers can canoe through the Amazon and look down through crystal-clear waters to see trees beneath them. The trees have evolved to keep their leaves, and one can see fish flitting through the branches, feeding on the trees' fruit. Life seems to fill every imaginable niche in this environment.

The Amazon is tens of millions of years old and home to a vast number of species. From the air, you can fly for hours over green expanses of forest, which gives the land a surface impression of uniformity. But some geologists hypothesize that the forest has expanded and contracted through time, which has created pockets of forest with particular species called refugia (Leakey and Lewin 1996, 109); for scientists, these can be thought of as biological islands with plants and animals unlike those in other areas of the forest. The suggestion is that this geologic history may help to explain the immense richness of species that the Amazon possesses. From electric eels and bird-eating spiders to blue morpho butterflies and manatees to the capybara—the largest rodent on the planet, which wanders the Amazonian forest looking like a guinea pig on growth hormones—the Amazon is full of unexpected creatures.

Scientists are constantly discovering new species. In 2017 the World Wildlife Federation and a Brazilian institution announced that in 2014 and 2015, 381 new species had been found in the Amazon. Among the 20 new mammal species discovered were the Araguaian river dolphin and the fire-tailed titi monkey (Valsecchi, Marmontel, Franco et al. 2017). In 2013 researchers announced the discovery of a new species of tapir. What was remarkable was the animal is large (over 220 pounds), travels in groups, and is relatively common along the upper Madeira River, where it is well known to locals (Cozzuol et al. 2013). There is currently no good figure for the total number of species in the Amazon. The region is too vast, and the resources devoted to an inventory to date have been far too small. But from the trees that define the forest to the insects that live upon them, the Amazon is immensely rich in species.

The scale of the Amazon River basin, which amazed early scientific explorers from Richard Spruce to Henry Walter Bates, long made it difficult to imagine that such a vast environment could be endangered. But far to the east, another forest's death has served as a warning. When the first Portuguese explorers arrived, they encountered the Atlantic Forest, which stretched from northern Argentina to northern Brazil. Despite its great length, it seldom reached over 200 miles in thickness, except in the very southern edge of its range, where it stretched into Paraguay. After discovery, the Portuguese first exploited the coastal region and then gradually moved to the interior, mostly settling in areas near the ocean so that they could export their main crop—sugarcane—to the mother country. Most of the country's major cities now lie in the region that was once covered by the Atlantic Forest. Perhaps less than 7 percent of the original forest remains—a fraction of a woodland that "once covered 466,000 square miles—an area larger than Texas and California combined—along the Atlantic coast of Brazil" (LaFranchi 1998, 12). Some parts of this forest appear in unexpected patches, where monkeys live at the edge of the Copacabana in Rio de Janeiro and diminutive owls nest an hour outside of São Paulo, the largest city in South America.

Despite its shrunken area and the fact that many sections are now second growth, the Atlantic Forest remains astoundingly rich in species. For this reason, the Atlantic Forest is a World Biosphere Reserve, a status designating an ecosystem that merits particular protection and recognition. According to the Nature Conservancy, the Atlantic Forest is home to "around 20,000 species of plants, representing 8 percent of the earth's plants. In fact, in the 1990s researchers from the New York Botanical Garden counted 458 tree species in 2.5 acres—more than the number of tree species in the entire U.S. eastern seaboard" (Nature Conservancy 2006; see also LaFranchi 1998, 12). This wealth of plant diversity supports a corresponding diversity in other species. The forest has twenty-one species of primates found nowhere else in the world.

What is amazing about the Atlantic Forest is that patches of it are so accessible. One can take a path at Praia Vermelha at the base of Sugarloaf Mountain that winds around the base of this tourist attraction, which holds a small remnant of the Atlantic Forest. Most of the people on the trail are Brazilians who come to see the huge butterflies and small monkeys in the heart of Rio de Janeiro, one of South America's great cities. As Warren Dean (1995) has argued in his magisterial history of the Atlantic Forest, what remains is a ghost of an ecosystem. Yet "international interest in the Atlantic Forest is heightened by conservation biologists' growing attention to the world's remaining centers of biodiversity" (LaFranchi 1998, 12). The argument has been made that saving the Atlantic Forest is hopeless and that the remaining areas of the forest will not survive past the middle of this century. Attention should therefore be focused instead on the Amazon (LaFranchi 1998, 13). But the incredible biodiversity of the Atlantic Forest makes people reluctant to abandon it, and some surveys have found positive news about the biological health of the forest. At the same time, the Atlantic Forest serves as a warning of what could happen to the Amazon. It is possible to kill an entire ecosystem.

The Amazon became an international environmental issue in the 1980s as people began to realize that if deforestation rates continued, this ecosystem could be destroyed. At the same time, a global tide of species loss made biodiversity a focus of popular attention. Geographically, the diversity of species increases sharply near the tropics. Most of the world's species exist in a band 30 degrees on either side of the equator. Some environments, such as the dry scrublands of northeastern Brazil, are surprisingly rich in species (Leakey and Lewin 1996, 103–4). But overall, the tropical rain forests are home to the most remarkable biodiversity on earth. As Richard Leakey notes, the result of this natural law is that much of earth's life lives in a surprisingly small space: "Termed the 'latitudinal species-diversity gradient,' this bold signature of nature has been known to biologists for many years. . . . Tropical rain forests are especially rich in biodiversity: they cover one-sixteenth of the world's land surface, yet are home to more than half its species" (Leakey and Lewin 1996, 103). As one might expect, tropical rain forests are central to current discussions surrounding biodiversity and species loss.

In a UNESCO publication, Tove Skutnabb-Kangas, Luisa Maffi, and David Harmon concisely defined biodiversity as the "total variability among genes, plant and animal species, and ecosystems found in nature" (2003, 53). In other words, biodiversity is a measure of the richness of life in an environment. It also seems to correlate with cultural and linguistic richness. Environments that foster a wealth of cultures and languages seem to be the same as those that create remarkable biodiversity (9, 38–39). The Amazon and Papua New Guinea are rich in both languages and species; indeed, the island of New Guinea is the most linguistically diverse region on earth, with over 1,000 languages (26). But these biological hotspots are under mounting pressure at the same time that languages and cultures are being assimilated at a rapid rate. Deforestation, overhunting, and dams are rapidly changing the ecosystems in the Atlantic Forest, the Amazon, and the Congo River basin, as well as Southeast Asia's forests.

One particular problem is that the areas of our planet with the greatest biodiversity are also those undergoing the most rapid population growth. While forests are growing in the wealthier north, deforestation is still continuing in tropical countries (Sloan and Sayer 2015). As Alex Ezeh noted in 2016, population growth in Africa in particular will lead to dramatic environmental changes: "One of the key drivers of environmental change globally is population growth. In 1950, Africa accounted for about 9% of the world population; by 2100, it is estimated to account for about 40% of the world population, with a projected total population of 4.4 billion people. Indeed, 83% of the projected increase in global population by 2100 will occur in Africa" (27). Global population growth impacts entire ecosystems, and much of the world's population growth in this century will take place in the regions with the greatest species density.

At the same time, temperature increases driven by global warming are increasingly heat-stressing trees and causing periods of drought in some regions. The number of areas in which there has been major tree mortality because of drought and heat is concerning, according to William deBuys: "For the years since 1970, . . . eighty-eight instances of such mortality spread from Zimbabwe to Alaska and Australia and Spain. Significantly, the rate of occurrence of such events increased markedly after 1998 and continued to accelerate through the 2000s" (2011, 254). One 2018 study by the World Wildlife Federation suggests that if temperatures within the Amazon rose by 4.5 degrees centigrade, half the species within "priority places" would go extinct. The same year, Thomas Lovejoy and Carlos Nobre wrote that large sections of the Amazon might no longer remain as forest: "We believe that negative synergies between deforestation, climate change, and widespread use of fire indicate a tipping point for the Amazon system to flip to nonforest ecosystems in eastern, southern and central Amazonia at 20–25% deforestation" (2018, 2340). Given these facts, is a global period of mass extinction looming?

Extinction

Our world has endured mass extinction before. Over the multibillion-year history of life on our planet, there have been five great extinctions in which most life disappeared: "This handful of major events, from oldest to the most recent, are: the end-Ordovician (440 million years ago), the late Devonian (365 million years ago), the end-Permian (225 million years ago), the end-Triassic (210 million years ago), and the end-Cretaceous (65 million years ago)" (Leakey and Lewin 1996, 45). For at least one of these extinctions, there is a clear explanation. Most scientists now agree that 65 million years ago, an asteroid or comet collided with the earth in the ocean off the coast of the Yucatán Peninsula, Mexico. This created a firestorm of energy, unleashed a massive tsunami, and heated the entire planet, which then slid into months of darkness. This event wiped out many life forms, of which the most famous were the nonavian dinosaurs. Other events are more mysterious, such as the end-Permian extinction, during which nearly all major life forms on earth died. There is little mystery, however, about the dramatic extinctions that are currently taking place. On Monday, March 12, 2018, the last remaining male northern white rhino died. In the

1960s there had been 2,000 of the animals. Now, after decades of poaching and habitat loss, only two female rhinos remained. Although researchers have stored sperm from northern rhinos, neither of these female rhinos is able to bear offspring (Nuwer 2018). Scientists have been preparing for this moment by exploring how to bring back the population using innovative stem cell technology (Calloway 2016). Still, at this moment this subspecies is functionally extinct. While stem cell science may help to save the northern white rhino (Calloway 2016), in the end it is no substitute for habitat preservation and wildlife protection. This is true not only on land but also at sea, where in 2018 studies found that the North Atlantic right whale population was trending toward extinction, with no births for the year and seventeen deaths (GrrlScientist 2018). The number of individual species impacted is overwhelming but is only one part of a larger picture.

Pollution, hunting, and deforestation can destroy not only species but even entire ecosystems with astounding speed. Richard Leakey and Roger Lewin describe the experience of two scientists who discovered a ridge in western Ecuador called Centinela. It was an environment as rich as it was vulnerable: "Among the riot of diversity that is nurtured by this habitat . . . were ninety unknown species, including herbaceous plants, orchids and epiphytes, which lived nowhere else. Centinela was an ecological island, which, being isolated, had developed a unique flora. Within eight years the ridge had been transformed into farmland, and its endemic species were no more" (Leakey and Lewin 1996, 243). Centinela is but one example of a larger process of extinction, which is not confined to western Ecuador but is taking place across the planet.

Scientists now argue that the current sweep of extinction is so dramatically different from that in the recent geological record that it should be recognized as something distinct. Some scientists contend that perhaps as many as 100,000 species a year go extinct (Leakey and Lewin 1996, 241). This devastation constitutes a "sixth extinction" comparable to the greatest mass extinctions in our earth's history (232–45). As Paul Martin has described, the damage inflicted by our industrialized society is only one part of a longer process in which humans have destroyed large mammal and bird species from North America to Australia (Martin 2005; R. Stone 2001, 111–20; Leakey and Lewin 1996, 170–94). Jared Diamond made the environmental damage of ancient cultures the major theme of his work *Collapse: How Societies Choose to Fail or Succeed* (2005); this book carefully describes how past societies so thoroughly damaged their environments that civilizations or cultures suffered. The world lost dramatic species—

from the moa, the largest bird that has ever lived, to the mammoth, which disappeared in North America shortly after the first humans arrived. Given humanity's dependence on its environment to survive, this destruction may seem difficult to understand. As Diamond's students asked him, what passed through the mind of the Easter Islander who cut down the last tree (419)? But these extinctions were only a forerunner for the far broader damage now being done to our modern world.

No part of our planet seems to be safe from species loss. Frog species are going extinct at a rapid rate globally for reasons that are hard to understand but may have something to do with an invasive fungus spread by human activity. In the oceans, overfishing threatens multiple species. Even where species survive, commercial fisheries are collapsing under the pressure of mounting global demand for fish. The cod fishery in the North Atlantic, for example, was scientifically managed into oblivion (Kurlansky 1998, 144–233). Despite a current fishing moratorium, the population has been slow to recover (Pedersen et al. 2017). This trend is a global phenomenon, but not all regions are equally affected. At the core of this process is the loss of tropical forest, which has the greatest riches of species on the planet and where vast numbers of species are disappearing.

Such an immense catastrophe is difficult to fathom. In the past, there was little concern about preserving dying species. The last thylacines (Tasmanian tigers) died in Australian zoos because nobody bothered to breed them. Of course, saving even a single species can be an overwhelming task that requires an immense amount of resources; it can be very expensive, and there often is no margin for error. Yet the total scale of the challenge is overwhelming. Some rare species, such as the Nepalese rhino, require both large amounts of territory and constant protection from poachers. There is no way that a global response to this problem could focus on using innovative technologies to save individual species. Instead, any such effort must concentrate on the broader problems that many species face. (For a list of these challenges, see Diamond 2005, 486–96.)

There is no consensus, however, that the cost of doing so is worthwhile. (For a short list of the arguments used against environmentalists, see Diamond 2005, 503–14.) Popularly, most people agree that the loss of a species is a tragedy. But preserving species often comes with a cost, whether it be preserving old-growth forests to save the spotted owl in the U.S. Northwest or fighting the illegal ivory trade to preserve elephants in Kenya. This has led to a tension between people advocating for environmental preservation and people who argue that employment and development have to be equally valued. In spite of environmentalists' quantification of the economic value of biodiversity (Leakey and Lewin 1996, 124–25), there remains a larger anti-environmental critique.

The Anti-environmental Critique

The argument of the anti-environmental movement can be broadly summarized around several key points. The environmental movement has created a narrative of constant environmental decline, even though there has been significant progress. Its strong political agenda has also warped its use of science. Critics argue that environmentalists do not create a nuanced or qualified picture of environmental trends, which are often complex and contradictory. Instead, they tend to create a bleak vision of the future as a political tool to mobilize support. Historically, however, many of their predictions have proved to be wrong. The success of the movement owes as much to its political work, especially within the educational system, as it does to the power of their arguments.

These critics argue that the pendulum has swung so far in the environmental movement's direction that development and employment are often threatened. In this narrative, the environmental movement is elitist and disconnected from the concerns of the working majority of Europeans and Americans. Many of the policies that the environmentalists advocate are simply not practical. For example, renewable energy sources have been touted for decades as an alternative to fossil fuels. But there are serious obstacles to their adoption, which the environmental movement glosses over. At root, these critics argue that much of the environmental movement is anti-science and anti-growth.

Much of the criticism of the environmental movement also has a strong free-market component. Detractors argue that the solution to environmental problems is not more government regulation but rather privatization. For example, one of the most influential pieces of environmental writing has been Garret Hardin's 1968 *Science* magazine article "The Tragedy of the Commons." In this work, Hardin argued that resources held in common, such as fisheries, tend toward disastrous overuse because individual actors can benefit from actions that are collectively disastrous. In response, Fred Smith has argued that this should not be seen as a market failure but rather a call for more privatization. This is true for many issues, including efforts to address species loss: "Note also that while many species of wildlife are threatened, domesticated species—pets as well as livestock—are prospering" (2002, 297). Smith maintains that if people see economic benefits from endangered species, such as elephants, then they will work to preserve them (308). Most environmentalists, however, would point to the many situations in which private property owners are making decisions that are profoundly destructive to the environment. In the 1980s, the poster child for environmental destruction might have been the cattle ranchers of the Amazon. Today, it might be the major soy farmers, who are also replacing the forest, partly to produce biodiesel. There are larger philosophical issues involved: does biodiversity have value only if it provides economic benefit? What are the economic benefits of the species that provide oxygen, purify water, and pollinate the plants we eat—in short, what is the value of the ecosystems that make the earth a livable planet? Leakey and Lewin have described this debate in detail (1996, 124–44). Yet it would be a mistake to characterize the anti-environmentalists' arguments as uniformly naive.

Southern Critiques of Environmentalism

The most recognized critics of the environmental movement have been northern authors, such as the Danish academic Bjørn Lomborg, who is a statistics professor at the University of Aarhus in Denmark. Nonetheless, there are also significant objections to the environmental movement in the developing world. One can clearly see that many of these arguments concern the Amazon. As mentioned earlier in the chapter, the Amazon came to prominence as an international cause in the 1980s, driven by rising concerns about global warming and the publicity associated with the death of Chico Mendes, an environmental and union activist in Brazil's Amazon. At this time, there was a great deal of media attention devoted to the Amazon, which attracted the support of public figures such as the rock star Sting. In environmental publications, the Amazon was described as being "the lungs of the Earth"; this was the region that generated oxygen for our planet.

In response to these concerns, there were thoughtful efforts to see how developed nations could help South American nations address the issue of deforestation. One popular answer that policy makers suggested was "debt-for-nature" swaps. Under these agreements, wealthier nations would forgive the debt of poor countries, which did not have the capacity to repay their debt in any case. In return, these nations would set aside certain areas as nature reserves. It seemed to be a win-win situation for all.

Within developing countries, however, such efforts were sometimes viewed as being very threatening. To understand why, you have to consider the historical and cultural context that shaped South American governments at the time. This is not to deny the serious damage that was being done to the Amazon. In 1990 documentary filmmaker Adrian Cowell released four videos that formed the *Decade of Destruction* series. Cowell's work documented the environmental and human costs of Brazil's Amazon policy. Viewers have been moved to tears watching the tragic encounters between native peoples and settlers or between gunmen and squatters.

Yet the beliefs and attitudes held by people in Brazil and other Amazonian countries are not invalid. If one were to summarize the views of many Brazilians and combine them with the writing of various authors on the Amazon, a skeptic's viewpoint might be as follows in the rest of this section.

Europeans have long imposed their views of an exoticized nature onto the Amazon, beginning with the first ideas of El Dorado, which led the first Spaniards to navigate down the Amazon. Europeans and North Americans continue to impose these images upon the Amazon, in part because it is a politically safe way for them to address environmental issues (Nugent 1994, 15–21, 214–15; Slater 2003a). Yet nobody in the United States, Germany, or Japan has to lose a job to fight deforestation in the Amazon.

Many people within South America have a cynical attitude toward both Europeans and North Americans (Christianson 1999, 189–91). From their perspective, northern countries have largely deforested their nations as part of the developmental trajectory (Nugent 1994, 19; Christianson 1999, 182). But now that Brazil and Peru want to follow in their path—and are preserving far more of their old-growth forest than the United States or Europe has (Stewart 1994, 23) and have set aside large areas as nature reserves—northern countries are telling them that they cannot do so. Moreover, these South American nations owe immense sums to these rich countries. There is no realistic hope that they can repay these debts unless resources such as the Amazon are developed.

South American governments also argue that the Amazon is not as vulnerable to development as environmentalists have proposed. One of the reasons that the Amazon is so species-rich is that, historically, the forest has waxed and waned, with periods when much of the Amazon basin looked more like a savanna with divided patches of forest (Leakey and Lewin 1996, 109). Nor is the forest in some primeval state. The Indigenous people have modified this forest for thousands of years. Some authors use the term "cultured forest" to capture the extent to which the forest's composition has changed. Native peoples burned extensive areas of forest. They created plantations of their favorite fruit-bearing crops, some of which have endured for centuries (N. Smith 1999, 32). They even fashioned canals to connect different branches of rivers together (Raffles 2002, 26–27, 34). After disease and slave raids caused the Amazon's population to collapse, the forest reclaimed many of these fields and plantations. But the impact on the soil and plant composition was profound, so that local peoples can readily identify areas where native peoples once lived even centuries after they left (N. Smith 1999, 24–28). The Amazon is not an untouched wilderness that is easily destroyed by human contact. One recent study found that 1 million people may have lived along the southern Amazon, where they had built large earth structures (de Souza et al. 2018). What Europeans had taken to be wilderness had been emptied of people by European diseases and slave raiders after contact. Many government officials and businessmen in Brazil believe that the people who have seized upon the Amazon as an environmental issue have only a vague idea of the region's nature and history.

For South American critics, the current effort to impose the environmental values of the developed world upon South American nations represents a modern form of imperialism. It is true that developed countries are no longer using military means to impose their control. Now, they implement their will by threatening to deny World Bank loans or funding for packages that serve key national interests. The idea of debt-for-nature swaps is particularly disturbing, because it represents a threat to national sovereignty. The United States has a long and sad history of interventions in Latin America, ranging from Haiti to Nicaragua and Colombia, and European nations have no greater legitimacy among southern governments and populations. How, then, do these northern nations have the authority to tell South America how to use land within its own territory?

We do not personally subscribe to the South American viewpoints described here—quite the opposite. But it is important to hear these voices. Many of the feelings surrounding this topic are raw. South Americans surely know how they are being portrayed abroad, and it angers them. There are clear cases when the people are articulating simplistic arguments, such as the man who successfully ran for governor in one of Brazil's Amazon states with the slogan "For every peasant, a chain saw." But more thoughtful arguments are also voiced by Brazilians and Peruvians, as well as by some North American experts. Environmental issues must be discussed in a social context if they are to persuade the people involved.

As Adrian Cowell's work makes clear, the people responsible for much of the environmental damage in the Amazon are the poor and the dispossessed, who act not from malice but from need. Simplistic narratives of the Amazon's destruction ignore the larger social and economic factors that drive deforestation. Without more nuanced views, it is difficult to gain the support of people who actually live in the Amazon, many of whom are now urban dwellers. The advocates for the forest need to understand different perspectives in order to craft broad alliances. It is true that there are "pro-growth" or "anti-environmental" sentiments in many developing nations. But dramatic growth can come with an equally dramatic cost, as China is now learning. Environmental perspectives do not break down on a clean north/south line, and environmental concerns are becoming more powerful in the developing world.

Atmosphere and Climate

It is possible to bring together all of the world's nations to address environmental issues, which is necessary if humanity is to combat the pollution of the planet's atmosphere. One positive example is provided by the global effort to eliminate chlorofluorocarbons (CFCs), which at one time were used in everything from refrigerators to Styrofoam cups (Kolbert 2006, 182–83). In the 1980s, researchers realized that in the upper atmosphere, CFCs broke down into chlorine, which served as a catalyst in reactions involving ozone. Although ozone is a poisonous gas at ground level and commonly thought of as a pollutant, in the upper atmosphere it serves to protect the planet from dangerous levels of ultraviolet radiation. In the mid-1980s, scientists documented significant holes in the earth's ozone at the poles. In 1987 the world came together with the Montreal Protocol, which began the phased elimination of CFCs, despite significant opposition from industry. The result has been that the global release of CFCs has plummeted. It will take probably more than half a century for the hole in the ozone to heal. But there is evidence that the holes have stopped growing and are beginning to shrink (Arctic Climate Impact Assessment 2004, 98–107). In this case, a global coalition was able to prevent an environmental disaster.

A similar effort will be needed to prevent the worst possibilities of global warming, which is widely perceived to be humanity's greatest challenge. Global warming is the heating of the planet driven by rising levels of carbon dioxide (CO_2) and other greenhouse gases in our atmosphere.

Atmospheric gases trap heat, without which it is unlikely that our planet could support life:

> The greenhouse gas effect is indispensable for life on the Earth; it is the weakness or excessive strength of the effect that is a matter for concern. The effective radiative (blackbody) temperature of a planet without an atmosphere is simply a function of its albedo (the share of incoming radiation that is directly reflected into space) and its orbital distance. The Earth (albedo 30 percent) would radiate at –18 degrees Celsius, compared to –57 C for Mars and –44 C for Venus, and all these planets would have permanently frozen surfaces. A planet ceases to be a perfect radiator as soon as it has an atmosphere some of whose gases . . . can selectively absorb part of the outgoing infrared radiation and reradiate it both downward and upward. (Smil 2008, 172)

In other words, greenhouse gases are essential to life on our planet because they capture enough heat to maintain the planet's temperature sufficient for liquid water to exist.

The problem is that humanity is changing the balance of these gases in our atmosphere by increasing the level of CO_2. This chemical is released through the burning of fossil fuels, as well as by deforestation. The loss of forests is particularly serious because it not only releases carbon but also changes the planet's reflectivity, or albedo (Smil 2008, 178). At the same time, methane is a potent greenhouse gas released by our farming practices, in particular our reliance upon cattle. CFCs and nitrogen dioxide are also greenhouse gases (177). Combined, these chemicals are increasing the quantity of the sun's energy that our atmosphere retains.

People have known that humanity was impacting the atmosphere for a long time. Swedish chemist Svante August Arrhenius described the basic mechanism for global warming in the nineteenth century (Kolbert 2006, 39–42). Scientists can measure the level of CO_2 in the atmosphere over a large span of time, even in the absence of modern measuring machines: "Atmospheric CO_2 levels are now known for the past 650,000 years thanks to the ingenious analyses of air bubbles from ice cores retrieved in Antarctica and in Greenland. During that period CO_2 levels never dipped below 180 ppm [parts per million] and never rose above 300" (Smil 2008, 175). In 1850 the CO_2 level had been roughly 280 ppm. In 1959, as Elizabeth Kolbert describes, the level was perhaps 316 ppm (2006, 44). As I write these words in July 2019, the Mauna Loa Observatory reports a CO_2 level of 412.93 ppm; Kolbert predicts it may reach 500 ppm by the mid-twenty-first century (2006, 44). A graph of CO_2 levels called the Keeling Curve provides evidence that greenhouse gases are rising at a dramatic rate (Christianson 1999, 167). This matches with careful calculations of temperature rise over time: "Consequently, it can be stated with a high degree of confidence that the mean temperatures during the closing decades of the twentieth century were higher than at any time during the preceding four centuries, and it is very likely that they were the highest in the past 13 centuries" (Smil 2008, 177).

As Gale Christianson (1999) and Jared Diamond (2005) have documented, even small changes in climate historically have had dramatic impacts on cultures as varied as that of the Maya, the Greenland Vikings, the Anasazi, and the inhabitants of the U.S. Great Plains during the Dust Bowl years. There is now mounting evidence for global warming from multiple measures, including the northward shift of species ranges, the rising elevations at which species are typically found, the bleaching of coral reefs, the pattern of record warm years, the thawing of permafrost, and the retreat of glaciers.

With global warming comes particularly dramatic possibilities. Ocean levels will rise, in part because of the melting of glaciers (particularly in Antarctica) as well as the Greenland ice cap. Recent data suggests that Greenland's ice sheet is melting far faster than scientists had predicted: "It is the acceleration that stuns scientists. Greenland's glaciers are adding up to 58 trillion gallons of water a year to the oceans, more than twice as much as a decade ago and enough to supply more than 250 cities the size of Los Angeles, NASA research shows" (Milstein 2007). Another study found that global sea level was rising faster than expected (Picazo 2018).

Warmer water also fills a greater volume. Scientists can already measure the warming of the oceans: "The strength of this warming signal varies by ocean and depth. North and South Atlantic warming, by as much as 0.3 C, reaches as deep as 700 m, whereas Pacific and Indian Ocean warming is mostly limited to the top 100 m" (Smil 2008, 182). The impact for some places, such as the Netherlands, Louisiana, Florida, and Bangladesh, is ominous (Arctic Climate Impact Assessment 2004, 40–43). In 2012 Hurricane Sandy caused $65 billion in storm damage—most of which was the result of flooding—in New York and New Jersey. This raised questions about how these states should prepare for higher ocean levels. As Lyman Stone has argued (2017), Puerto Rico was so damaged by Hurricane Maria in September 2017 that it has experienced a significant outflow of migration; other Caribbean islands face serious dangers from hurricanes that will grow stronger with global warming. How do nations deal with climate migration? India is constructing a high-tech fence that is 2,100 miles long, in part because it fears that 15 million Bangladeshis might flee their country for India as rising waters flood coastal areas (Friedman 2009). It is a common observation to say that many of the countries that will suffer the most (such as the Pacific Island nations of the Maldives and Tuvalu) are those that have contributed the least to global warming (Flannery 2005, 287; for a description of island loss in the Pacific, see Pearce 2007, 55–62).

Throughout the text we have sought ways for you to link information about globalization to your own life. We have also provided you with factual information about a wide variety of nation-states and issues they face. While there are many estimates circulating concerning the number of climate refugees in the future, the estimate that is referred to most frequently in the literature belongs to the International Organization for Migration, which suggests that by 2050 there could potentially be 200 million climate refugees (Goodell 2017, 182). Other estimates are higher; scholar Peter Singer sets it at 750 million (McAdam 2016).

Small Island Developing Nations

In the following case study we consider climate change issues facing Small Island Developing Nations (SINs), a set of more than forty-one countries. Specifically, here we examine issues facing Tuvalu, a protectorate of New Zealand; the Maldives, an independent country; and the Marshall Islands, a protectorate of the United States. In this case study we explore the relationship among large countries responsible for a high percentage of emissions and SINs deeply impacted by sea level change, as well as the cost to people not having an international designation as climate refugees by the UN High Commissioner for Refugees. We will also explore what happens to nation-state demographics and global diasporas when large numbers of individuals from SINs immigrate to places able to accommodate them, but their arrival creates pressures between new arrivals and prior citizens.

A standard argument presented in much of the climate change literature looks at the obligations of big polluters to attend to the damage caused to smaller nonpolluting nations. In 2007, the UN created a committee called the Warsaw International Mechanism for Loss and Damage (Goodell 2017, 180). It was charged with determining how to compensate nation-states for loss. This committee, however, has not made recommendations regarding how peoples will move in the event of catastrophic global warming. Clare

Heyward and Jörgen Ödalen (2016) propose the notion of a "Free Movement Passport for Territorially Dispossessed Climate Migrants" whereby those displaced could freely choose where to relocate. Yet this suggestion may be impossible to implement because of historical relations, climate conditions, religion, and current nation-state bilateral relations.

Tuvalu

Originally the Ellice Islands, Tuvalu became a member of the British Commonwealth with its independence on October 1, 1978. With a 2016 population of roughly 11,000 people, no portion of the islands rises more than ten feet above sea level. Currently, under the Pacific Access Category (a preferential visa status in New Zealand), any Tuvalu resident can apply for permanent residency in New Zealand, another Pacific Rim nation with similar climates and a stable, settled population of Tuvalu citizens to welcome them. As of 2018, there were about 3,500 Tuvalu citizens residing in New Zealand. General calculations anticipate a roughly 1 percent increase in the percentage of Tuvalu immigrants by 2020 without global warming (Worldometer 2018). Even if the entire Tuvalu population were to resettle in New Zealand, they would make up only .23 percent of New Zealand's population. Most recently, several individuals have filed lawsuits in Australia and New Zealand seeking to settle permanently as refugees, but their cases have been denied because there are no international provisions for climate refugees.

The Maldives

This Muslim island nation is close to India and is perceived to be within both Indian and Australian spheres of influence. The Maldives have long been a tourist mecca for much of the world. By January 2018, however, countries such as the United States, the UK, and Australia issued travel advisories due to increased attacks and threats of attacks on both tourists and secular Maldivians. The national religion is Islam, and no non-Muslim may hold office. In February 2018, a state of emergency was extended due to perceived corruption and threats to national security. In the case of extreme global warming, Sri Lanka, with a 2016 population of roughly 21.2 million citizens, has been identified by some policy makers and scholars as an appropriate new home for the Maldives' 420,000 citizens (Heyward and Ödalen 2016; Vaha 2017).

If this ratio remains the same and the entire population of the Maldives were resettled in Sri Lanka, there would be a 2 percent infusion of Muslim Maldivians to a predominantly Buddhist state that has a record of religious conflict. For example, in February 2018, conflicts broke out between Muslims and Buddhists in Kandy, Sri Lanka, and a state of emergency was declared on March 6, 2018. In the case of a global climate emergency, it may seem advantageous to resettle to an island in a contiguous geographic area with a similar climate, yet while many scholars and policy makers see the benefits of such a plan, religious tensions and political instability may preclude such a decision.

Finnish scholar M. E. Vaha suggests that social policies for resettlement may be based on the availability of what she terms "a global compensation scheme" (2017, 8; see also Heyward and Ödalen 2016) wherein climate refugees would have free passage to any country of their choosing and both sending and receiving nations would be compensated. She argues that Finland possesses many desirable social and political amenities and could take in a large number of climate refugees, but she cautions that the geographic move from a tropical climate to an arctic climate could impede such activity. What is important to note about this example is that global political instability due to ISIS terrorism and religious conflict may prevent a best-case scenario move. The currently negative attitudes toward refugees on the part of many Europeans reinforce the fragile nature of this suggestion.

Marshall Islands

The Marshall Islands originally formed part of the UN Trust Territory of the Pacific Islands. In 1986 they became an independent nation and in 1991 joined the UN. From 1947 to 1968 the United States conducted nuclear tests there, ultimately rendering a number of atolls—most roughly seven feet above sea level—uninhabitable. The 2011 population was roughly 53,000 individuals. In 1986 a Compact of Free Association was signed, permitting Marshallese to live and work permanently in the United States in partial reparation for the destruction of their lands. Around 3,200 people have settled in Springdale, Arkansas, largely linked to the chicken processing industry, but a proposal to resettle 53,000 individuals in the United States would no doubt create quite a backlash. What is important to note here is that this many individuals have the right to resettle in the United States.

These three communities all face similar devastation. The current focus of proposed policies has clung to what William Neil Adger and his colleagues term "a lexicon on danger" (2011, 2). These authors suggest it may be time instead to not only build resilience among residents but also attend to a stronger emphasis on place, because they submit that paying attention to identity in place matters. For those people living in the Marshall Islands, settling in the United States involves perhaps the least amount of paperwork. For those in Tuvalo, resettlement in New Zealand presents possible legal challenges but few sociocultural issues. For those in the Maldives, resettlement in Sri Lanka may contribute to continuing political instability. As Sri Lanka is less developed than either the United States or New Zealand, the economic pressures are potentially more severe. Heyward and Ödalen's (2016) notion of a Free Movement Passport for Territorially Dispossessed Climate Migrants may be the best solution.

The Arctic

While sea level rise in particular will devastate people living in small island nations, the impact of global warming is likely also to be dramatic at the earth's poles. While all parts of the world will be affected, not all parts will heat up equally. For a number of reasons, the impact in the Arctic will likely be especially severe, and it is now in places like Alaska that the effect of global warming is becoming most apparent. The ice cap that has covered the North Pole for "at least 1 million years" is fading and will likely disappear this century (Davis 2005). Some predictions suggest that it could be gone by as early as 2040, while other models expect it to have declined by roughly half by the end of this century (Revkin 2006; Arctic Climate Impact Assessment 2004, 24–25, 35, 82–83; Flannery 2005, 144). Ice melting in the Antarctic also has the potential for disastrous rises in sea level (Flannery 2005, 147–49). There is no question, however, that the ice cap is shrinking and that the ice cover itself is becoming thinner.

In the past, it had long been thought that the area under the ice was largely sterile. Recent biological investigations have revealed, however, that there is a diverse ecological system below the ice. How will the plants and animals that have evolved over geologic time to live with the ice adapt to its disappearance? Some seals will likely go extinct: "Adapting to life on land in the absence of summer sea ice seems highly unlikely for the ringed seal as they rarely, if ever, come onto land. Hauling themselves out on land . . . would expose newborns to a much higher risk of being killed

Some nations are already planning how to respond to global warming. For example, the Netherlands is preparing to abandon some land for use as a flood plain while redesigning homes that will float in key areas. Kiribati, Tokelau, Tuvalu, and the Marshall Islands are considering building seawalls around their respective nations. To what extent are such plans positive? Could they be considered problematic because they undermine efforts to fight global warming?

by predators. Other ice-dependent seals that are likely to suffer as sea ice declines include the spotted seal, which breeds exclusively at the ice edge in the Bering Sea in spring, and the harp seal, which lives associated with sea ice all year" (Arctic Climate Impact Assessment 2004, 59).

Other animals that live on the ice will likely disappear as well, from the walrus to seabirds (Arctic Climate Impact Assessment 2004, 59). A primary example is the polar bear. In December 2006, U.S. interior secretary Dirk Kempthorne proposed "listing polar bears as a 'threatened' species on the government listing of imperiled species. . . . 'Polar bears are one of nature's ultimate survivors, able to live and thrive in one of the world's harshest environments,' Kempthorne said. 'But we are concerned that the polar bear's habitat may literally be melting'" (Heilprin 2006, A-1). In recent years, polar bears on the southern edge of their range are thinner in the spring; they are also having fewer cubs, and fewer of these are surviving (Arctic Climate Impact Assessment 2004, 58). One 2016 study (Pilford et al. 2017) also found that polar bears now have to swim significantly greater distances than in the past, as the distance between pack ice and the land has grown. Another study in 2017 (Hamilton et al.) found that with climate change polar bears in Svalbard, Norway, spent less time in areas inhabited by their typical prey, ringed seals, so they now have to travel greater distances to find food. The future of this species is uncertain.

Many of the changes that global warming will set into motion will lead to a cascade of further trends, which may also contribute to the planet's warming. As forests spread northward, for example, they will absorb more carbon, but they will also absorb more sunlight than the snow-covered tundra. The overall effect will contribute to planetary warming. Equally important, as the Arctic Ocean is uncovered, it will also be transformed from an environment that reflects most sunlight to one that absorbs most of it. Finally, much of the northern land is made up of permafrost, which

> The Arctic is warming far faster than other regions of the globe. A large portion of Arctic peoples are Indigenous. How do you think these two facts will affect the ability of Arctic peoples to shape debates about global warming? What duty do people living in the Southern Hemisphere have toward their neighbors to the north? It is also true that international migration will likely challenge major powers. How should a nation respond when a climate catastrophe sends waves of refugees across its borders?

is soil that has remained frozen for a lengthy period of geological time. As this melts, it may release large amounts of methane (a potent greenhouse gas) into the atmosphere, especially from vast reserves in Siberia (Arctic Climate Impact Assessment 2004, 38; Pearce 2007, 90–100). One 2017 study (Kohnert et al.) found that a warmer climate resulted in increases not only in the biological release of methane but also in its release from geologic sources. This creates the possibility for a powerful feedback loop.

There are also concerns that methane hydrates in the ocean could be released: "The release of methane from this source is a less certain outcome of climate change than the other emissions discussed here because it would probably require greater warming and take longer to occur. If such releases did occur, however, the climate impacts could be very large" (Arctic Climate Impact Assessment 2004, 38–39). Indeed, just such a phenomenon is one of the hypotheses (the clathrate gun hypothesis) used to explain the Permian Extinction, the greatest mass dying in the Earth's geologic history—the time when life itself nearly ended (Flannery 2005, 199–201). Scientific publications raise the possibility of sudden and catastrophic global warming as a result (Sergienko et al. 2012).

Events in the Arctic have implications for the entire planet (Arctic Climate Impact Assessment 2004, 34–35). They also raise geopolitical questions. Canada, Denmark, Russia, and the United States are currently arguing over travel rights through the newly opening sea-lanes, as well as maritime borders, as each nation strives to lay claim to the resources of the Arctic seabed (Funk 2007). These environmental and political changes will have complex and enduring impacts on Indigenous peoples, who make up "roughly 10% of the current population of the Arctic" (Arctic Climate Impact Assessment 2004, 7). One of the most famous examples of this process is in Shishmaref, Alaska, which lies on an island off the Alaskan coast. With the waning of ice cover, powerful waves from major storms now are causing rapid coastal erosion. The entire community will likely be forced to evacuate, given the ocean's advances (Kolbert 2006, 7–10). This community is not unique. As a people heavily dependent upon food from the ocean, many Eskimo/Inuit communities have long lived on the shorelines and hunted out on the ice. Now, communities from Nelson Lagoon in Alaska to Tuktoyaktuk in Canada are threatened (Arctic Climate Impact Assessment 2004, 78–81). Other changes are also serious. Migration patterns for some animals are changing. Hunters notice that animals arrive at different times of the year or use new routes. This impacts the hunters' ability to feed their communities, as many northern peoples still rely on game in their diet (16–17, 61, 71–72). Indigenous peoples are also seeing the arrival of new bird species such as the robin, which they have never seen in their communities before (45).

Global warming presents a serious challenge to the culture and folkways of northern peoples from Siberia to Greenland. For example, the Sami people of northern Scandinavia find that their reindeer herds are also threatened by climate change (Arctic Climate Impact Assessment 2004, 106, 108–9). Because native communities have long traditions in an area and often depend upon the land for their livelihood, they have a rich store of Indigenous knowledge that can complement scientific observations about global warming. Their reports contribute to our understanding of the changes that global warming is already making in the north (92–97).

Arctic peoples are some of the first to be able to observe global warming's effects, but its effects are now becoming manifest globally. In the South Atlantic, the first hurricane in 500 years of recorded history reached Brazil (Flannery 2005, 136). It used to be thought that hurricanes could not form in this part of the Atlantic, in part because the waters are too cool. But with Hurricane Catarina (also known as Cyclone Catarina) in March 2004, this no longer seems to be true (Davis 2005). And in the United States, Central America, and the Caribbean, there is rising concern that hurricanes may be growing more powerful because ocean waters are warming. If this proves to be true, even developed countries will have difficulty adapting to these changes. Hurricane Katrina flooded New Orleans on August 29, 2005, because the levees failed. The subsequent disaster laid bare the multiple institutional, financial, engineering, and leadership failures that made the city vulnerable. But if hurricanes are strengthening, we will have less room for error.

No place will escape global warming's impact. One issue embodies this fact. In the long term, as the acidity (pH) of the oceans increases, the lime in shells may begin to dissolve (Flannery 2005, 186). One study in the United States in 2008 reported that the "acidity is much higher than expected in the ocean just off the West Coast, hitting the relatively shallow waters of the fruitful continental shelf during spring and summer" (Learn 2008, A-1). There is no doubt that the CO_2 responsible for the acidity came from manmade sources. "The chemical signature of the carbon dioxide makes clear it is from fossil fuel combustions, and not natural sources such as volcanoes," the researchers said (A-12). Once the pH reaches 7.5, the shells of sea life will "dissolve faster than their hosts can create them" (A-12). How will such a profound change ripple throughout the marine ecosystem as the base of the food chain dissolves into the acidic oceans?

In December 1997 the world's industrialized nations negotiated the Kyoto Accord, which was designed to prevent future increases in CO_2 emissions. This would not stop global warming, but it would help to keep the process from accelerating. The United States had deep concerns about the agreement because it exempted developing economies such as that of China and India (Kolbert 2006, 153–57). European countries argued that the developed world had to show leadership and develop new technologies if it was to ask similar sacrifices of emerging economies. In the end, President George W. Bush decided not to uphold the accord, although he had supported it during his campaign (157–58).

There are numerous and vocal critics who argue that global warming is not taking place, that it is a natural process, or that it will not necessarily have negative impacts (Kolbert 2006, 158–59; Flannery 2005, 156; for the best critique of global warming as a phenomenon, see Michaels 2004; for a rebuttal, see Pearce 2007, 10–17). But most of these arguments are not by scientists, and they are not published in peer-reviewed journals or by academic presses (that is, presses associated with an institution of higher education). In academia, rigor is ensured by a process of peer review in which articles are sent out to experts in the field. Scholars carefully read these papers and respond to the journal editor with a detailed evaluation of its strengths and weaknesses, as well as a recommendation regarding publication. Of course, many times, reviewers do not agree. They may have political or personal interests that cause them to oppose publications. But good works survive this process and are published, having met a high academic standard. Books published by academic presses pass through a similar process. There is still a debate over global warming, but it is distinctive in that it no longer takes place within an academic or scientific framework.

The scientific consensus is so strong that most publications critiquing global warming are issued by conservative think tanks or with the support of industry backers. Michael Crichton's novel *State of Fear* (2004) also contains an attack on the scientific argument for global warming, which attracted media attention. But articles and books like these no longer generally survive the peer-review process, although critics point to bias within the process itself. Overall, the work on global warming that is recognized for its rigor and sophistication now takes place on the side of those scientists who believe that it is happening. (For the ongoing debate over global warming, see Kolbert 2006, 162–70.)

Global warming will be difficult to address because of our demographic reality. It is true that fertility rates are dramatically declining in some areas, such as Japan, Russia, and most of Europe (L. Stone 2017). This will lessen the pressure on resources in these nations, permit forests to expand, and decrease the human footprint. But even as global fertility rates decline, there is so much momentum behind population growth that the planet will still see a substantial increase in Asia, Africa, and Latin America for decades to come. In Africa in particular, the future is one characterized by staggering growth in population (Cleland and Machiyama 2017). In the long run, demographers predict that the population for the entire planet will likely decline after reaching a peak around midcentury. This means that there is reason to be hopeful about those species that make it through this bottleneck. But in the meantime, humanity will face a difficult challenge as it strives to preserve the natural environment in a world with more people than at any time in history. In this sense, the current generation will make choices that will be of unique and lasting importance.

While global warming is perhaps the greatest environmental threat facing the planet, it is only one of many forms of atmospheric pollution, which impacts not only other species but also people. This is particularly true for Asia in general, and China in particular:

> The symptoms of industrial pollution are everywhere in Asia, where pedestrians wear surgical masks to filter the air and urban smog is sometimes so thick that Beijing's Forbidden City is rendered nearly invisible behind a cloud of soot. Just this month, Chinese authorities canceled flights at Beijing's main airport amid especially heavy pollution, and shuttered highways in and out of the city. The implications for human health are obvious: studies show pollution is shortening life spans in northern China by five years or more. Intel engineers in

> Oregon are now discovering that rotten air is also taking a toll on electronics in China and India, with sulfur corroding the copper circuitry that provides neural networks for PCs and servers and wrecking the motherboards that run whole systems. (Rogoway 2013, D-6)

Intel Corporation has responded by setting up a special testing facility that exposes computer motherboards to high levels of pollution. The goal is to ensure that computers built in Asia will not be damaged by the corrosive effects of air pollution (Rogoway 2013). But what does it mean for human health when the pollution is so severe that it corrodes the copper in computers? The problem of climate change is so immense that it can overshadow other issues that impact human health, from the release of nuclear radiation into the Pacific Ocean from the damaged Fukushima power plant to the spread of plastic particulates throughout all the world's oceans. All life on our planet, including human life, is challenged by global pollution, of which CO_2 is only the most dangerous element.

Conclusion

In many respects, environmental issues are the ultimate international problem. Pollution does not recognize borders. The costs of inaction are high. It takes comprehensive agreements and global cooperation to address issues such as ozone depletion and global warming. At the same time, local actors can have significant effects. While the United States as a nation has not taken the lead in the fight to stop global warming, the state of California has. Even small nations such as Denmark, which is making a dramatic shift to renewable energy, can have a powerful impact through their example. On many environmental issues, cities have also taken the lead. Curitiba, Brazil, has become famous for its example as a sustainable urban area. People are not powerless, as Tim Flannery argues: "Climate change is very different from other environmental issues, such as biodiversity loss and the ozone hole. The best evidence suggests that we need to reduce our CO_2 emissions by 70 percent by 2050. If you own a four-wheel-drive and replace it with a hybrid fuel car, you can achieve a cut of that magnitude in a day rather than half a century. If your electricity provider offers a green option, for the cost of a daily cup of coffee you will be able to make equally major cuts in your household emissions" (Flannery 2005, 6). If current predictions are correct, almost everyone who reads these words will live to see dramatic changes brought about by global warming and global population growth. But it is possible to shape this future with political will and to avoid the bleak visions that are now forecast.

➤ VOCABULARY

biodiversity
biological hotspot
chlorofluorocarbons (CFCs)
sixth extinction
debt-for-nature swaps
Kyoto Accord
methane hydrates
Small Island Developing Nations (SINs)
Keeling Curve
greenhouse gases
World Biosphere Reserve

➤ DISCUSSION AND REFLECTION QUESTIONS

1 *Why might environmental issues reflect globalization perhaps more powerfully than other thematic issues presented in this book?*

2 *How do northern nations perceive the future of the Amazon, and how do southern nations perceive its future?*

3 *What are the policy implications resulting from the fact that the areas of the world with the greatest biodiversity also are undergoing the most rapid population growth?*

4 *Is the cost of saving an individual species worth it?*

5 *What are the key points of the anti-environmental movement?*

6 *What is a debt-for-nature swap? Why might individuals in the Global South problematize this type of assistance from the Global North?*

7 *What is the relationship between rising sea levels and emigration?*

8 *How do you believe your country should adjudicate rights of current citizens facing displacement due to rising sea levels?*

9 *The text suggests that native communities threatened by climate change have rich knowledge that can complement scientific knowledge. Should policy makers work with their knowledge? How?*

10 *Why is it likely that nations that have not contributed in any major way toward global warming may suffer the most, particularly in the Pacific?*

ACTIVITY 1: ANALYZE Examine the brief data set below. Assume that nation-states have to take in the same percentage of climate refugees by 2050 as the percentage of greenhouse gases for which they are responsible. Peter Singer estimates 750 million refugees by 2050 (McAdam 2016). Using the following table, calculate the number of people to be taken in. Then create a bar graph that shows the same data.

Country	World Resources Council estimates (1850–2011) of percentage of greenhouse gases	Number of people to be taken in
U.S.	27%	
European Union	25%	
China	11%	
Russia	8%	
Japan	4%	

Source: From McAdam 2016. Data adapted from Goodell 2017, 187.

Now transfer the data to a bar graph by country or to a graph with an x and y axis presenting countries, percentage of gases, and number of people if the global climate refugee population is 200 million.

ACTIVITY 2: REFLECT Identify the current population of the state, province, or country you are living in using any online forum such as Worldometer (http://www.worldometers.info/world-population/population-by-country/). The International Organization for Migration projects that possibly 200 million people may be climate refugees by the year 2050 (Goodell 2017, 182). This is roughly the current 2018 population of Pakistan. How do you make sense of this number or put it into the context of your life? Write without stopping for twenty minutes, beginning with either the phrase "200 million is approximately the number of . . ." or "If 200 million climate refugees were resettled from their homelands . . ."

ACTIVITY 3: EXTEND The Union of Concerned Scientists (http://www.climatehotmap.org/global-warming-solutions/small-islands.html) suggests that in order to protect small island nations, "the U.S. needs to reduce heat-trapping emissions by at least 80 percent below 2000 levels by 2050." What is one choice you and one of your friends can make that could help reduce emissions?

References

Adger, N., J. Barnett, F. S. Chapin III, and H. Ellemor. 2011. This must be the place: Underrepresentation of identity and meaning in climate change decision-making. *Global Environmental Politics* 11 (2): 1–25.

Allison, E., A. Perry, M.-C. Badjeck, W. N. Adger, K. Brown, D. Conway, A. Halls, et al. 2009. Vulnerability of national economies to potential impacts of climate change on fisheries. *Fish and Fisheries* 10 (2): 173–96.

Arctic Climate Impact Assessment. 2004. *Impacts of a warming Arctic.* New York: Cambridge University Press.

———. 2010. UN rejects ban on tuna export, global sale of polar bear skins. *Oregonian*, March 19. Retrieved March 20, 2010, from http://www.oregonlive.com/newsflash/index.ssf?/base/international-27/1268929733151470.xml&storylist= international.

Bailey, R., ed. 2002. *Global warming and other eco-myths: How the environmental movement uses false science to scare us to death.* Washington, D.C.: Forum.

Barlow, M., and T. Clarke. 2002. *Blue gold.* New York: New Press.

Barnett, J. 2001. Adapting to climate change in Pacific Island countries: The problem of uncertainty. *World Development* 29 (6): 977–93.

Bentley, C. 2016. Trying to confront a massive flood risk, Jakarta faces "problem on top of problem." Public Radio International, September 15. Retrieved July 10, 2019, from https://www.pri.org/stories/2016-09-15/trying-confront-massive-flood-risk-jakarta-faces-problem-top-problem-0.

Benton, M. J. 2003. *When life nearly died: The greatest mass extinction of all time.* New York: Thames and Hudson.

Callaway, E. 2016. Stem-cell plan aims to bring rhino back from brink of extinction. *Nature* 533 (7601): 20–21.

Campbell, D. 2005. *Land of ghosts: The braided lives of people and the forest in far western Amazonia.* New York: Houghton Mifflin.

Christianson, G. E. 1999. *Greenhouse: The 200-year story of global warming.* New York: Walker and Company.

Cleland, J., and K. Machiyama. 2017. The challenges posed by demographic change in sub-Saharan Africa: A concise overview. *Population and Development Review* 43 (S1): 264–86.

Council on Foreign Relations. 2017. Deforestation in the Amazon. Infoguide, Interactive Storyboard. Retrieved on July 20, 2019, from cfr.org/amazon.

Cowell, A. dir. 1990. *Decade of destruction.* Four-part documentary series. Oley, Pa.: Bullfrog Films.

Cozzuol, M. A., C. L. Clozato, E. C. Holanda, F. H. Rodrigues, S. Nienow, B. de Thoisy, R. A. F. Redondo, and F. R. Santos. 2013. A new species of tapir from the Amazon. *Journal of Mammalogy* 94 (6): 1331–45.

Crichton, M. 2004. *State of fear.* New York: Harper Collins.

Davis, M. 2005. Melting away. *The Nation*, October 7. Retrieved December 16, 2007, from www.thenation.com/doc/20051024/davis.

Dean, W. 1995. *With broadaxe and firebrand: The destruction of the Brazilian Atlantic Forest.* Los Angeles: University of California Press.

deBuys, W. 2011. *A great aridness: Climate change and the future of the American Southwest*. Oxford: Oxford University Press.

de Souza, J., D. Schaan, M. Robinson, A. Barbosa, L. Aragão, B. Marimon Jr., B. S. Marimon, et al. 2018. Pre-Columbian earth-builders settled along the entire southern rim of the Amazon. *Nature Communications* 9 (1): 1125.

Diamond, J. 2005. *Collapse: How societies choose to fail or succeed*. New York: Penguin.

Doherty, B. and E. Ro. 2017. World Bank: Let climate-threatened Pacific Islanders migrate to Australia or New Zealand. *The Guardian*, May 8. Retrieved from https://www.theguardian.com/environment/2017/may/08/australia-and-nz-should-allow-open-migration-for-pacific-islanders-threatened-by-climate-says-report.

Ezeh, A. 2016. Addressing planetary health challenges in Africa. *Public Health Reviews* 37 (1): 27.

Flannery, T. 2005. *The weather makers: How man is changing the climate and what it means for life on earth*. New York: Grove Press.

Friedman, L. 2009. How will climate refugees impact global security? *Scientific American*, March 23. Retrieved March 3, 2010, from http://www.scientificamerican.com/article.cfm?id=climage-refugees-national-security.

Funk, M. 2007. Cold rush: The coming fight for the melting North. *Harper's*, March 23, 44–55.

Goodell, J. 2017. *The water will come: Rising seas, sinking cities, and the remaking of the civilized world*. New York: Little, Brown.

GrrlScientist. 2018. Extinction looms for North Atlantic right whales. *Forbes*, March 29. Retrieved July 10, 2019, from https://www.forbes.com/sites/grrlscientist/2018/03/29/extinction-looms-for-north-atlantic-right-whales/#1595d6425cd6.

Guggenheim, D., dir. 2006. *An inconvenient truth*. Documentary film. Distributed by Paramount Classics.

Hamilton, C. D., K. M. Kovacs, R. A. Ims, J. Aars, and C. Lydersen. 2017. An Arctic predator-prey system in flux: Climate change impacts on coastal space use by polar bears and ringed seals. *Journal of Animal Ecology* 86 (5): 1054–64.

Hanson, E. P. 1944. *The Amazon: A new frontier*. New York: Headline Series, Foreign Policy Association.

Hardin, G. 1968. The tragedy of the commons. *Science* 162 (December): 1243–48.

Heilprin, J. 2006. Polar bears' lives rest on thinning ice. *Oregonian*, December 28, A-1, A-4.

Hertsgaard, M. 1999. *Earth odyssey: Around the world in search of our environmental future*. New York: Broadway Books.

Heyward, C. and J. Ödalen. 2016. A free movement passport for the territorially dispossessed. In *Climate justice in a non-ideal world*, edited by C. Heyward and D. Roser, 208–26. Oxford: Oxford University Press.

Kohnert, K., A. Serafimovich, S. Metzger, J. Hartmann and T. Sachs. 2017. Strong geologic methane emissions from discontinuous terrestrial permafrost in the Mackenzie Delta, Canada. *Scientific Reports* 7 (1): 5828.

Kolbert, E. 2006. *Fieldnotes from a catastrophe: Man, nature, and climate change.* New York: Bloomsbury.

Kurlansky, M. 1998. *Cod: A biography of the fish that changed the world.* New York: Penguin.

LaFranchi, H. 1998. Bye-bye to Brazil's bio-paradise. *Christian Science Monitor,* December 7, 12–13.

Leake, J. 2010. U.N. climate chief "got grants through bogus claims." *Sunday Times* (London), January 24. Retrieved March 3, 2010, from http://www.timesonline.co.uk/tol/news/environment/article6999975.ece.

Leakey, R., and R. Lewin. 1996. *The sixth extinction: Patterns of life and the future of humankind.* New York: Anchor Books/Doubleday.

Learn, S. 2008. Gases tipping ocean's balance. *Oregonian,* May 23, A-1, A-12.

Lomborg, B. 2001. *The skeptical environmentalist: Measuring the real state of the world.* New York: Cambridge University Press.

Lovejoy, T., and C. Nobre. 2018. Amazon tipping point. *Science Advances* 4 (2): 2340.

Martin, P. S. 2005. *Twilight of the mammoths: Ice Age extinctions and the rewilding of America.* Berkeley: University of California Press.

McAdam, J. 2016. Fact check Q and A: As the climate changes are 750 million refugees predicated to move away from the flooding? *The Conversation,* August 3. Retrieved March 10, 2018, from https://theconversation.com/fact check-qanda-as-the-climate-changes-are-750-million-refugees-predicted-to-move-away-from-flooding-63400.

Mendelsohn, R., A. Dinar, and L. Williams. 2006. The distributional impact of climate change on rich and poor countries. *Environment and Development Economics 11*:159–78. doi: 10.1017/S1355770X05002755.

Mercer, J. 2010. Disaster risk and reduction or climate change adaptation: Are we reinventing the wheel? *Journal of International Development 22*:247–67. doi: 10.1002/jid.1677.

Michaels, P. J. 2004. *Meltdown: The predictable distortion of global warming by scientists, politicians, and the media.* Washington, D.C.: Cato Institute.

Milman, O., and M. Ryan. 2016. Lives in the balance: Climate change and the Marshall Islands. *The Guardian,* September 15. Retrieved February 20, 2018, from https://www.theguardian.com/environment/2016/sep/15/marshall-islands-climate-change-springdale-arkansas.

Milstein, M. 2007. Greenland ice melt shocks scientists. *Oregonian,* September 9, A-1, A-10.

Monastersky, R. 2006. Climate science on trial. *Chronicle of Higher Education,* September 8, A-10–A-15.

Nature Conservancy. 2006. *The Atlantic Forest of Brazil.* Retrieved November 15, 2008, from http://www.nature.org/wherewework/southamerica/brazil/work/art5080.html.

Nisbet, M. 2003. The skeptical environmentalist: A case study in the manufacture of the news. January 23. Retrieved November 14, 2008, from https://www.csicop.org/specialarticles/show/skeptical_environmentalist_a_case_study_in_the_manufacture_of_news.

Nugent, S. 1994. *Big mouth: The Amazon speaks.* San Francisco: Brown Trout.
Nuwer, R. 2018. Sudan, the last male northern white rhino, dies in Kenya. *New York Times,* March 20. Retrieved July 10, 2019, from https://www.nytimes.com/2018/03/20/science/rhino-sudan-extinct.html.
O'Connor, G. 1998. *Amazon journal: Dispatches from a vanishing frontier.* New York: Plume.
Parry, M., O. Canziani, J. Palutikof, P. van der Linden, and C. Hanson. 2007. *Climate change 2007: Impacts, adaptation, and vulnerability.* Cambridge: Cambridge University Press.
Pearce, F. 2007. *With speed and violence: Why scientists fear tipping points in climate change.* Boston: Beacon Press.
Pedersen, E. J., P. L. Thompson, R. A. Ball, M. J. Fortin, T. C. Gouhier, H. Link, and A. Gonzalez. 2017. Signatures of the collapse and incipient recovery of an overexploited marine ecosystem. *Royal Society Open Science* 4 (7): 170–215.
Picazo, M. 2018. Global sea level rise on faster pace than expected. Weather Channel, February 14. https://www.theweathernetwork.com/us/news/articles/global-sea-level-rise-us-flood-rain-nasa-el-nino-la-nina-pacific-climate-melting-ice-greenland-fossil-fuel/95694.
Pilfold, N. W., A. McCall, A. E. Derocher, N. J. Lunn, and E. Richardson. 2017. Migratory response of polar bears to sea ice loss: To swim or not to swim. *Ecography* 40 (1): 189–99.
Pilkey, O. H., L. Pilkey-Jarvis, and K. Pilkey. 2016. *Retreat from a rising sea: Hard decisions in an age of climate change.* New York: Columbia University Press.
Raffles, H. 2002. *In Amazonia: A natural history.* Princeton: Princeton University Press.
Revkin, A. 1990. *The burning season: The murder of Chico Mendes and the fight for the Amazon rain forest.* Boston: Houghton Mifflin.
———. 2006. Open Arctic Sea likely by 2040, study says. *Oregonian,* December 12, A-7.
Rogoway, M. 2013. The gunk in the machine: Intel is trying to make circuitry less vulnerable to the pollution that's pervasive in the developing world. *Oregonian,* October 13, D-1, D-6.
Sergienko, V. I., L. I. Lobkovskii, I. P. Semiletov, O. V. Dudarev, N. N. Dmitrievskii, N. E. Shakhova, . . . and A. S. Salomatin. 2012. The degradation of submarine permafrost and the destruction of hydrates on the shelf of the East Arctic seas as a potential cause of the "methane catastrophe": Some results of integrated studies in 2011. *Doklady Earth Sciences* 446 (1) (September): 1132–37.
Skutnabb-Kangas, T., L. Maffi, and D. Harmon. 2003. *Sharing a world of difference: The world's linguistic, cultural, and biological diversity.* Paris: UNESCO/WWF/Terralingua.
Slater, C. 2003a. Fire in El Dorado, or images of tropical nature and their practical effects. In *In search of the rain forest,* edited by C. Slater, 41–68. Durham: Duke University Press.
———, ed. 2003b. *In search of the rain forest.* Durham: Duke University Press.

Sloan, S., and J. Sayer. 2015. Forest resources assessment of 2015 shows positive global trends but forest loss and degradation persist in poor tropical countries. *Forest Ecology and Management* 352:134–45.

Smil, V. 2008. *Global catastrophes and trends: The next fifty years.* Cambridge: MIT Press.

Smith, F. 2002. Enclosing the environmental commons. In *Global warming and other eco-myths,* edited by R. Bailey, 293–318. Washington, D.C.: Forum.

Smith, N. 1999. *The Amazon River forest: A natural history of plants, animals, and people.* New York: Oxford University Press.

Spotts, P. N. 2006. Global warming: A few skeptics still ask why it's happening. *Christian Science Monitor,* December 8. Retrieved December 16, 2007, from http://www.csmonitor.com/2006/1208/p01s03-usgn.html.

Stewart, D. I. 1994. *After the trees: Living on the TransAmazon highway.* Austin: University of Texas Press.

Stone, L. 2017a. The great baby bust of 2017. *In a State of Migration* (blog), November 29. Retrieved February 20, 2018, from https://medium.com/migration-issues/the-great-baby-bust-of-2017-2f63907402fc.

———. 2017b. How low will Puerto Rico's population go? *In a State of Migration* (blog), November 17. Retrieved February 20, 2018, from https://medium.com/migration-issues/how-low-will-puerto-ricos-population-go-c8d108ac8b3b.

Stone, R. 2001. *Mammoth: The resurrection of an Ice Age giant.* London: Fourth Estate.

United Nations. n.d. Small Island Developing States. Sustainable Development Goals Knowledge Platform. Retrieved February 20, 2018, from https://sustainabledevelopment.un.org/topics/sids/list.

Vaha, M. E. 2017. Hosting the Small Island Developing States: Two scenarios. *International Journal of Climate Change Strategies and Management* 10 (2): 229–44. doi:10.1108/IJCCSM-10-2017-0183.

Valsecchi, J., M. Marmontel, C. L. B. Franco, D. P. Cavalcante, I. V. D. Cobra, I. J. Lima, . . . and V. Monteiro. 2017. Atualização e composição da lista–Novas Espécies de Vertebrados e Plantas na Amazônia 2014–2015. *Brasília/DF e Tefé/AM: WWF e Instituto de Desenvolvimento Sustentável Mamirauá.*

World Wildlife Federation. 2018. Wildlife in a warming world. March. Retrieved July 19, 2019, from http://c402277.ssl.cf1.rackcdn.com/publications/1149/files/original/WWF_-_Wildlife_in_a_Warming_World_-_2018_FINAL.pdf?1520886759.

Worldometer. 2018. Environmental Disasters Raise Refugee Numbers. Retrieved November 11, 2019, from www.worldwatch.org›environmental-disasters-raise-refugee-numbers.

TWELVE **Where to Go Next?**

➤ SYNOPSIS

As you work your way through your undergraduate curriculum, it is important to look toward potential careers that an international studies major may lead to. This chapter lays out a variety of options for career development, including jobs in government, business, the military, higher education, and nongovernmental organizations. An annotated set of references at the end of the chapter further frames your prospective job search.

➤ SCAFFOLDING

As you read through this chapter, think about how you would answer each of the questions below.

Are you completely familiar with required coursework and sequencing for your major?

Have you always dreamed of a particular type of international job?

What do you know about requirements and skill sets for entry-level positions in this area?

Who are the individuals on your campus best able to assist you in your search?

➤ CORE CONCEPTS

Your interest in international events and situations may take you into job spaces that you never imagined.

Both human resources and electronic resources can serve to give you the most accurate sense of how to proceed in your job search.

You can be engaged internationally in activities that are not linked to your career.

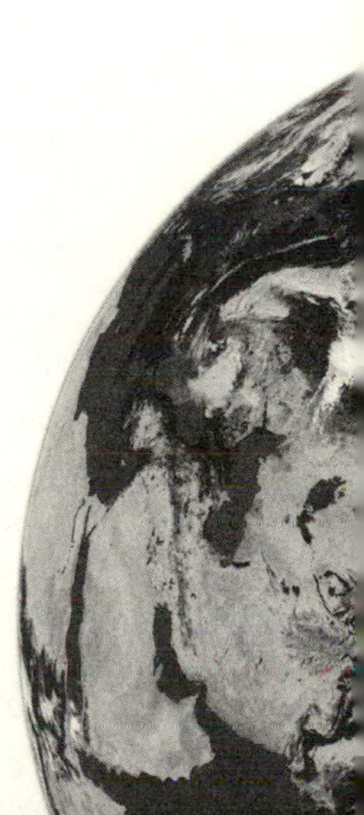

As an international studies major, you would probably like to know more about the different career opportunities that are available to you. There are four main paths that most graduates follow: government, business, NGOs and international organizations, or jobs for which further education may be required. The last category includes a wide range of different opportunities, such as Teaching English to Speakers of Other Languages (TESOL in the United States and TEAL or TESL in Canada), study abroad advising, international student advising, international admissions at universities and colleges, and teaching international studies at the postsecondary level. This chapter describes how to find a career in each of these paths and gives information on everything from preparing for the State Department exam to finding internships in consulates. It also discusses the advantages and disadvantages of master's and other graduate programs and how to decide which program best meets your needs. Throughout, we have tried to give information on career paths that is relevant for students in both the United States and Canada.

Government Career Paths

There are a variety of ways to use your international studies background to enter government service. Perhaps the best known of these is to join the Foreign Service, now a division of the Department of State. Foreign Service officers work in one of five areas: Consular Affairs, Economics, Management, Political Affairs, and Public Diplomacy. On the U.S. government website, there is a questionnaire you can fill out that will help you decide which of these tracks is appropriate for you and your interests (http://careers.state.gov/officer/career-track.html). General information about the exam can be found at the State Department website (http://www.state.gov/careers). This site contains a great deal of information about this career path.

Almost all branches of the government have some international responsibilities, from Homeland Security to the Department of Agriculture. But there are several key institutions or positions that you might consider, which include roles as a civil service officer, a Foreign Service specialist, or an attorney. You could also work in diplomatic security, the Peace Corps, the U.S. intelligence community, or the U.S. Agency for International Development. The latter organization might be particularly attractive for students who are also interested in working with NGOs. Some colleges either provide symposia or training sessions for the Foreign Service exam through their career centers or specific departments like international studies or political science. Some professional test centers, like Kaplan, also provide workshops. At the end of this chapter, we list a variety of Foreign Service exam preparatory materials.

Another possible career path is to join the armed services, mostly likely as an officer candidate. If you choose this path, you will take a language aptitude test. If you score well, you may be sent for advanced language training at one of several sites. Perhaps the best known is the Defense Language Institute. The U.S. Department of Defense maintains an extensive list of strategic languages for U.S. national security. The Defense Language Institute has tracked exactly how many weeks it takes to achieve a particular skill level in each language. No matter which language you study, you will spend more than forty hours per week for up to a year and a half working only to develop your language skills. With this background, it is possible for you to apply to be a Foreign Area Officer (FAO) within the armed services.

Once you have completed training as a regular branch officer (such as infantry, artillery, or signal), you will begin training as an FAO. When possible, you will be kept within your area of regional and language expertise. If, however, nonlanguage skills are in higher demand or the need is great, it is possible that you would serve in a geographic or language area outside of your primary area of expertise. This occurs more often among those who are not officers but rather enlisted personnel in areas like interrogation. Ultimately, you could end up serving as an interpreter, working in specific areas of language and culture program design, or working at one of the service academies teaching language and culture. Keep in mind that if you are interested in using your language capabilities, you should also develop other skill sets; simple proficiency in a particular language, even one with important security implications for the United States or Canada, is not highly regarded by itself. In contrast, if you have public policy training plus language capability, or technology skills with language skills, you would be a very attractive candidate.

Business

Business careers offer graduates a broad range of opportunities, from teaching English as a second language to working in a multinational corporation in the United States or being stationed in another country. Among the many advantages of international business careers is that they can prepare you well for work in NGOs or even the government. You will have options later. In addition, it may be possible to live very well in developing countries if your salary is matched to that of your home country. But these jobs also come with some risks. You may find yourself stationed in successive countries over time, which can be hard if you have a spouse or partner. It can be challenging to raise a family abroad if you know that you are going to return to your home country someday. For these reasons, as people progress in their careers, they often choose to return to their home countries while still working with international issues. You should be mindful of these constraints as you make your choice, even though the opportunities are exciting.

Students considering an international career should think about the particular skills that companies want. Employers generally look to hire people who can work in a multicultural setting, not only to interact in a culturally sensitive manner but also to help frame the marketing of the corporation. They want to identify people who can tolerate ambiguity and have strong social skills. A facility with language and knowledge of a major world tongue are desirable. It is perhaps less important which language is chosen than the ability to master that language. But you should not assume that you will necessarily be hired to work in an area directly tied to your language knowledge; you will have to be flexible. Remember, too, that cultural skills are often as important as language ability.

Corporations need people who can help them avoid making cultural mistakes. If possible, a study abroad program may be a valuable way to develop not only language ability but also multicultural skills. The vast majority of U.S. students still study in Europe; consider studying in a country that is not traditionally a focus for study abroad. Your family or loved ones may need some reassurance, but be persistent. Most professionals in your school's study abroad office are quite willing to talk one-on-one with parents and guardians who are nervous about their children studying outside of their home country, particularly in regard to safety and security.

For many students, the financial and life commitments entailed by a semester or year abroad are simply not realistic. But many schools are also developing short-term study abroad programs that often last for two weeks. Some schools also have international capstone experiences in which senior students work on a project to help communities abroad. You should meet with a study abroad advisor if this interests you, because he or she can help to explain such issues as how your credits will transfer and how you can use your financial aid. Some programs may also have scholarships, or you may even receive funds for foreign study from governments abroad. Finally, the Rotary Club and many similar organizations distribute scholarships. There are many books available on this topic for exploring these possibilities, and your study abroad advisor can point you in the right direction.

It also makes sense to consider internships. Most universities have internship programs. You can generally also arrange your own internships with the support of a faculty member, who can do an independent study course with you. These classes are created by an agreement between a faculty member and a student, both in the subject of study and in the requirements to complete the course. There are many different areas in which you might intern. If you are in a large urban area, there may be a consulate nearby that would appreciate an intern. Even some small urban areas may have an honorary consulate that might welcome support. You do not have to be a citizen of that particular nation in order to work at the consulate. Do not worry about working with a consulate in your particular region of interest. The experience itself is what matters—as well as the letter of reference that you can get afterward.

Most major U.S. cities also have a branch of the World Affairs Council, which is an excellent place to develop skills. There are likely also NGOs in your area working with international populations, whether it be supporting refugees or helping arts organizations. In cities, look for international trade centers or research institutes for businesses. A call to your local chamber of commerce can help you to identify these. An internship in one of these areas can help you to build your résumé, develop important experience, and learn more about the business world.

There are other ways to develop multicultural experiences. If you live at home, see if your family might be willing to host a foreign student for a year. Attend international events on your campus. If you are attending a residential campus, see if your university has an international hall or floor; most colleges and universities do. Explore the possibility of tutoring someone learning English in exchange for having them tutor you in their language. Listen to world music. Read novels set in other countries or written by foreign authors. Watch foreign films. When you can afford to dine out, have your meal at a restaurant from a region you know little about. Avoid even minor infractions of the law (such as obtaining or making a fake I.D.) that could give you a criminal record, which could restrict your choices later. For all international travel, you need to have appropriate credentials to enter a new country and return to your home country;

passports are the most broadly used credentials. Even if you do not have immediate plans to travel, get a passport now.

Before your senior year, you should visit the campus career center. Follow the job postings. Work on a draft of your résumé and have someone at the career center critique it. When you have a class with a faculty member with whom you have a good relationship, ask him or her for a letter of recommendation at the end of the class. Do not wait until two years later, when the faculty member may be on sabbatical or has left for another institution. Participate in informational interviews with people in fields that you find interesting; that is, meet with people not to apply for a job but only to learn about their work. These interactions take some courage to arrange, as you need to pick up the phone and make the call. But most people are willing to take a half hour to speak to someone considering their career path. Be flexible. Many colleges and universities have a career day when they bring employers to campus to do interviews. Attend these well before your senior year. Dress professionally, bring copies of your résumé, and talk with as many corporations as possible. It is good to participate in interviews even if you are not certain you are interested in a job; just getting the experience is important. Both the career center and the international studies program likely have books for those considering an international career. If they are not available on campus, go to your local public library.

If you wish to work abroad for a short period of time, you should consider the TESOL track (described more fully later in the chapter). Most certificate programs at universities are at least one year long, and master's programs range from two to three years. There are also shorter certificate programs through what is termed the Cambridge certificate program, or CELTA. They range from one month to six weeks and typically cost in the range of $1,500 to $2,500. They exist all over the world; you could be in a place like Thailand and be teaching and studying at the same time. To learn more, do a Web search for CELTA programs.

For many people interested in a career in international business, a master's degree, a master's in business administration, or a master's in international management will be necessary. There are many schools with strong programs, and a Web search will quickly find many of these. But a visit to your school's business school advisor or faculty member is probably a more useful way to gain information. If you are interested in a particular school, phone and ask if you can speak with an advisor at the institution. One question to pose is if they would give you the names and phone numbers of some students in the program. You should be careful not to make your decision primarily based on what these students say (you may catch them on a bad day), but they can give you a different perspective. Carefully research the institution online. Does the school discuss its placement record and the resources it makes available to its graduates? Does it have opportunities for internships or study abroad? Can you speak with alumni in your area? It's worth taking the time to do careful research. If you do not want to earn an MBA, a master's in a clearly international discipline (such as international studies) may also be a good path for you. Finally, consider finishing your MBA or other master's program in another country so that you have the chance to complete a truly international experience. There are many websites and books that can help you to make these choices, but it is also best to speak with an advisor or faculty member. Actually, speak to more than one, because each will have his or her own perspective. Be courageous.

Working for Nongovernmental Organizations and International Organizations

Nongovernmental organizations are primarily outreach programs providing service or assistance, often in the form of development aid, crisis management, education, and health. Many NGOs have both domestic and international programs. They are sometimes restricted to one country, but most often they have missions expanding beyond one nation-state. Individuals directing programs can be in-country nationals or expatriates. The programs may be international in scope—their boards of directors and organization headquarters may be outside of the country where they deliver assistance—or their leadership and organization may lie within the country where they work. Sometimes NGOs work side by side with governmental organizations, and sometimes they are actually at odds with the government of the country they are in. Aid workers have frequently developed their skill sets on the job, but many have completed graduate or undergraduate work in a field related to international development. Most students in the United States are familiar with the Peace Corps. But there are a number of other options. One resource for identifying these opportunities is Caitlin Hachmyer's *Alternatives to the Peace Corps* (2008). In terms of further education, there are more than ninety-five graduate programs in development listed within the United States, and varied master's programs throughout the United States and Canada focus on particular skills. The Association of Professional Schools of International Affairs ranks professional schools throughout the United States and Canada.

You should know that your career working for an NGO will probably give you less monetary rewards than other career pathways related to international studies. When preparing to apply to an NGO, keep in mind that such agencies often like to see the same business and organizational skills that are attractive to other employers. These jobs also tend to be highly competitive. Even if you wish to work for an NGO, you may need to pay your dues by first working for the government or in business. To find descriptions of graduate programs in international development, several search engines may be helpful. The website GradSchools.com (http://www.gradschools.com/ListingFunctions/FindAProgram.aspx) allows you to search for specific United States–based programs in international development under the main areas of either international studies or business with the subfield "international development." If you are in Canada, two main centers are the Comparative, International and Development Education Centre at the University of Toronto and International Development Studies at McGill University in Montreal.

Many NGOs also do work in the field of international conflict resolution, human rights, global public health, peace studies, and gender and global change. Graduate work in any of these areas would also provide the combination of academic studies, grant-writing experience, internships, and project-based learning necessary to be a competitive applicant for an NGO position.

International organizations are another possible career pathway. These bodies are created by multiple countries to achieve a particular goal. Some examples of international organizations include the United Nations, the Organization of American States, the World Bank, the International Monetary Fund, the International Committee of the Red Cross, and the Organization for Economic Cooperation and Development. This is a very brief list. These jobs tend to be very competitive, and the hiring procedures vary widely among them. In particular, the United Nations has a reputation for having an extremely slow and bureaucratic hiring process. But these jobs can also be very rewarding, giving people the opportunity to work in areas that can bring meaningful changes. Some jobs also come with substantial perks, such as the relatively high pay at the International Monetary Fund and World Bank. Each of these organizations has a Web page that contains information on the organization and its hiring procedures.

Jobs That Might Require Further Education

An international studies major provides a solid undergraduate background to enter a master's-level professional program. Of particular relevance are four jobs in higher education: international student advising, study abroad advising, international admissions and credentials evaluation, and Teaching English to Speakers of Other Languages.

International Student Advising

International student advisors are part of the international education team at all institutions of higher education that admit students from outside their home countries. Most U.S. and Canadian universities and community colleges employ these advisors, who monitor students at their institutions to ensure that the students are in compliance with relevant immigration rules, check for their successful completion of programs of study, communicate as necessary with the education advisor at the students' respective embassies, and ensure that the students receive all assistance necessary to succeed in their academic programs. To work at this level, a master's degree is required. Many international student advisors have completed degrees in student affairs and/or counseling. Some have completed degrees in TESOL (discussed below). Very few universities have dedicated preparatory programs for individuals interested in these positions. One that does is Lesley University in Boston, Massachusetts, which offers a master's program in international higher education and intercultural studies. Another possibility is to complete a master's degree in international studies. If you are interested in such a position, we suggest that you interview one of the international student advisors at your institution and ask them about their career path.

It is not necessary for you to be from the country where you wish to work. Some of the most successful advisors are individuals who have actually been international students themselves. In all cases, though, individuals who wish to serve as international student advisors will need to put in service time—either via a paid or unpaid internship—at one or more institutions prior to applying for a position.

To find out more about these positions, please consult either NAFSA: Association of International Educators (www.nafsa.org) or the Canadian Bureau for International Education (www.cbie.ca/). Both organizations sponsor annual conferences as well as regional conferences with presentations relevant to international student advising. It is possible to volunteer at these conferences and receive reduced rates for attending them.

Study Abroad Advising

As with international student advising, a master's-level degree is required for most positions in study abroad advising. Study abroad advisors typically manage all study-away activities for their universities. This includes term- and year-length study programs, various types of internships, and short-term study-away opportunities varying from two to six weeks. Advisors are expected to have completed some type of overseas study program themselves prior to advising others. Both NAFSA and the Canadian Bureau for International Education have professional development workshops at their annual conferences for individuals just joining the field. A typical master's degree program could be in the same fields as discussed for international student advising, with the addition of region-specific area studies programs, such as Latin American studies.

International Admissions

Most individuals working in international admissions have moved from regular admissions appointments into the international arena. That is, the skill set they first develop is related to domestic student recruitment and retention. It is useful to be a detail-oriented person in this field, particularly because of the range of education, grading, and transcript systems you will come in contact with. Some level of experience in the general admissions office as a work-study student or student worker will give you a sense of the hectic nature of this position. Because international education systems vary so widely in the United States and Canada, individuals interested in things such as international grade equivalencies or whether credentials are real or fraudulent may find this a fascinating field. While a master's degree is not essential for an entry-level position, degrees in either student personnel or business affairs would be helpful for promotion to leadership positions.

TESOL

Teaching English to Speakers of Other Languages is another field that is linked quite logically to an interest in other countries and cultures. While there are certificate-level programs that can be completed at the undergraduate or post-baccalaureate level, a master's degree in TESOL would allow you to teach English to speakers of other languages at the university level both in your home country and abroad. The international professional organization TESOL (www.tesol.org) can assist you with your investigation of various programs, as can the American Association of Applied Linguistics (aaal.org).

Teaching International Studies at the Graduate or Undergraduate Level

To teach at the community college level, a master's degree is essential, while a PhD is necessary for the university level. Because our field is interdisciplinary, you could complete an advanced degree in almost any social science field and be a strong candidate for a teaching position in international studies. Questions you may wish to ask yourself before you apply to a program include whether you are most interested in being a generalist or have a particular regional or thematic area of focus. Are you particularly concerned about the Middle East, Africa, or the Caribbean? Are you more interested in international development, women and gender, international health, or language and area studies? Do you wish to attend a program with a particular reputation, or one with a strong alumni and career network? Are you bound by geographic location? The more you know about where you would like to teach and exactly what you would like to teach, the easier it will be for you to choose your graduate program. All social science disciplines have professional organizations, such as the International Studies Association, the American Association of Geographers, and the American Anthropological Association. Frequently, these associations publish directories of graduate programs in the United States and Canada. These programs are ranked. You can also find out what types of financial aid are available. Do not hesitate to talk with your professors about their recommendations for particular programs that best suit your needs.

For many of you with university teaching and research goals, a PhD will ultimately be required. You may choose to complete a master's degree at one time and then subsequently complete your PhD, or you may attend a school that allows you complete your master's in a seamless manner as you finish your doctoral requirements. There are significant advantages to the latter path. Most master's programs provide less financial aid than doctoral programs do. They also generally require two years to complete, as well as possibly a thesis. On the other hand, as a student admitted to a PhD program (at a school with an integrated master's/PhD program), you can sometimes apply for a master's after a single year of coursework, and you are much more likely to receive a strong financial aid package. While it can take time to locate schools with these programs (Yale is one example), it is worth considering them.

Traveling to attend a school of choice in the field is usually worth the effort, inconvenience, or expense. It is generally not wise to receive your graduate degree from the same school where you went for your undergraduate education; people may think that you went to graduate school there because you were place-bound or could not get into other schools. It is also generally believed that you will have a greater diversity in your education if you attend more than one institution. That said, there may be an exception if your university is particularly well known in an area that is important to you.

When applying to universities, think hard about the location of the school. Some programs in Europe are less expensive than programs in the United States. In places like Scandinavia, the Netherlands, and Germany, some programs are offered completely in English. A PhD program generally takes six or seven years to complete (although people sometimes finish in five years or less). You want to be somewhere you will be happy. Pick a limited number of schools to apply to; four to five is usually a good number. At least one school should be a backup that you are more confident will accept you. Give the faculty member or members whom you ask for a reference at least three weeks to write it; a month is even better. Give them a copy of your personal statement and let them know things about yourself that you'd like the admissions office to know.

When working on your application, spend a lot of time on your personal statement. This matters a great deal in the admissions process. Rewrite and proofread it until you are sick of it, then have others whom you trust read it. You should look at the school's website to find if there is someone there whom you are interested in working with. There is no point in attending a great university if the only possible advisor is someone with interests that do not match yours. It is best to choose a department where you can work with more than one lead advisor; if you have a difficult work relationship with one, you can turn to the other. Refer to the faculty member's work in your application. Suggest that you have a particular area/topic that you would like to investigate for your PhD (you will not be held to this). Research carefully the particular requirements for your program.

What is the language requirement, and when does it have to be fulfilled? It is often a good idea to pick up the phone and try to call some of the faculty members and the departmental registrar. Ask if they will give you the name of a graduate student to talk to. Then call them. Check to make sure that the people you want as advisors will not be on sabbatical the year that you arrive. Look at the course offerings and make sure that the program has enough depth that you will have the choices you want. Do not be shy about talking to the departmental registrar concerning teaching assistantships and financial aid. But be positive: you are selling yourself. Do not get too personal, and do not come across as needy.

Most graduate schools still require Graduate Record Exam (GRE) scores, although this is changing. The GRE is a multiple-choice test that examines your ability in logic, mathematics, and language. For students with test anxiety, the GRE can be a formidable obstacle. If you qualify for accommodations such as extra time, be sure to request them. There are books about preparing for the GRE, and some testing services provide training. Some preparation helps, but after a couple of weekends, you will probably hit a saturation point. Do not cram the night before; you want to walk into the test rested. You can retake the test, but it is offered a limited number of times per year. There is also a charge each time you take it, just as there are application fees for each graduate application. Your acceptance and rejection letters from the universities you apply to may seem quite random: you could receive a full offer from one school, with tuition assistance and a stipend, only to be turned down by others. It is important to try not to put your ego on the line and to have a backup plan. The process can be time-consuming, exhausting, and difficult. But there are few things more exciting in life than a letter of admission to graduate school. After I (Shawn Smallman) received mine, I had to walk to the grocery store to buy food for dinner for my housemates. I took the letter in my pocket so that I could stop and reread it over and over as I went down the aisles—it just seemed impossible.

Final Thoughts

While your career is important, it is only one part of your life. If you do not follow an international career path, we hope that this book and your college course have interested you enough that you will want to remain internationally engaged. That can take many forms, from travel plans and music choices to personal friendships. Many international studies courses begin by showing you how international factors affect your life, including security problems, financial investments, and the immense reach of globalization. You will be a more informed citizen, and it may open new life opportunities to you. All of these are important factors. But an international perspective also makes for a richer perspective in the best tradition of liberal education. We hope that whatever path you take, you choose to remain interested in, and curious about, global affairs.

➤ VOCABULARY

Department of Homeland Security
international organizations
TESOL, TESL, and TEAL
Foreign Area Officer

ACTIVITY 1: ANALYZE The résumé template that follows is shared with permission by a young undergraduate, Chiara Nicastro, who has demonstrated much success in scholarship applications and academic honors programs, most recently a Fulbright to Spain. Please be respectful of this private information. Look over the formatting in this document. It has been truncated to give you a sense of what to write. Note the location of her study abroad information and language and other skills proficiency. There is no job objective listed at the top, as you may have often seen in the past. Begin to build your own résumé with the following subheadings: Education, Professional Experience, Skills and Qualifications. Identify four of your own courses that have helped shaped your study and list them as Chiara has done.

Full Name

Accurate phone number. Accurate email. Linked-in URL

EDUCATION:

Bachelor of Arts International Studies Major and Women's Studies Minor September 2017

- Portland State University, Portland, Oregon
- Oregon Consular Corps Scholar 2015–2016, PSU McNair Scholar 2017, Dean's List Student, National Honors Society Member
- Courses in Intercultural Communications, Forced Migration and Exploitation, Women Activism and Social Change, and United States & Foreign Policy

University of San Jose, Costa Rica January 2016–June 2016

- Courses in Women's Health, Environmental Politics, Spanish, and Cultural Studies
- Two week case study in Cuba on Cuban Life: After Opening Borders with U.S.
- Volunteer English teacher at local school with junior high students for four months

University of Queretaro, Mexico June 2014–August 2014

- Spanish Language Intensive

PROFESSIONAL EXPERIENCE:

Work-Study Summer Institute for Intercultural Communication April 2017–Present

- Assisted event-planning and organization with the Intercultural Communication
- Institute (ICI) for the Summer Institute for Intercultural Communication (SIIC) 2017
- Attended SIIC Session 1: Deconstructing and Challenging Personal and Institutional Inequities and One-Day Workshops
- Operated ICI two online databases; and conduct research for library and on participates registrations to help create future branding

Communications Intern at Made In a Free World June 2015–September 2015

- Managed all social media sites; completed data entry and created demographics of users and the nonprofit, online outreach and met with local businesses, develop programs to celebrate donors
- Maximize Made In A Free World's visibility and research strategies for finding and growing a more network
- Assisted with hiring and training fall Interns and other application paperwork
- Attend and facilitate meetings with supervisor and other staff members, submit weekly reports

ADDITIONAL WORK EXPERIENCE:

McNair Scholar Summer Research Internship January 2017–Present

- Conducted and published research on Refugee Resettlement in Portland

SKILLS/QUALIFICATIONS:

- Outgoing, enthusiastic, creative, and resourceful
- Language Proficiency: English native speaker; Spanish- excellent listening, fluent speaking, reading; good writing
- Experience with event planning and volunteer management
- Strong organization skills
- Ability to work independently and multitask under pressure
- Experience and passionate about narratives and storytelling
- Excellent verbal, written, and interpersonal communication skills
- Computer skills in MS Word, MS Excel, MS PowerPoint, Salesforce, Photoshop, and social media

References Given Upon Request

ACTIVITY 2: REFLECT A recent undergraduate at our institution received two prestigious graduate school offers in Middle East studies to Research 1 schools in Washington and Arizona. She suggests the following for anyone thinking of graduate school. Review these steps and turn them into your own checklist for your future applications.

- Forge relationships with your professors; they have been to grad school and can offer advice as well as write recommendation letters.
- Use summer vacation before your last year to research and pick out the schools you are interested in applying to. Make note of their application deadlines; some are as early as October.
- Apply to more than one school so you will have options.
- Summer is also a great time to study and sign up for the GRE.
- Give yourself time to write narratives and ask for feedback from professors.
- Give professors several weeks to write recommendations and send reminders as the deadlines approach.
- Ask for help. Reach out to people who have been through the process.
- Try to look at the process as practice for the years to come when you will be applying for funding.

ACTIVITY 3: EXTEND Go to the U.S. government site for the Foreign Service: https://careers.state.gov/work/foreign-service/officer/. Assume you are going to take the exam and actually apply. Identify which sections of the website will help you. Spend at least one hour going through the various sections of this site. Make sure you know when the nearest exam to you will be offered and how much it will cost. Note: it is necessary to be a U.S. citizen to take this exam. Other countries have their own websites and career paths. Please consult the website from your home country. Also, many of the Foreign Service Officer test resources in the United States and Canada are available through alternative media: apps, Facebook, e-books. These resources are not listed below, but a basic Internet search will pull them up.

References

General International Education Career Resources

Busse, M., with S. Joiner. 2010. *The idealist guide to nonprofit careers for first-time job seekers*. Atlanta, GA: Hundreds of Heads.

Joiner, S., with M. Busse. 2008. *The idealist guide to nonprofit careers for sector switchers*. Atlanta, GA: Hundreds of Heads.

Mueller, S. L., and M. Overmann. 2014. *Careers in international education, exchange, and development*. 2nd ed. Washington, D.C.: Georgetown University Press.

Job Websites

Idealist, idealist.org (this website pulls all relevant positions within a 25- to 100-mile radius of your current location).

International Jobs.com, http://www.internationaljobs.com/ (this website includes both private sector and U.S. government positions).

Foreign Service Resources (United States)

Clark, R. 2016. *The Complete FSOT study guide*. New York: Aegis Group.

Dorman, S. 2003. *Inside a U.S. embassy: How the Foreign Service works for America*. Washington, D.C.: American Foreign Service Association.

FSOT flashcard study system. 2017. Beaumont, Tex.: Mometrix Test Preparation.

FSOT practice questions (Set #2). 2017.Beaumont, Tex.: Mometrix Test Preparation.

Grayson, F. N. 2006. *Foreign Service officer exam: Preparation for the written exam and the oral assessment*. Hoboken, N.J.: Wiley (Cliffs Test Prep).

Krasowski, J., ed. 2005. *American Foreign Service officer exam*. 4th ed. Laurenceville, N.J.: Thomson/Peterson's.

Linderman, P., and M. Brayer-Hess. 2002. *Realities of Foreign Service life: True stories of rescued golden retrievers and the people who love them*. Lincoln, Neb.: iUniverse (Associates of the American Foreign Service Worldwide).

Wilson, L. W. 2016. *Hack the FSOT: Biographic questionnaire edition*. Scotts Valley, Calif.: CreateSpace Independent Publishing Platform.

Intercultural Education Preparation

Leeds-Hurwitz, W. 1990. Notes in the history of intercultural communication: The Foreign Service institute and the mandate for intercultural training. *Quarterly Journal of Speech* 76 (3): 262–81. doi:10.1080/00335639009383919.

Paige, R. M., A. Cohen, B. Kappler, J. Chi, and J. Lassegard. 2004. *Maximizing study abroad: A student's guide to strategies for language and culture learning and use*. Minneapolis: University of Minnesota.

International Development Careers

Career Opportunities in International Development. n.d. Retrieved April 2, 2018, from glenn.osu.edu/career/.../career.../Career%20Opportunities%20in%20 International%20.

Hachmyer, C. 2008. *Alternatives to the Peace Corps: A guide to volunteer opportunities*. 12th ed. Oakland, Calif.: Food First Books.

Mueller, S. L., and M. Overman. 2008. *Working world: Careers in international education, exchange, and development.* Washington, D.C.: Georgetown University Press.

Russell, D. 2013. *Choosing a career in international development: A practical guide to working in the professions of international development.* College Station, Tex.: Virtualbookworm.com.

University of Oxford International Development Resources: https://www.careers.ox.ac.uk/international-development/.

USAID. https://www.usaid.gov/careers.

Social Change Graduate Programs

Claremont Lincoln University. Graduate program with a focus on social change: Master of Arts in Social Impact (fully online). Retrieved from https://www.claremontlincoln.edu/programs/social-impact/.

Powell, J., ed. 2001. *Education for action: Undergraduate and graduate programs that focus on social change.* 4th ed. Oakland, Calif.: Food First Books.

THIRTEEN **Conclusion**

As we observed in the introduction, globalization is the dominant force of our time, with profound social, political, and cultural consequences for all of us. Predicting the future is always a dangerous task, and many scholars have made predictions—such as the end of the United States' unique position of power—only to be proved wrong over time. While nothing is determined, some demographic, environmental, and political trends are clear, and it would be difficult to change these without great political will. An overview of these trends will allow you to reflect on how they will impact your life and your local community. Given that globalization affects every individual, how do you—or how will you—think of your role in the global community and your allegiances? What are our responsibilities in this international order? In the latter part of the chapter, we look at two profiles of key individuals who have made the connection from the local to the global through civic engagement in order to address major global problems, Chinese artist Ai Weiwei and New Zealand prime minister Jacinda Ardern.

Imagining the Future

In terms of security, some trends are complex. One of the more serious issues will be the international community's inability to prevent nuclear weapons proliferation. While individual nations may make the choice to abandon their nuclear development efforts—as has happened in the past in Brazil and South Africa, for example—the fact remains that the international community does not appear capable of stopping nations that are determined to acquire nuclear weapons. In the future, therefore, we are likely to see more nations with nuclear weapons, some of which obtain them as a response to their neighbor's development of nuclear capability in a so-called domino effect. Over the long term, it is likely that the danger from Islamic terrorism will decrease because, historically, few terrorist threats have endured for extended periods, and there is no clear reason why this threat would be different. But the increased complexity of security threats will lead to the rising influence of human security as an ideal. Traditional security concerns will remain paramount, particularly in Asia, where many nations will have to adapt to the rapid rise in the power of China and India and the relative decline of Japan. The power of nationalism, unresolved border issues, and the changing balance of power among states in the region means that, globally, a major war is most likely to take place on this continent in the decades to come. In contrast, Europe will continue to benefit from the peace brought by the European Union at the same time that its relative military and diplomatic influence fades globally.

In terms of economic globalization, we will see the continuing power of neoliberalism and ongoing tensions around the world—particularly in the European Union between those who seek a workforce-based set of solutions to economic problems and those who seek a traditional market-based set of solutions. Populism and protection of the nation-state and multinational corporate resources will be dominant themes. We will also see the rising power of states as creative problem solvers that draw on their nation-state contexts to solve their financial woes instead of depending on multinational, one-size-fits-all remedies. Iceland is perhaps the best example of this phenomenon. It is also true that the world will continue to see its economic center of gravity shift toward Asia, although the United States will not suffer an absolute decline in economic power.

Regarding political globalization, the international order will have to adapt to the relative rise in the power of Africa, Latin America, and Asia as these three world regions gain in population, with the most dramatic increase to come in Africa. The major European states—Germany, France, and Britain—will fall in most measurements of power. In their place, we will likely see India and China increasingly shape the global power dynamic. They will be augmented by other nations that may acquire new political influence to reflect their economic rise, such as Brazil or Mexico, should they be able to overcome their political problems. This will increase the pressure to reform the United Nations to create a new global architecture that will reflect this modern-day power balance rather than the one prevalent in 1945. Overall, the two great world powers will be China and the United States. Historically, many wars between Great Powers were caused by the rapid rise of one power, which threatened the power of another. If China's rise is to avoid conflict, it will take not only skillful diplomacy but also greater influence on the part of regional associations and international bodies. At the same time, democracy is likely to retain its political attraction, and many authoritarian states are likely to see regime changes. This is the greatest challenge facing China, which currently relies on economic growth and nationalism for legitimacy. Should the nation face difficult times, these are unlikely to prove sufficient.

In terms of cultural globalization, the world is likely to see significant migration because of broad differences in birth rates among world regions, as well as political and economic instability resulting in pressures that pull individuals from one space to another. Despite Europe's efforts to maintain its identity, it will become increasingly pluralistic in terms of religion and will face great pressure from migration from North Africa. Japan will find it hard to avoid some increases in immigration, which will lead to difficult political choices. And the United States will continue to see the rising power of its Latino population. These trends all mean cultural globalization will deepen as populations become increasingly diverse. Linguistically, we will continue to see the waning of small languages, while globally, the dominance of English will be challenged at the regional level by the rise of Chinese, Spanish, Hindi, Russian, Bahasa Malaysia, and Arabic (Graddol 1997).

In the area of development, an increasing number of countries will make the transition from developing to developed status. This has already happened in South Korea and Chile and may happen in the next two decades in Argentina, Mexico, and Turkey, if these nations can address their current financial and political challenges. More importantly, given their population and geographic size, China, India, and Brazil will also achieve developed status in this century. This will lead to a more complex world in terms of development aid, as these nations become increasingly important donors. At the same time, the World Bank will continue to weaken and the role of the Asian Development Bank will grow. At the local level, microfinance lending institutions will permit local development to occur, regardless of what is happening on state, regional, and international levels. The growth of cryptocurrencies may also weaken the economic power of states.

Patterns of food distribution, production, and consumption will continue to change. The number of countries deemed "food insufficient" will increase. As groundwater depletion and salinization become growing problems for nations such as Pakistan and Saudi Arabia, both global and local tensions will increase. Nation-states will become more possessive of their resources, even as the WTO and TRIPS strive to maintain global control. Countries dependent on single foodstuffs (monocropping) for export will continue to be buffeted by the winds of political instability, weather changes, and market demands. With global warming, some regions will face increasing challenges in terms of producing food, which is particularly true in the Middle East and North Africa. These pressures will force nations to adopt new agricultural and water management practices (Mancosu et al. 2015).

The world will continue to face health concerns such as the danger of epidemic disease, as the Korean MERS outbreak in 2015 demonstrated. The increasing density of human populations, the development of antibiotic resistance, and the spread of insect vectors with global warming will mean that "plagues" are not just a legacy of our past. In the end, the urban civilizations of the classical world were devastated by both malaria and Justinian's Plague. It will take great investments and wise public-health policy—not to mention luck—if we are to avoid a similar health disaster in our age. Given the rise of antibiotic-resistant bacteria and fungi, the global community will need to make major investments in nontraditional antibiotics and vaccines. At the same time, as many public-health specialists note, we may face a double burden as chronic diseases such as diabetes escalate. While increasing wealth creates the opportunity to respond to these challenges, the optimism of the 1950s seems naive today.

With regard to energy, petroleum will continue its slow decline for the next half century. This will not be because of declining supply but rather because of the rapid growth of solar and wind energy, combined with the further development of electric cars. With global warming widely agreed to be the greatest threat of our age, the political pressure to move away from fossil fuels will be overwhelming in the long term. This will remain true despite the emergence of political leaders who wish to advocate for the use of a particular fossil fuel, as has been the case with President Trump and coal in the United States. For the Arab world this transition will pose immense challenges, as these nations will face a slow but steady decline for the region's major export. States that lack good renewable resources will confront difficult decisions regarding other forms of energy, such as nuclear power. Still, over the next decade, environmental concerns and technological breakthroughs—such as new battery technologies and hydrogen storage—will lead to a move away from petroleum and toward expanded choices for energy.

The environmental future is one filled with challenges. It seems clear that the world will not be able to prevent global warming in the near term.

Even with breakthroughs in fuels for transportation, the use of fossil fuels for electricity will continue this trend, although it may slow. With the diminishment of the earth's polar ice cap in the North, the globe's albedo will change (that is, the region will reflect less sunlight), which will cause a positive feedback loop in which the ocean will absorb more of the sun's energy. The result is that rather than resolving the issue, the international community instead will be trying to prevent catastrophic change and manage living in a warming world. There will be clear losers in this effort—Bangladesh and the Netherlands, Florida and Louisiana. Some Pacific Island nations will disappear. The future for coral reefs and the species that live under or on the Arctic ice appear bleak. But there may be some winners, too, such as Canada, Denmark, and Russia, as new areas open to agriculture or transportation from Greenland to the Northwest Passage (Easterbrook 2007). For animal species, however, there will only be loss, which will be exacerbated by the looming peak in the planet's global population in the mid-twenty-first century, particularly in Africa. Environmentalists will struggle to ensure the survival of key species, with the hope that the declining human populations after midcentury will lead to better natural conditions for the very long term. This will be a hard period in the earth's history.

Global Citizenship

Given the scale of these changes and the impact they will have upon all of us, what are your responsibilities? At the start of this text, we introduced you to the idea of global citizenship. Global citizens view themselves as actors in relation to all of humanity, with particular rights and responsibilities apart from any owed to one's nation-state (Pike 2008). This idea is widely debated, with some people questioning whether global citizenship exists. From the viewpoint of the critics, the international order above the scale of the nation-state is largely defined by anarchy. You cannot have a passport as a global citizen. Any obligations that you have are those that pertain to your nation alone. Within this framework, the ideal of global citizenship is idealistic and unrealistic (Dower 2000, 555–57). Still others question whether it is again the Global North that is defining for the rest of the world how we should behave in various contexts.

The concept of global citizenship is particularly contested in an era defined by war, migration, and nationalism. Yet we all have multiple allegiances, some of which are below the state (such as to our local community) and some of which lie above it (humanity's need to fight global warming). In reality, many global processes are undermining traditional ideals of national citizenship, and these challenges are likely to increase (Urry 2000, 68–74).

The issue of global citizenship may be inescapable. While this concept may seem rather vague, Nigel Dower (2000, 553) and others have made the point that this vision of global citizenship has deep historical roots that reach back to classical civilization. People have been debating the competing ethical demands placed upon people by their shared humanity (global citizenship) and their allegiance to their nation (patriotism) for more than two millennia, from golden age Athens to ancient China. Many authors stress that the scale of global problems requires people to redefine their sense of self and to demand institutions that will "exercise global responsibility" (553). Dower emphasizes, however, that belief in global citizenship does not entail belief in global government; rather, it requires a shift in perspective, such that people and populations are concerned with the needs of humanity on a global scale (553). Within this perspective, we see a strong ethical component to this concept of global citizenship.

As authors, we also share an ideology that includes a commitment to the belief in the value of global citizenship, in the sense that our actions have implications for others. We want to be explicit about our own perspective. We are all global actors, whether it be because of the commodity chains in which we are embedded, the votes that we cast, or the beliefs that we advocate. This reality carries a moral obligation with it. We recognize that in practical terms, the idea of global citizenship is complicated. There are many challenges to the idea of global citizenship, and the duties that it entails can be interpreted in widely differing ways. We don't believe that you need to choose between populism/nationalism and global citizenship; that is, you can be a good national citizen and at the same time a good global one. What's important is that you don't let others define what is ethical for you. You should know what you wish to decide and why. If you can't think of yourself as a global citizen, can you be globally minded?

Biographies

Ai Weiwei and Jacinda Ardern personify some or all of the dimensions of global citizens described above. Peggy McIntosh describes six capacities of mind when describing global citizenship: "(1) the ability to observe oneself and the world around one; (2) the ability to make comparisons and contrasts; (3) the ability to 'see' plurally as a result; (4) the ability to understand that both 'reality' and language come in versions; (5) the ability to see power relations and understand them systemically; and (6) the ability to balance awareness of one's own realities with the realities of entities outside of the perceived self" (2005, 23).

As you read these individuals' stories, try and identify which of McIntosh's descriptors apply to each of them. In a way, these life stories are a kind of portrait of global leaders. Perhaps you will recognize some of your own traits in theirs. Neither of these individuals sets out to become model global citizens or expected to cross disciplines and regions or become engaged in international issues. As you reflect upon their stories, think about the common threads in their experience—how they planned for their futures, only to take a different course. Were there hints that someday they would become actors on a global stage? Are there parallels between their lives and your own?

Ai Weiwei

Ai Weiwei (艾未未) is an accomplished Chinese artist and political activist who was born in Beijing in 1957. His father, Ai Qing, was a noted Marxist intellectual and poet (Callahan 2014, 908) who was nonetheless exiled and experienced persecution in the 1960s and 1970s. Despite this fact, Ai Weiwei took part in political protests as early as the 1970s. He came to the United States in 1981 and spent twelve years living here before returning to live in Beijing in 1993. Over time, he became increasingly critical of the authoritarian regime there, which deeply impacted his artistic expression. One quote perhaps captures the transgressiveness of Ai's work, which addresses powerful social and political issues: "His art is revolutionary. It includes an installation made from 1,001 wooden doors and windows wrested from destroyed Ming and Qing dynasty houses, backpack stuffed installations representing the schoolchildren killed in the 2008 Sichuan earthquake, and an image of Tiananmen Square that foregrounds an underwear-flashing young woman (a casual version of the skirt-lifting women who terrified royalist soldiers during the French Revolution)" (Yaeger 2011, 553).

His art based upon the 2008 Sichuan earthquake was particularly powerful. This earthquake killed nearly 70,000 people, and approximately 375,000 people were severely injured. Thousands of schoolchildren died as their schools collapsed. There was intense popular outrage at what was viewed as shoddy "tofu" construction. After Ai Weiwei perceived that the government was not launching an adequate investigation into why these buildings collapsed, he worked to organize Chinese citizens to do so themselves. Additionally, he organized an art installation in Germany using children's backpacks (Callahan 2014, 905), attracting attention and shocking viewers. Ai Weiwei was also an avid blogger at a time before social media had displaced blogs' influence. The introduction to Ai's book notes that when the government deleted his blog in May 2009, it eliminated not only more than 2,000 posts but also millions of reader comments. He responded by moving to Twitter and published his blog posts as a book in 2011 (Weiwei 2011, xvii).

In this situation, Ai's arrest was inevitable. He had publicly criticized government policy and developed a global following that made him appear untouchable. In response, his art studio was torn down, and a few months later in 2011 he was arrested at the airport and held for eighty-one days. By his own description, despite his mistreatment (which included a beating so severe that he later suffered a cerebral hemorrhage) he set out to befriend his guards as an act of psychological warfare (Callahan 2014, 904, 912). After a firestorm of international protest, Ai Weiwei was freed. In 2015 the Chinese government permitted Weiwei to leave China. He now lives in Berlin with his family and is an internationally known artist whose work has been exhibited everywhere from the Tate Modern in London to the Fukushima nuclear exclusion zone in Japan.

Ai Weiwei is a complex figure who has described himself as not being a deep political thinker (Callahan 2014, 913). William Callahan has portrayed him as being in some respects like a medieval court jester who uses humor to speak to power (906–7). Still, Callahan suggests that Ai Weiwei is best understood as a citizen-intellectual (915). To his critics, he is someone who enjoys playing to Western media and is more popular outside China than he is influential within it. Still, he has also proved to a persistent critic of Western states too. Much like the Nobel Peace Prize–winning poet Liu Xiaobo (刘晓波), he has challenged the Chinese government by peaceful means, overcome imprisonment and persecution, and created a vision of a China that is neither authoritarian nor corrupt.

Jacinda Ardern

Jacinda Ardern, New Zealand's prime minister, rose to international fame for her swift condemnation of terrorist attacks on worshippers in a series of mosques in March 2019. Addressing her nation first in Maori and then in English, Ardern modeled compassion and competence. Ultimately, the New Zealand parliament banned assault rifles and semiautomatic weapons.

Ardern completed her undergraduate work at Waikato University, majoring in political science and public relations. She was finishing her study abroad program overseas at the University of Arizona when 9/11 occurred. Arden then served as president of the Socialist Youth organization from 2008 to 2010. In this capacity, she traveled to Norway after one young man with an assault rifle attacked a Socialist Youth camp and killed seventy-seven young people. Her presence in the United States during 9/11 and the knowledge that young people who were part of her organization had been killed in Norway spurred her continuing activism.

During her leadership term for Socialist Youth, she traveled widely to numerous foreign countries supporting activities to help refugees and fight global poverty and climate change. These experiences and her commitment to global leadership have led her to engage in political controversies around climate change, social media, global poverty, and the health of women and children.

After serving in the New Zealand parliament, she rose to the position of Labour leader only twelve weeks before being elected prime minister. Ardern was then sworn in on October 26, 2017. Tracy Withers notes she is "the South Pacific's youngest prime minister since 1856" (2017).

While much press coverage has explored her pregnancy and delivery of her young daughter while in office, it is her political platform and diplomatic persona that distinguish her work as a global citizen. Ken Ross singles out her strengths as a problem solver and her "talented advocacy": "Ardern, like her 'local hero' Norman Kirk, is principally a problem solver; she has deep humanitarianism summed up in [Kirk's] much quoted 'all Kiwis [New Zealanders] want is someone to love, somewhere to live, somewhere to work and something to hope for'" (2018, 2).

In a speech delivered to the New Zealand Institute of International Affairs on February 27, 2018, Ardern articulated the strength of her commitment to global and local social change:

> This is my first formal comment on issues relating to international relations, but not my first encounter with them. In fact, the relevance and importance of our place in the world, and the clues to navigating such significant global disruption, have always started at home. I spent some of my early childhood during the 1980s in a small

> town in the Bay of Plenty called Murupara, before moving to the dairy-farming town of Morrinsville. It would be easy to feel isolated from the world, impervious to what was happening around you. But the size of the town has rarely isolated anyone from the reverberations of international events. The removal of tariff protections right through to the 1987 stock exchange crash all had their impact. And just as globalisation has been felt through the past few decades, so too will the effects of the next industrial revolution and the changing nature of work. (2018b)

Deeply committed to impacting climate change, Ardern demonstrates awareness of the role powerful nations play in the lives of members of small island nations: "We're small, and our contribution to the global emissions profile is even smaller, but we are surrounded by island nations who will feel the brunt of climate change acutely" (Lester 2019). She has chosen to engage deeply with her constituents and with world leaders. She has chosen to make a difference.

Hope and the Future

We have chosen to end the book with these two examples because they make the point that global citizenship entails the idea of civic engagement. You may not agree with what each of these people is fighting for, but what is important is that they both choose to act on their beliefs to help other people on a scale that ultimately has global implications. Ai Weiwei and Jacinda Ardern first looked beyond their local communities for different reasons. Both then reinvested in their communities, ultimately pulling the world onto their stages. They stepped up to serve as change agents.

One of the challenges with a book such as this is that it can quickly become a litany of global problems. Some of these issues—from global warming to population growth—are unlikely to be entirely solved in our lifetimes. But that does not mean that these problems cannot be mitigated through civic engagement, new ideas, and public policy. Through this work, we have sought to make you aware of the major economic, political, social, and biological trends that are accompanying globalization and will impact everyone's lives. You have been exposed to different views and should now be able to think critically about these perspectives, to decide which arguments appear persuasive to you, and to reflect on what information you may be missing. Ultimately, we want you to think about the idea of global citizenship in a way that does not leave you feeling overwhelmed by our planet's problems but rather instilled with a sense of responsibility for addressing humanity's concerns through means that are both possible and necessary.

References

Ai, Weiwei. 2011. *Ai Weiwei's blog: Writings, interviews, and digital rants, 2006–2009*. Edited and translated by L. Ambrozy. Cambridge: MIT Press.

———. 2013. *Weiwei-isms*. Princeton: Princeton University Press.

Ai, Weiwei and A. Pins, eds. 2014. *Ai Weiwei: Spatial matters—art architecture and activism*. Cambridge: MIT Press.

Ardern, J. 2018a. Engaging with an uncertain world: Jacinda Ardern gives an outline of her government's approach to international affairs. *NZ International Review* 43 (3): [May–June]. Retrieved June 21, 2019, from https://www.questia.com/library/journal/1G1-540903267/engaging-with-an-uncertain-world-jacinda-ardern-gives..

———. 2018b. Speech delivered to New Zealand Institute of Foreign Affairs, February 27. Retrieved July 10, 2019, from http://www.scoop.co.nz/stories/PA1802/S00264/ardern-speech-to-nz-institute-of-international-affairs.htm.

Callahan, W. 2014. Citizen Ai: Warrior, jester, and middleman. *Journal of Asian Studies* 73 (4): 899–920.

Dower, N. 2000. The idea of global citizenship—a sympathetic assessment. *Global Society* 14 (4): 543–67.

Easterbrook, G. 2007. Global warming: Who loses—and who wins? *Atlantic Monthly*, April. Retrieved January 8, 2010, from www.theatlantic.com/doc/200704/global-warming.

Graddol, D. 1997. *The future of English*. British Council. Digital edition created by the English Company (UK) Ltd. Retrieved January 16, 2010, from www.officiallanguages.gc.ca/docs/f/Future_of_English.pdf.

Lester, A. 2019. The roots of Jacinda Ardern's extraordinary leadership after Christchurch. *New Yorker*, March 23.

Mancosu, N., R. Snyder, G. Kyriakakis, and D. Spano. 2015. Water scarcity and future challenges for food production. *Water* 7 (3): 975–92.

Martin, B. 2013. *Hanging man: The arrest of Ai Weiwei*. New York: Farrar, Straus and Giroux.

McIntosh, P. 2005. Gender perspectives on educating for global awareness. In *Educating citizens for global awareness*, edited by N. Noddings, 22–39. New York: Teachers College.

Obrist, H. U. 2011. *Ai Weiwei speaks: With Hans Ulrich Obrist*. London: Penguin UK.

Pike, G. 2008. Reconstructing the legend: Educating for global citizenship. In *Educating for human rights and global citizenship*, edited by A. Abdi and L. Shultz, 223–38. Albany: SUNY Press.

Ross, K. 2018. Jacinda Ardern—ready for global diplomacy? Ken Ross assesses the new prime minister's capacity to perform on the world stage. *NZ International Review 43* (2): 2.

Sorace, C. 2014. China's last Communist: Ai Weiwei. *Critical Inquiry* 40 (2): 396–419.

Urry, J. 2000. Global flows and global citizenship. In *Democracy, citizenship, and the global city*, edited by E. F. Isin, 62–78. New York: Routledge.

Withers, T. 2017. New Zealand prime minister Jacinda Arden interview. *Bloomberg Business Week*, November 6, 28.

Yaeger, P. 2011. The Almost-All-Asian Issue: Channeling Ai Weiwei and the Grass-Mud Horse. *PMLA 126* (3): 553–54.

Acknowledgments

A large number of people worked to make this book possible. Patrice Ball, Robert Halstead, and Cara Clark Martinez carefully edited drafts of these chapters. Janice Smith, in particular, has served as not only a superb copy editor but also a reflective mentor to both of us in terms of process and text organization. Nathan Houtz did research for this text, especially for the security chapter, where his work was invaluable. Tasia-Jana Tanginoa proved to be an expert on the United Nations; her research greatly improved the political globalization chapter. Michael Bonham and Jamie Biesanz did work on Antarctica that was also key to the political globalization chapter. Grace Lamb and Megan Jessup-Varnum helped to research maps. Jenny Shipman did outstanding research on a number of topics, particularly Brexit. Steph Gaspers, with help from David Banis, designed the world map at the start of the text. Chiara Nicastro allowed us to use her job search materials. Andrew Russo and Mingma Dorji Sherpa provided case study data for us. Grace Lamb did important research on health and cyber issues. Margaret Everett, Aomar Boum, and Christina Caponi allowed us to use their photos. We also want to recognize our Portland State students who read different drafts of this work and provided important feedback. Additionally, we are grateful to our current and former international studies colleagues who have brainstormed extensively with us: Aomar Boum, Stephen Frenkel, Pronoy Rai, Leopoldo Rodriguez, and Birol Yesilada. We are grateful as well to our subject librarians Linda Absher and Rick Mikulski. We have derived inspiration from published work by the Institute for Global Citizenship at Macalester College. Elaine Maisner and the editorial and marketing teams at the University of North Carolina Press proved to be outstanding partners. Finally, we would both like to thank our families, who supported us through the process.

Index

Page numbers in italics refer to illustrations.